MAJOR LABELS

MAJOR LABELS

A HISTORY *of* POPULAR MUSIC *in* SEVEN GENRES

KELEFA SANNEH

PENGUIN PRESS | NEW YORK | 2021

PENGUIN PRESS
An imprint of Penguin Random House LLC
penguinrandomhouse.com

LIBRARY OF CONGRESS CATALOGING-IN-PUBLICATION DATA
Names: Sanneh, Kelefa, author.
Title: Major labels : a history of popular music in seven genres /
Kelefa Sanneh.
Description: New York : Penguin Press, 2021. | Includes index.
Identifiers: LCCN 2021008355 (print) | LCCN 2021008356 (ebook) |
ISBN 9780525559597 (hardcover) | ISBN 9780525559603 (ebook)
Subjects: LCSH: Popular music—History and criticism.
Classification: LCC ML3470 .S25 2021 (print) | LCC ML3470 (ebook) |
DDC 781.64—dc23
LC record available at https://lccn.loc.gov/2021008355
LC ebook record available at https://lccn.loc.gov/2021008356

Printed in the United States of America
1 3 5 7 9 10 8 6 4 2

Designed by Amanda Dewey

CONTENTS

INTRODUCTION

Wearing Headphones

WHEN MY FATHER WAS LYING in a hospital bed in New Haven, Connecticut, struck down by a sudden illness, and the doctors and nurses were searching for any sign that he was still alive, my mother decided that he needed a soundtrack. She brought his Bose noise-canceling headphones to the bed and we took turns playing him his favorite music. Over the next week, as we kept him company and said goodbye, one of the albums we put into heavy rotation was *Clychau Dibon*, a shimmering collaboration from 2013 between Catrin Finch, a Welsh harpist, and Seckou Keita, a kora player from the Casamance region of Senegal, in West Africa—not far from where my father had grown up, in the Gambia.

The kora, a harp-like device with twenty-one strings held taut between a wooden neck and a calabash body, was my father's favorite instrument— no doubt it reminded him of the village life he left behind when he was a teenager. He named me after a legendary warrior who is the subject of two of the most important compositions in the kora tradition, "Kuruntu Kelefa" and "Kelefaba." And I once spent a surreal summer in the Gambia as a kora student, taking long daily lessons from a teacher with whom I communicated mainly in improvised sign language. I remember how excited my dad had been when he discovered that harp-and-kora album, a warm and atmospheric hybrid that sounded instantly familiar to him. Sometimes when people talk about loving music, this is what they mean. You hear something that resonates with some fragment of your biography, and you feel you wouldn't mind if those were the last sounds you ever heard.

Often, though, falling in love with music is a more complicated and contentious process. When I was growing up, I thought of my dad's beloved kora cassettes as finger-chopping music, because of the keening voices of the griots, who sounded to me as if they were howling. I had no interest in it, just as I had no interest in classical composers who were often heard in my house, and whose creations I learned to play on the violin, starting when I was five. Like most kids, I liked the idea that music could carry me out of my house and into the streets, into the city, and beyond. I started by asking my mother to buy me a cassette of Michael Jackson's *Thriller*, because everyone at school was talking about it. And soon I moved on to early hip-hop, old and new rock 'n' roll, and eventually punk rock, which transformed my moderate interest in music into an immoderate passion. Punk taught me that music didn't have to express consensus; you didn't have to sing along with whatever was coming from the family stereo, or whatever you saw on television, or whatever the kids at school were into. You could use music as a way to set yourself apart from the world, or at least *some* of the world. You could find something to love and something—perhaps lots of somethings—to reject. You could have an opinion, and an identity.

Does that sound obnoxious? Probably it does, and probably it would have sounded even more obnoxious if you had asked me to explain it when I was a teenager, newly converted to the gospel of punk. But I think that musical fandom tends to be at least a little bit obnoxious or embarrassing, which is why it's so easy to make fun of obsessive listeners, whether they are pretentious music snobs or wide-eyed pop stargazers, owlish record collectors in basements or aggressive "stans" on social media. (The term "stan" comes from a track by Eminem about a fan who is morbidly and romantically fixated on him; both the track and the term reflect a widespread belief that there is something shameful and scary and *unmanly* about fans' hunger for their idols.) We can, for the sake of politeness, agree to disagree and not to mock one another's musical tastes. But even those of us who are nominally grown-ups may find that we never quite outgrow the sense that there is something profoundly good about the music we like, something profoundly bad about the music we don't, and something profoundly wrong with everyone who doesn't agree. We take music personally, partly because we learn it by heart; songs, more than movies or books, are designed to be experienced over and over, made to be memorized. We take it personally, too, because we often listen to it socially: with other people, or at least while *thinking* of other people. Especially in the late twentieth century, American popular music grew increasingly tribal, with different styles linked to different ways of dressing, different ways of seeing the world. By the 1970s, different genres had come to stand for different cultures; by the 1990s, there were subgenres and sub-subgenres, all with their own assumptions and expectations.

In some ways, this is a familiar story. Many people have a vague idea that in the old days, popular music was *popular,* and that somehow popular music got increasingly fragmented and obscure. We put on our headphones and escape from the world into our own curated soundtracks. But at the same time, many fans have kept faith with the idea that music brings people together, assembling audiences that cross boundaries. The truth, of course, is that both of these ideas are important and true. Popular songs or styles or performers can erase boundaries, but they can also erect new ones. The early hip-hop records, for instance, sparked a movement that drew fans from all over the planet. But that movement also helped sharpen a generational divide, giving young Black listeners a way to renounce the R&B that their parents loved. And in the 1990s, country music became more suburban and more accessible. But it nevertheless remained a world apart from the pop mainstream. (Country music gained new listeners, in fact, by portraying itself as a gentler, more tuneful alternative to the increasingly truculent sounds of nineties rock and hip-hop.) Often, the economics of the music industry helped reinforce these divisions. Radio stations encouraged listeners to think of themselves as partisans, loyal to their favorite stations. Record stores arranged their wares by genre, hoping both to enable efficient shopping and to inspire serendipitous discoveries. And record companies scrambled to identify audiences and trends, searching for ways to make the listening public a little less unpredictable.

It is easy enough to acknowledge the evident diversity of popular music. But "diversity" is a rather uninspiring term, conjuring up a polite and static world where people have the serenity to accept one another's differences. More often, popular music has been not merely diverse but divisive, riven by crossover successes and cruel excommunications, rival fan bases and sneering feuds; full of musicians and listeners who keep finding new ways to set themselves apart. This is the divisive spirit I first heard in punk, and through punk I learned to hear it everywhere, even in my father's kora music, which he loved partly because it represented the world from which he had set himself apart. Unlike virtually all of his many siblings and half siblings, my father left his country and his family in order to build a very different life in America, where he became a celebrated scholar of global Christianity and Islam. He didn't pretend to share my infatuation with popular music, but he couldn't have been too surprised by my interest in the stubborn and restless people who made it and loved it, and by the fractious musical communities they created.

The Bose headphones that my dad wore in that hospital bed were brand-new. A week earlier, I had given them to him for Christmas; a week later, we brought them home from the hospital and they were mine again. I am wearing them now as I write, listening to mixes of wordless house and techno tracks on the music-sharing platform SoundCloud. This is background music for me, and maybe comfort music; it's what I often turn to when it's time to read or write. But even a serene, gently propulsive DJ set is in some sense an argument: it rewrites the unsettled history of the disco movement; it elevates a handful of tracks over innumerable others; it endorses a particular view about how they ought to be combined. Electronic dance music is infamous for its proliferating categories, which can seem absurd to anyone not inclined to investigate the basic distinction between house music and techno, let alone the subtler distinctions that separate, say, progressive house from deep house. But those differences matter greatly to a DJ, not least because they help determine who shows up to the party and who sticks around. Dance music, no less than country or hip-hop, brings people together by keeping *other* people out. These musical tribes pull and they push, drawing some of us close while keeping others of us outside. And sometimes they come to feel like home.

Literally Generic

I am always a bit puzzled when a musician is praised for transcending genre. What's so great about that? In visual art, "genre painting" refers to works that depict normal people doing normal things. In publishing, "genre fiction" is the down-market counterpart of literary fiction. And moviegoers talk about "genre films," a term applied to films that fulfill the basic obligations of a certain genre, like horror movies or heist movies—and, it is often implied, do no more than that. But in popular music, genres are all but inescapable. In the old days of record stores, every record in the store had to be filed *somewhere*. And even streaming services find it useful to rely on these categories; if you want to explore Spotify, the first option you are offered is to browse by "Genres & Moods." The idea of transcending genre suggests an inverse correlation between excellence and belonging, as if the greatest musicians were somehow less important to their musical communities, rather than more. (Did Marvin Gaye transcend R&B? Did Beyoncé?) Sometimes musicians are praised for mixing genres, although I'm not convinced that mixture is necessarily better than purity, or a more reliable route to transcendence. It is strange, anyway, to praise genre mixing without also praising the continued existence of the genres that make such mixing possible.

Musicians, I have learned, generally hate talking about genres. And reasonably enough: it's not their job. Virtually every music interview I have conducted has elicited some version of the sentence "I don't know why it can't just be 'good music.'" No doubt this sentiment captures something true about many musicians, especially accomplished ones. They *hate* being labeled. And they think more about the rules they break than about the ones they follow, reveling in a sense of freedom—especially in the recording studio. (I wouldn't know firsthand: although I eventually moved from playing violin in my high school orchestra to playing guitar and bass in bands, I never achieved anything beyond rudimentary competence, and that only sometimes.) But typically musicians have a sense of who their peers are, even if they insist that comparisons are worthless. Typically, too, they have a sense of industry and audience expectations, even if they say they love to confound them. Often their comments, like their albums, reflect a series of assumptions that they're scarcely even aware of: about what qualities might make a track acceptable to radio programmers; about what sorts of collaborations might be considered valuable, or surprising; about how songs are made and when they are finished. Country singers, for instance, have sometimes bucked country tradition by recording their albums with members of their touring bands instead of Nashville session musicians. But most *non*country singers probably didn't even know this tradition existed. You can't really rebel against a genre unless you feel part of it, too.

In many conversations and books about music, genre obsessives are the enemy. They are the mercenary record executives, intent on fitting each new act into a neat little box, just to make life easier for the marketing department. And they—we!—are the myopic music critics, too busy categorizing music to truly listen to it. Still, this book is a defense of musical genres, which are nothing more or less than names we give to communities of musicians and listeners. Sometimes these have been physical communities, revolving around record stores or nightclubs. More often, they have been virtual communities, sharing ideas and opinions through records and magazines and mixtapes and radio waves; especially in the era before social media and before the Internet, fans sometimes had to take it on faith that there were other people out there listening, too. I think the story of popular music, especially over the past fifty years, is a story of genres. They strengthen and proliferate; they change and refuse to change; they endure even when it looks as if they are dying out or blending together. (It seems that every decade or so, a genre becomes so popular that people worry it is disappearing into the pop mainstream.) The persistence of genres—the persistence of labels—has shaped the way music is made and also the way we hear it. And so this book aims to acknowledge that. This book is literally generic.

It can be slightly deflating to view popular music this way, and I don't think that's a bad thing. Pop music, broadly defined, has a tendency toward irreverence, and yet it is often discussed in worshipful tones, as the product of a succession of charismatic geniuses. And indeed, many of those familiar geniuses play a role in these histories, from Johnny Cash to the members of N.W.A. But if you emphasize genres, you inevitably find yourself thinking about the *other* stars, too—the hitmakers who don't tend to get celebrated in blockbuster movies. Like Grand Funk Railroad, for a time one of the most popular rock bands in America, even if many critics couldn't figure out why. Or Millie Jackson, an R&B trailblazer who couldn't quite reconcile herself to disco. Or Toby Keith, who epitomized so much about what people loved, and hated, about country music in the 2000s. Many of the musicians in this book *didn't* transcend their genres, sometimes because they didn't care to try, and sometimes because they tried and failed. Some of them battled the perception that their music was "generic" in a pejorative sense—as if any musical act embraced by a particular community must therefore be unimaginative. But this criticism of "generic" music is merely a restatement of the most common criticism of popular music in general: that there is something corrupting about certain kinds of popularity. Over the past half century, many musicians and listeners have belonged to tribes. What's wrong with that?

Excellent/Popular/Interesting

In 2002, I was hired as a pop critic at *The New York Times*, a dream job that allowed—or, rather, obliged—me to do almost nothing except listen to music and write about what I was hearing. In 2005, the newspaper sent me to the California desert to cover the Coachella music festival, an event so influential that it helped jump-start an entire economy of American outdoor music festivals. I scrambled from stage to stage, trying to see and hear as much as I could, while lingering over any performances that seemed especially excellent or popular or interesting. Those were my standards, at festivals and in general: I wrote about music that was excellent or popular or interesting, in that order of importance, with a special focus on musicians who satisfied at least two of those criteria, and extra scrutiny aimed at musicians who fulfilled only the last and least one. (Too much music coverage, I think, is devoted to music that is supposed to be interesting, despite arousing no particular passion in either the general public or the person doing the story. If it's not popular and it's not excellent, are we *sure* it is nonetheless interesting?) By the time I arrived at Coachella, I had long since gotten used to the cognitive dissonance of essentially going to parties for work, clutching my notepad like a weirdo while wandering among oblivious revelers. I never loved music festivals, perhaps because of the enormously privileged musical life I led: as a resident of New York with a prominent music-writing job, I had access to every club and concert in probably the most exciting city on the planet; no festival could rival that. But Coachella was by no means an unpleasant assignment, especially once you managed to navigate the complicated hierarchy of VIP areas.

I was sitting on a very important lawn one night with some friends, after most of the music was finished, when a stylish guy with a big smile wandered up: Yasiin Bey, the rapper who was then known as Mos Def. I had interviewed him once, a few years before, and he gave me a warm handshake and an unexpected greeting.

"I'm sorry you didn't like the album," he said.

I had forgotten about that. Six months earlier, I had described his most recent album, *The New Danger*, as "dreary." I braced for confrontation.

Bey kept smiling. "But *I* did," he said, with a shrug. It was an extraordinarily graceful response to a highly awkward but unavoidable situation.

Musicians have a right to feel wounded when writers who have been friendly in person publish negative reviews. Then again, they probably wouldn't feel much better if those writers were *un*friendly in person. Partly for that reason, I generally avoided interviews during my years at the *Times*. Usually I was just one more listener with a CD, or a concert ticket, and some strong opinions about whatever I was hearing.

Some of those opinions have changed and softened—indeed, *The New Danger* sounds a bit better to me now than it did in 2004. More often, though, I find myself still enjoying now what I did back then, whether or not the listening public ever agreed. And I am skeptical, in any case, of the way we all revise our opinions over time, the better to conform with contemporary peer pressure. In this book, I try to focus on the way popular music was heard at the time that it was released, which means I rely heavily on contemporaneous interviews and articles, as well as metrics like album sales and singles charts. It is no secret that these figures can be manipulated by record companies, although it is also true that many such efforts fail; there is a reason why not every hyped-up release makes it to the top of the charts. And throughout pop history, charts like the ones compiled by *Billboard*, the music industry's definitive weekly magazine, have shaped broader perceptions of success and failure, sometimes complicating familiar stories in interesting ways. (Some of the most excellent and interesting records in history were not popular—at least, not at first.) Our historical musical data are noisy and patchy: the record companies had a rough idea of how many people bought each album, but no way to measure how often those albums were played. But measurements like *Billboard* charts can serve as a useful corrective to the distorting effects of history and hagiography. It takes nothing away from the astonishing legacy of Aretha Franklin, for instance, to observe that she had only two No. 1 singles in her career: "Respect," her defining 1967 hit, and "I Knew You Were Waiting (for Me)," her 1987 collaboration with the English heartthrob George Michael. Franklin had one of the greatest voices of her era, but she was generally not—judging by the numbers—a pop star.

I pay attention, too, to what contemporary critics were saying. Not because these opinions were necessarily correct, or even influential. During my own time as a critic, I quickly realized that I had relatively little power, beyond the ability to occasionally aim some extra attention at an unknown performer. And this seemed like a healthy state of affairs. Among music critics, what looks like power is more often prescience, the ability to identify a hit before it hits. (I was never much good at that part of the job.) But even without make-or-break power, critics have retained a certain influence, because their collective judgments affect the way musicians are regarded, and how they regard themselves. Performers whom critics disdain sometimes come to conceive of themselves as populist rebels, waging war against a stuffy musical elite. And performers whom critics adore can sometimes help shape the general perception of what a genre should sound like, even without drawing huge audiences. Of course, as a critic myself, I am hardly unbiased about criticism and the people who practice it: by way of disclosure, I know a number of them, and wrote occasionally for some of the publications I quote in this book, including *The Source, The Village Voice,* and *Rolling Stone.* As a result, I don't have a particularly exalted view of the job. Music critics are just people who listen to lots of music and find ways to share their thoughts—which generally tend, in my experience, to be *less* judgmental than the thoughts of casual fans.

Part of the fun of revisiting older writing about music is the opportunity to be reminded how judgments and reputations can change. Many modern listeners might scarcely believe, for instance, that some knowledgeable listeners once considered Prince a sign of everything that was wrong with R&B. In the past few years, there has been an intense effort to reassess a number of musical careers, especially ones characterized by misbehavior or offensive views. This is not a new phenomenon: musicians and styles are constantly rotating in and out of vogue, sometimes for good reason and sometimes for no obvious reason at all. Many contemporary listeners want to be reassured that the performers they love are also people they would like—a common enough desire, although probably a more radical one than some listeners realize. (A playlist of unimpeachably good-hearted, well-behaved musicians would probably not resemble anyone's idea of a greatest-hits collection.) There is something intriguing about older music that meets the requirements of newer listeners, but there is also something intriguing about all the older music that doesn't, for whatever reason. Anyway, this book isn't meant to tell you what to listen to now. It's meant to tell you something about what everyone else has been listening to, and why.

Divide and Conquer

There is an idea, common and possibly even accurate, that music changed in the 1960s. Usually this claim involves the Beatles, and youth culture, and something about the Vietnam War. But the Beatles broke up at the end of the sixties, and this is a book about what happened afterward, over the next fifty years, as told through the stories of seven major genres. The first three are the most venerable: rock 'n' roll, R&B, and country—older genres that remained so popular, and so distinctive, that they came to seem like permanent features of the American cultural landscape. The next three are younger: punk rock, hip-hop, and dance music—upstarts that inherited different versions of the rebellious spirit that once animated rock 'n' roll. And the last genre is pop, which is barely a genre at all. At various times, "pop" has referred to the entirety of popular music, or merely to those performers who don't have a genre to call home; it arrived only relatively recently, and unexpectedly, as a genre unto itself.

This structure is necessarily more hospitable to some performers than others. And the story told here is necessarily a partial one. Classical music is excluded, and so is jazz, which by the time these stories begin had largely drifted away (or been cut off) from the world of pop charts and hit singles and big concert tours. Likewise, the story of modern popular music has generally not been a story of blues and folk and gospel and other traditional forms that survive with little help from the mainstream music market-place. This book is a reflection of my lifelong fascination with America, where I have lived since I was five, and so the focus is firmly on American pop—and, sometimes, its British counterpart. It does not attempt to do justice to the wider world of global music, including my father's beloved kora music. (I hope he would understand, especially because he is the reason my family came to America in the first place.) And Latin genres, which could and should be the subject of an entire book like this one, mostly developed in parallel to the ones set down here. Latin music makes only occasional appearances in these stories, although it has lately become central to the sound of American pop—in an account of the *next* fifty years of popular music in America, Latin genres would doubtless play a dominant role.

A story about musical genres is necessarily a story about conflict, as anyone who has watched the animated film *Trolls World Tour* can attest. (In it, tribes of trolls devoted to different genres wage war—and, rather less convincingly, make peace.) Performers and listeners alike figure out how and when to police the borders of their communities and argue about the status of those who find ways to "cross over." Often, crossing over means "going pop," abandoning your genre to make music that is meant to be more universally appealing. But the process can work in reverse, too, at moments when a genre gets popular enough to make pop stars jealous. "Gone Country," from 1994, was a wry Alan Jackson hit about singers moving to Nashville in search of country cred. ("She's gone country, look at them boots," Jackson sang. "She's gone country, back to her roots.") And in 2020, the former teen star Justin Bieber complained that the Grammy Awards had categorized him as pop instead of R&B. "I grew up admiring R&B music and wished to make a project that would embody that sound," he explained on Instagram. Performers, when they deign to talk about genre, can be strikingly ambivalent, reaffirming their genre affiliations while simultaneously claiming total music freedom. In many genres, a stronger sense of cultural identity can enable a looser sense of musical identity: in the eighties, hair-metal bands struck exaggerated rock 'n' roll poses while recording the mushy love songs known as power ballads. They were eventually displaced by a generation of so-called alternative-rock bands, some of whom couldn't quite decide if they wanted to bury old ideas of rock 'n' roll glory or bring them back to life.

When I was in high school, in the early 1990s, popular music was going through an unusually tribal phrase, and maybe that is why I wanted to write a tribal book. Many people who are roughly my age can still remember the taxonomies that defined their teenage years: some schools had metalheads and kids in cowboy hats; some schools had goths and classic rockers; nearly every school had a cluster of hip-hop fans, and many had a faction of ravers; different parts of the country had different kinds of punks. There was even, in 1990, a multi-genre music festival called A Gathering of the Tribes. (It helped blaze a trail for Lollapalooza, which began the next year.) One of the organizers was Ian Astbury, from the British band the Cult, who was proud to bring together a wide range of alternatives to mainstream pop: the punk pioneer Iggy Pop, the hip-hop group Public Enemy, the folk duo the Indigo Girls, and many others.

"Us and them doesn't exist any more," Astbury told the *Los Angeles Times*, although of course the festival's organization was not quite so ambitious. The tribes, after all, were supposed to be *gathering*, not disappearing.

Again and again, moments of heightened visibility for musical genres have also been moments of existential anxiety—moments when they seem on the point of disappearing. In the 1980s, some people worried about the long-term viability of R&B, precisely because of its success: with stars like Michael Jackson and Prince defining the sound of mainstream pop, how could R&B maintain its identity and its audience? In the 1990s, the success of Nirvana thrust "alternative" culture into the mainstream, creating both an opportunity and a paradox for a generation of formerly underground bands. And these days, the dominance of hip-hop is so total that the term itself is under some stress: if most of the most popular songs in America can be described, more or less, as "hip-hop," then where does that leave all the rappers and producers who *don't* tend to make pop hits? On music-streaming services, the top songs tend to be hip-hop hybrids that exist just beyond the reach of genre. Slow-rolling beats with synthetic snare rolls; moody and sometimes spooky electronic ambience; sullen vocals, often under-enunciated, that split the difference between singing and rapping. Has the problem of genre been solved? Is it possible that, when we finally have easy access to just about any song we want, many of us end up wanting to listen to the same thing?

This is not usually the question we ask about ourselves, especially in contemporary America, where conventional wisdom holds that our divisions are deeper and more destructive than ever. It is still the case, in some places and some times, that music can bring people together, across partisan and other divides. But the energy and anger that characterize many modern political debates reflect something important, too, about the very human—and perhaps very American—tendency to draw boundaries, and heighten differences, and to define ourselves as much by what we hate as what we love. For more than half a century, listeners, especially in their formative years, have used popular music to define their identities. And for as long as it serves this function, popular music will necessarily be divisive, bringing us together while also pushing us apart.

1.

ROCK

The Kingdom of Rock 'n' Roll

ONE EVENING IN 1962, a thirteen-year-old girl named Pamela was pleased to see, on her television, a twenty-two-year-old man from the Bronx called Dion DiMucci. He was the former lead singer of Dion and the Belmonts, and a preeminent teen idol—one of the biggest stars in rock 'n' roll. The girl was more than pleased, in fact. "DION!!!" she wrote in her diary. "Oh Help!!! I'm so excited, I think I'll just DIE!!! I was runnin' around, chokin' and cryin' and yellin' and screamin'."

Like many American teenagers in the 1960s, Pamela was obsessed with rock stars. And as she grew older, her obsession grew more intense, in tandem with the increasing intensity of its objects. A few years after Dion came the Beatles, and in particular Paul McCartney. "Every day I sent Paul a retardedly corny poem written on an aerogram and sealed with a kiss," she recalled. She had a particularly vivid memory of a Paul McCartney trading card emblazoned with a photograph that some other fans might have considered infelicitous. "You could actually see the shape of his balls being crushed by the tightness of his trousers," she later wrote. She and her similarly besotted friends called themselves the Beatlesweeties, and they composed romantic Beatlecentric stories for one another, imagining themselves into the Beatleish lives of their idols.

But Pamela soon realized that she was sweeter still on someone else: Mick Jagger, from the Rolling Stones, whom she and her friends had always found "dirty" and "sloppy"; she was discovering that these qualities were no longer so off-putting. "With my precious Paul, I never really got past the hoping stage, but now I dared to imagine Mick with his widewale corduroy trousers down around his ankles," she remembered. Her diary entries recorded her fantasies, which were becoming distinctly physiological. "Someday I will touch and feel him, I know it," she wrote. "Mick, my dear, dear PENIS!"

The young diarist eventually turned her passion for rock stars into a lifestyle, and then a literary career. She is Pamela Des Barres, and in 1987 she included those diary entries in her first book, *I'm with the Band: Confessions of a Groupie.* The title is accurate enough: Des Barres was for years a leading light in the Los Angeles rock 'n' roll scene, and her adult life turned out to be even more interesting than her girlhood diary. (Her Jagger prediction, for example, proved accurate soon enough.) But the true subject of her book was rock stardom itself. Few people have ever written as insightfully, or as sympathetically, about the peculiar enthusiasm that gives the genre of rock 'n' roll its mythic reputation, or about the complicated bond that unites performers and fans—and, just as important, divides them. Often in the book, Des Barres and her idols seem to be trying to figure out exactly how they are supposed to relate to each other. After all, Des Barres was not just a fan but a minor celebrity, and also a recording artist: a member of the GTOs, or Girls Together Outrageously, a rock 'n' roll performance-art troupe that released an album on an imprint owned by Frank Zappa, the rock eccentric who served as their mentor. Still, she was clear-eyed about the seductive power of rock stardom, and about the corresponding imbalance of power in many of the relationships she had. "I wondered if I was going steady with the best guitar player in the world," she thought while she was dating Jimmy Page, from Led Zeppelin. As part of the arrangement, she was expected to savor the band's forthcoming album:

> On his day off, we stayed in my bedroom, listening to the test pressing of *Led Zeppelin II* over and over again while he took reams of notes. I had to comment on every solo, and even though I believed the drum solo in "Moby Dick" went on endlessly, I held my tongue and went on pressing his velvet trousers and sewing buttons onto his satin jacket.

By the time Des Barres published her book, the rules of this world had been codified. It was 1987, and MTV was thriving, fueled by a particularly glamorous and decadent form of rock 'n' roll that came to be known as hair metal. Even people with no interest in rock 'n' roll had a pretty good idea by then of how rock stars were supposed to look and act. Rock stars outlived the Los Angeles scene that Des Barres chronicled, and they outlived the eighties, too. By the 2010s, the term "rock star" was commonly used to describe mildly quirky CEOs, faintly charismatic politicians, slightly unconventional athletes, and sometimes—although not so often—professional musicians. Sometimes it seemed as if "rock star," as a description or a general term of praise, had left the genre itself behind. A song called "Rockstar," by Post Malone featuring 21 Savage, was one of the biggest hits of 2017, and an entirely *different* and unrelated song called "Rockstar," by DaBaby featuring Roddy Ricch, was one of the biggest hits of 2020. Both tracks were about rock stardom as a form of celebrity, or a state of mind. (Post Malone declared, "I feel just like a rockstar," while DaBaby asked, "Have you ever met a real nigga rockstar?") And both tracks were hip-hop—not rock 'n' roll.

In the late sixties, though, rock stars were new. So new, in fact, that they didn't really have a name yet. The term "rock star" is mostly absent from Des Barres's book, even though rock stardom is her subject; in one typical diary entry, written in the early months of 1970, she refers to her world, instead, as the "pop-star circle," not the "*rock*-star circle." *Rolling Stone,* which was the rock 'n' roll publication of record for many decades, didn't regularly use the term until the 1970s. The first prominent occurrence of "rock star" in *The New York Times* came on October 5, 1970, in a front-page headline: JANIS JOPLIN DIES; ROCK STAR WAS 27. (The term was not used exclusively; the accompanying article described Joplin, variously, as a "rock singer" and a "pop singer.") The deaths of Joplin and Jimi Hendrix, in 1970, and then Jim Morrison, from the Doors, in 1971, helped to popularize the idea of rock stardom, reinforcing the link between rock music and drugs and alcohol, while also fostering the impression that the life of a rock star was wild and dangerous and, as a consequence, quite possibly short.

The rock-star era started around the time that Des Barres's diary was growing more explicit, at the end of the 1960s. And her evolving tastes tracked the genre's evolving sense of itself. Dion and McCartney, her early favorites, were not rock stars, in the modern sense, but she threw them over for Jagger, Page, and others, who certainly were. Many listeners thought they heard something changing, as the rock 'n' roll sixties gave way to the rock-star seventies. When McCartney released his second solo album, *Ram*, in 1971, *Rolling Stone* published a despairing review by the critic Jon Landau, who called it "incredibly inconsequential" and "monumentally irrelevant," a sign of cultural decline. He argued that *Ram* represented "the nadir in the decomposition of Sixties rock thus far," confirming what the breakup of the Beatles had suggested. "These days groups are little more than collections of solo artists," he wrote. "The idea of a group as a unit with an identity of its own has become increasingly passé."

By the time Joplin was memorialized as a "rock star" on the front page of the *Times*, the music had already shed some of its older associations. In the fifties, Elvis Presley's paradigm-changing rock 'n' roll records had been so broadly popular that they appeared atop the pop, R&B, and country charts simultaneously. But the path of rock 'n' roll grew more singular. In the fifties, rock 'n' roll split from country; in the sixties, it split from R&B; and in the seventies, it split from pop, developing its own media and its own benchmarks. Now rock 'n' roll bands were being judged by their albums, not their singles; record and ticket sales, not pop-chart performance, determined which bands were on top. ("Stairway to Heaven," arguably the definitive Led Zeppelin song, helped the group sell tens of millions of copies of *Led Zeppelin IV*, even though the track wasn't released as a single.) At the same time, though, the music was splintering, attracting a host of new modifiers that threatened to turn the genre into a collection of subgenres: acid rock, soft rock, folk rock, progressive rock, arena rock, art rock, punk rock. In 1977, when Presley died, one of his many obituaries was written by the critic Lester Bangs, who generally appreciated the increasing weirdness and rudeness of rock music, and who was predictably contemptuous of Presley's late-career incarnation as a Las Vegas oldies act. Bangs compared Presley, unfavorably, to Hendrix and Joplin, and, more favorably, to the Pentagon, which was not a band but the headquarters of the US Department of Defense. Each, he wrote, was "a giant armored institution," hailed for its "legendary" power. "Obviously we all liked Elvis better than the Pentagon," Bangs continued, "but look at what a paltry statement that is." Even as he mocked Presley, though, Bangs found himself missing the so-called King of Rock 'n' Roll, because he missed the days when the kingdom of rock 'n' roll had been coherent enough to have a so-called king. "I can guarantee you one thing: we will never again agree on anything as we agreed on Elvis," he wrote. "So I won't bother saying good-bye to his corpse. I will say good-bye to you."

In the 1970s, many musicians and listeners seemed to share Landau's and Bangs's sense that rock 'n' roll was decomposing or disintegrating. And many of them responded by doubling down, insisting that rock 'n' roll was not merely a musical category but an identity, a flag to wave. There was a rash of rock 'n' roll songs about rock 'n' roll, which tended to be rather nostalgic. "American Pie," the 1971 hit by Don McLean, was a wistful eulogy for the good old days of rock 'n' roll—but so, too, was Led Zeppelin's "Rock and Roll," which was released the same year. ("It's been a long time since the 'Book of Love,'" roared Robert Plant, paying thunderous tribute to an oldie from 1957.) Sometimes these rock stars seemed to be delivering backhanded compliments to the genre they were supposed to love. "I remember when rock was young," Elton John sang in "Crocodile Rock," adding that "the years went by and rock just died"; the sweet, fifties-inspired tune helped sweeten a rather sour tale of cultural decline. "Long Live Rock," by the Who, from 1974, followed its puffed-up title with a deflating afterthought: "Long live rock—be it dead or alive." And Mick Jagger offered the aging genre an affectionate shrug: "I know it's only rock 'n' roll, but I like it."

The defining attribute of rock 'n' roll in the seventies was self-consciousness, and in this sense the seventies never ended. Self-conscious rock 'n' roll turned out to be surprisingly versatile, and surprisingly durable. Ever since the seventies, rock bands have had to find ways to acknowledge their allegiance to a genre that is not at all young and not at all dead. And ever since the seventies, virtually every rock 'n' roll movement has portrayed itself as a kind of reformation, on a mission to revive the spirit of some golden age, real or imagined. Generations of musicians and listeners have viewed "rock" as an identity worth fighting over, which has created a never-ending debate over what constitutes "real" rock. Unlike country music, which sanctified rural white lifestyles, or R&B, which catered to multigenerational Black listeners, rock 'n' roll does not generally derive its identity from the demographics of its audience. (It may be the case that white suburban dads, for instance, are disproportionately likely to love rock music these days. But rock bands cannot earn credibility by bragging about their popularity among white suburban dads.) Instead, rock 'n' roll has endured as a musical tradition that successive generations have engaged with—it is the most traditional, perhaps, of any major pop genre. It is also the most spiritual. Rock 'n' roll is regularly described not as a set of practices or a particular sound but as a presence, emerging anywhere there are true believers, in rough accordance with the formula that Jesus gave to his disciples: "Where two or three are gathered together in my name, there am I."

If rock 'n' roll is an eternal spirit, then it must also be eternally itself—capable of being revived but not fundamentally changed, despite the progression of new styles and poses. One of the most effective revivalists over the years has been Bruce Springsteen, who was a bit of a throwback even when he first emerged, in 1973. He understood that "rock star" was both a job and a character. ("I know your mama, she don't like me 'cause I play in a rock 'n' roll band," he sang in "Rosalita.") This enthusiasm for rock 'n' roll history is part of what made him prescient: he realized that, from the seventies onward, the future of rock 'n' roll would belong to the past. ("There *is* no future in rock 'n' roll," Mick Jagger said in 1980. "It's only recycled past.") Springsteen became a top-of-the-heap rock star in 1975 with the release of *Born to Run*, an album that put him on the cover of both *Time* (ROCK'S NEW SENSATION) and *Newsweek* (MAKING OF A ROCK STAR). And then Springsteen did something even more impressive: he remained a rock star, enduring for decades as one of the most popular singers in the country, and one of the most reliable ticket sellers. He was still among the biggest names in rock in 2017, when at the age of sixty-eight he began a solo theatrical residency, singing songs and telling stories in a Broadway theater, five nights a week, for more than a year. Even without his band, he played the part of rock 'n' roll true believer, sometimes waxing sermonic between songs. "There is no love without one plus one equaling three," he exclaimed during the show. "It's the essential equation of art, it's the essential equation of rock 'n' roll." He chuckled at his own teenage faith in rock 'n' roll and marveled at how little had changed since then. "It's the reason true rock 'n' roll—and true rock 'n' roll bands—will never die!"

Abunchanoise

Over the course of 1970, the Beatles released their final album, *Let It Be*, all four members released solo albums, and, on December 31, Paul McCartney began the legal process that culminated in the official breakup of the band. As a consequence, some listeners began to consider a question that probably sounded reasonable then, although it sounds very unreasonable now: Who would be the next Beatles? Many of the proposed answers were rather far-fetched, even back then. There was Badfinger, known for spirited and catchy rock songs; the band's strongest claim to Beatleness was its status as the first band signed to Apple Records, the Beatles' label. (Badfinger had a handful of hits but never ascended to the rock 'n' roll elite.) In 1976, a band called Klaatu released an album with so little information, and so many Beatlesy flourishes, that a number of listeners grew convinced that the band was the Beatles in disguise. (Klaatu, as people soon discovered, was a progressive-rock band from Canada, now best remembered for "Calling Occupants of Interplanetary Craft," a curiously affecting space ballad that became a minor pop hit when it was covered by the Carpenters.) But there was one act that tried to follow in the Beatles' footsteps and, in some ways, succeeded—selling out Shea Stadium in Queens, even more quickly than the Beatles had, and becoming for a time one of the most popular bands in America.

The band's name was Grand Funk Railroad. Today the members are probably best remembered for "We're an American Band," a cowbell-powered tribute to the rock-star lifestyle, and for their effortful versions of a couple of sixties hits, "The Loco-Motion" and "Some Kind of Wonderful." Often, though, they are not remembered at all; many listeners who hear the name now might wrongly but reasonably assume, as I did for years, that it belonged to some sort of funk band. In fact, the guys from Grand Funk Railroad played what might be called hard rock: critics described their music as "loud," or "powerful," or "straight-ahead." Mainly, though, critics described it as lousy. Writing in *The New York Times*, in 1972, Loraine Alterman rendered a judgment that was unsparing but not at all unusual. "Anyone with a trace of taste in rock music can't seriously say that Grand Funk has produced any music in the slightest degree memorable except for its deafening racket," she wrote. The same year, the band released a greatest-hits compilation that included, on the record sleeve, a collage of newspaper stories, many of them unflattering:

GRAND FUNK IS LOUSY
RECORD OFFICIALS PUZZLED BY GRAND FUNK'S SUCCESS
HOT GROUP GETS THE COLD SHOULDER AT HOME

Grand Funk Railroad was probably the first popular rock 'n' roll band to define itself in opposition to rock critics, who were a fairly new species. *Rolling Stone* was launched in 1967; its founding publisher was Jann Wenner, an ambitious fan and journalist from San Francisco who figured out that there would be an audience for a magazine that took rock 'n' roll seriously—that is, a rock 'n' roll magazine that took *itself* seriously. This was a good idea, especially since the tastes of critics and everyday rock fans tended, then, to coincide. In 1969, *The Village Voice,* New York's leading countercultural newspaper, began publishing a column called Consumer Guide, written by a stern but openhearted critic named Robert Christgau, who assigned letter grades to albums, as if they were homework. Christgau later wrote that back then, rock critics like him were generally in sync with the listening public. "Not all of the most popular rock was good," he wrote, "but most of the good rock seemed to be popular." The rise of Grand Funk, though, was a sign that in the seventies, rock critics and rock fans were beginning to diverge—permanently, it turned out. *Rolling Stone* once referred to Grand Funk Railroad, rather sniffily, as "the world's biggest car radio." And Christgau reviewed six of the band's first seven albums, giving them marks ranging from C- to C+.

From a distance of decades, the Grand Funk Railroad discography scarcely seems controversial: the band's fuzzy, bluesy rock songs sound exactly the way you might expect them to; it is not hard to understand why a young listener looking for loud rock 'n' roll may have settled on Grand Funk and been satisfied, at least for a time. Some critics fought against their own potential irrelevance by fighting for Grand Funk. Dave Marsh, from the raffish Detroit rock magazine *Creem,* praised Grand Funk, lustily but not quite convincingly, for being "in touch with... the spirit of American youth"; similarly, Christgau eventually professed admiration for the group's "populist sincerity." In *The New Yorker*, Ellen Willis, who was one of the most insightful rock critics of that era or any other, published a column titled "My Grand Funk Problem—And Ours." (The title was a mischievous reference to "My Negro Problem—And Ours," a despairing 1963 essay about racism by Norman Podhoretz.) Willis had initially dismissed the band as "abunchanoise," but then, as she noticed that millions of young people were buying the albums, she was seized by a discomfiting thought: "Hadn't my parents reacted the same way to Little Richard?" When the essay was published in 1972, Willis was thirty, and yet she felt herself wondering if she was already out of touch. The new teenagers had found their own music, only it was rock 'n' roll, which was supposed to be *her* music. The rise of Grand Funk seemed to her like further proof of "the fragmentation of the rock audience." In the old days, rock 'n' roll had stood on one side of the generation gap—the rising side. Now there was a generation gap within the genre. Where rock 'n' roll had once scandalized and polarized American culture, now a new crop of bands was doing something similar to rock 'n' roll itself. And they were doing it by making music that sounded, even to many rock fans, like "abunchanoise."

In the sixties, writers sometimes used the term "acid rock" to refer to bands that summoned up a countercultural spirit, often through trippy lyrics and squally electric guitars. The term was regularly affixed to Hendrix, whose playing and persona suggested psychedelic exploration, and also to bluesy and raucous bands like Cream, featuring Eric Clapton, and Blue Cheer, whose joyfully unrefined songs were destabilized by wild, cork-screwing guitar solos. The "acid" in "acid rock" indicated a connection to San Francisco hippie culture, but bands like Cream were helping to push rock 'n' roll away from hippies and into the post-hippie era. In 1971, in the *Los Angeles Times*, the critic John Mendelssohn cited "Cream and its imitators" as the chosen soundtrack of a new generation of fans who prized "distortion-laden volume and exhibitionism" above all else. "These kids generally came to eschew the relatively benign psychedelics favored by their elder brothers and sisters in favor of barbiturates and cheap wine,"

Mendelssohn wrote disapprovingly. "Their music asks absolutely nothing of the listener—everything is moronically simple, extremely loud, and re-peated so mercilessly that one can be barbituated and/or drunk beyond recognition and still not miss a thing. The whole phenomenon is quite ter-rifying." More recently, the cultural sociologist Deena Weinstein observed, with less alarm, that these new bands had catered to a large but often overlooked audience: blue-collar white men who embraced many elements of the sixties counterculture (drugs, denim, long hair, loud guitars) while rejecting its starry-eyed idealism in favor of a more overtly macho ethos, enthralled by the imagery of power and dominance. These guys were a "melding of hippie and biker," she wrote, and they needed music to match their sensibility.

For a while, no one knew quite what to call this post-acid sound. One term was "downer rock," which seemed to describe both the lumbering rhythms of the music and the firmly anti-idealistic sensibility of its fans, not to mention the drugs they liked to take. In 1971, *Billboard* anointed Grand Funk Railroad "kings of the downer-rock youth underground." Around the same time, *Rolling Stone* was celebrating a strange and mes-merizing band from Birmingham, England—"the dark princes of downer rock," the magazine wrote. The band was Black Sabbath, and in those early days some listeners found the music confusing. The band's self-titled debut album, from 1970, was far too strange to be generic: it started with the sound of rain and then bells and then the guitar and bass, tolling together in slow motion. Nothing in the singer's voice promised the thing that rock 'n' roll singers used to promise: a good time. He wheezed, "What is this that stands before me? / Figure in black which points at me." After about five minutes, the tempo increased from an eerie plod to an ominous gallop, which felt like a kindness. Black Sabbath was radical, and (despite little radio play) radically popular, which reportedly surprised some executives at the band's record company. Some critics were aghast: Robert Christgau described Black Sabbath as "the worst of the counterculture on a plastic platter." (In reference to the band's spooky lyrics, he added, "I've been worried something like this was going to happen since the first time I saw a numerology column in an underground newspaper.") Lester Bangs, on the other hand, appreciated the band's "dark vision of society and the human soul" and, more important, the "obsessive, crushing blocks of sound." Like the early rock 'n' rollers, some decades earlier, Black Sabbath made music that seemed so simple, so single-minded, that many grown-ups had trouble taking it seriously.

In time, a term emerged for Black Sabbath, and for a universe of more or less like-minded bands: heavy metal. The two words had been memorably joined in 1968, by the Canadian band Steppenwolf, in "Born to Be Wild," which also served as the theme song for the 1969 outlaw movie *Easy Rider*. When John Kay intoned, "Heavy metal thunder / Racing with the wind / And the feeling that I'm under," it seemed clear that he was talking about a motorcycle, but in the years that followed, perhaps partly by coincidence, "metal" and "heavy metal" entered the rock 'n' roll glossary. (In 1970, a review of Led Zeppelin in *The New York Times* referred to "the twin metallic shrieks of Jimmy Page's guitar and Robert Plant's vocals.") A musical shift was underway, too, as bands began to realize that they could build songs not around lyrics or chord progressions but around riffs—simple, heavily rhythmic guitar phrases. Mendelssohn was right about the growing importance of "distortion-laden volume." Through a howling amplifier, a single guitar note could hold its own against the rest of the band. And a six-string guitar chord could sound even tougher when reduced to its three-note essence, octaves and a fifth, neither major nor minor—a power chord. Tony Iommi, the guitarist from Black Sabbath, was a wizard of power chords, which suited both his musical sensibility and his hand: as a teenager, he had lost the tips of two fingers in a factory accident.

Like many musical revolutionaries, the members of Black Sabbath didn't realize quite how revolutionary they were. Ozzy Osbourne, the lead singer, sometimes sounded confused when asked about the band's fascination with the devil—this despite the fact that he sang lyrics like, "My name is Lucifer, please take my hand," and despite the fact that on the inside cover of the band's debut album, the text is inscribed within an upside-down cross. "All the tracks on the first album were a warning against black magic," he told one interviewer. And he tried to explain that "War Pigs," from the group's second album, *Paranoid*, was a protest song. "It's about VIP people who are sitting there saying, 'Go out and fight,' and all the everyday people are forced to, but the VIPs never do," he said. But when people think about "War Pigs," they don't usually think about Osbourne's earnest invocation of "the poor." They think about Iommi's eerie guitar and Osbourne's opening couplet: "Generals gathered in their masses / Just like witches at black masses." What's memorable is the way Osbourne evokes not merely war's cost but its seductive appeal. Part of what made Black Sabbath seem new—part of what made heavy metal seem new—was a disinclination to be uplifting, or hopeful, or self-righteous. Often, the music seemed primarily concerned with evoking evil and cruelty, and only secondarily concerned with condemning it. Sometimes not even secondarily.

When Ellen Willis was figuring out how she felt about Grand Funk Railroad in 1972, she mentioned the possibility that "the enormous success of bands like Grand Funk and its English counterpart Black Sabbath" might "re-create a cohesive rock community." This was a lot to ask, but the rise of heavy metal really did help define a particular "rock community" in the seventies, making the sprawling genre feel a bit more like a tribe again. In 1970, another English band, Deep Purple, released an influential album of fast and muscular riff rock called *Deep Purple in Rock*. The cover depicted the five members carved into Mount Rushmore: the ultimate "rock" band. A 1974 feature in *Time*, about how rock 'n' roll was splintering into subgenres, described heavy metal as the form of rock favored by "young teen-agers just experimenting with marijuana"—the rock 'n' roll of rock 'n' roll, you might say.

Led Zeppelin was a leading light, drawing some of the biggest crowds even while remaining rather uncategorizable; the band's epic songs and albums were remarkably delicate, lightened by influences from folk music and country blues. "It really annoys me when I see the band categorised as 'heavy,' and put into bags with people like Grand Funk," Jimmy Page told the *New Musical Express* in 1972. Unlike Black Sabbath, Led Zeppelin made music that was difficult to imitate. But Robert Plant, the lead singer, was the platonic ideal of a rock star, beloved for his glorious voice and his equally glorious golden curls, strutting and preening, transported by the music. Led Zeppelin helped standardize the idea that a rock concert should be a grand spectacle, and in 1976, the band released an audacious and entertaining live concert film, *The Song Remains the Same*, with extended instrumental interludes accompanied by filmed sequences, some fictional and some better than fictional. (More concert films should include footage of the band's manager in the back of a police car.) Many of the decade's biggest new rock bands found their own ways to be spectacular. Alice Cooper dressed in a kind of vampire drag, and put on a stage show that often overshadowed his music. Queen built quasi-metallic mini symphonies, using parts that shouldn't have fit together: Brian May's molten guitar, Freddie Mercury's expansive tenor, Broadway-esque keyboards, un–rock 'n' roll harmonies. Later in the decade came KISS, wearing black and white face paint and breathing fire, even as they insisted they were simply trying to uphold the genre's traditions. "KISS has never been anything but a right-on-the-line straightforward rock 'n' roll band," explained Paul Stanley, the lead singer, who portrayed a character known as the Starchild. The band's most famous chorus was proof of its devotion to the genre, and also proof that the genre had become synonymous with decadence: "I wanna rock and roll all nite / And party every day."

None of these hard or heavy bands were beloved by critics, and all were, in different ways, deeply uncool, secure in the knowledge that everyday kids—and maybe some hippie-biker types—got it, even if the tastemakers didn't. These were *populist* rock bands, a description that probably would have seemed redundant a decade earlier. In the sixties, rock 'n' roll was presumed to be simultaneously crowd-pleasing and cool; in the seventies, it seemed as if bands often had to choose. Christgau eventually concluded, in 1979, that the previous ten years had severed the link between popularity and excellence. "The decade's best music," he wrote, had been "semi-popular," as opposed to popular—beloved by an emerging elite of careful listeners, both professional and amateur. Meanwhile, Peter Frampton, formerly of a band called Humble Pie, went solo and eventually released a concert album that made him a mainstream heartthrob and, for a time, one of the biggest rock stars in the world, to the surprise of many critics, even the ones who liked him. And in Boston, five guys called themselves Aerosmith and, borrowing unashamedly from the Rolling Stones and other established rock stars, became arena headliners themselves, famed for the intensity of their fan base, the Blue Army, named for their devotion to denim. Steven Tyler, the lead singer, later recalled that the band was particularly popular in "rust-belt towns: Toledo, Cincinnati, Cleveland, Detroit." The first *Rolling Stone* cover story on Aerosmith, from 1976, began, half fondly, with a scene out of a horror movie:

> They came staggering across the parking lot in the still, brackish Michigan dusk and advanced on Pontiac Stadium—one of those monstrous modern sports arenas—like a boozy army of hard hats whose intention it was to dismantle the place. They looked like hell. Nobody dresses up for concerts anymore. They gobbled reds and chug-a-lugged beer. Some fell on their faces and tumbled down the hill.

This is one way to define rock 'n' roll: the term—the genre—belongs to whoever has the biggest army, whoever is most apt to drunkenly howl its name, whoever is most intent on claiming the ground. (In the gnomic words of Steven Tyler, "Our music is rock 'n' roll, and rock 'n' roll is rock 'n' roll.") It is a fittingly democratic definition, and it reveals a pattern beneath the seemingly endless fragmentation of rock. From the seventies onward, a long string of raucous and undeniably unhip bands have made the genre their own. In every generation, there are people who consider this state of affairs a fate worse than death for a once-proud genre. But even this complaint concedes that the genre is not dead—that it staggers on, zombielike, fueled by beer and a vaguely working-class identity and a fistful of reds, or whatever gets you the highest the cheapest.

Less Monstrous and More Glamorous

"Ladies and gentlemen, rock 'n' roll." Those were the first words broadcast on MTV when the network was launched, in the summer of 1981. The name stood for "music television," of course; the idea, a dead-simple stroke of genius, was simply to play music videos all day long. (Part of the genius was that record companies paid for the videos, and provided them free to MTV, as a form of promotion.) It doesn't appear that a lot of thought went into that opening statement, or the musical commitment it signaled—in 1981, it must have seemed obvious that a brash musical upstart should be identified with rock music. When the network declined to play a video by the R&B star Rick James, one executive explained that the channel's "rock audience" wasn't interested in "R&B or disco." This exclusive posture soon proved unsustainable; not even MTV could resist the appeal of Michael Jackson, who became an MTV mainstay after the release of *Thriller* in 1982. But rock 'n' roll remained central to the network, which became, in turn, increasingly central to rock 'n' roll.

Although some R&B fans were offended by this focus, so, too, were some rock fans, who worried about what the network might do to their genre. *Rolling Stone*, which had been suspicious of the heavy-metal explosion of the 1970s, was even more hostile to the MTV revolution, at least at first. In 1983, the magazine published a cover story that was advertised as an exposé: INSIDE MTV: THE SELLING OUT OF ROCK & ROLL. (It was illustrated with a Warhol-style portrait of Michael Jackson and Paul McCartney, who had just filmed the video for their duet "Say Say Say.") The author, Steven Levy, noted that MTV was "becoming a factor in the selection of which rock & roll songs get recorded and which bands get recording contracts," and he wrote that on MTV, there were few traces of "the musical energy and optimism of the Sixties." Levy's complaints were many: he was concerned about the lack of R&B and country music, the "violence and sexism" of some videos, and the fact that viewers were encouraged to be "passive" consumers. Mainly, though, it seemed that Levy—and perhaps, by extension, the editors at *Rolling Stone*—simply didn't care for much of the music on MTV. He noted that the channel "makes stars out of the likes of Adam Ant," the theatrical British singer affiliated with the cresting "new pop" movement. To Levy, this looked like dumbing down, not to mention derockification. "The stars of the future will more likely be the superficial, easy-to-swallow Adam Ants than the enigmatic Bob Dylans," he wrote.

Some musicians agreed. In *I Want My MTV*, an oral history of the network, Howard Jones, another theatrical English singer, fondly remembered MTV as an ally, supporting him and his fellow pop stars in their battle against the "macho" rock establishment. "That whole explosion of MTV was quite significant in the sense that it gave the finger to rock 'n' roll," he recalled; the network helped a generation of flamboyant British pop stars briefly conquer America. At the same time, though, MTV was *obsessed* with rock, which had anyway grown more theatrical during the seventies. (Even Bob Dylan briefly took to wearing white face paint, during his 1975–1976 *Rolling Thunder Revue* tour. In Martin Scorsese's fictionalized documentary of the tour, from 2019, Dylan claimed, deadpan, that he had stolen the idea from KISS.) "Anyone who wasn't theatrical was done," remembered Dee Snider, elsewhere in the book. Snider led the band Twisted Sister, and became an unlikely rock star in 1984, after MTV began playing the music video for "We're Not Gonna Take It," the band's breakthrough single. "Videos inspired a resurgence of metal—heavy metal has never gone away, but it had a really big moment in the '80s," he said. "Metal owes MTV for that. But MTV owes metal." In the case of Twisted Sister, being "theatrical" meant embracing a caveman version of drag-queen chic. In the "We're Not Gonna Take It" video, the band members did battle against a furiously uptight dad who was too straight to understand his son's love of rock 'n' roll. The song was rather quaint, with a Christmas-carol tune and a hilariously underwhelming guitar solo. Even so, the song got more exposure the next year, when the Parents Music Resource Center, a group that sought to expose harmful and offensive records, appeared at a US Senate hearing and adduced "We're Not Gonna Take It" as an example of how rock 'n' roll can promote violence. Snider was there, and he tried to reassure the senators, telling them that he was a faithful Christian and family man. Under cross-examination by Senator Al Gore, though, Snider was forced to concede that the band's fan club was called SMF Fans of Twisted Sister, and that the initials stood for "Sick Mother Fucking."

Snider was happy enough to wave the banner of heavy metal, but sometime between Black Sabbath and Twisted Sister, the music once described as "downer rock" had morphed into something closer to "upper rock." In the early eighties, hard rock and heavy metal were ruled by raging bands like AC/DC, Iron Maiden, and Judas Priest, whose songs were brisk and exuberant. This was party music, slightly camouflaged—Judas Priest, for instance, cultivated a menacing black leather image but was known for singing about "Living after midnight / Rocking to the dawn." MTV helped a generation of mainstream American kids discover how much fun this music could be, while also encouraging the bands to emphasize all the fun they were having. One band that didn't need much encouragement was Van Halen, a California band anchored by a pair of brothers from Holland, and featuring perhaps the most extroverted singer of his generation, David Lee Roth. Starting in the late seventies, Van Halen perfected a Day-Glo variant of heavy metal; Eddie Van Halen, the band's virtuoso guitarist, deployed state-of-the-art squiggles and swoops, and he popularized a technique sometimes called "tapping," with both hands on the frets. (His electric guitar could evoke a bank of synthesizers, sped up and spliced together.) Unlike many virtuosos, Eddie Van Halen had a knack for making virtuosity seem like a good time, and all the early Van Halen albums sound as if they were recorded at house parties, with the party noise somehow edited out. More important, perhaps, was the band's fan base. "Van Halen from the outset was a band that appealed to both males and females, and our audience reflected that popularity," explained Noel E. Monk, who was for a time the band's manager. "Lots of wannabe head-banging teenage boys, and plenty of nubile young ladies just dying for a chance to meet one of the guys in the band." In a memoir of those years, Monk remembered taking the band to England in 1978, to open for Black Sabbath. "When I looked out into the crowd every night, it seemed like 98 percent of the audience was young (and not so young) men," he wrote. This demographic datum had a catastrophic effect on the members' postshow routine.

As any savvy manager knows, a rock band that draws women as well as men is much more likely to fill arenas and even stadiums, as Van Halen eventually did. And in the wake of Van Halen's success, a generation of California bands—some local, many transplants—realized that newish styles and sounds, borrowed from heavy metal, could help them attain old-fashioned rock stardom. None did more to establish the new template than Mötley Crüe, a seemingly simple rock band that turned out to be a complicated cultural hybrid. (The umlauts, purely decorative, were inspired by Löwenbräu beer, not the seventies hard-rock band Blue Öyster Cult.) In *The Dirt*, their cheerful and salacious oral history, written with the critic Neil Strauss, the members of Mötley Crüe explained their musical lineage. One obvious influence was KISS, although Mick Mars, the guitarist, *hated* KISS; he hated hippies, too, despite loving sixties rock. Nikki Sixx, the bassist, had a punk-rock phase but was concerned that the movement had become "too mainstream." Tommy Lee, the drummer, once played in a Beach Boys–influenced band, even though he thought the Beach Boys were "stupid sissy shit"; he only did it because he was so excited to be in a "real rock band." And Vince Neil, the lead singer, had previously dressed in all white, as the leader of a scrappy but glamorous California party band called Rock Candy. In other words, by the time Mötley Crüe came together, "rock 'n' roll" meant many different things; somehow, the members synthesized these strands into a mixture that didn't feel mixed up at all.

There is no way to overstate the importance of the band's look, which was tough and androgynous: tight leather and lots of metal studs, seductive makeup and professionally teased hair. The members were inspired by glamorous bands of the 1970s, especially one called the New York Dolls, but also by apocalyptic films like *Mad Max* and *Escape from New York.* Although Tommy Lee was appropriately and effectively frenetic, none of the other members were known for musical proficiency. "We're not great, we're just all right," Nikki Sixx said in 1986. But their appearance and their attitude hinted at the insanity of their lives, which were defined not only by ceaseless partying but also by brutal drug addictions, violent assaults involving both men and women, and more near-death experiences than any four people might reasonably hope to survive. When Nikki Sixx was asked to explain why the band's second album was called *Shout at the Devil*, with a pentagram on the cover, he told a journalist from *Creem* that the band members hadn't sold their souls to Satan but to rock 'n' roll. "I like to think that we're a lot like the Rolling Stones of the '80s. They would live their life to the fullest and their songs revolved around their lifestyles, and that's what we do," he said, and he expanded on the album's title. "Shout at your teachers, police, politicians, anybody that's an authoritative figure that puts you down or doesn't let you achieve what you want to do in life. Shout at the motherfucker, do what you want to do. That's what it's about."

One of many kids who got the message was Chuck Klosterman, a Mötley Crüe fan from rural North Dakota who grew up to write *Fargo Rock City*, a book of autobiographical essays about the genre that came to be known as hair metal. Klosterman took pride in being a metal guy, and yet he understood that eighties metal wasn't really a subculture but a mainstream phenomenon, both in popularity and in ethos. "Instead of telling an alienated kid that it was okay to be different, metal seemed to say, '*You're not different at all,*'" Klosterman wrote. "In fact, you're hyper-normal. In fact, you're extremely popular and totally cool." MTV spread the message, helping Mötley Crüe sell millions of albums and boosting countless other bands that looked vaguely similar, even if they weren't quite as feral. Def Leppard, from England, and Bon Jovi, from New Jersey, teamed with canny collaborators (the producer Mutt Lange and the songwriter Desmond Child, respectively) to create addictive hair-metal pop songs, with synthesizers alongside the guitars. A band called Whitesnake, led by a former Deep Purple singer named David Coverdale, formed a successful partnership with a model, Tawny Kitaen, who starred in a series of hit videos for the band. (The subsequent MTV success of bands named White Lion and Great White hardly dispelled the perception that hair metal was unusually formulaic.) Some rock veterans successfully reinvented themselves for the hair-metal era, including Aerosmith, who had helped inspire it, and Heart, a great seventies hard-rock band led by sisters Nancy and Ann Wilson, who were given a makeover. In the MTV history, Ann Wilson recalled, "The idea was to transform us into porn kittens." It turns out that many people at MTV had mixed feelings about hair metal. They believed, accurately, that the network's reliance on big-haired men (and occasionally women) in spandex undermined "the cool, cutting-edge image we were presenting," in the words of one executive. But they also realized that it tended to draw higher ratings than any other kind of music.

In retrospect, the hair-metal movement probably crested in 1987, when Guns N' Roses released *Appetite for Destruction*, a blockbuster that even hair metal's detractors could appreciate. I was eleven then, and I remember sitting in a friend's bedroom as he showed the cassette to me—shyly, as if it were pornography. On an inside cover was the painting, by Robert Williams, for which the album was named. It depicted a woman, half-naked and unconscious, slumped against a fence; a robotic skeleton, presumably her assailant, standing over her; and a blood-red monster, possibly an angel of vengeance, descending fast. The band members seemed even scarier and more dissolute than the guys from Mötley Crüe; in photographs, they tended to look slightly dirty and more than slightly dazed. The lead singer, Axl Rose, had a snarling, screeching voice, more extreme than his contemporaries', even while Slash, the guitar player, favored elegant bent notes that gestured back toward earlier forms of rock and the blues. The next year, the director Penelope Spheeris released *The Decline of Western Civilization Part II: The Metal Years*, a mesmerizing documentary that captured the glee and desperation of the Los Angeles hair-metal scene. (It was a sequel to a documentary about the Los Angeles punk scene.) In the film, also-ran musicians, aching for stardom, share the screen with big names like Paul Stanley from KISS. Stanley appears wearing no makeup, or at any rate no more makeup than the lingerie-wearing woman he is caressing; in 1983, the members of KISS had scraped off their face paint in recognition of the fact that rock music had grown less monstrous and more glamorous. As the camera pulls back, we see that Stanley is actually caressing three different women. "I think heavy metal is the true rock 'n' roll of the eighties," he says. "And rock 'n' roll was basically music made by people who were thinking with their crotches."

The Edge of Wuss Cliff

One of the defining qualities of hair metal was that people hated it—the bands' shameless preening and obvious hunger for adulation made them easy to sneer at, and they knew it. *Rolling Stone* panned Mötley Crüe's second album; the review said, "You'd almost think it was developed by MTV's marketing staff." And Jann Wenner, the magazine's publisher, considered Bon Jovi so unimpressive that he apparently lobbied to keep the band out of the Rock & Roll Hall of Fame, which he helped steer. He told his biographer, Joe Hagan, "What does Bon Jovi mean in the history of music? Nothing." (Bon Jovi was admitted in 2018, nearly a decade after becoming eligible; Mötley Crüe, eligible since 2007, is still waiting.) One of the running themes in *Fargo Rock City* is that Klosterman loves the music that rock snobs love to hate. *"Shout at the Devil* was my *Sgt. Pepper's,"* he writes, knowing that some readers will recoil from the comparison between Mötley Crüe and the Beatles. But snobbery is essential to fandom, especially music fandom, because adoring one thing inevitably means disdaining something else. Even as a boy, Klosterman was not immune. He remembers that *Hysteria*, the top-selling 1987 album by Def Leppard, felt to him like a betrayal, partly because it was so popular, especially among "vapid cheerleaders" and "girls named Danielle who wore Esprit tank tops." He had an even more complicated relationship to Poison, a band originally from Pennsylvania that was known for an unusually feminine version of glam and for a peppy sound that was more "hair" than "metal." (*Rolling Stone*: "An annoying parade of limp three-chord clichés and breathy harmonies.") Klosterman loved Poison, but he kept his love a secret, because he knew that the local metalheads—snobs, too, in their own way—didn't consider Poison to be "'real' metal." For him, and doubtless not a few other high school kids, Poison was a guilty pleasure.

As it happens, Poison is the first rock band I ever saw in concert, in April 1988, at the Centrum in Worcester, Massachusetts. Poison was opening for David Lee Roth, who had split from Van Halen a few years before. The concert wasn't my idea—it was a friend's birthday, and his parents were generous enough to take a bunch of seventh graders out to a show. I didn't know much about either act, besides their cassette covers, and I was perplexed but not put off by the look of *Look What the Cat Dragged In*, Poison's debut, which showed all four guys wearing heavy eye makeup and red lipstick. I seem to remember squinting down at the stage, where the members of Poison didn't look quite as camera-ready, or as transgressive, as they did on the album cover. And maybe I remember, too, some of David Lee Roth's stunts—footage from that tour reveals that his set included a boxing-ring sequence, a steel-drum interlude, and plenty of guitar shredding by Steve

Vai, who was the main attraction in his band. But most of what I remember is thoroughly generic: the guitars were loud, everyone was wearing jeans, some people were smoking cigarettes that didn't smell like cigarettes, and the men's room line was so long that some guys peed in the bathroom sinks instead. It all seemed very rock 'n' roll.

The next year, in 1989, my family moved from Belmont, Massachusetts, to Hamden, Connecticut, a suburb of New Haven, where, because the television received fewer broadcast channels, my parents were finally convinced to subscribe to cable. For the first time in my life I had in-home access to MTV, which had begun to divide its programming into a bunch of genre-specific shows: *Yo! MTV Raps* for hip-hop; *Club MTV* for pop and dance music; *Headbangers Ball* for heavy metal; *120 Minutes* for what was beginning to be called "alternative" music; *Dial MTV*, a countdown show, for the most popular videos station-wide. "Ladies and gentlemen, rock 'n' roll" was no longer a sufficient enticement; the network was now acknowledging the power of musical fragmentation. Even so, there was still plenty of hair metal on MTV, and one of the most popular videos that summer, when the cable technician came to wire our television, was "Heaven," the breakthrough hit by a glammy band called Warrant. The video starts with the sound of a strummed acoustic guitar and a close-up of Jani Lane, the blond lead singer, looking earnestly into the camera, delivering some pensive doggerel about a faded picture and faded memories. He's just marking time until, after nearly a minute, the rest of the band arrives, along with a crashing three-chord chorus and a perfectly vague refrain: "Heaven isn't too far away / Closer to it every day."

There had always been a gap between the idea of hair metal and the sound of hair metal. Plenty of listeners noticed that although the bands' lyrics were full of boasts about "kicking ass on the wild side," as Vince Neil once sang, the music tended to be a good deal tamer. Most albums from the era were stocked with sturdy midtempo songs, driven by simple guitar riffs that chugged and sometimes squealed. But then, once or twice per album, the chugging would temporarily cease so that the lead singer could move a little closer to the microphone and sing something quieter and more earnest: a power ballad. The form arose in the 1970s, as various rock 'n' roll acts discovered, seemingly in parallel, that even rock fans were not immune to the considerable charms of a sentimental love song. For "heavy" bands in particular, the power ballad represented a chance to dramatically cut both the tempo and the volume. "Stairway to Heaven," by Led Zeppelin, was one early example, although it may be too long and too unpredictable to qualify. (When I was in junior high school, "Stairway to Heaven" was a common slow-dance song, despite the perilous acceleration near the end. I can still recall the burning shame I felt, swaying awkwardly with my dance partner, as John Bonham's drums began to clatter and I tried to figure out whether the slow dance was over.) Another early example was "Without You," a perfectly overwrought specimen by Badfinger, from 1970, although most people know the breezier cover version by the roguish singer Harry Nilsson, which became one of the most popular singles of 1972. The power ballad was not then considered an integral part of rock 'n' roll tradition—in fact, the term was still not widely used in 1981, when Journey released "Don't Stop Believin'," a masterpiece of hard-rock melancholy that endures as perhaps the most beloved power ballad ever recorded.

In the 1980s, the power ballad went from being a rock 'n' roll sideshow to the main attraction. Mötley Crüe had "Home Sweet Home," Poison had "Every Rose Has Its Thorn," Def Leppard had "Love Bites," Whitesnake had "Is This Love." (Needless to say, White Lion had "When the Children Cry," and Great White had "The Angel Song.") The popularity of the form was proof that slow, sentimental songs never really go out of style. But the power-ballad boom also illustrated the paradoxical way musical genres often evolve, with image and sound pulling in different directions. The hair-metal bands used fashion and rhetoric to portray themselves as rock 'n' roll extremists, advertising an intensified version of seventies rock stardom. But over the years, this movement grew less single-minded, as musical movements usually do—reaching out, as Klosterman noticed, beyond metal-head boys to attract listeners who were neither metalheads nor boys. It seems likely that the bands' commitment to rock 'n' roll pageantry made it easier for them to record mawkish love songs, driven by acoustic guitars or pianos, without anyone wondering whether they were leaving rock 'n' roll behind. One of Aerosmith's last big hits was "I Don't Want to Miss a Thing," by the pop songwriter Diane Warren—it wasn't particularly rock 'n' roll, except for the fact that it was an Aerosmith power ballad, which made it rock 'n' roll, by definition. Often, in popular music, the more you look and act the part, the more freedom you have to alter the script.

The popularity and musical impurity of hair metal were also vulnera-bilities, though, because the mismatch between the genre's rebellious image and its mild sound became increasingly conspicuous. In retrospect, it's clear that some listeners were craving a purer, narrower form of rock 'n' roll. (In rock 'n' roll, as in many human endeavors, eras of expansion and dilution tend to give rise to eras of retrenchment and purification, and vice versa.) According to the conventional wisdom, hair metal died in the fall of 1991, killed off by a single event: the release of a song called "Smells Like Teen Spirit," by a previously obscure band called Nirvana. The song had a rudimentary four-chord riff and no real guitar solo; the music video, set in an underlit high school gym, featured a lead singer with matted hair, a baggy striped T-shirt, and a mumbly voice. Somehow, this song became a hit, and then a movement, popularizing a subgenre known as grunge, and the broader musical sensibility that was sometimes called alternative. Surely the end of hair metal couldn't have been that simple?

The evidence suggests that the myth is probably true. I was a junior in high school when "Teen Spirit" hit, and although I didn't care much for it, I remember how inescapable the song suddenly was, and how quickly MTV filled with like-minded bands. In *I Want My MTV*, Peter Mensch, who managed Def Leppard, described the 1992 MTV Video Music Awards as an "apocalyptic" moment: Def Leppard, performing a ludicrous ode to teen-age defiance called "Let's Get Rocked," seemed disastrously out of place. (It probably didn't help that the lead singer, Joe Elliott, possibly hoping to approximate grunge fashion, wore a beret and a bright blue overcoat that resembled a dressing gown.) Kip Winger, the hunky leader of a hair-metal band called Winger, claimed that Nirvana's video effectively made his band nonviable. "I watched 'Smells Like Teen Spirit' and I thought, *All right, we're finished,*" he said. "We all knew it. It was obvious." In 1993, Winger was featured on the network's hit animated show *Beavis and Butt-Head,* about two cretinous metalheads who watch videos and go on dumb adventures.

"These guys live on the edge," Butt-Head snickers, when a Winger video appears on their television.

"Yeah—the edge of *wuss cliff,*" says his sidekick, Beavis.

Right about the time Kip Winger gets to the leering refrain—"She's only seventeen / Daddy says she's too young, but she's old enough for me"—Butt-Head finally asks Beavis to change the channel. "Let's find something that *rocks,*" he says. The show later compounded the insult by introducing a character named Stewart Stevenson, a Christian bed-wetter who always wore a Winger T-shirt.

The end came about as quickly as Kip Winger says it did. Winger never had another big hit—and neither, for the most part, did Van Halen or Def Leppard or Poison or Warrant or Whitesnake (or White Lion or Great White). Guns N' Roses released *Use Your Illusion* parts I and II, a rather exhausting pair of albums, in 1991, and disintegrated before managing to record a proper follow-up. Mötley Crüe kept going, but the band's first post-grunge single, "Hooligan's Holiday," showed how much had changed. The band had split with Vince Neil and enlisted a new singer, John Corabi, who had a stronger voice and, by all accounts, a milder personality. The new Mötley Crüe song was bluesy and brooding, and the music video was full of ironic white-on-red slogans that seemed to have been inspired by the artist Barbara Kruger. A band that had helped invent the sound and look of mainstream rock in the eighties now wanted to be perceived as part of the growing "alternative" movement. Alternative to what?

Alternative Everywhere

Nirvana had an idea. Kurt Cobain, the leader, had no particular interest in "alternative rock" as a genre, but he certainly did see himself as a member of the rock 'n' roll opposition. As Nirvana was transformed, in the course of a few months, from an underground favorite to a worldwide chart-topper, Cobain tried to make sure listeners understood that the band, which had been nurtured in Seattle's post-punk scene, wasn't like the other bands on the radio. "We're not going to be proud of the fact that there are a bunch of Guns N' Roses kids who are into our music," he said, as "Smells Like Teen Spirit" was taking off. In 1992, when Nirvana was on the cover of *Rolling Stone*, Cobain positioned himself as a rock 'n' roll pied piper, leading America's impressionable youth away from mainstream bands. "Hopefully, they'll like our music and listen to something else that's in the same vein, that's a bit different from Van Halen," he said. Elsewhere, he complained about the indignity of having to face autograph-seeking fans in Bruce Springsteen T-shirts—he hated the idea that Nirvana had become just another arena rock act. In the liner notes to *Incesticide*, a 1992 compilation, he issued a warning to his new listeners. "If any of you in any way hate homosexuals, people of different color, or women, please do this one favor for us—leave us the fuck alone! Don't come to our shows and don't buy our records."

And yet Nirvana's music seemed to send a different message. It was inviting: catchy and dramatic, often alternating between self-effacing verses and roaring sing-along choruses. In that sense, Cobain's songs, especially the hits, were less confrontational than his interviews. This was still loud guitar music, based on rather simple chord progressions—still rock 'n' roll, in other words. And so there was never a sharp musical demarcation between "true" alternative-rock bands like Nirvana and all the mainstream bands that were, as Cobain once put it, "jumping on the alternative bandwagon." Nirvana's success helped popularize a number of other Seattle exports: Pearl Jam, Soundgarden, Alice in Chains, and the one-off supergroup Temple of the

Dog. (Cobain mocked Pearl Jam as a "corporate" band, but Pearl Jam turned out to be both one of the decade's most successful bands and one of its most uncompromising, doggedly committed to its own sound and principles.) The label "alternative" seemed to fit a trio of maverick West Coast rock bands that had broken through before Nirvana: the Red Hot Chili Peppers, Faith No More, and Jane's Addiction. "Alternative" also described, sort of, two of the most popular new rock bands of the 1980s, R.E.M. and U2, who emerged from decidedly nonmainstream rock scenes in Athens, Georgia, and Dublin, Ireland, respectively. Most important, "alternative" was the label affixed to just about every quirky or brooding rock band that had any success in the 1990s—"alternative" was a broad catchall that became increasingly, and paradoxically, synonymous with rock 'n' roll itself.

Radio programmers noticed the change and began using "alternative" as the name for a format that was broad enough to cover everything from devotedly weird college stations to the big-market powerhouses that focused on top-selling rock bands. There was a *Billboard* chart called Modern Rock, which was supposed to be an alternative to the magazine's Album Rock chart, which was renamed Mainstream Rock in 1996. But often, the distinctions were hard to parse. For instance, "You Oughta Know," the intense but infectious song by Alanis Morissette, went to No. 1 on the Modern Rock chart, No. 3 on the Album Rock chart, and No. 6 on the pop chart. Morissette, a Canadian pop star who reinvented herself as a rock trail-blazer, was not nearly as splenetic as Cobain, but her wordy songs were perhaps even more at odds with the party-every-day sensibility of eighties rock. (Many of her lyrics didn't sound like rock lyrics, or lyrics at all: "Let's talk about life for a while / The conflicts, the craziness, and the sound of pretenses falling.") Her breakthrough album, *Jagged Little Pill*, became one of the most influential and popular rock albums of the modern era, selling more than fifteen million copies in America; "alternative" was everywhere. In 1995, an article in *Billboard* defined "alternative" as "one of those radio terms nobody can quite define, but which everybody wants to make money off"; the article noted that the format embraced acts as varied as the Offspring, a punkish rock band, and Sheryl Crow, a faintly rustic singer-songwriter, alongside countless more obscure performers. One of the only things everyone seemed to agree on was that "alternative" was short for "alternative rock": an alternative form of rock 'n' roll, rather than an alternative *to* rock 'n' roll.

Nirvana had proudly set itself apart from generic rock. But in the aftermath of Cobain's death, by suicide, in 1994, generic rock sounded and looked more and more like Nirvana. Long-haired rockers gave themselves haircuts, and some embraced baggier clothes and thrift-store chic. Even mainstream rock stations began to sound rather downcast, full of songs in minor keys, with anguished lyrics, often imperfectly enunciated, and guitar players who mostly resisted the urge to show off. One of the decade's many post-Nirvana successes was Stone Temple Pilots, a formerly funky band from San Diego that settled upon a moodier sound and, in 1992, released *Core*, a debut album that sold millions of copies. This success would have been unimaginable in the pre-Nirvana rock world—for starters, *both* of the band's first two singles, "Sex Type Thing" and "Plush," were tormented songs about women being violently assaulted. But Stone Temple Pilots had no particular connection to an underground rock scene, or to college radio stations; from the start, this was a rock band for everyday rock fans. (In the 2000s, Scott Weiland, the lead singer, joined with former members of Guns N' Roses to form a kind of pre-grunge/post-grunge supergroup, Velvet Revolver.) Collective Soul, Candlebox, Live, Bush, Seven Mary Three: none of these bands were cutting-edge or underground, and none were consumed, Cobain-like, by the possibility that the wrong sorts of listeners might turn up at concerts. But all of them provided proof that in the nineties, being a band that played "rock," as opposed to some subgenre of it, meant sounding a bit like Nirvana. And some underground groups found that real rock stardom was suddenly within reach, including the Smashing Pumpkins, a formerly indie band from Chicago that specialized in loud but dreamy rock songs that suffered not at all when they were transplanted from clubs to arenas.

It is not fair to say that the alternative era was just the hair-metal era with a few tweaks to the music and fashion. The post-Nirvana hunger for new and unusual music helped enliven the airwaves by boosting a wide range of performers. (There is something admirable about a radio format that can champion both the Offspring and Sheryl Crow.) And the traveling festival Lollapalooza, which was launched by Perry Farrell, from Jane's Addiction, in 1991, and originally ran through 1997, brought popular and obscure rock bands together with rappers and cult favorites—a whole spectrum of alternatives. Even so, the alternative era, no less than the hair-metal era, had its share of traditions and clichés. Male rock voices got lower and huskier, moving away from the clarion shrieks that had ruled hard rock ever since Led Zeppelin. And singers seemed compelled to pretend that they were having less fun than they really were, rather than more. It was startling to hear Cobain proclaim, "I feel stupid and contagious." But confessions of self-loathing soon seemed inescapable: "I'm a creep" (Radiohead); "I'm a loser, baby" (Beck); "I'm a loser and a user" (Green Day); "I'm just a sucker with no self-esteem" (the Offspring); "I'm a freak" (Silverchair). A song about anguish is not necessarily any more meaningful than a song about partying, let alone any better.

The oddest thing about the post-Nirvana era was how long it lasted. In 1991, there was good reason to think that the so-called grunge movement was a fad and that the country's obsession with noisy Seattle bands would last only a few years. But Nirvana has been so influential, for so long, that the revolution it inspired now seems preordained: *of course* Nirvana, or a band like Nirvana, was going to come along. The move from hair metal to grunge mirrored a broader cultural shift toward more casual styles and attitudes, and so maybe it was inevitable that rock stars would evolve from tight spandex to loose jeans, from revelry to rumination, from high screeches to low moans.

One thing stayed the same, though: these new rock stars turned out to be just as polarizing as the old 1980s rock stars had been, maybe more so. *Spin* magazine had been founded in 1985, to provide a hipper and more entertaining alternative to the rather staid rock 'n' roll coverage of *Rolling Stone*, and in the 1990s the magazine became closely identified with the alternative-rock boom. As the nineties ended, though, and "alternative rock" and "mainstream rock" became near-synonyms, it grew harder to figure out which band was on which side. In 2000, the *Spin* cover subjects included such radio-friendly "alternative" bands as Papa Roach, Matchbox Twenty, and, most controversially, Creed, a group from Florida that streamlined and amplified the grunge template, adding tougher riffs and grander choruses, sung by a self-regarding front man named Scott Stapp. The members of Creed were Christian, a fact that inspired the magazine to mention, rather disdainfully, the band's "'Up With Jesus' lyrics." An executive from VH1, MTV's sibling network, offered some notably faint praise of Creed. "They're very derivative of classic '60s and '70s rock," he said. "And they're very derivative of grunge. But they're also very much their own band." Even this rough treatment was too gentle for some *Spin* readers, one of whom unburdened himself in the letters section of a subsequent issue:

> I would rather see Britney Spears on the cover for an entire year. Scott Stapp and his moronic band play music for mindless, pathetic dolts. I'm offended that writer Gavin Edwards actually compared Led Zeppelin fans to Creed fans. And if Stapp's idol, Jim Morrison, were still alive, he'd vomit on the singer's greasy-ass chest.

People who hated bands like Creed often hated them for one of two reasons. Some, like the *Spin* letter writer, thought Creed was "moronic," which is the kind of insult typically hurled at raucous and unpretentious rock bands, especially those with young fans. In the world of rock 'n' roll, of course, "moronic" need not be an insult—over the years, many rock stars have demonstrated the musical value of moronity, feigned or otherwise. (The correspondent compared Creed unfavorably to Led Zeppelin and to Jim Morrison, from the Doors, but both Led Zeppelin and the Doors were often described in similar terms, sometimes even by their fans. A review in

Creem once praised the "stupid-rock punch" of *Led Zeppelin II*. And Lester Bangs once lauded Morrison as a "Bozo Dionysus.") Others hated Creed and their peers out of a hunger not for intelligence but for innovation, which made more sense. Nearly a decade after Nirvana's breakthrough, it seemed time for a new template.

By the time Creed made the cover of *Spin*, one alternative to alternative had already emerged: rap rock, a hybrid codified by the furious protest band Rage Against the Machine, and taken up, in various forms, by top-selling acts such as Korn, Kid Rock, and Limp Bizkit. In the 2000s, this hybrid was sometimes described as "nü-metal," a term that emphasized both the riffs and the importance of novelty. (The umlaut was purely decorative, and probably disparaging, because the term, like "hair metal," was mainly used by detractors.) Unlike nth-generation grunge, these bands worked hard to be cutting edge, inviting DJs into their lineups, collaborating with rappers, and experimenting with percussive guitar techniques. Linkin Park emerged as the most popular band from this tradition, and one of the most popular bands of the new century, refining the innovations of its predecessors to create an earnest and efficient nü-metal hit-making machine.

With the exception of Rage Against the Machine, whose riotous leftist anthems made just about every other rock band seem timid, this music was never really cool. These new rock stars tended to be white, and their love of hip-hop often led them to imitate rappers, not always deftly. With his backward red baseball cap and crotch-grabbing bravado, Fred Durst, from Limp Bizkit, emerged as a pop-culture punching bag, notwithstanding his band's elastic riffs. It was easy to mock him and the others as hip-hop wannabes, but I really liked some of these bands. I remember a particularly thunderous Korn performance from 2002, at Madison Square Garden, where the band's murky and propulsive songs made the arena feel like a pulsating underground lair. (Jonathan Davis, the lead singer, encouraged the fans to bellow along with "Faget," his chronicle of high school bullying, which built to a darker, more unsettling version of grungy self-loathing: "I'm a faget!") I liked that Linkin Park was willing and able to serve as an effective backing band for Jay-Z, on a collaborative album called *Collision Course*; it seemed appropriate that the country's biggest rock bands should reckon with hip-hop, rather than ignoring it, as many of their predecessors had done. If the future of mainstream rock 'n' roll was inclusive and sometimes embarrassing—well, that didn't seem like the worst possible fate for the genre.

Nü-metal soon ran aground, a victim of the increasing unpopularity of the figurehead Durst, and of a growing consensus that rapping is difficult and perhaps best left to the professionals. Once you have heard Jay-Z effortlessly unspooling rhymes over Linkin Park's riffs, it may be harder to get excited about the band's own rapper, Mike Shinoda. Astonishingly, though, the post-grunge movement lumbered onward: one of the most popular mainstream rock bands of the 2000s was Nickelback, a Canadian group that honed a rather utilitarian version of the nineties sound. When I reviewed a Nickelback concert for *The New York Times* in 2002, I wrote that the songs combined "grunge's limited sonic palette with hard rock's unlimited bombast," and I wondered, noting the workaday tunes and witless banter, whether the whole show had been a sly parody. Evidently it hadn't, because Nickelback kept selling records and making hits, including "Photograph," a likable power ballad that got new life in the 2010s as a social media meme. (In 2019, President Donald Trump tweeted a version of the "Photograph" meme that had been turned into a criticism of Joe Biden.) When Nickelback was announced as the halftime entertainment for a Detroit Lions game on Thanksgiving 2011, an anti-fan started a petition urging the Lions to "think about their fans before choosing such an awful band to play at halftime," and asking, "Does anyone even like Nickelback?" Something about the petition captured people's imagination, although the show went on as scheduled—at halftime, the band took the field to play "When We Stand Together," a remarkably vague and stiff protest song. ("We must stand together, there's no giving in / A hand in hand forever, that's when we all win.") In some ways, Nickelback was merely the newest version of the old Grand Funk Railroad phenomenon: the popular rock band disdained by connoisseurs and critics—including me, in this case.

Something was changing, though: by 2011, after a run of nearly a decade, Nickelback was no longer making big hits in America—and few other rock bands were, either. A Nielsen report revealed that during the 2010s, most of the top-played songs on American "alternative rock" radio stations were by relatively anonymous bands like Cold War Kids and AWOLNATION, neither of which had any members whom the average music fan could name or recognize. Meanwhile, all ten of the top-played songs on "mainstream rock" radio were from the nineties, mainly by antique grunge bands like Nirvana and Pearl Jam. In the nineties, Nirvana and Pearl Jam helped push alternative rock into the mainstream. But in the 2010s, even mainstream rock was simply one more alternative. Possibly no new mainstream rock band enjoyed more success in the decade than Imagine Dragons, which drew from pop and electronic music to make songs that were catchy, if rather mild-mannered. American listeners in search of a band more fully devoted to rock 'n' roll might have gravitated to, say, Five Finger Death Punch, known for a shouty and riff-driven hybrid of metal and alternative rock—a big name, but only within the smallish circle of listeners who liked that sort of thing. In the 2010s, rock music in America—real, loud rock music, not some gentle or artsy variant of it, played by new or newish bands and not elderly veterans— was alive but relatively obscure, at least when compared to hip-hop or pop. And newly minted rock stars typically weren't considered celebrities. It was as if Ellen Willis's prophecy had finally come true, in a way she might not have expected, or enjoyed. She had wondered when the "rock community" might once more feel "cohesive." The answer was: when the genre shrunk.

Heavy Metal Rules

One of the most entertaining rock videos of the 1980s never made it into rotation on MTV. It had no stars, no plot, and virtually no music. It was called *Heavy Metal Parking Lot*, and it consisted of seventeen minutes of footage from outside a Judas Priest concert at the Capital Centre, an arena in Landover, Maryland. The film became a cult favorite in the 1990s, circulating on bootleg videocassettes, because it so pungently captured the partisan enthusiasm of the fans. A man with feathered hair and a zebra-striped sleeveless T-shirt summed up the musical philosophy that held sway in the parking lot—and, no doubt, in similar parking lots throughout the country. "Heavy metal *rules*," he said. "All that punk shit sucks, it doesn't belong in this world, it belongs on fuckin' Mars, man. What the hell is punk shit? And Madonna can go to hell, as far as I'm concerned. She's a dick." He sounded as if he were reciting a catechism, and in a way he was: "Heavy metal definitely rules: Twisted Sister, Judas Priest, Dokken, Ozzy, Scorpions—they all rule!"

Not every story about the growth of heavy metal leads to Mötley Crüe and the hair-metal boom. In fact, while the band was sometimes promoted as heavy metal, Nikki Sixx disagreed. In a 1986 interview with *Kerrang!*, a rock and metal magazine, he said, "We never *were* heavy metal." (He preferred to think of Mötley Crüe as simply a "sleazy" rock 'n' roll band.) Plenty of metalheads probably agreed. Arguments over the identity of heavy metal grew louder in the 1980s, and the genre's contours grew correspondingly sharper. The success and intensity of groups like Judas Priest inspired what was known as the new wave of British heavy metal, or NWOBHM, an initialism that was, fittingly, better suited to obsessive fanzines than to casual conversation. Iron Maiden, which helped define NWOBHM, had a flair for imagery: the angular lettering in the band's logo seemed designed to be etched into jean jackets, and the album covers invariably featured the band's mascot, Eddie, a skinless, wild-eyed apparition that looked terrific on a concert T-shirt. The band was generally ignored by American radio stations, but the imagery served as a form of peer-to-peer marketing; many people doubtless saw the logo before they heard the music, which was galloping and energetic—although not nearly as gruesome or fiendish, truth be told, as Eddie might have led them to believe.

From its earliest days, heavy metal was superlative music, with bands competing to be the most extreme: in 1968, Blue Cheer, the trailblazing acid-rock group, was advertised as "the heaviest sound going." Black Sabbath, with slow tempos and grim lyrics, seemed heavier still. Deep Purple was brawnier. Judas Priest, with those black leather outfits, was tougher. A band like KISS, meanwhile, was great fun but not particularly extreme, which helps explain why KISS was essentially written out of the heavy-metal canon. And so while groups like Mötley Crüe were conquering Los Angeles and, in time, MTV, the British bands cultivated a more obsessive audience. American listeners followed along in new magazines like *Kerrang!*, which was founded in 1981, and in smaller, smudgier publications, where they could find pen pals and swap cassettes. Soon this British wave inspired an American one: a movement of bands that sought to further refine the British sound by making it faster and scruffier. Bruce Dickinson, from Iron Maiden, had a semi-operatic voice, and he sang as if he were leading his metalhead troops into glorious battle. But these American bands often had singers who snarled instead, and they often dressed like high school troublemakers, in jeans and high-top sneakers, with hair that was long but relatively unstyled. Many guitarists adopted a venerable metal technique known as palm-muting: using the heel of the picking hand to silence the strings between strokes, creating a chugging rhythm instead of letting them ring and reverberate. And they did it at impossible speeds, unleashing furious barrages that made established metal bands like Judas Priest seem rather stately and sedate by comparison.

A writer from *Kerrang!* referred to this style as "thrash metal," and the term stuck to a whole generation of bands, including one with a name that ensured it could never really renounce metal: Metallica. The drummer, Lars Ulrich, was a Danish immigrant who paid close attention to the latest underground sounds from Britain and Europe, and he resolved to form a *real* metal band, one that would function as a rejection of the cheerful and glamorous scene then ascendant in Los Angeles. To underscore the point, Ulrich and his bandmates initially wanted to call their 1983 debut album *Metal Up Your Ass*, but they settled for a less confrontational title: *Kill 'Em*

All. While hair-metal bands were conquering MTV, Metallica refused to make music videos, which made them seem like the leaders of an underground outlaw faction. Like the punk rockers, these thrash metalheads defined themselves in opposition to mainstream rock, but many were, like the zebra-striped man in the Maryland parking lot, similarly suspicious of punk. Compared to metal, punk seemed too artsy, too cozy with elite rock critics, too trendy—or else, as in the case of hardcore punk, too crude, and insufficiently attentive to musicianship. (Metal bands were expected to have at least one member who could really shred, and ideally more than one.) The thrash-metal partisans may not have wanted to be mainstream, but they didn't exactly want to be freaks, either. Even as they pledged allegiance to the strange subculture of metal, these bands also presented themselves as regular guys, devoted to nothing weirder than loud riffs and cold beverages. James Hetfield, Metallica's rhythm guitarist and lead singer, was once photographed wearing a T-shirt with a parody of the band's first album cover. It read "ALCOHOLICA: DRANK 'EM ALL," and where the original had a hammer and a pool of blood, this one had a Smirnoff bottle and a pool of vodka.

Metallica emerged as the dominant thrash-metal band, but there was plenty of competition. A former Metallica guitarist named Dave Mustaine formed a band called Megadeth, playing an angular and imaginative version of thrash, with zigzagging riffs heading off in unexpected directions. And then there was Slayer, admirably fast and mean, propelled by a drummer, Dave Lombardo, whose playing sounded as if it were driven by pure hatred and a few spare limbs. In this scene, what set Metallica apart was not so much the band's ferocity as its relatively traditional musical sensibility: the members knew how to shape riffs into memorable songs, and they suspected that they might be able to win fans far beyond the thrash underground. *Ride the Lightning*, the second Metallica album, arrived in 1984, and it contained Metallica's version of a power ballad: "Fade to Black," a suicide note in song form, which started with acoustic guitar and then grew louder and faster. In 1989, Metallica at last released a music video, for a song called "One." The full version was nearly eight minutes long, and it found a home on MTV despite looking and sounding like nothing else on the network: footage of the band was intercut with scenes from *Johnny Got His Gun*, a 1971 film about a wounded veteran; the music unspooled as a miniature thrash symphony, building to an ecstatic guitar solo and a machine-gun rhythmic finale.

"One" helped send Metallica into the stratosphere: the band's next album, *Metallica* (often known as *The Black Album*), arrived in 1991, and it was stern but accessible, full of midtempo hard rock and even a proper love song, "Nothing Else Matters," a power ballad with orchestral ornamentation. The album was an unprecedented success, with more than sixteen million copies sold in America. It is probably the most popular heavy-metal album of all time—except, of course, for the fact that many heavy-metal listeners may not recognize it as a heavy-metal album at all. In the fall of 1991, the band made the cover of *Rolling Stone* (METALLICA: FROM METAL TO MAIN STREET), and Kirk Hammett, the lead guitarist, confessed that some metalheads he knew didn't care for the band's new sound. "Friends of mine who are really hard-core fans have said, 'Well, the album's not as heavy. You guys aren't as heavy as you used to be,'" he said. His response was philosophical: "How do you define heavy?"

The Power of Evil

Something about heavy metal inspires listeners to get carried away. Fans listening to those early Black Sabbath albums couldn't help but imagine that they were being granted access to a realm of evil spirits, even though Ozzy Osbourne tried to explain that he had no interest in "black magic." After being fired from Black Sabbath, for conspicuous insobriety, in 1979, Osbourne emerged as a solo act and cemented his reputation as a heavy-metal maniac by apparently decapitating two animals with his teeth: a dove, on purpose, at a meeting with record executives in 1981, and a bat, by accident (he thought it was fake), at a concert in Iowa in 1982. A few years later, Osbourne was sued, separately, by two different sets of parents, who alleged his song "Suicide Solution" had inspired their sons to commit suicide. Neither lawsuit succeeded, but they helped enshrine Osbourne as not just a musical pioneer but a public menace. An enemy of polite society. A legend.

Often when we say that a particular sort of music has a bad reputation, we mean that it is thought to be mediocre. Heavy metal had the other kind of bad reputation: it was thought to be evil, or at least to contain evil elements. The genre's signature hand symbol was the "devil horns," an index-and-pinkie salute that was popularized by Ronnie James Dio, who sang with a Deep Purple successor band called Rainbow, and also with Black Sabbath after Osbourne's departure. Throughout the 1980s, there were reports that Satanists were using heavy metal to lure young people into cults that practiced ritual violence. (There was never any conclusive proof that these cults actually existed, although there were reports, here and there, of violent criminals who were fascinated by satanic iconography.) The Parents Music Resource Center (PMRC) hearing, in 1985, only strengthened this bad reputation, and although Dee Snider wanted to make clear that he and his band were firmly anti-evil, other groups seemed to benefit from the attention. One of the stars of the hearing was W.A.S.P., a rather ridiculous shock-rock band. The group was denounced for having released a single called "Animal (F**k Like a Beast)," which depicted on its cover a man wearing a puzzling and seemingly impractical contraption—a codpiece with a built-in buzz saw. The PMRC's list of offensive songs included, alongside pop hits by Prince and Cyndi Lauper, a song by a band called Venom. It is easy to chuckle at the PMRC, but in this case the council chose fairly wisely, because Venom, a band associated with the NWOBHM, did in fact sound like a politician's bad dream. The first two Venom albums, *Welcome to Hell* (1981) and *Black Metal* (1982), were truly gnarly, with lyrics that barked allegiance to Satan, and playing that was fast and loose; the members made it easy for listeners to imagine that they were in the aural presence of true evil. Venom's commitment to musical extremism was what helped inspire thrash bands like Metallica to create a sound that was faster and more frenzied—more *metal*, you might say.

Of course, metalheads who flocked to Metallica in search of frenzy eventually had to contend with *The Black Album* and its midtempo songs; despite the name they chose, the members of Metallica were ultimately less interested in upholding metal purity than in realizing and expanding their own vision of rock 'n' roll. By the time Metallica hit the mainstream, some devoted metalheads had already defected to Slayer, which guaranteed listeners a ballad-free experience. The band's classic 1986 album, *Reign in Blood*, hurtled through ten songs in less than half an hour, with Tom Araya, the bassist and singer, barking lyrics about death and vengeance and hellfire; the opening song, "Angel of Death," chronicled the life of Josef Mengele, the Nazi doctor known for his cruel experiments on prisoners in concentration camps. (Slayer became a PMRC target.) In 1989, *Spin* sent Reverend Bob Larson, a pastor known for warning about the dangers of heavy metal, on tour with Slayer, to see if the musicians were as depraved as their songs. What he discovered on the tour bus, somewhere in West Germany, was a rock 'n' roll band doing rock 'n' roll things: watching horror movies, drinking beer, killing time. "The worst corruption I could find was one slightly used *Playboy* magazine they looked at again and again," he wrote. Although Slayer had a song, "Altar of Sacrifice," that described a Satanic human sacrifice, none of the members had any particular interest in satanism. Larson seemed rather disappointed that the members of Slayer were not satanic true believers but just four guys playing energetic music for their fans.

By 1989, when Larson boarded Slayer's tour bus, the metal treadmill had already produced something more extreme than thrash. A band called Possessed, made up of Venom fans from California, had released an album called *Seven Churches*, in 1985, which stripped some of the rock 'n' roll swagger from thrash metal: the guitarists used a technique known as tremolo, repeatedly picking down and up on the same note, creating buzzing swarms of sound; Jeff Becerra, the singer and bassist, didn't just snarl, he growled. In the years that followed, bands like Death and Morbid Angel followed this blueprint, honing a frenzied but highly technical style: death metal. Where the thrash bands had been suspicious of mainstream success, the death-metal bands were positively allergic to it. Some of them took blasphemy seriously (Glen Benton, from Deicide, had an upside-down cross permanently branded into his forehead), and virtually all of them delivered unintelligible lyrics about physical brutality and degradation. A band from Buffalo, New York, called Cannibal Corpse became known for writing some of the genre's most repulsive lyrics; *Tomb of the Mutilated*, from 1992, included a track called "Necropedophile," which was written, like many Cannibal Corpse songs, in the first person. (One of the milder couplets: "The dead are not safe / The lifeless child corpse I will violate.") That album also included one of death metal's biggest hits, "Hammer Smashed Face," which the band performed during a brief but memorable scene in *Ace Ventura: Pet Detective*, the 1994 Jim Carrey comedy. There was always something funny about death metal, especially to outsiders, who were less likely to marvel at the crosshatched guitar lines than to smirk at the genre's rather adolescent obsession with noise and violence—death metal, like most of its precursors, was incorrigibly uncool.

Throughout the eighties and nineties, there was always a new subgenre of heavy metal, with a new claim to extremism. If death metal was insufficiently brutal, you could opt instead for grindcore, a style played so fast that the rhythmic pulse became nearly as indecipherable as the lyrics. (*Reek of Putrefaction*, the 1988 debut by a British band called Carcass, sounded less brutal than alien: a compendium of vibrations and explosions and grunted words from medical textbooks.) If you believed that heavy metal ought above all to be *heavy*, then you might have been entranced by doom metal, which built upon the ominous grandeur of early Black Sabbath; by the late 1980s, doom metal had inspired a grimier, punkier offshoot known as sludge metal. Meanwhile, the success of Metallica expanded the audience for all kinds of metal. In 1992, a Texas band called Pantera released an album called *Vulgar Display of Power*, which was unclassifiable but extremely influential, mixing thrash riffs with concussive rhythmic interludes, hints of bluesy rock 'n' roll, and belligerent vocals; the album's most popular refrain had Phil Anselmo, the lead singer, shouting, "Are you talkin' to me?" The album sold millions, and the similarly belligerent follow-up, *Far Beyond Driven*, made its debut at No. 1 on the album chart. Pantera never crossed over beyond the metalheads, but the band's success showed just how many metalheads there were.

Sometime over the years, metal shed its modifier, "heavy," and the genre's relationship to rock 'n' roll grew more strained. Being "metal" often meant being in some sense extreme, and indeed "extreme metal" became an umbrella term for many of the harshest—and perhaps, therefore, most authentic—expressions of the genre. (*Terrorizer*, a British metal magazine, was launched in 1993; one of its slogans was "The World's No. 1 Extreme Music Magazine.") In some ways, this perverse musical philosophy was merely an exaggerated version of age-old rock 'n' roll defiance, but there was something paradoxical about the way many of these bands sought to be simultaneously repellant and attractive. The musicians sometimes compared themselves to horror-movie directors, intent on giving the audience a great show and maybe a good fright. Unlike punk rockers, metalheads accepted and expected a certain amount of theatricality. When Black Flag, a hardcore punk band, played a gig with Venom in 1986, Henry Rollins, Black Flag's lead singer, was not impressed. "It's all lights and make-up," he wrote in his tour diary, which he later published. He was offended that the band members used roadies instead of doing their own schlepping and tuning, and he thought the band's leader, known as Cronos, spent too much time worrying about his hair. "Venom suck," Rollins wrote. "What a bad joke. They don't sweat and they probably don't even fuck."

How "metal" did metalheads really want their favorite metal bands to be? The thrash bands turned out to be less antagonistic than they first appeared; even the bloodthirsty guys from Slayer seemed to have no particular agenda beyond a desire to play loud and have fun. But in the 1990s, a furor erupted in Northern Europe that pushed the ethos of metal to its logical conclusion. The bands there played a style that was called black metal, after the old Venom album. Where many metal bands had treated satanism as a goof or a gimmick, a group of bands in Norway tried to figure out what it might mean to be truly "evil." Almost from the start, the music was overshadowed by violence and destruction, which made the musicians' favored costumes—leather armbands with metal spikes, ghost-white makeup known as corpse paint—seem threatening, rather than hokey. One of the landmark albums was *Hvis Lyset Tar Oss*, by a solo act called Burzum, which appeared in April 1994. The next month, the man behind Burzum, Varg Vikernes, was sent to prison, having been found guilty of stabbing a fellow musician to death and setting fire to three churches. And yet Burzum's music was not exactly ferocious: the album's title means "If the Light Takes Us," and it starts with three long and smudgy midtempo songs, with rudimentary guitar playing and vocals that sound like screams from down the hall; the mood is grim (one of the most popular black-metal adjectives) but also rather wistful, especially during the fourth and final track, an atmospheric keyboard piece that lasts fourteen minutes. Not long before his conviction, Vikernes gave an interview to a magazine called *SOD*, or *Sounds of Death*, in which he portrayed himself as a member of a revolutionary vanguard. "We want to create the most possible fear, chaos, and agony so that the idiotic and friendly Christian society can break down," he said, and he claimed that his music was a crucial part of this effort. "It tears apart the soul of the listener, and through it we spread death and devastation."

When I was a teenage punk, I viewed metal with suspicion. I respected the commitment to musical extremism, but I wasn't interested in virtuosity, and lyrics about murder and Satan didn't capture my imagination. As I grew older, I came to appreciate the glory of a precision-crafted riff, and also the secret sensuality of heavy metal: its determination to achieve transcendence through sheer intensity, its physical exuberance. (Part of the reason great riffs are fun to listen to is that they sound as if they are fun to play.) But black metal was the form that really sucked me in, precisely because it was so perverse. It was as if the bands had gone all the way through the Cannibal Corpse version of brutality and emerged somewhere on the other side, making music that could be discomfitingly serene. Instead of roaring about Satan, the singers often screeched about nature, reviving or inventing old pagan myths as part of their program to oppose Christianity—or, as Vikernes sometimes called it, "Judeo-Christianity." Vikernes is essentially a neo-Nazi, and although he rejects the term, he has written about his desire to "throw millions of non-Whites out of Europe," and his determination to stand against "Jewish world domination." (In 2009, Vikernes was released from prison, unrepentant, having served sixteen years of a twenty-one-year sentence.) In Central and Eastern Europe, especially, a horde of black-metal bands made records that were sometimes implicitly or explicitly neo-Nazi: the lyrics extolled nature and national or ethnic pride; the music sometimes blended black-metal chaos and ambience with ancient local folk traditions.

I have spent countless hours listening to this music, drawn in by its fearsome beauty and by the way it confounds common ideas about the limits of musical acceptability. Of course, I understand why so many people think we would be better off if no one made or listened to music like this, and perhaps they're right. If it is true that music can be a force for good, then it must also be true that music can be a force for evil. I suspect, though, that the moral influence of music is typically slight, and in any case unpredictable. The popularity of black metal, for instance, has lately inspired a whole constellation of furiously *anti*-fascist black metal bands, striving to demonstrate that grimness and goodness can coexist. Part of the power of music is its ability to plunge you into an alien culture, blurring the line between observer and participant: by listening to, say, Burzum, you become, at least for a time, the kind of person who listens to Burzum. (I used to sometimes shop at a record store in the East Village that stocked lots of black metal, including

CDs from bands that were explicitly neo-Nazi. It was located in the basement of a reggae store, which may say something about the way seemingly discordant musical communities can sometimes coexist.) Must we convince ourselves—or pretend—that our favorite bands are making the world a better place before we can appreciate them? Metal bands have been conjuring the power of evil ever since Ozzy Osbourne first howled about a "figure in black." The power of evil seemed real enough then. Is it any less real, or any less compelling, when the singer really means it?

Cock Rock

"It's a drag, man, the way people dig evil—not evil itself, but the *idea* of it." Keith Richards was aboard the Rolling Stones' private airplane in the summer of 1972, talking to the novelist Terry Southern, who was working on an article for *Saturday Review*. Southern was trying to get Richards's response to a pamphlet that had been circulated at a recent Rolling Stones concert, by a group that called itself Men Struggling to Smash Sexism. The pamphlet accused the band of perpetuating sexist oppression through the songs they sang and the atmosphere they created:

> If you are male, this concert is yours. The music you will hear tonight is written for your head. It will talk to you about *your* woman, how good it is to have her under your thumb, so that she talks when she's spoken to. Men will play hard, driving music for you that will turn you on, hype you up, get you ready for action.... We resent the image the Stones present to males as examples we should imitate.

If "Under My Thumb" was not evil, then it was certainly nasty. It was first released in 1966, a sour chronicle of sexual conquest, with Jagger sneering at "the girl who once had me down," and crowing, "The change has come / She's under my thumb." You could hear the song as a heartless celebration, if you liked, or else you could hear it as the interior monologue of a bitter man in a cruel relationship. On that airplane, Richards apparently declined to be drawn into a discussion of his band's complicity in sexism—to him, the pamphlet seemed like yet another example of listeners' tendency to hear their darkest fantasies in his music. "It's *their* fascination with evil that locks us into this projection of it," he said. Perhaps he was still thinking of the band's disastrous appearance at a festival at Altamont Speedway, in California, in 1969, where four people died—one of them, an eighteen-year-old Black attendee named Meredith Hunter, stabbed to death by a member of the Hells Angels, the motorcycle club, which was supposed to provide security. (Hunter had been brandishing a gun, and his alleged killer was acquitted of murder.) The Rolling Stones were playing "Under My Thumb" when it happened.

The problem with the Rolling Stones, if it was a problem, was also a problem with rock 'n' roll more generally. The maleness of rock 'n' roll was echoed in the rock-star culture that surrounded it, in which famous men were expected to carry on commitment-free relationships with starstruck women who loved them, or the idea of them. Many of these relationships now seem obviously abusive. Des Barres writes that her diary fantasies did not spring to life until she was nineteen, but one of her best-known contemporaries was Lori Mattix, who has said that as a fifteen-year-old, she had sexual encounters with David Bowie and Jimmy Page. In a 2015 interview, Mattix confided no regrets, describing her experiences with Bowie as "so beautiful," and saying that she felt "blessed" by Page, even though he had broken her heart. But three years later, amid growing awareness of sexual abuse, Mattix told *The Guardian* that she was starting to rethink her relationship with Page. "I never thought there was anything wrong with it, but maybe there was," she said. "I don't think underage girls should sleep with guys."

In 1970, the underground newspaper *Rat* published a landmark essay titled "Cock Rock: Men Always Seem to End Up on Top"; it was later attributed to Susan Hiwatt, which was evidently a pseudonym. (Hiwatt was a British amplifier company.) "Getting turned on to 'Under My Thumb,' a revenge song filled with hatred for women, made me feel crazy," Hiwatt wrote, adding, "When you get to listening to male rock lyrics, the message to women is devastating." Even so, the severity of this message bothered her less than its ubiquity. "All the names on the albums, all the people doing sound and lights, all the voices on the radio, even the D.J.'s between the songs—they are all men," she wrote. In her experience, Janis Joplin was a singular exception, and so Joplin's death marked a turning point. "When she died," Hiwatt wrote, "one of the few ties that I still had left with rock snapped." Her essay was both a work of criticism and a letter of resignation.

Ellen Willis, by contrast, heard "Under My Thumb" less as an insult than a challenge. "Early rock," she conceded, in a *New Yorker* essay from 1971, was "sexist in all the obvious ways." But she preferred the Rolling Stones' swaggering approach to some of the alternatives. "[A] diatribe like 'Under My Thumb' is not nearly so sexist in its implications as, for example, Cat Stevens's gentle, sympathetic 'Wild World,'" she wrote. Where the Rolling Stones portrayed the woman as an adversary, Stevens, a quavery folk-inspired singer who emanated sensitivity, portrayed the woman as a potential victim: "But if you want to leave, take good care / Hope you make a lot of nice friends out there / But just remember there's a lot of bad, and beware." To Willis, this was proof of a double standard that was more insidious because it wasn't overtly hostile. "It's hard to imagine a woman sadly warning her ex-lover that he's too innocent for the big bad world out there," she wrote. In a *Village Voice* essay from 1977, she explained that part of what she loved about rock 'n' roll was its rudeness, an attitude that seemed to her inherently radical, sometimes in spite of itself. "Music that boldly and aggressively laid out what the singer wanted, loved, hated—as good rock-and-roll did—challenged me to do the same, and so, even when the content was antiwoman, antisexual, in a sense antihuman, the form encouraged my struggle for liberation," she wrote. "Similarly, timid music made me feel timid, whatever its ostensible politics."

Like many critics, Willis heard rock 'n' roll through the lens of her own conviction that the genre could and should be politically righteous, a force for "liberation." She shared this conviction with generations of listeners and musicians, many of whom have taken it for granted that rock 'n' roll has a certain liberatory essence. In this and countless other ways, the Rolling Stones were unusually canny, finding ways in their music to acknowledge the underlying tension between two competing notions of liberation: the political sort, which may require discipline and compromise, and the personal sort, which tends to refuse those things. Many of their most urgent-sounding songs, like "Gimme Shelter" and "Street Fighting Man," were artfully ambiguous, evoking political tumult without delivering any message clear enough to qualify as a protest. Over the years many observers noted, with alarm, that the Rolling Stones, once young and dangerous, had grown old and safe, content to rake in huge sums on the touring circuit. (In 1983, *Rolling Stone* published an article on what was then a growing trend: bands like the Rolling Stones were starting to be underwritten by major corporations; Jovan, a brand of cologne, had sponsored the band's 1981 tour.) I remember taking the subway up to Van Cortlandt Park, in the Bronx, in 2002, for an unnecessarily grand press conference at which the Rolling Stones announced details of their forthcoming tour; a blimp and a financial services company were both prominently featured. But when I saw them play live, a few months later, at Madison Square Garden, I was stunned at how well they had aged. Keith Richards sounded like no rock guitarist I had ever heard; his licks, interrupted by little bursts of silence, were rocks skipping across the surface of a bumpy sea. Meanwhile, Jagger strutted and preened, a fifty-nine-year-old with nothing to prove and nothing to be embarrassed about—a brilliant rock star who had never pretended to be anything more, or less.

In the fifties and sixties, rock 'n' roll had been celebrated (and sometimes denounced) as an example of American integration in action: a universal genre, made and consumed by Black and white people alike. But by the seventies, this myth was undercut by the reality of pop segregation.

Black music was typically categorized as R&B or soul, while rock 'n' roll was redefined as a white genre, albeit one with debts to Black precursors, especially blues singers. Seventies rock was sometimes faulted for not living up to the genre's universalist identity—indeed, a 1972 article in *Rolling Stone* described a different pamphlet (or possibly the same one), distributed at a different Rolling Stones concert, making a connection between the band's putative sexism and its broader failure to be inclusive. "Rock music should be everyone's music," the pamphleteers wrote. "Rock culture should be everyone's culture." Certainly musical segregation tended to harm the professional prospects of Black musicians, who typically found R&B stardom less lucrative than the rock 'n' roll equivalent. And certainly there were plenty of Black musicians making brilliant rock-inspired music in the seventies, ranging from Sly Stone to George Clinton to Chaka Khan. But to classify them as belonging to the rock 'n' roll world, instead of the R&B world, would be to enrich rock 'n' roll and impoverish R&B. Would that be an improvement? It is fair to object that musicians can (and usually do) work in more than one genre. But it also seems important not to distort the reality of the seventies, during which the world of rock 'n' roll was in many ways less integrated than it had been before.

When rock 'n' roll split from R&B, in the sixties, it lost much of its Black audience, and therefore its pretension to universality—it could never again claim to be the sound of America. Not coincidentally, rock 'n' roll lost its horns around the same time: the saxophone, once an integral part of the rock 'n' roll sound, was nearly gone from the genre by the early seventies, except for the occasional solo. Now the dominance of guitars was total, and the electric guitar was more and more perceived as a "white" instrument. Seventies rockers tended to be self-conscious about their position as white stars in a genre with an illustrious Black history. The Rolling Stones returned endlessly to the blues masters who inspired them and sometimes made a point of touring with Black opening acts. (It is possible to hear "Brown Sugar," the band's much-loved and much-loathed song about slavery and interracial sex, as an autobiographical allegory: the story of white

British musicians whose "cold English blood runs hot" when they hear Black American music.) But some rock bands pushed the other way, eager to carve out a musical identity for rock that would be independent of its roots in blues and Black music. Critics sometimes used "blues" as an insult, shorthand for plodding and predictable instrumental passages. A perceptive writer known as Metal Mike Saunders, who championed heavy bands, praised *Led Zeppelin II* for taking "a crucial first step away from blues and excess jerkoff solos"; a review of Fleetwood Mac in *Rolling Stone* noted with approval that the group had moved away from "laborious blues/rock jams"; *Time*, in its 1974 explanation of heavy metal, defined the genre as "heavy, simplistic blues played at maximum volume." Disparaging the blues became a way for rock stars to portray themselves as modern, or honest. In 1978, Tom Petty, who was just starting to be celebrated for his tough and tart rock 'n' roll, told *Sounds*, a British magazine, "I never really copped to the blues," although he did express admiration for old R&B records. And in an interview in *BAM*, a San Francisco rock magazine, Alice Cooper, the vampire-drag hard rocker, explained his disdain for the blues in demographic terms. "We're not going to play Delta Blues," he said. "I don't give a damn about how many times his baby left him. We're upper middle-class suburban brats that had anything we wanted. We never *had* a blues period."

Cooper's evocation of middle-class suburban normalcy was, of course, rather at odds with his life on the stage, where he played a character named Alice (his real name was Vincent Furnier), who was supposed to look, he once explained, like a "cheap whore," and whose wardrobe included thigh-high leopard-print boots, along with ever-present black eye makeup radiating outward like exploded mascara. This was another seventies change: a growing expectation that male rock stars should embrace elements of drag. The Rolling Stones were pioneers in this regard, too. One of the pamphleteers suggested that the band's view and treatment of women was linked to a retrograde idea of masculinity, and accused the group of reinforcing the idea that "the only real men are those who want to be like John

Wayne or Mick Jagger." But Jagger's prancing and pouting were a partial rebuke to the John Wayne model of masculinity. In an essay called "Confessions of a Gay Rocker," the critic Adam Block wrote about the "sexual ambiguity" that informed the image of the Rolling Stones, particularly Jagger, whom he described as "a heterosexual who liked to flirt with boys." (Block mentioned "Schoolboy Blues," an unreleased Rolling Stones song from 1970, possibly recorded as an act of contractual sabotage, in which Jagger sings, "Oh where can I get my cock sucked? / Where can I get my ass fucked?") Jagger never claimed to be anything but heterosexual. But many fans suspected, or hoped, that he was romantically involved with his friend David Bowie, who identified himself as bisexual in a 1976 *Playboy* interview—and became, in the years that followed, probably the first pop star ever to face rumors that he was secretly straight.

Counter-Countercultural

The rock-star years of the 1970s were also the high-water mark for something people called glitter rock, a subgenre that embraced camp and theatricality. Bowie was part of this loosely defined movement, and so was Alice Cooper, as well as Roxy Music, Gary Glitter, and Marc Bolan, the dreamy (in both senses) leader of T. Rex. By some definitions, Elton John also fit: his music had little in common with the glitter template, which emphasized affected vocals and fizzy electric guitars, but his tendency to take the stage in outrageous, star-spangled outfits made him seem like a fellow traveler. Under the influence of glitter, also known as glam, many mainstream male rock stars, including Mick Jagger, began to experiment with makeup and flowing fabric. And in New York, a couple of influential bands helped turn glitter rock into something less artsy. One was the New York Dolls, whose music, sassy and sneering and tough, helped inspire the first wave of punk bands. The other was KISS, with its comic-book look and "rock and roll all nite" lyrics—the members realized, like Alice Cooper before them, that it was possible to be simultaneously a freakish rock star and an all-American guy.

The glitter-rock movement generally presented itself as straight. Elton John was an exception: in a 1976 *Rolling Stone* cover story, he disclosed that he was bisexual—though no more bisexual, he suggested, than the rest of the world. ("I think everybody's bisexual to a certain degree," he said. "I don't think it's just me.") He did not publicly identify himself as gay until 1992. Elton John was also an exception in another respect: unlike most of the glitter-rock stars, he was not a traditional heartthrob. In 1974, he was described by *NME* as a "balding, bespectacled plumpoid," a great musician and performer who succeeded despite "breaking every single rule for '70s visuality." More typically, though, performers found that glam and glamour only enhanced their positions as men who drove women wild. When a male musician put on tight pants, a frilly top, and some makeup, it was often just because he wanted to dress like a rock star. By the end of the seventies, that was pretty much how rock stars dressed.

When glitter and glam returned in the 1980s as hair metal, the ethos was much more KISS than Bowie. Part of what made hair metal so amusing was the fact that the stars' flamboyant appearance was unconnected to any similarly provocative musical or cultural identity. Sometimes the stars themselves scarcely seemed to know how or why they had ended up dressing just like the women they dated. "Girls liked us," recalled Phil Collen, from Def Leppard, in the MTV oral history. "We were a rock band, but we didn't want to look like other bands who had greasy hair and greasy jeans. Our girlfriends let us borrow their clothes." In *The Dirt*, Vince Neil remembers playing an early gig with Mötley Crüe at a biker bar, with the band dressed in typical regalia: "stiletto heels, hair spray, red-painted fingernails, hot-pink pants, and make-up." Why? Because it looked cool, apparently. Chuck Klosterman remembers that in his North Dakota town, the pretty boys of Poison "almost seemed like some sort of gay propaganda." The joke, of course, was that Poison, like many of the hair-metal bands, seemed to have no agenda at all. Agendalessness is what made the hair-metal scene seem contemporary and fun, setting it apart from more earnest, old-fashioned forms of rock 'n' roll.

In a sense, Vince Neil in stiletto heels at a biker bar did represent a kind of "struggle for liberation," though not quite the same kind as Ellen Willis had undertaken. In different ways, the eruption of disco, the insurgency of punk, and the growth of electronic pop music all damaged the idea that rock 'n' roll was on the side of progress, or was inherently hip. And so the resurgence of "pure" rock 'n' roll, in Los Angeles and on MTV, was often perceived as musically reactionary, a backlash against various musical revolutions. Hair metal was often perceived, too, as *politically* reactionary, and not only because the bands generally declined to write protest songs. Many of them unapologetically embraced groupie culture and filled their videos with underdressed women who tended not to have speaking roles. Warrant, in particular, was mocked and criticized for a 1990 video called "Cherry Pie," in which a model, Bobbie Brown, has a piece of cherry pie land in her lap and is sprayed with a fire hose, as the singer, Jani Lane, exclaims, "Looks so good, bring a tear to your eye / Sweet cherry pie." In fact, the video, bright and playful, was a good deal less annoying than the lumbering song, thanks largely to Brown, who was a more exuberant screen presence than any of the band members. (Years later, in her memoir, Brown wrote that she had found the accusations of sexism "ridiculous," calling the clip "a sexy, playful little video for a sexy, playful song.")

It is no simple thing to be a heartthrob—traditionally, a boyish man who appeals largely to girls and women. The hair-metal rock stars were heartthrobs, and so they were criticized both by listeners who wished they weren't so laddish and by listeners who wished they weren't so girly. Rock critics insulted them just as fiercely as the metalheads in Klosterman's North Dakota. And yet heartthrobs are important. When people think about the gender imbalance in rock 'n' roll, they often concentrate on the imbalance among performers, and they look for ways in which the industry and culture of rock 'n' roll have frustrated women musicians and would-be musicians. There is no shortage of stories to tell: when the Wilson sisters, from Heart, talk about being made over into "porn kittens," they are doubtless speaking for many women who were similarly marketed, and many more whose careers suffered because they weren't. But the point of popular music, surely, is not to employ and enrich musicians, but to delight listeners. And so one way of judging how a type of music treats women is to ask how much it appeals to women as consumers. From this point of view, the hair-metal movement was a success, and maybe a leap forward; bands like Bon Jovi and Def Leppard and even Mötley Crüe were notable, unlike their seventies predecessors, for attracting huge audiences that were largely female. *Mainly* female, maybe—it's hard to get good statistics. There are limits to this sort of analysis, of course, because it may measure what listeners are willing to settle for, as opposed to what they actually want. But that is true of all genres and all audiences. And there is no reason to think that the fans who packed arenas for hair metal were especially ambivalent or unusually unsatisfied.

These hair-metal heartthrobs generally did not see themselves as feminists, of course. On the contrary, they were part of a generation that helped to sever rock 'n' roll from liberal politics, partly by insisting that rock 'n' roll should be fun and that liberal sensitivity was not. (Joey Allen, Warrant's lead guitarist, once defended the "Cherry Pie" video by appealing to the genre's unwritten bylaws: "Spraying down a girl with a fire hose? It's rock 'n' roll, give me a break.") "Rock music has become depoliticized," one marketing executive explained to *Rolling Stone* in 1983. In the same magazine a few months later, Bob Pittman, who was the CEO of MTV, laid out the network's rock 'n' roll manifesto. "In the Sixties, politics and music fused," he said. "But there are no more political statements. The only thing rock fans have in common is the music." Some older rock stars retained their belief in the power of rock 'n' roll idealism: in 1988, Neil Young released a video for his song "This Note's for You," which used Michael Jackson and Whitney Houston look-alikes to mock corporate pop. And established rock and pop stars convened for philanthropic collaborations like "We Are the World," a 1985 single benefiting humanitarian aid to Africa, and *A Very Special Christmas*, a 1987 album that raised money for the Special Olympics. But arguably the most prominent rock 'n' roll cause of the 1980s was a self-interested one: a broad movement against censorship, objecting to efforts by the PMRC and others to marginalize music with explicit lyrics. (The PMRC campaign led to a compromise in which American record companies agreed to create a classification system, labeling certain albums as "explicit"; Walmart and some other retailers declined to stock "explicit" albums in their stores.) This was a way in which the liberationist urge persisted within rock 'n' roll: singers insisted on the right to sing whatever they wanted.

In the worlds of hard rock and heavy metal, an abiding anti-hippie ethos led to a kind of counter-countercultural attitude. Two of the T-shirts shown in *Heavy Metal Parking Lot* are emblazoned with anti-anti-war messages that were popular at the time: "Kill 'Em All / Let God Sort 'Em Out!" and "DON'T GET MAD / NUKE THE BASTARDS." And some of the metal bands, like Black Sabbath before them, created anti-war songs that evoked mayhem more vividly (and sometimes more sympathetically) than they evoked peace. When Bruce Dickinson, from Iron Maiden, howled, "Run to the hills / Run for your life," he was decrying the slaughter of indigenous Americans by the "white man," but the refrain sounded more triumphant than mournful. Heavy metal is typically fascinated by brutality, and that fascination animates putatively anti-war songs like "One," by Metallica, and "War Ensemble," by Slayer. Even "Angel of Death," Slayer's account of Josef Mengele's Nazi war crimes, can't help but glamorize its subject, especially because it denounces Mengele using words like "infamous," which sounds like a heavy-metal compliment. It is a song about violence and evil, by a band *obsessed* with violence and evil.

Few records better express the complicated message of eighties hard rock than *G N' R Lies*, by Guns N' Roses, which appeared in 1988, a year after *Appetite for Destruction*. It was a strange hybrid, not really an album, with four songs that were live, or pseudo-live, and four that were mainly acoustic. One of the acoustic ones, "Patience," was a sublime rock ballad—perhaps the decade's best. Another, "Used to Love Her," was essentially a two-line crack about a whiny lover: "I used to love her / But I had to kill her." The song was delivered as a joke, although in the years to come, Axl Rose was sued for violent assault by his ex-wife, and he exchanged lawsuits alleging violence with an ex-girlfriend. The most startling song, though, was "One in a Million," the monologue of a "small-town white boy," fed up in Los Angeles. "Police and niggers—that's right / Get out of my way," Rose snarled. In the second verse, it was "Immigrants and faggots"; in the third, "Radicals and racists." The song caused an uproar, though not one that did any serious damage to the band's career, and the next year, in *Rolling Stone*, Axl Rose claimed that he had used the word "nigger" as a kind of protest. "I don't like being told what I can and what I can't say," he said. He explained that the song was inspired by specific situations: "Black men" he had seen hawking "stolen jewelry" and fake drugs in downtown LA; an immigrant worker who once chased him out of a store; a man who tried to rape him while he was hitchhiking. (Rose didn't apologize, although the song was conspicuously omitted from a multidisc Guns N' Roses reissue in 2018.) Perhaps accidentally, the song captured the conflicted position of mainstream rock 'n' roll in the late eighties: defiant and resentful, increasingly out of place in the chaos of the big city.

The rise of grunge changed that, though perhaps not as much as one would think. Certainly Cobain was committed to reviving the idea of rock 'n' roll as a progressive force, and was opposed to people like Axl Rose, whom he called "a fucking sexist and a racist and a homophobe," in an interview in *The Advocate*, the LGBT magazine. He said, "You can't be on his side and be on our side." (Cobain and Rose had a hostile encounter backstage at the 1992 Video Music Awards, the same one where Def Leppard was upstaged by the grunge insurgency.) And yet grunge helped rock 'n' roll become more musically isolated by popularizing a scrappier, purer form of hard rock. By rejecting the bloated rock "establishment," the alternative movement also pushed rock 'n' roll even further away from its history as Black music:

saxophone solos now seemed laughably uncool; no one wanted or expected guitar players to indulge in bluesy jamming; and many bands had realized they could do without backup singers, who were often Black women. Even the name "alternative rock" suggested a musical tradition whose heroes were eccentric white bands like the Velvet Underground and R.E.M.—one that didn't seem to have much to do with Black rock 'n' roll pioneers like Sister Rosetta Tharpe and Ike Turner and Chuck Berry. The rise of alternative rock helped reinforce an old idea that had seemed new only a few decades earlier: that rock music was white music.

I don't think it is necessary to lament this evolution. Genres change, and the existence of predominantly Black genres in America, a majority-white country, basically ensured, as a mathematical certainty, that there would also be predominantly white genres. Why shouldn't rock 'n' roll have become one of them? The biggest surprise, perhaps, is that rock 'n' roll turned out to be more culturally versatile than most of its early fans expected. Like motorcycles or tattoos, rock 'n' roll can mean different things in different times and places. One of the most unexpected rock 'n' roll stories in recent decades has been the rise of Christian rock. The first Christian rock album to be certified platinum, for sales of a million copies, was *To Hell with the Devil*, from 1986, by a Christian hair-metal band called Stryper that was not known for its light touch—members tossed pocket-size Bibles into the crowd during concerts. But in the mid-1990s and 2000s, a new generation of Christian rockers found mainstream success: not just Creed but also Jars of Clay, P.O.D., Switchfoot, Evanescence, Daughtry, the Fray, and Lifehouse. Many of them, including Creed, resisted or rejected the label "Christian rock," because they didn't want to be pigeonholed. There had always been Christians in rock music, depending on how you define "Christians"; Bono, from U2, spent his whole career singing about his Christian faith and his Christian doubts. But as mainstream rock grew more distant from its countercultural roots, the Christian faith came to seem progressively less remarkable within it. Two of the most successful rock bands of recent decades, the Killers and Imagine Dragons, are led by members of the Church of Jesus Christ of Latter-day Saints, formerly known as Mormons, and fans scarcely seemed to notice, or care. Or maybe, in the twenty-first century, mainstream rock fans dig evil less than they dig good.

The Opposite of Noise

There was another path for rock 'n' roll. In the summer of 1969, *Newsweek* celebrated two investitures. One was depicted on the cover: Queen Elizabeth II placed a crown on the head of her son Prince Charles, thereby signifying that he was the heir apparent to the British throne. Inside, tucked near the back of the issue, the magazine described something more interesting, and possibly more consequential: the emergence of a new kind of rock 'n' roll, and a new kind of rock star. The "rock-music scene," according to the article, had been "a world of male groups, of pounding, thunderous music that drowns out the words, which are rarely of moment." But now, "a new school of talented female troubadours" was emerging, ready to give rock 'n' roll "the feminine touch." According to *Newsweek*, the most prominent of these new rock 'n' roll heirs was Joni Mitchell. Within a couple of years, she would be known as a fiercely original singer and writer, but in those days she was often cast, rather condescendingly, as an ingenuous pixie. The article characterized Mitchell's singing style as "natural" and "flower-fresh," and suggested that her home in Laurel Canyon, in the Hollywood Hills, was an urban refuge. "I'm a little in awe of cities, being raised in a prairie town in Saskatchewan," Mitchell said. "I owe it to myself to live where there's greenery."

This idea—that many listeners craved a respite from noisy rock 'n' roll—was evidently widespread at the dawn of the seventies. In 1971, *Time* found a different way to celebrate this emerging sound, with a cover that featured a drawing of a man with a mustache and shoulder-length brown hair, along with a decisive headline: THE NEW ROCK: BITTERSWEET AND LOW. The man was James Taylor, a folk balladeer, and the magazine hailed him as the antidote to "ear-numbing, mind-blowing acid rock," which was, readers were assured, in decline. A few years later, an article in *The New York Times* portrayed Taylor as "a refreshing relief after the ear-splitting excesses of late-sixties psychedelic music." And in 1972, an Associated Press article hailed the singer-songwriter Carole King as the "queen" of "soft rock"—which was, the article explained, the antithesis of "hard rock." There was something slightly dismissive about the way these singers were celebrated for being quiet. The opposite of noise, after all, is silence, and it sometimes seemed that these strummers were merely providing the next best thing. Not everyone welcomed this refreshment. "If I ever get down to Carolina I'm gonna try to figure out a way to off James Taylor," Lester Bangs once wrote, making reference to one of Taylor's best-loved songs, "Carolina in My Mind." Bangs was deliberately exaggerating the contrast between his own hotheadedness and Taylor's infuriatingly mellow music and demeanor. If Taylor was out to slay the beast of raucous rock, then Bangs would have to slay *him* first.

"Carolina in My Mind" appeared at the end of 1968, on James Taylor's self-titled debut album, which was issued by Apple, the Beatles' record company. Taylor's voice was warm and slightly conversational, but the mood was not necessarily light: he was only twenty, but he had already spent time in a psychiatric hospital, and he had begun what would become a yearslong struggle with heroin addiction. The song's narrator is desperately homesick, and possibly dopesick, too: "Hey, babe, the sky's on fire—I'm dying, ain't I? / I'm gone to Carolina in my mind." In 1973, a *Rolling Stone* reporter asked James Taylor about Joni Mitchell's latest release, *For the Roses*, an unsparing album that seemed to chronicle the demise of a relationship. "I'd be very interested to hear it, because I really love Joni's music," Taylor said. "Everyone who writes songs writes autobiographical songs, and hers are sometimes really disarmingly specific." This was a coy answer, because Taylor was by then Mitchell's ex-boyfriend, and fans wondered if he had inspired her new songs; he was being interviewed alongside another singer-songwriter, Carly Simon, who happened to be his new wife. Part of the appeal of this music was voyeuristic: listeners loved the idea that they were hearing an honest account of a real life, right from the person who lived it, even though the truth was often more complicated. The biggest hit of James Taylor's career was "You've Got a Friend," which went to No. 1 on the pop chart. The song, an incessantly hummable declaration of loyalty, helped establish Taylor as one of his generation's most popular singer-songwriters, even though in this case he was merely a singer: the song was written by his friend Carole King, who recorded her own version for her album *Tapestry*, which had also appeared in 1971, and which soon dwarfed Taylor's albums, and just about everyone else's, too.

King's career traced a path from an older kind of rock 'n' roll to a newer one. Working with Gerry Goffin, she had cowritten some of the most infectious hits of the early sixties, including "Take Good Care of My Baby," by Bobby Vee, and "The Loco-Motion," by Little Eva. But *Tapestry*, which was recorded after she moved to Laurel Canyon, sounded earnest and homemade, as if she had somehow matured from a pro into an amateur. The cover was a snapshot of King in front of a window, partly obscured by her pet cat, which peered into the camera. And the album ended with "(You Make Me Feel) Like a Natural Woman," which she had cowritten for Aretha Franklin, who made it an enduring hit. Compared to Franklin's soaring version, this rendition, with King accompanying herself on piano, seemed almost like a demo, and perhaps that was why so many people loved it. *Tapestry* generated a pair of big radio hits ("It's Too Late" and "I Feel the Earth Move"), but it was the kind of album that people seemed to want to bring home and live with. It became one of the bestselling albums of all time, and it helped invent a more intimate form of rock stardom. *Tapestry* often seemed to address listeners as if they were confidants, sharing stories and giving advice. "You're gonna find, yes you will / That you're beautiful as you feel," King sang, and the couplet would not be out of place in any of a few dozen inspirational songs that have found a home on the pop chart this century.

King generally declined interviews, but she was sometimes portrayed as part of a movement of "liberated women" leading a musical insurgency. This characterization was a way of acknowledging that the singer-songwriter movement was largely defined by women performers, in marked contrast to more raucous strains of rock 'n' roll. "Singer-songwriter" could be a flexible category: Joni Mitchell and Carly Simon were sometimes grouped with mellow performers like Linda Ronstadt, who was primarily an interpreter—her country-inflected hits tended to be cover versions, not original compositions. (One of Ronstadt's songwriters was Karla Bonoff, who released an excellent but rather unheralded self-titled debut album in 1977.) Judy Kutulas, a historian and cultural critic, has suggested that the world of singer-songwriters was "a space that critics regarded as feminized," and that the format "helped to bridge the gap between the sexual revolution and the feminist one": instead of celebrating free love, many of these songs chronicled the complications of romantic relationships. Indeed, Kutulas connects this genre to the enactment, starting in 1970, of no-fault divorce laws in a number of states. A 1974 cover story in *Time* about Joni Mitchell and other "rock women" noted, regretfully, that "Rock women seldom have successful marriages," though of course this was scarcely less true of rock *men*. When *Rolling Stone* asked James Taylor in 1973 why he and Carly Simon had gotten married, he said playfully, "That's the way we always heard it should be." He was referring to a song of Simon's, "That's the Way I've Always Heard It Should Be," about a woman contemplating marriage and all the sorrows it can bring.

The world of singer-songwriters overlapped with the world of so-called soft rock, a tradition in which gentleness was valued not because it enabled intimate self-expression but for its own sake. The tag stuck to Ronstadt and to a few members of her band, who left her employ and started a country-rock group that became one of the most popular bands in rock 'n' roll history: the Eagles. Critics tended to disregard this music, especially critics who thought that easy-listening rock 'n' roll ought to be a contradiction in terms. But the term "soft rock" could denote not merely restraint but also expansion, as the musicians mixed rock 'n' roll not only with country, as the Eagles did, but also with R&B and jazz. "Soft rock" described, more or less, the duo Steely Dan, whose slick compositions were buoyed by astonishing musicianship, and enhanced by arch lyrics that hinted, softly, at perversion. "I crawl like a viper / Through these suburban streets," Donald Fagen sang, over an appropriately slithery groove. (Decades later, the smoother, funkier seventies soft-rock records were retrospectively reclassified as "yacht rock," a term that conferred upon them a kitschy sort of credibility.) In most discussions of rock 'n' roll, though, "hard" was more often a compliment than "soft" was. In the 1980 edition of *The Rolling Stone Illustrated History of Rock & Roll*, the critic Dave Marsh criticized Neil Young's beloved 1970s solo recordings for being, in essence, not rock 'n' roll enough. Young's albums with Buffalo Springfield and Crosby, Stills, Nash & Young made him a sixties rock star, but in the seventies, Marsh wrote, Young became "a singer/songwriter more in the mold of James Taylor or Joni Mitchell." Marsh suggested that he no longer sounded like a "major artist" but rather a mere purveyor of "soft rock."

"Soft rock," unlike "hard rock" or "heavy metal," never developed into a proud tribal identity. Musicians tended to reject the label, and in fact soft-rock musicians tended to avoid labels altogether, which is one reason why the tradition seemed to fade out as louder bands proliferated. But soft rock has been everywhere ever since. Many of the most enduring rock acts of the seventies were classified as "soft." There was the triumvirate of grand balladeers: Barbra Streisand, Neil Diamond, and Barry Manilow, all of whom were more "soft" than "rock," gesturing back to the musical world that existed before rock 'n' roll. Elton John, though glittery, was soft rock, too—a piano-playing singer-songwriter with an asterisk. (The asterisk is an acknowledgment that John only wrote the open-hearted tunes; his lifelong collaborator Bernie Taupin typically wrote the lyrics, which could be cryptic.) Fleetwood Mac, the onetime blues band, was transformed into a soft-rock sensation by the addition of a pair of California singer-songwriters, Stevie Nicks and Lindsey Buckingham; in 1977, the band released *Rumours*, a perfectly bittersweet album full of "relationship" songs that eventually outsold even *Tapestry*. And Billy Joel, a piano-playing singer-songwriter in love with rock 'n' roll history, felt his songs were too muscular for the category; in a 1997 *Rolling Stone* interview, he acknowledged the subtext of sex and sexuality that lurks beneath some of these arguments. "I'm perceived as a mainstay of soft rock—which to me is like soft cock," he said. "I hate that. Fifty percent of the music on my albums is hard rock." There was something affecting about hearing Joel, by then one of the most successful singers in the world, trying to convince a *Rolling Stone* reporter that his brand of rock 'n' roll was hard, or semi-hard.

The term "soft rock" is often associated with the AM radio stations of the 1970s, which played only the most palatable hits—as opposed to the newer stations on the FM band, which were more likely to play raucous, album-oriented bands like Led Zeppelin. By the eighties, all kinds of music were moving to FM radio, which delivered higher fidelity, though over shorter distances; the AM airwaves increasingly filled with various sorts of talk. But the spirit of soft rock lived on: power ballads were conspicuously soft and incontrovertibly rock, and "soft rock" is a good description for many of the songs that have dominated radio over the decades, whatever genre they emerged from. For instance: "Lady," by the pop-country singer Kenny Rogers, in 1980; "Say You, Say Me," by the mellow R&B singer Lionel Richie, in 1985; "Can't Help Falling in Love," by the British reggae band UB40, in 1993; "Breathe," by the country singer Faith Hill, in 2000; "I'm Yours," by the laid-back strummer Jason Mraz, in 2008; "Perfect," by the unpretentious British singer-songwriter Ed Sheeran, in 2017. Some genres endure because people are devoted to them; others, like soft rock, endure because they are useful catchall categories, and because no one cares enough to police their boundaries. If "soft rock" denotes a tradition of songs, often about romantic love, that are neither fast nor frenzied and that convey a sense of intimacy, then "soft rock" is not really a genre at all but a mode, important to a wide range of genres and fundamental to popular music.

Confessional

Every discussion of singer-songwriter music takes place in the shadow of Bob Dylan, who helped invent the form but kept reinventing himself, providing his fans so much delight and so much frustration that they sometimes found it hard to tell which was which. In 1970, in *Rolling Stone*, the critic Greil Marcus began his review of Dylan's latest, *Self Portrait*, by asking, "What is this shit?" Marcus emerged in the decades that followed as one of the most insightful scholars of Dylan, which is no small distinction, and his review was not a pan, or not merely a pan. It ran more than seven thousand words, a treatise on the general if not invariable greatness of Dylan, and on the America that he loved to sing about. *Self Portrait* seemed designed to undermine the myth of Dylan as the ultimate singer-songwriter, because it was a double album consisting mainly of cover versions. The title was paradoxical, and so was Marcus's argument, which was that by recording so many covers, Dylan seemed to "turn inward," inviting listeners to wonder about his complicated personal motivations, instead of helping them think about the wider world. (Why on earth did he decide to interpret "Blue Moon," one of the most familiar songs in the American songbook?) In this view, *Self Portrait* is a wry comment on the glorification of singer-songwriters, because Dylan is mainly declining to be one. But it is also a prime example of singer-songwriter solipsism, because these cover versions are interesting mainly for what they reveal about Dylan's sense of himself. Dylan taught his many disciples the importance of getting into character, and also the futility of it. No matter how sophisticated your fans, they will always imagine that whatever you are singing tells them something about who you "really" are.

Joni Mitchell may have seemed, at first, like a folk singer willing to give listeners simple truths about herself, and about us. *Ladies of the Canyon,* her 1970 album, included "Big Yellow Taxi," a wistful song about environmental degradation that remains one of her most popular, with a refrain fit for a pin-back button: "They paved paradise, put up a parking lot." The next year, she released *Blue,* which was even better: it helped invent a form that is now familiar, the breakup album. And while the words were sometimes memorably plain ("I hate you some, I love you some"), the way she sang them was thrillingly unpredictable. Lines ended early or late, hinting at a powerful undercurrent of syncopation; a flat, half-spoken stanza might suddenly curl up into the high end of her range. She was a visual artist as well as a performer, and for her the most important part of being a singer-songwriter was the solitary nature of it, the absolute control. ("How many times do you hear about painters working together?" she once asked, by way of comparison.) With every album, she seemed less like a member of a movement—let alone, as *Newsweek* had once suggested, a remedial presence, come to give rock 'n' roll a "feminine touch." Some singer-songwriters seemed convinced that they were called to be poets, but Mitchell seemed more interested in being a composer, instead, and her albums grew more astonishing. She built songs that were closely attentive to the complex rhythms of the English language, and her music had a sense of swing and melodic play more often associated with jazz. Like Dylan, Mitchell was widely and accurately hailed as a genius, so intensely venerated by fans that a critic once described the atmosphere at her concerts as "excessively devotional." And like Dylan, she was restless and sometimes confounding. In 1977, she released *Don Juan's Reckless Daughter,* which featured the singer in blackface on the front cover, and which was wordy but spookily mesmerizing. (Not everyone was impressed. "I'm sure it's boring, but I'm not sure how boring," wrote Robert Christgau, who nevertheless gave the album a passable B-.) The follow-up was *Mingus,* a notably less popular collaboration with the jazz bassist and composer Charles Mingus, which demonstrated both the range of her musical vision and, perhaps, the limits of her fans' tolerance. "I'd rather be crucified for changing," she said, than for "staying the same."

Singer-songwriters didn't wave the flag of rock 'n' roll the way the heavy-metal pioneers did. And yet they were evidently part of the rock 'n' roll world, and arguably at the center of it. From early in his career, and despite his many attempts to complicate his own story, Bob Dylan was regarded as a totem of authenticity: a performer whose music was in some undefinable sense the real thing. (When Dylan traveled to Princeton to receive an honorary degree, in 1970, he was hailed at the ceremony as "the authentic expression of the disturbed and concerned conscience of Young America.") Often, other rock stars were judged by their ability to perform in a way that felt somehow true. In 1970, when the British rock 'n' roller Rod Stewart released his second solo album, *Gasoline Alley*, a review in *Rolling Stone* praised "the authenticity of his phrasing," which gave his music "gentleness and depth." As the decade progressed, though, Stewart evolved: no longer a reliable purveyor of twangy, slightly rustic rock 'n' roll, he cultivated a playboy image and crafted hits like "Hot Legs" and, in 1978, "Da Ya Think I'm Sexy," a shameless disco tune that went to the top of the pop chart. Many critics and old fans weren't impressed, and by 1979 *Rolling Stone* had lost patience, noting that a singer who once seemed "instantly authentic" was now making ridiculous music that "carries no conviction." If one archetype of rock 'n' roll was a fistful of guys making loud guitar music, another archetype was one guy with a trusty acoustic delivering astringent lyrics in an astringent voice—Dylan, or some version of him. Stray too far from either version of rock 'n' roll authenticity, and you might end up a mere pop star, beloved but not respected, at least not by rock 'n' roll fans.

There were plenty of singer-songwriters who earned the same kind of respect that Dylan did, if not the same quantity, making stubbornly idiosyncratic music that was rock 'n' roll in spirit, though not in sound. Leonard

Cohen's doleful albums and doleful poems made him a cult idol. Randy Newman honed a sweet kind of sarcasm, eventually evolving from critical success to Hollywood A-lister. (He became a constant presence at the Academy Awards, acclaimed for his contributions to the soundtracks of animated films.) There were country-inflected singer-songwriters like Townes Van Zandt and John Prine. And Tom Waits sang bluesy, greasy songs that could sound rough-hewn or clumsy, depending on your taste. This music was cool and literary, and the solitary nature of its creation lent it an added sense of integrity and individuality. Listeners could imagine that these songs had been created at a righteous distance from the corrupting music industry, by lone misfits disinclined to be part of any social organization, even a band. This music suggested that the singer-songwriter tradition could extend beyond soft rock.

And then there was Paul Simon, one of the most beloved singer-songwriters to emerge from the 1960s: as half of Simon & Garfunkel, he wrote "The Sound of Silence" and "Bridge Over Troubled Water" and other songs so popular, and so earnest, that they quickly came to seem like modern hymns. Because his voice is boyish, not grainy, and because he carried himself less like a troublemaker than like an eager student, Simon has sometimes been underrated. On his solo albums, he developed a marvelously light touch and a taste for livelier rhythms. The song "Mother and Child Reunion," from 1972, was recorded in Jamaica, under the influence of a rather new genre called reggae; it was an upbeat elegy named for a chicken-and-egg entrée Simon had seen on a Chinatown menu. In 1986, Simon staged an unexpected career comeback with *Graceland*, an Afropop classic that was also the only contemporary album I recall my parents listening to. Like lots of people my age, I grew up on *Graceland*—my mother, who is South African, taught Zulu and other Southern African languages at Yale, which means she was one of the few American listeners who understood all the lyrics. But I'm not convinced that nostalgia alone explains why I have found just about all of Simon's solo albums so captivating. I think *The Rhythm of the Saints*, the clattering 1990 follow-up to *Graceland*, deserves more celebration than it gets, and I think *So Beautiful or So What*, from 2011, was a late-career highlight, using snippets of old gospel music to fortify Simon's shrugging lyrics about love and death. Friends sometimes wonder if I'm trolling them when I say that, over the years, Simon has given me much more pleasure than Dylan, or Joni Mitchell, or any of the other legendary singer-songwriters. I enjoy the nervous prolixity of his lyrics. ("May twelve angels guard you while you sleep," he once sang, and he let the lyric reverberate for a moment before reconsidering: "Maybe that's a waste of angels, I dunno.") And I like the way he keeps these lyrics moving by grafting them onto sprightly rhythms from around the world. He is an unapologetic practitioner of cultural appropriation, and he has worked hard to find unexpected sources of inspiration, and to avoid anything that sounds merely nostalgic or retro. Simon's career is proof that the singer-songwriter tradition can extend beyond soft rock, and beyond rock 'n' roll altogether.

In this sense, "singer-songwriter" is a term that can apply to just about any performer who combines lyric and melody in a memorable way, and the term is especially useful for performers who aren't exactly rock 'n' roll. Bob Marley, the reggae immortal, was also an honorary rock star; "Redemption Song," a solo acoustic recording that is among his most beloved, makes him sound like one of the greatest singer-songwriters of all time. You might apply the term, too, to Kate Bush, whose songs were omnivorous and slightly theatrical; in the early eighties, when scores of British singers were conquering the charts with electronic pop songs, Bush's sublime compositions seemed to have been beamed in from another planet. Sinead O'Connor's 1987 debut album, *The Lion and the Cobra*, was a singer-songwriter classic, even though her defining hit, a few years later, was an interpretation—a devastating version of "Nothing Compares 2 U," by Prince. Influential singer-songwriters emerged from the post-punk underground. Björk, from Iceland, left her band the Sugarcubes to create stupefying mini symphonies that were entirely her own; Nick Cave, from Australia, left his band the Birthday Party and remade himself into a theatrical balladeer. In the 1990s, a little-known indie rocker named Liz Phair released a mordant and sharply observed album called *Exile in Guyville,* which became first an indie obsession and then, in time, a generational touchstone—surely one of the most influential singer-songwriter albums ever recorded.

The role of singer-songwriter seemed to be more hospitable to women performers than many other rock roles, and in 1997, a concert tour called Lilith Fair affirmed this affinity. The tour was cofounded by the Canadian singer-songwriter Sarah McLachlan, and though it was billed as "A Celebration of Women in Music," the headliners reflected a tradition of what the critic Ann Powers called "feminine folk-pop": Sheryl Crow, Tracy Chapman, Jewel, the Indigo Girls, and McLachlan herself. The tour was a success, although it also raised tricky questions about "women's music," a category that seemed to include all music made by women but that also functioned as a kind of pseudo-genre, with its own expectations and stylistic conventions. Indeed, this fact is part of what made the tour possible: the headliners were similar enough to draw a crowd of like-minded fans. Some fans complained that by suggesting that "women in music" meant "singer-songwriters," the tour was diminishing the wide variety of music made by women. Jennifer Taylor, a Canadian musicologist, observed that the fair's musical identity was "clearly flawed," because it echoed an old-fashioned idea of what kind of music women should make. "The image of a lone, self-accompanied female musician with an acoustic instrument, stoically delivering confessional lyrics does not challenge traditional representations of femininity informed by white, middle-class respectability," Taylor wrote. By its second year, the tour had broadened its vision, and the main stage included rappers and R&B singers: Missy Elliott, Queen Latifah, Erykah Badu. No doubt Lilith Fair was improved, as any enterprise would be, by the addition of this trio. But I've always been a bit puzzled by criticism of the tour's initial incarnation: it seems unfair to assume that women's music—but not men's music—must challenge the social order. And if, as the original Lilith Fair suggested, there is a large and largely female audience for women strumming guitars and singing "confessional" lyrics, well, what's wrong with that?

In retrospect, the 1990s were a new golden age for confessional singer-songwriters, particularly but not solely women. Tori Amos sold millions of albums full of lavish story songs; Beck revealed himself to be both a quirky alt-rocker and an earnest balladeer; Ani DiFranco amassed a huge cult following with an acoustic guitar and sheafs of fervid lyrics. Because many traditionally African American musical traditions involve intensive collaboration, the term "singer-songwriter" tends to be less useful in describing hip-hop and R&B stars, who often compose alongside their producers. But in rock and pop, singer-songwriters thrived—the term denoted not a particular sound, but a way of working, and a huge field of precursors to draw from, or push against. Fiona Apple, a veteran of the original Lilith Fair, became one of the most acclaimed musicians of her generation, singing songs that were furiously intense and fearlessly, dizzyingly personal; each album seemed like a world of its own. Out of the mainstream, countless singer-songwriters built their own idiosyncratic bodies of work; for decades I have nursed an obsession with Daniel Bejar, the Canadian singer-songwriter who records as Destroyer, and whose lyrics are packed with cryptic in-jokes that no one fully understands, including him. For the biggest names in music, identifying as a singer-songwriter meant embracing a certain seriousness of purpose. Taylor Swift was a country star who became a pop star, but she has always portrayed herself as primarily a songwriter; she once disparaged "songs that sound like they were cooked up in a lab" with "eight songwriters." In fact, Swift is both a brilliant songwriter and a brilliant collaborator, and she has worked with cowriters on nearly all of her albums. That's nothing to be ashamed of, of course. Writing and singing your own songs is just one approach to music making. But evidently it remains, even after all these decades, a singularly prestigious approach—being a singer-songwriter is the kind of thing even a pop star might brag about.

Making Progress

At the dawn of the 1970s, it seemed clear—to some people, anyway—that the future of rock 'n' roll was going to turn out very differently than it did. In 1967, the Beatles had released *Sgt. Pepper's Lonely Hearts Club Band*, showing the world how, using orchestration and studio trickery, a rock 'n' roll album might evoke the immersive pleasure of watching a movie, rather than the kicky thrill of listening to the radio. Singles were being replaced by albums, which were evolving into so-called concept albums, unified in theme but diverse in sound. And some bands were abandoning short, sharp love songs to experiment with intricate compositions and mythopoetic lyrics. To some of these musicians and their fans, it seemed absurd to imagine that rock 'n' roll bands would forever stick to three-minute love songs, when there was so much more musical terrain to conquer. Some of them thought that rock 'n' roll might merge with classical and jazz to create a singular music of the future, drawing from the best of all the traditions. And all of them were sure that in order to remain relevant, rock 'n' roll had to keep making progress.

At first, "progressive rock" was a radio format, referring to stations where DJs were allowed to play album cuts and other noncommercial tracks. But in the early seventies, "progressive rock" also denoted a handful of ambitious bands, mainly British, that hoped to push rock 'n' roll forward by embracing extravagance: odd instruments and fantastical lyrics, complex compositions and abstruse concept albums, flashy solos and flashier live shows. The goal was to create what Jon Anderson, from the progressive-rock band Yes, called "a higher art form." These bands loved to show off their instrumental prowess: Keith Emerson, the keyboard virtuoso from Emerson, Lake & Palmer (ELP), loved to play as fast as he could and sometimes faster; Robert Fripp, an austere guitar scientist, led a fearsome band called King Crimson, using precise dissonance and off-kilter rhythms to make a ferocious but precise racket. Bill Bruford, a virtuosic drummer who played with both Yes and King Crimson, once said he wanted to give listeners "a little glimpse of the future." In some ways, this music was diametrically opposed to the burgeoning heavy-metal scene—these bands wanted not to drag rock 'n' roll down but to lift it up into the rarefied realm of high art. Many critics hated it. In 1974, Lester Bangs took in an ELP performance and came away appalled by the arsenal of instruments (including "two Arthurian-table-sized gongs" and "the world's first synthesized drum kits"), and by the band's apparent determination to smarten up rock 'n' roll by borrowing from more respectable sources. ELP had reached the Top 10 in both Britain and America, with a live album based on its bombastic rendition of *Pictures at an Exhibition*, by the nineteenth-century Russian composer Modest Mussorgsky. Carl Palmer, the drummer, told him, "We hope, if anything, we're encouraging the kids to listen to music that has more quality"—and "quality" was precisely the quality that Bangs loathed. He reported in *Creem* that the members of ELP were soulless sellouts, participating in "the insidious befoulment of all that was gutter pure in rock."

It is easy to mock the various pretensions and follies of the progressive-rock bands. Yes toured with sets designed by Roger Dean, the artist who painted the band's extraterrestrial album covers. Dean's innovations included enormous, saclike pods from which the musicians could dramatically emerge. (A pod inevitably malfunctioned, trapping a musician inside and prefiguring a famous scene from *This Is Spinal Tap*, the rock 'n' roll mockumentary.) But one needn't affirm the genre's considerable pretension in order to appreciate its audacity. Yes used lovely multipart vocal harmonies to create songs that were, by turns, gently pastoral and gloriously futuristic. In 1972, a Yes song called "Roundabout" became an American radio hit, helping spark a progressive-rock boom in America, and later that year Yes released *Close to the Edge*, a three-song magnum opus. When the British progressive-rock pioneers toured America, they played arenas; by the end of the decade, progressive American bands like Styx and Kansas were playing arenas, too, and so was Rush, a progressive-rock band from Canada. This was a populist sort of avant-garde movement, led by self-styled visionaries whose biggest fans were not artsy college kids but cheerful young people who howled from the bleachers. Young men, more precisely: Bruford, the drummer, once ruefully conceded that throughout his career, women "generally and rather stubbornly stayed away" from his performances. The bands, obsessed with technique and equipment, and unusually uninterested in love songs, confirmed many stereotypes about what men want. But they also made some great music—for a time.

The question of progress bedeviled many of the prog bands: the ethos, which implied constant transformation, was at odds with the sound, which was identifiable and therefore stuck. Robert Fripp solved this problem by disbanding King Crimson just as the group was releasing *Red*, a progressive-rock highlight. "The band ceased to exist in 1974, which was when all English bands in that genre should have ceased to exist," he said later. Once some album-side-long songs had been recorded, and some snippets of classical music appropriated, it was not obvious how further progress might be made, especially since the bands now had big crowds to please. But in modified form, this music proved surprisingly well suited to the mainstream. A mechanical engineer from Toledo, Ohio, named Tom Scholz drew from progressive rock to create Boston, a band that became, in the late seventies, one of the biggest names in hard rock. Yes simplified and "modernized" its music, as the guitarist Steve Howe put it, and had a No. 1 American hit in 1983: "Owner of a Lonely Heart." And Genesis, one of the progressive pioneers, transformed into a top-selling pop act while spinning off three successful solo careers: Peter Gabriel, the singer, became a pop star, and so did the drummer, Phil Collins, and the bassist, Mike Rutherford, who led Mike + the Mechanics. The most popular progressive band of all was Pink Floyd, although it might be more accurate to call Pink Floyd semi-progressive, because the band avoided the highly structured, ostentatiously virtuosic instrumental passages that helped define the form. Pink Floyd is responsible for three of the bestselling albums in music history: *Dark Side of the Moon*, *Wish You Were Here*, and *The Wall*, all of which drew some of their immersive power from restraint. The songs seemed to unfurl in slow motion, creating a sensation that many listeners found extra-musical ways to intensify. Pink Floyd's vague but robust ongoing connection to psychedelic drug culture was part of what helped the band retain its underground reputation, even as it was outselling virtually every rock band that was considered mainstream.

One slightly heartbreaking aspect of progressive rock was the musicians' admiration for non-rock music, which tended to be rather one-sided. Frank Zappa, whose sprawling discography included progressive rock and much besides, formed a late-life alliance with Pierre Boulez, the French composer and conductor. But in general, these bands were ignored by the classical-music establishment—and, for that matter, the jazz establishment. Bill Bruford, for instance, had always wanted to play jazz, but despite releasing some potent jazz-influenced records, he concluded that he lacked the ability, crucial to great jazz performers, to "mutate on a whim." There was in the seventies a movement called jazz-rock, but many of the bands in it, like Chicago, functioned in practice as rock bands with horn sections. (One of Chicago's lead singers, Peter Cetera, became a soft-rock hitmaker in the eighties.) From the other side came jazz fusion, which enlivened jazz with the blare and the blocky rhythms of rock 'n' roll: John McLaughlin, an English guitarist who had played with Miles Davis, led a dazzling fusion group called Mahavishnu Orchestra; another Davis collaborator, the keyboard player Chick Corea, started his own imaginative and unpredictable band, Return to Forever. And yet on the whole, rock 'n' roll remained firmly in the world of popular music, separate from the festivals and institutions that nurtured jazz and classical music. Over the years, there have been occasional exceptions, as when rock luminaries compose soundtracks, or when jazz or opera singers record pop songs and find themselves on commercial radio. But these are generally recognizable as "crossover" events, a term that acknowledges that each tradition has staked out its own terrain, permitting only occasional trespassers.

In the long run, the grand and sometimes fussy bands of progressive rock were upstaged by a humbler and seemingly less ambitious tradition that emerged at about the same time. The Grateful Dead began performing around San Francisco in 1965, and unlike some other bands from the era, the Dead never transcended the hippie subculture—the band grew as the subculture grew, even when it was supposed to have stopped growing. "Heads are the only people who have ever come to see us, and it used to be that if we played some places, no one would come see us because there weren't any heads in the town," explained Jerry Garcia, the lead singer, to *Rolling Stone* in 1970. "Today there is no place without its hippies." Where the progressive bands dreamed of creating the future, the Dead embraced a hippie identity that was starting to seem rather old-fashioned, and yet the members pursued their own version of musical progress. The idea was not to create a new genre, or to make radical changes from album to album. The idea was to improvise, much the way jazz musicians do, finding new musical inspiration at every concert, altering the grooves and digressions just enough so that musicians and listeners could share the sensation of going somewhere new. This was a subtle kind of audacity. As a boy I heard in Sunday school that the Dead represented something uncanny and possibly pernicious, and so I remember being disappointed the first time I heard the band, on some cassette, sounding friendly and old-timey, a little bit like country music. I started to get it a few years later, in college, when I encountered *Anthem of the Sun*, from 1968, which begins with a shuffling, sparkling song that evolves first into a raucous rock jam and then into a noisy collage of prerecorded sounds. And in time I grew to love the Dead's shaggy, sideways version of rock 'n' roll grandeur: the way the extended jams built not upward but outward, spreading and crisscrossing; simple ripples, creating dizzying patterns.

Until Garcia's death, in 1995, and then in various diminished forms afterward, the Grateful Dead built a community that made progressive rock seem old-fashioned: rather than obsessing over a handful of albums, Dead fans created a decentralized network of tape traders. The Dead also created a tradition that was eagerly taken up by other groups. The Allman

Brothers, from Macon, Georgia, were often classified as a "Southern rock" act, but they were exploring much the same terrain as the Grateful Dead, at much the same time, hunting for moments of inspiration in bluesy overtures and jazzy explorations that sounded pleasantly endless. "Mountain Jam," a sublime and unpredictable improvisation from the group's 1972 double album, *Eat a Peach*, lasted so long that it had to be split between sides two and four. The world of jam bands, as they were known, was about as unhip as the world of progressive rock, but it proved more self-sustaining than even Garcia might have predicted, continuing on long after the hippies had begun to die out. Dave Matthews Band drew big crowds, from the nineties onward, with songs and jams that were mellow but twitchy. And Phish drew from both progressive rock and the jam-band tradition; starting in 1983, in Vermont, the group built a huge following without ever recording any song that could be described as a hit. At a 2004 Phish concert in Coney Island, at the minor-league baseball stadium there, I overheard a fan complaining that one new song, "Crowd Control," sounded like a "radio song." (He needn't have worried, because radio stations evidently disagreed.) In my review I noted, rather pointedly, how much the band meant to its community of fans—and how little it meant to anyone outside that community. Phish recordings have never entranced me the way live Dead recordings do, or the way my favorite progressive-rock albums do. But I think that if I saw Phish today, I would be less inclined to criticize the band's insularity and more inclined to marvel at the size and longevity of the world the members created for themselves and their listeners.

By comparison, the world of progressive rock shrunk markedly once the seventies were over. The genre's decline, a bit like disco's, had its own momentum: once "progressive" became a dirty word, fewer bands wanted to be associated with it—even the ones, like Yes, that helped invent it. But progressive rock, broadly defined, can never disappear, because there will always be musicians who want to experiment with long songs, big concepts, complex structures, and fantastical lyrics. A band called Tool reimagined progressive rock for the nineties, precise but unremittingly heavy, all rumbles and hums. And in Sweden, bands like Meshuggah and Opeth brought progressive precision to extreme metal. Often, though, latter-generation progressive rock has been rather clandestine. In 1997, the alternative-rock band Radiohead released *OK Computer*, a landmark album that was profoundly prog: grand and dystopian, with a lead single that was more than six minutes long. But when a reporter asked one of the members whether Radiohead had been influenced by Genesis and Pink Floyd, the answer was swift and categorical: "No. We all *hate* progressive rock music." If you like, you can hear a trace of the genre in the intricate compositions and virtuoso harp playing of the singer-songwriter Joanna Newsom, or in "Pyramids," the ten-minute slow jam by Frank Ocean that blends Afrocentric mythology with a narrative about sex work. Some traditions start underground and then burst into the mainstream, but progressive rock was a story written backward: an arena sensation that lives on as a cult favorite, and maybe also a universal tendency.

Old-Time Rock 'n' Roll

As the original progressive-rock musicians tried to conjure a rock 'n' roll future into existence, ahead of schedule, some musicians were already trying to conserve its past. By 1970, rock 'n' roll was something like twenty years old, depending on when you started counting, and not everybody was convinced that it needed any more so-called progress. Levon Helm spoke for many rock fans when he named 1957 as the year when "the rock and roll craze was at its explosive peak." Helm watched Elvis Presley playing *The Ed Sullivan Show* in January of that year, and a few months later he got together a band of his own; he was a drummer, spellbound by the "jungle beat" of Bo Diddley, and by Jimmy Van Eaton, who played with Jerry Lee Lewis. Not long afterward, he joined the Hawks, the backing band for a hardworking rock 'n' roller named Ronnie Hawkins, who made his money on the touring circuit. By 1962, Helm recalled in his memoir, the Hawks already seemed like "one of the last of the old-time rock and roll bands," which says something about just how quickly a new trend can become a historic cultural relic.

Before long, Helm and his bandmates found a new star to support, a folk singer who was seeking to become less folky: Bob Dylan. After a couple of years with Dylan, Helm and the others had amassed a handful of songs, and they decided to strike out on their own, as a band called the Band. Like the Hawks, the Band was proudly old-fashioned; John Simon, who produced the group's first two albums, said that the music was "more like buried treasure from American lore than new songs by contemporary artists." Critics and not a few listeners agreed: the Band made the cover of *Time* in 1970, accompanied by an article that suggested that the group might be as good as the Beatles. The songs were stately and refined, with loping rhythms and warm harmonies drawn from folk, country, and earlier iterations of rock 'n' roll. This music, *Time* suggested, was intended not for "groupies and would-be groupies" but for grown-up listeners who were thoughtful and perhaps a little nostalgic. The Band continued to work with Dylan, who was, likewise, happy to be out of date. Sometimes Dylan seemed to be writing his own version of American music history: in 1975, he released one of his most popular and enduring albums, *Blood on the Tracks*, which consists of ten songs that could almost be old standards. His language, sometimes casual and sometimes artfully archaic, contributed to this impression: "'Twas in another lifetime, one of toil and blood / When blackness was a virtue and the road was full of mud."

A longing to be less contemporary was, ironically, one thing that Dylan had in common with many of his contemporaries. He and the Band were both part of the country-rock movement that was ascendant in the early seventies; rockers were attracted to country music precisely because the genre seemed a bit old and quaint, offering a link to an earlier version of

America. ("The old, weird America," Greil Marcus called it, in his 1997 book about Dylan and the Band and American folk music.) Gram Parsons, one of the movement's most important figures, was a hip Harvard dropout who reinvented himself as a countercultural country maverick; he spent time with the Rolling Stones while they recorded *Exile on Main St.*, their bleary masterpiece from 1972. That album was full of songs that evoked venerable American musical traditions, including "Torn and Frayed," in which Mick Jagger successfully impersonated a country singer in a dusty honky-tonk. "Just as long as the guitar plays / Let it steal your heart away," he drawled, accompanied by a pedal steel guitar that sounded as wistful as he did.

By the end of the seventies, of course, pioneers like Dylan and the Rolling Stones were themselves emissaries from the past, having been making records since 1962 and 1963, respectively. *Rolling Stone* magazine had a name inspired by both the Stones and Dylan's 1965 single "Like a Rolling Stone," and although *Rolling Stone* was widely perceived to be a magazine about rock music, it was also—and sometimes chiefly—a magazine about the late sixties. Some of the best and funniest passages in Joe Hagan's biography of Jann Wenner, the magazine's founding publisher, detail Wenner's close and complicated relationship with rock royalty, which was paid constant and kind attention in the magazine's pages. (Paul McCartney, for many years, was an exception—partly, it seems, because Wenner adored John Lennon instead.) In a 1981 article, inspired by the latest Rolling Stones tour, Wenner declared that the band was "redefining rock & roll by asserting new standards for a totally modern music" and "charting new territory"; he praised them for their newfound "maturity" and sobriety (he reported that "beakers full of L.A. cocaine are nowhere to be seen"), and he called the group "a living treasure." This last claim, at least, was true enough: in 1981, the Rolling Stones remained, astonishingly, as popular as they had ever been, if not more. The band had recently released *Tattoo You*, which turned out to be the last of the definitive Rolling Stones albums. The lead single, "Start Me Up," went to No. 2 on the *Billboard* pop chart, and they never again ascended so high.

Part of the reason why the Rolling Stones did not seem obsolete in 1981 was that so many of the younger bands were eager to sound old. Wenner wrote that the Stones' only serious rock 'n' roll rival was Bruce Springsteen, who had been both celebrated and derided as a first-rate throwback since before he was famous. In 1974, the critic Jon Landau wrote, in a Boston weekly newspaper, "I saw rock and roll future and its name is Bruce Springsteen"; this was high praise, although what Landau really loved about Springsteen was the way he summoned the past, reviving in Landau the excitement he had felt a decade earlier, when he was obsessed with sixties rock 'n' roll. Springsteen's band even included, in Clarence Clemons, something most rock bands had long since learned to live without: a saxophone player. (The review helped Springsteen but it also helped Landau, who soon afterward became Springsteen's longtime coproducer and manager.) Years later, *The Rolling Stone Illustrated History* offered a more skeptical judgment of Springsteen. "The whole of his musical persona is haunted by an unsettling sense of *déjà vu*," the entry read. "True, he upholds a tradition. But does he add anything to it?" Springsteen eventually won over most of his detractors, both by getting serious and by getting even more popular. *Nebraska*, from 1982, was shockingly austere, recorded cheaply and simply, entirely solo, the better to focus listeners' attention on Springsteen as a singer-songwriter. And the follow-up, *Born in the U.S.A.*, was a smash, with a title track that came to evoke the eighties as a whole: a patriotic song if you just listened to the refrain, or a protest song if you just listened to the verses ("Went down to see my VA man / He said, 'Son, don't you understand'"), or both if you listened all the way through.

It was harder to criticize Springsteen for nostalgia once he was being celebrated as the voice of a generation. And besides, by the early eighties, déjà vu was growing more prevalent in rock 'n' roll. A band called the Knack had been briefly celebrated, in 1979, for leading a rock resurgence against the dark forces of disco with "My Sharona." (The Knack turned out to be more or less what many disco acts were accused of being: a one-hit wonder.) Tom Petty proved much sturdier: an upstart rock star with plenty of memorable tunes and a chip on his shoulder. In an age of proliferating genres, he made traditional rock 'n' roll seem defiant again, even if his songs, by turns nervy and jangly, weren't quite as traditional as he said they were. Just as Petty denied being influenced by the blues, he rejected any link to contemporary trends. "We're not a heavy metal band, and we're not a new wave group," he told *Musician* magazine in 1981. "We're an American rock band." Similarly, Huey Lewis, John Mellencamp, and, later in the decade, Melissa Etheridge all found success by making rock music that was proudly old-fashioned: inspired by the sixties, untouched by metal. Dire Straits, from England, became a worldwide success with a glimmering, transfigured version of seventies blues rock. And some old-school rock stars found new audiences: ZZ Top, a Texas blues band formed in 1969, prospered on MTV; Steve Winwood, a veteran of the sixties scene in England, topped the American pop charts in 1986 and again in 1988, twenty-five years after his musical career began; Eric Clapton, a contemporary of the Beatles, remained the definitive rock guitar god for decades.

I was only a kid, but I still remember how, in the 1980s, old rock records seemed nearly as prevalent as the latest hits. In *Back to the Future*, the most popular film of 1985, Michael J. Fox's character traveled back in time to 1955, where he amazed the audience at a high school dance by performing Chuck Berry's "Johnny B. Goode," even though it wasn't released until 1958. (The soundtrack included a rerecorded version of "Johnny B. Goode" alongside "The Power of Love," the film's theme song, by Huey Lewis and the News, which became a No. 1 hit.) And a generation of viewers would forever associate "Old Time Rock & Roll," the 1978 Bob Seger song, with *Risky Business*, the 1983 film in which Tom Cruise, wearing a dress shirt with white briefs and white tube socks, lip-synchs the lyrics. "Today's music ain't got the same soul," Seger roars, voicing a sentiment that was slowly becoming a rock 'n' roll cliché.

Rock 'n' roll nostalgia wasn't new: Sha Na Na, a kitschy fifties revival act, played Woodstock in 1969, and the self-consciousness of the seventies bands—all those rock 'n' roll songs about rock 'n' roll—was a form of nostalgia, too. But in the eighties, a new radio format emerged: classic rock, playing sixties icons alongside some of the big names of the seventies, including Led Zeppelin and Pink Floyd. Unlike some radio-format names, like MOR, for "middle of the road," which thrived in the sixties and seventies, this one was well judged because it sounded serious and discriminating. These stations pledged allegiance to rock, promising to play only the greatest bands. It helped, no doubt, that many of these bands were still touring and still selling tickets, even if they were no longer making hits: I clearly remember sitting in a friend's car and listening to a local classic-rock DJ, in 1989, as he talked excitedly about an upcoming tour by the Who. Many of the DJs—and, no doubt, many of the listeners—seemed to agree with Seger's complaint: in the world of classic rock, the old guys *were* rock 'n' roll, while the pop charts offered only a weak imitation of it. Young listeners had more and more options besides rock 'n' roll, and older listeners had fewer and fewer memories of life before it. Accordingly, rock 'n' roll was aging.

In a way, the rise of grunge only hastened this process. Kurt Cobain was an insurrectionary, but one with a keen appreciation of rock 'n' roll history: the punk-rock rebellion that inspired him was more than fifteen years old, and the first Nirvana single was a cover of "Love Buzz," a 1969 song by a Dutch band called Shocking Blue. Many of the nineties alternative bands, much like the country-rock hipsters before them, had discovered the charms of vintage culture: thrift-store clothes, used records. In Britain, a so-called Brit-pop movement emerged, full of bands that were artfully but indisputably indebted to the Beatles and the Rolling Stones; the biggest of them, Oasis and Blur, made great records that were self-consciously traditional, especially compared to the various British DJs and producers who competed for the attention of listeners and critics. And in the 2000s, Coldplay, less hip but more approachable, became for a time the most popular rock band on the planet, partly by departing from this tradition, and deemphasizing traditional rock 'n' roll. The band's focal point was not some guitar god but Chris Martin, the piano-playing lead singer, who became, through his marriage to the American actress Gwyneth Paltrow, a global celebrity.

America produced its own response to Brit pop: a cohort of bands, led by the Strokes and the White Stripes, that found smart and sometimes thrilling ways to reimagine rock history. ("Last Nite," the incendiary 2001 breakthrough single by the Strokes, has an introduction based on "American Girl," a 1977 Tom Petty song.) This seemed impudent at the time, and less so as time went by, and it became clearer that all modern rock bands were borrowing styles and sounds, if not entire riffs, from their predecessors. By the 2010s, even heavy metal was growing rather retro: fans talked lovingly of new bands that evoked "classic death metal," or "old-school black metal," and some of the tribal enmity faded as fans came to realize that these subgenres were not rival factions but merely options at a musical buffet, among which young bands could pick and choose.

There is still loud and proud rock 'n' roll, but for most contemporary listeners, the genre has faded in cultural importance, even as the music remains ubiquitous. Rock endures as a set of tools and moves so commonplace that many listeners hardly notice them. The pop heartthrob Shawn Mendes, for example, generally performs with a band, and often wields a guitar as he sings. But neither his fans nor his detractors seem inclined to argue over whether he is a "real" rock 'n' roll musician, because the term simply isn't meaningful enough to generate a spirited argument. Progressive-rock bands thought that rock 'n' roll was evolving and improving, and they couldn't wait to hear what was next. But nowadays, rock history seems not linear but cyclical. There is no grand evolution, just an endless process of rediscovery and reappraisal, as various styles and poses go in and out of fashion. To a surprising extent, though, the canon endures. If you tell someone today that your favorite kind of music is rock music, they will probably—and probably accurately—assume that you love many of the same bands that Pamela Des Barres loved when she was making the scene in Los Angeles: the Beatles, the Rolling Stones, maybe Led Zeppelin. Rock 'n' roll seems to have become repertory music, a new great American songbook for Americans who don't much care for the old great American songbook (which has become, in turn, the new classical music, taught in conservatories and beloved by connoisseurs). There was a night in 1969, not long before the Altamont disaster, when Des Barres found herself among the amplifiers at a Rolling Stones concert, watching the audience from Jagger's perspective. "Everyone came together; surging like a sea to the stage, thousands of eyes never leaving MJ's magical being," she wrote in her diary. "Such power with a capital P." Perhaps she imagined, then, as many people did, that the Rolling Stones would endure indefinitely and that no one would ever really take the place of Jagger and the other heroes she adored. Over half a century, lots has happened in the world of rock 'n' roll. It often seems, though, that the genre never really found rock stars to replace the original bunch. Millions of eyes still staring hungrily, after all these years.

2.

R&B

An Exclusive Music

I N THE SUMMER OF 1960, an entrepreneur from Detroit placed an ad in *Cash Box*, a music-business magazine. FROM OUT OF THE MIDWEST COMES A NEW LABEL DESTINED TO TAKE ITS PLACE AMONG THE LEADERS OF THE INDUSTRY, it read. The label was called Tamla, and its founder, the ad explained, was ONE OF THE YOUNG, DRIVING GENIUSES OF THE MUSIC BUSINESS TODAY. This last opinion may not have been widely shared at the time, but it was sincerely held by at least one person: Berry Gordy Jr., the so-called genius himself, who had written the copy. He was the proprietor of a cluster of Detroit labels that came to be known, collectively, as Motown, and that soon outpaced even the bold prediction in the ad. At its height, in the mid-1960s, Motown seemed to release nothing but hits, enough of them to justify the claim, printed on its records, that its music was "The Sound of Young America."

Berry was indeed "driving" and driven, and his genius lay in his ability to pursue two seemingly incompatible commitments at the same time. He wanted to run the best and biggest record company in the world. But he was also devoted to rhythm and blues, a genre defined by many evolving musical considerations, and a single demographic consideration: the term "rhythm and blues" has traditionally been reserved for Black music, a fact that has been, at various times, a source of pride and frustration for the musicians whose work is classified that way. At the time Gordy was starting his record company, R&B still occupied a rather marginal place in the music industry. Popular R&B records could and did enter the musical mainstream, but the genre itself operated in a scrappy world of independent labels and promoters. The cultural critic Amiri Baraka wrote that R&B was originally "an exclusive music," by which he meant that in its first incarnation, it was "performed almost exclusively for, and had to satisfy, a Negro audience."

Baraka published those words in 1963, in *Blues People*, his landmark study of the complicated relationship between race and music. In the sixties, R&B was growing less exclusive, thanks in large part to the efforts of Gordy, whose optimism and ambition were often echoed in the records he released. One of Motown's early hits was "Way Over There," by the Miracles, Smokey Robinson's group. It was an upbeat song about a long-distance romance:

> *I've got a lover, way over there*
> *On the mountainside, and I know that's where*
> *I should be*

In his autobiography, *To Be Loved*, Gordy connected the lyrics, written by Robinson, to his own professional ambition. "For me," he wrote, "'way over there' was where my dreams were—for Motown, for happiness, for success." Listeners may have assumed it was a love song, but Gordy couldn't help but hear, in Robinson's words, his own obsession with crossover success.

That success was not quite automatic. "Way Over There" peaked at No. 94 on the *Billboard* Hot 100, the definitive pop chart. By then, Motown had already earned its first No. 1 pop hit with "Please Mr. Postman," by the Marvelettes, and soon the label was a fixture on the chart. One sign of Berry's success came on November 30, 1963, when *Billboard* suddenly stopped publishing its long-running R&B singles chart, which listed the most popular R&B records in shops and on the radio. The genre, as the magazine defined it, had become largely indistinguishable from mainstream pop, making a separate R&B chart superfluous. The chart was reinstated in 1965, announced with one of the magazine's abbreviated headlines: BB HAS NEW R&B PAGE. Inside was the reinstated Hot Rhythm & Blues Singles chart. At the top, naturally, was a Motown release: "My Girl," by the Temptations, which stayed there for six weeks and eventually made it to the top of the pop chart, and in some sense remains there; it is one of those songs that came to seem eternally contemporary, an American classic. The biggest Motown hits of the sixties, like "My Girl," seem to preexist musical taste itself: these are the songs that we all know and (unless we are exceedingly contrary) like, no matter what kind of music we *really* like.

Baraka published a sequel to *Blues People* in 1967: it was called *Black Music*, and although it was largely devoted to jazz, which Baraka adored (and, as proof of his adoration, sometimes reviled), he included a chapter on recent developments in R&B. His verdict was mixed. He loved the genre's extravagance, its use of romantic language to evoke emotional extremes of "wild joy" and "deep hurt." But he thought that the Motown sound was, by comparison, rather tame; he called it "a slick citified version of older R&B-Gospel influenced forms." Baraka was the kind of critic who used "slick" as an insult, to describe music that had been cleaned up and watered down for casual listeners. But his critique was widely shared, including by some of Motown's biggest stars, who had begun to fear that the label's cheerful style was out of step with a tumultuous country. Marvin Gaye later recalled the day, in 1965, when a radio DJ interrupted one of his songs—"Pretty Little Baby," an ethereal Top 40 hit—in order to tell listeners about the riots in Watts, Los Angeles. "My stomach got real tight and my heart started beating like crazy," Gaye remembered. "I wondered to myself, With the world exploding around me, how am I supposed to keep singing love songs?"

The golden age of Motown was also the golden age of R&B, and it only lasted a few years. The label's famous claim to represent "The Sound of Young America" started appearing on its records in 1966, by which time Motown's form of R&B was already under threat. Listeners who had grown tired of "slick" and "citified" Motown were turning to singers with raspier voices and, often, fiercer sensibilities: James Brown, Otis Redding, Aretha Franklin. This was R&B, too, but fans embraced a new name for it: they called it soul music, because "soul" promised authenticity. "Soul" also functioned as an implicit challenge, suggesting that any other kind of music, including Motown-style R&B, was relatively soulless. Sometimes the challenge was explicit. In a 1967 interview, Redding criticized Motown for putting together its records in the studio, rather than allowing all the musicians to play live. "It's mechanically done," he said dismissively. And Franklin, a Detroit singer whom Motown had somehow failed to sign, released her sublime *Lady Soul* album in 1968. On the back cover was an essay by the rock critic Jon Landau, who argued, plausibly, that Franklin was at the "vanguard" of a new cultural movement. "It is Aretha more than anyone else," he wrote, "who has given contemporary rhythm and blues their most effective expression, bringing the soul message to new mass audiences." He used the terms almost interchangeably, while nevertheless suggesting that "soul" was something more than just a genre—it had a "message," too. By the end of the decade, in 1969, *Billboard* acknowledged the shift: it abandoned the term "R&B" and gave the old chart a new name: Soul Singles.

So what happened to R&B? That is a question that musicians and listeners have been asking ever since, at Motown and far beyond. It turns out that the genre would survive the "soul" rebellion, and the many rebellions that followed. The story of R&B after the golden age is the story of an embattled and self-conscious genre, forever grappling with its complicated relationship to the mainstream, and with its own history. Ever since the sixties, R&B singers have been right at the center of American popular music, from Stevie Wonder to Michael Jackson to Beyoncé. But each new decade has brought new claims that the genre is dead, or dying, or deserves to die. Starting in the eighties, a growing number of R&B singers vowed that they weren't like those *other* R&B singers, or that they weren't "merely" R&B singers, or that their music wasn't really R&B at all. This ambivalence about the genre itself must have something to do with its continuing identity, even after all these decades, as Black music, and maybe the Blackest music. In the 2000s, when I was a full-time music critic, I noticed that hip-hop shows, at least in New York, drew crowds that were racially mixed. Virtually any rapper with momentum would attract a sizable contingent of young connoisseurs, many of them white, Latino, or Asian American. (Part of what those connoisseurs surely liked, of course, was the idea that this music was too uncompromising, too inaccessible, for mainstream white listeners.) At R&B concerts, by contrast, audiences were generally older, and predominantly—sometimes nearly entirely—African American. Indeed, the durability of R&B is, in part, testimony to the continuing salience of race in America, and the continuing reality of segregation in our musical communities as elsewhere. In the early eighties, *Billboard* acknowledged this reality by giving its Soul Singles chart a provocative new name: Black Singles. And the magazine continued to chart the country's favorite "Black" records until 1990, when the editors finally returned, after a two-decade hiatus, to an older term for the music—a term that, like the tradition it refers to, still hasn't quite gone out of fashion: "rhythm and blues."

Race Records

People who listen to R&B today surely don't spend much time thinking about the two letters themselves: the name can resemble one of those brand names, like AT&T and ESPN and KFC, that no longer officially stands for anything at all. But there was a time when "rhythm and blues" was a roughly accurate description of a musical formula. It emerged in the 1940s, as a catchall classification for popular—and, often, danceable—records made by Black musicians. One pioneer was Louis Jordan, master of a frenetic style known as jump blues, who did as much as anyone to make the old big bands seem demure, bloated, and obsolete. *Billboard* had been publishing a chart of top records in "Negro territories" since 1942, first as Harlem Hit Parade and then as Race Records. But in the summer of 1949, the magazine started using the title Rhythm and Blues, a decision that helped push the term into the common vocabulary. (In the same issue, *Billboard* also renamed its folk music chart, using a different catchall term: Country and Western.) Throughout the 1950s, the *Billboard* R&B chart was as miscellaneous as its name would suggest, full of performers who now seem just about un-classifiable. One innovator who appeared on the R&B chart was Dinah Washington, a sophisticated jazz singer who found sly ways to emphasize the beat. Another was Bo Diddley, whose reedy electric guitar helped codify a sound that rock 'n' roll bands have been re-creating ever since.

By the time Berry Gordy placed that ad in *Cash Box*, in 1960, the world of R&B was lucrative and chaotic; he was determined to thrive in it imme-diately, and to leave it behind eventually. Gordy was a songwriter before he was a mogul, and by his own account an ambitious one. (His first compo-sition, "You Are You," was inspired by Doris Day, partly because she was widely popular; he was, he says, "thinking of general audiences," even though he was only twenty.) In his autobiography, Gordy described the way he forged strategic friendships in the R&B industry: he did favors for Black DJs, and cultivated *Jet* and *Ebony*, the leading Black magazines. But he also recalled the nerve-racking meetings that Motown held every Friday morning, at which he would decide which new songs were worthwhile and which were "garbage." Explaining the difference, he wrote that "garbage, to me, was anything that we didn't think would reach the Top 40." For Gordy, making R&B hits was important but not sufficient: the whole idea of Mo-town was to create R&B records that would transcend the genre and go pop. At one point, he remembers, one of his executives made a case for "Can

I Get a Witness," the Marvin Gaye record. "I took it home last night and my kids could dance to it," the executive told Gordy. "White kids."

This miniature focus group did its job well. "Can I Get a Witness" was released in the fall of 1963, and *Billboard* eliminated its R&B chart just as the song was nearing the top. But "Can I Get a Witness" crossed over, eventually reaching No. 22 on the pop chart; it stands as a quintessential example of the Motown formula. Like many of the label's golden-age hits, this one was written by Eddie Holland, Lamont Dozier, and Brian Holland, who were known as Holland-Dozier-Holland, or H-D-H. They had a knack for cheerful, upbeat compositions, with melodies and backbeats that fit together as neatly as a tailored suit. You might say that they emphasized the rhythm and deemphasized the blues: people who heard "Can I Get a Witness" on the radio might not have noticed, at first, that Gaye was complaining, not celebrating. He wanted to know, "Is it right to be treated so bad / When you've given everything you had?" Among the many people who loved the song were the members of the Rolling Stones, who recorded a sparser, more petulant version for their debut album the next year. "Can I Get a Witness" was propelled by a jingling backbeat, a Motown trademark, which became one of the most admired and imitated sounds in popular music. You can hear it in "Substitute," by the Who, which was inspired by a different Motown hit—its title comes from a line in "The Tracks of My Tears," by Smokey Robinson and the Miracles. You can hear it in "Good Vibrations," by the Beach Boys—that beat helped set the jubilant chorus apart from the mopey verses. You can even hear it in the theme song from *Sesame Street*, which was recorded in 1969, and which used a variant of the Motown sound to evoke the simple joy of children at play.

If it now seems odd that Marvin Gaye and the Rolling Stones would be singing the same song, that says something about the way in which, starting in the late sixties, the terms "R&B" and "rock 'n' roll," came to denote two different genres—one firmly Black and the other increasingly white. But in 1963, these terms sometimes overlapped. It was Alan Freed, a white

Cleveland disc jockey, who popularized the term "rock 'n' roll," in the fifties, to describe the music he was playing. But most of what he was playing was R&B. One of the singers Freed loved was Fats Domino, a New Orleans R&B singer who is now celebrated as a rock 'n' roll pioneer. Dave Bartholomew, a Black songwriter and producer who worked with Fats Domino, was one of many who thought that rock 'n' roll was not a new phenomenon but an old one, repackaged by outsiders. "We had the rhythm and blues for many, many year," he said in an interview conducted for a 1995 documentary. "And here come in a couple of white people, and they call it rock 'n' roll—and it was rhythm and blues, all the time."

Many listeners and scholars now agree that the emergence of "rock 'n' roll," as a term, also signaled the emergence of a new genre, one that drew largely from R&B but also from some of the more raucous forms of country music. But it is also true that, for a number of years, "R&B" and "rock 'n' roll" were treated as rough synonyms, precisely because the music was so mixed up. When the first Beatles record was released in America, it was released on Vee-Jay, a Black-owned R&B label based in Chicago. *The Beatles' Second Album*, from 1964, included versions of three different Motown hits, including "Please Mr. Postman." (Gordy was thrilled, although he had second thoughts about having granted the Beatles a discount on the royalty rate.) The spirit of this mixed-up era was captured in the *Teenage Awards Music International*, better known as the *T.A.M.I. Show*, a 1964 concert and concert film known for its astonishing lineup: the Rolling Stones, the Beach Boys, and Chuck Berry, as well as James Brown, Marvin Gaye, and the Supremes.

No act was more important to Motown in the sixties than the Supremes, led by Diana Ross, who was both the beneficiary and, at times, the victim of Gordy's obsession with going pop. The group succeeded by making sublime R&B records, often written by H-D-H, and they did as much as any act to propel the twinned sounds of R&B and rock 'n' roll. In 1965, when *Time* declared that rock 'n' roll was "the sound of the sixties," the Supremes were included on the cover, and inside, the magazine called them "the reigning female rock 'n' roll group." But Ross herself described the Supremes as "less wild than most of the big beat music you hear today"; the Supremes, she later wrote, stood out because of their "elegance" and "sense of sophistication." For Gordy, the Supremes' seemingly endless string of hits was merely a start. He was sure that the group could transcend popular music altogether, and to that end, he compelled the Supremes to gussy up their live show with grown-up songs like "You're Nobody Till Somebody Loves You," the Dean Martin hit. His goal was to turn the Supremes into a top-tier supper-club act. (He once said he wanted them to compete not with pop stars but with "superstar entertainers like Frank Sinatra, Tony Bennett, and Sammy Davis Jr.") He achieved this goal and, later on, came reasonably close to achieving another, more ambitious one: to establish Ross as a mainstream movie star.

In the decades to come, many people would remember the golden age of R&B as a time of musical integration, when genres and audiences freely mixed. "In the sixties all music forms fused together," Smokey Robinson once said. "The walls came down." But this mixed-up moment was also the period during which rock 'n' roll began to be redefined—permanently, it would seem—as white music. Nelson George, a cultural critic and a former *Billboard* editor, is an incisive and influential scholar of modern R&B; in 1988, he published a landmark book, *The Death of Rhythm & Blues*, which told a skeptical story about the genre's evolution. George argued that Freed used the term "rock 'n' roll" mainly to "disguise the blackness" of the music he was playing. And he wrote that the integrated *T.A.M.I. Show* was not a triumph but a travesty, and an ominous sign of things to come. In George's view, white rock stars like Mick Jagger, from the Rolling Stones, who were the headliners, scarcely deserved to share a stage with R&B's top performers, and he faulted the young audience for not noticing the qualitative difference. "That they could cheer as Mick Jagger jiggled across the stage doing his lame funky chicken after James Brown's incredible, camel-walking, proto-moon-walking, athletically daring performance—greeting each with equal decibels—revealed a dangerous lack of discrimination," George wrote. "To applaud black excellence and white mediocrity with the same vigor is to view them as equals, in which case the black artist in America always loses." In his view, the *T.A.M.I.* era was an era in which white imitators were starting to outshine Black originators.

It's true, of course, that Jagger's footwork was no match for Brown's— although when you watch the footage, it's also not hard to see why Jagger, with his catlike insolence and aggression, has inspired so much applause, across so many decades. But even readers who disagreed with George about the alleged "mediocrity" of the Rolling Stones could appreciate his broader point: as the triumph of R&B was transformed into the triumph of rock 'n' roll, white performers became more central to that story, and Black performers became more marginal to it, even in retrospect. (These days, when people talk about sixties rock, they generally aren't referring to the Supremes.) Partly as a result, many people in the R&B world began to use a new term: they called it "soul music."

Soul Music Is Ours

Because "soul" suggested authenticity, it fit established performers like Ray Charles and Nina Simone as neatly as emerging stars like Otis Redding. And because "soul" is something you can have, as well as something you can play, the term was linked to identity, and Black identity in particular. When *Billboard* started calling its R&B chart a "soul" chart, in 1969, the editors asserted that "the term 'soul' more properly embraces the broad range of song and instrumental material which derives from the musical genius of the black American." In 1974, Michael Haralambos published *Right On*, a book that documented the way that DJs at Black radio stations talked about soul music as if it were not just a musical genre but the manifestation of a racial essence. "The black man sings from his soul," said Lee

Garrett, known as Rockin' Mr. G, from WGPR, in Detroit, "and this is where the term 'soul music' originates." Fred Goree, from another Detroit station, WCHB, said, "Calling it 'soul music' is a way of identifying it, putting a stamp on it, and saying soul music is ours." White people could make soul music, too, but the term was a reminder that this music, unlike rock 'n' roll, did not belong to them, and never could.

For many of the old R&B singers, the goal had been to conquer the pop charts by charming white listeners—Motown even had an in-house charm school, run by Maxine Powell, who taught aspiring stars how to win over white America. "My philosophy was, don't antagonize the enemy, obligate him," she said. "Be warm, I told them, be natural, be poised, and be positive." But many listeners wanted something more defiant. After James Brown was criticized for releasing "America Is My Home, Pt. 1," a kind of anti-protest song (it was explicitly patriotic, and implicitly pro-military), he rebounded with "Say It Loud—I'm Black and I'm Proud," which still sounds radical today: an exercise in concussive minimalism, consisting of nearly nothing but a warlike beat and a warlike chant. Brown, the drill sergeant, barks out the first part of the refrain, and an army of schoolchildren yell back the second part. In 1968, this track was not only a No. 1 R&B hit but also a No. 10 pop hit, meaning that white listeners liked it, too—which meant, in turn, that Motown's version of R&B was now old-fashioned, and that its anti-antagonistic approach to crossover success needed to be updated.

In fact, Motown didn't have a choice. Its leading hitmakers, the H-D-H collective, essentially stopped writing for Motown in 1967, as part of a financial dispute with the label, and left altogether in 1968. Gordy tried to replace them by convening the Clan, a new group of songwriters that included Gordy himself. The Clan turned out a song called "Love Child," which was designed to show listeners that the Supremes could do more than sing lighthearted love songs—it was designed, you might say, to shift the group's focus from R&B to soul. The lyrics told the story of a husbandless mother and her fatherless baby, but Ross's delivery was incongruously cheerful, as if she were singing the theme song to an inspirational television show:

> *Love child*
> *Never meant to be*
> *Love child*
> *Born in poverty*

The song was a No. 1 hit, the eleventh of the twelve Supremes singles that went to the top of the pop chart. But Ross's soul-singer makeover didn't last long—apparently she herself didn't find "Love Child" entirely convincing. "The lyrics were good," she later remembered, "but those sweet romantic love songs like 'Come See About Me' were more real to me." (This was one difference between Ross and Gaye: even with the world exploding around her, she wanted to keep singing love songs.) After one final concert with the Supremes, in Las Vegas, Ross went solo in 1970, and eventually found her musical identity thanks to another transformation: an engagement with nightclub culture that helped her create a string of glorious disco records.

The person who did the most to help Motown endure and thrive in the soul-music era was Norman Whitfield, a brilliant producer who combined a taste for avant-garde arrangements with a colloquial sensibility. (Gordy described one of Whitfield's early productions, approvingly, as "street.") Working with Barrett Strong, his frequent songwriting partner, Whitfield composed "I Heard It Through the Grapevine," which was a big hit for Gladys Knight & the Pips in 1967, and then an even bigger hit for Marvin Gaye the next year. Gaye's version was sly and insinuative, echoing the paranoia in the lyrics, and it introduced a darker, less cheerful version of the Motown sound. Working primarily with the Temptations, Whitfield and Strong forged a new style known as psychedelic soul, which Gordy didn't initially support. He argued that "Cloud Nine," a 1968 Whitfield production for the Temptations, had "a message that could be interpreted the wrong way." (The chorus celebrated joy, and perhaps intoxication: "I'm riding high on cloud nine.") Gordy soon changed his mind, and the song was a success, which effectively settled the argument in Whitfield's favor. By then, Gordy was less controlling than he had once been, because he was less present at the label: by the time the song was released, he had already moved his family to Los Angeles and was himself spending less time in Detroit. That left Whitfield free to do just about whatever he liked, using Motown—the discography of the Temptations, in particular—as a laboratory for R&B experimentation. In 1972, "Papa Was a Rollin' Stone," by the Temptations, went to the top of the pop chart, even though it was nearly seven glorious minutes long (the album version was twelve), sustained by little more than a perfect bassline and a few artfully placed hand claps.

By the end of the sixties, the definition of music-industry success had changed: for ambitious R&B acts, the goal was not merely to make hit singles but to make important albums, just as the biggest and most respected rock 'n' roll bands were doing. (In this area, as in many others, James Brown led the way. In 1963, he had released *Live at the Apollo*, a live album that was an unexpected smash; not long after its release one distributor reported, delightedly, that the album was "selling like a single.") In 1969, Motown's soul-focused rival, Stax, released *Hot Buttered Soul*, by Isaac Hayes, which consisted of four long tracks. Sly and the Family Stone perfected their own form of psychedelic soul, culminating with *There's a Riot Goin' On*, an eerie and transfixing masterpiece from 1971. The same year, Aretha Franklin released *Aretha Live at Fillmore West*, which included a warp-speed version of her signature song, "Respect," alongside covers of the Beatles ("Eleanor Rigby") and Simon and Garfunkel ("Bridge Over Troubled Water"). For sixties R&B singers, crossover success usually meant a place on the pop charts; for seventies soul singers, crossover success sometimes meant a place in the record stores, and perhaps on FM radio, too, alongside the *rock* stars.

One of the greatest surprises in the Motown story is how a rather conservative, unapologetically hit-driven record company managed to excel in this new era. This was partly due to Whitfield's experimentation, but also to the evolution of a former teen pop star known as Little Stevie Wonder, who had been signed to Motown since he was eleven. In the early seventies, emboldened by his track record of sixties hits, Wonder negotiated a new contract that granted him unusual autonomy, and then set about following his obsessions, one of which was a notably unsuccessful group called Tonto's Expanding Head Band. The group was officially a duo but really a trio: it consisted of one American, one Englishman, and one modular synthesizer, which the two men had customized. Wonder went to work with the synthesizer and its custodians, and emerged, in 1972, with an electronically produced soul album called *Music of My Mind*. It was the start of a five-album arc, ending in 1976 with *Songs in the Key of Life*, that helped establish Wonder as one of America's greatest musical figures, in any genre. His music was radically inclusive, embracing nearly everything: gospel, jazz, progressive rock, folk music, Broadway balladry. He came across as both a great composer and a convivial host, always trying to get his fellow party-goers to sing along.

Marvin Gaye, like Stevie Wonder, was a Motown hitmaker who decided that hits weren't enough. Sometime around 1970—more than five years after the day when he had cringed at the sound of his own innocuous "love songs" on the radio—he told Gordy that he wanted to make a protest album. Gordy did not agree; he asked, "Protest about what?" If Gordy was playing the role of the mercenary record executive, he was also asking a good question. And part of the genius of the album that Gaye made was that it echoed the same good question instead of pretending to answer it. The term "protest album" suggests fiery assertion, but Gaye's version was wispy, even dreamy. Its title, *What's Going On*, had an invisible (but audible) question mark, and its languid compositions flowed together into one long song. Gaye's political program was compelling, though vague: opposed to war, unemployment, pollution, and despair; in favor of God and love; notably ambivalent about drugs. According to Raynoma Singleton, an early Motown executive, Gordy initially hated the album, but released it, in 1971, only after Gaye threatened to go on strike. Of course, the album was a success: it sold well, sent three singles to the top of the soul chart (and the Top 10 of the pop chart), and endures as perhaps the most celebrated album in the history of Motown. This is how it often happens in popular music: by the time an artist, or a label, or a genre has its biggest triumph, things are beginning to fall apart.

Selling Soul

By the early seventies, Motown was more well-known than ever, although not as dominant as it once had been. It was the home of Marvin Gaye, Stevie Wonder, and Diana Ross—a blue-chip record label whose boss, Berry Gordy, had come to be viewed as the godfather of Black music. But virtually all of the label's hits were coming from established acts from its sixties heyday, which meant that the sound of young America was getting older. At the same time, the soul-music insurgency was evolving: "soul" was coming to seem less like an idealistic uprising and more like a sustainable and profitable market sector. In the aftermath of the civil rights movement, a number of activists were shifting their focus from integration to self-reliance, stressing the importance of building Black institutions. In this context, the maturation—and commodification—of soul music seemed like progress, because it was a sign of Black cultural independence. In 1971, the publishers of *Tiger Beat*, the teen magazine, launched a Black counterpart, *Right On!* That same year, a Chicago-based dance revue called *Soul Train* earned national distribution, giving Black music a weekly television showcase. One of its main sponsors was a Black-oriented cosmetics company that had recently gone public: Johnson Products, maker of Afro Sheen. A Harvard Business School report, commissioned by Columbia Records, portrayed soul music as a doubly valuable genre, capable of both nurturing careers and vaulting stars into the mainstream; the report emphasized "the strategic importance of soul [radio] stations as one of the most effective vehicles for getting on to the top 40."

The Harvard report was issued in 1972, the year after Columbia had launched its own soul music label, Philadelphia International Records, created in partnership with a pair of shrewd Philadelphia producers, Kenneth Gamble and Leon Huff. In a 1972 interview with *Jet*, Gamble laid out a grand vision for the label. "We don't want to be branded as a company, for example, that pushes only R&B," he said. "That's already been done and it's sort of an outmoded concept." If this was a veiled criticism of Motown, it was nevertheless delivered in the spirit of Berry Gordy, who was always looking to expand beyond R&B, even as his legacy was becoming more and more inseparable from the genre's history. Similarly, Gamble and Huff succeeded, spectacularly, by failing to do what they had promised to do: leave the genre behind.

For a time in the 1970s, Philadelphia International Records was the most important R&B label in the world, popularizing a silky style that came to be known as Philly soul, or "TSOP (The Sound of Philadelphia)," which was the name of a 1973 Gamble and Huff production recorded by the Philadelphia International house band MFSB. (*Those* initials stood for "mother, father, sister, brother"—and also, more memorably, for "motherfuckin' son-of-a-bitch," a phrase the musicians apparently used as an expression of approval.) "TSOP" went to No. 1 on both the soul and the pop charts, and it helped define the sound of R&B in the post-Motown era. The music was designed to be accessible: smooth and plush, sweetened by strings and a horn section. And yet "TSOP" was not a typical pop song—in fact, it wasn't a pop song at all but a rhythmic dance track, with virtually no vocals. For a while, it served as the theme to *Soul Train*. And it was an example of how soul music, in the seventies, could go pop without *becoming* pop.

Where the sound of Motown, at least at first, was buoyant and optimistic, the sound of Philadelphia International was wistful and often nostalgic, as if to suggest that the golden age of R&B had already come and gone. Working with Thom Bell, a brilliant songwriter and producer, Gamble and Huff specialized in finding underappreciated soul veterans and making them sound somewhat new. They had a breakthrough hit in 1972 with "Me and Mrs. Jones," by Billy Paul, a singer from an earlier era: he had released his first record twenty years earlier, in 1952. The O'Jays, who had been recording since the early sixties, made their Philadelphia International debut in 1972, with *Back Stabbers*, a classic album full of bittersweet melodies and disheartened lyrics—it captured the painful sensation of disillusionment that so often sets in once love, or idealism, has begun to fade. The label also resurrected the career of Harold Melvin & the Blue Notes, a veteran local act, by putting the spotlight on Teddy Pendergrass, the group's drummer, who became first its lead singer and then, as a solo act, one of the decade's great balladeers.

The term "slow jam" did not enter into wide circulation until sometime after 1983, when an R&B group called Midnight Star released a song by that name, which became a cult favorite. But the slow jam, as a form, was really born in the seventies, thanks to balladeers like Pendergrass and others. In 1973, two years after *What's Going On*, Marvin Gaye released *Let's Get It On*, which was a different kind of concept album, all about love and sex; the title track is a seduction song that has become an archetype. (All these years later, those first three guitar notes still conjure up a world of dim lights and strong incense; in film, those familiar notes often function as a punch line, as when, in one of the Austin Powers movies, Dr. Evil sips an aphrodisiac and then gazes lovingly at his humorless henchwoman.) No soul singer focused more single-mindedly on seduction than Barry White, who paired his deep voice with lustrous grooves and symphonic arrangements to perfect his own brand of make-out music, a musical sibling of Philly soul. Throughout the 1970s, White had consistent success on R&B radio and less consistent success on pop radio ("Can't Get Enough of Your Love, Babe," from 1974, was his only No. 1 pop hit), and some critics seemed to wonder how seriously to take him—or how seriously he took himself. An article in *DownBeat*, the jazz magazine, described White's music as "bogus" and "overblown," and indeed words like that were increasingly affixed to the genre of R&B itself. To be sure, White's silky productions were not necessarily more "bogus," or less honest, than James Brown's grunts and groans, but listeners were not wrong to notice a change. Part of the appeal of classic soul music was that the singers promised to tell the truth. Seventies slow jams sounded less raw and more luxurious, emphasizing the importance of pleasure in both music and lyric: the singers promised to tell you whatever would make you feel good.

In the aftermath of *Let's Get It On*, Gaye began planning a tour. It was a triumphant moment: the title track had been his first pop No. 1 since "I Heard It Through the Grapevine" in 1968, and Gaye was by then one of the most beloved singers in the country. But he later remembered feeling as if he had something to prove. "Everyone was talking about new funk groups like the Commodores, Earth, Wind & Fire, and Kool and the Gang," he recalled. "Well, Kool was cool, but I could be just as funky as the funkiest dude in the neighborhood." Gaye's reference to "the neighborhood" was an acknowledgment that these bands were often thought to have a stronger connection to African American communities than the love-song specialists did, perhaps because they seemed to hold less appeal for non-Black listeners. Nelson George, the historian, quoted a chart expert who noted that R&B-to-pop crossover peaked during the period from 1967 to 1973; after that, records from the R&B charts were more likely to stay there and less likely to ascend the pop charts. (In other words, soon after the Harvard Business School report, the R&B-to-pop pipeline began to narrow.) George framed this decline as a "disaster," a sign that the music industry was growing less hospitable to Black artists in the disco era. But in the long run, perhaps the decline in pop radio play also helped R&B maintain its identity as Black music, increasing the relative value of R&B acts who were particularly popular with Black listeners.

Throughout the seventies, a cohort of funky R&B bands—not just the

Commodores, Earth, Wind & Fire, and Kool and the Gang, but also Rufus, Ohio Players, and many others—recorded energetic and inventive albums full of songs that are now considered R&B classics. One of the most beloved of these bands was also one of the least accessible: Funkadelic, along with its alter ego, Parliament, both of which were led by George Clinton, a former Motown songwriter who left Motown far behind. In his autobiography, Clinton summed up his relationship to mainstream R&B when he recalled his early concerts in Detroit, during which he sometimes wore only a sheet, and sometimes teased the high rollers in the front row by stealing their drinks and dumping them over his head. "There was a rumor going around that I peed on Berry and Diana at a performance," he wrote, "but that was just the wine running down my bald head and coming off the sheet."

Clinton excelled as both a bandleader and a mythmaker. In the P-Funk universe, each album, each concert tour, was a new installment in an ongoing saga of cosmic liberation through funky music. Severe judgments, like "America eats its young" (the name of a 1972 Funkadelic album, and a mournful song on it), sat side by side with sex jokes, science-fiction fantasies, and glorious, meditative electric guitar solos from Eddie Hazel. Clinton's spirit was exuberant and excessive, and his fans have tended to respond in similar terms. One of them is the scholar Cornel West, who has celebrated this music as a singular expression of Black identity. "Funkadelic and Parliament defy nonblack emulation," he wrote, arguing that Clinton's body of work "unabashedly exacerbates and accentuates the 'blackness' of black music, the 'Afro-Americanness' of Afro-American music—its irreducibility, inimitability, and uniqueness." But "Blackness" is a slippery quality, especially in popular music, where the character of a song is determined, in part, by the people who choose to listen to it. There are many musical features that are identified with African American culture: the minor pentatonic scale, certain forms of syncopation, bent notes, call-and-response patterns, improvisation. But often, the most useful definition of musical Blackness is simpler and more flexible. Wherever Black listeners are disproportionately listening to music made by Black musicians, that music will be, in a meaningful sense, Black music—no matter what it sounds like.

Who was listening to P-Funk? R&B radio stations sometimes played hits by Parliament and, to a lesser extent, Funkadelic. But so, sometimes, did underground rock stations. And in many ways Clinton continued to stand self-consciously apart from the mainstream of 1970s Black music, long after his encounter with Berry Gordy and Diana Ross. He thought that hybridity, not purity, was the defining feature of his music and his audience. "We were too white for black folks and too black for white folks," Clinton recalled proudly. "We were a source of confusion. And that's exactly how we wanted it." But he also found ways to emphasize Black identity, perhaps as a way of acknowledging or strengthening his connection to Black listeners. In 1975, Parliament released "Chocolate City," a funk track driven by the dream of a White House with an all-Black cabinet:

> *Richard Pryor, Minister of Education*
> *Stevie Wonder, Secretary of Fine Arts*
> *And Miss Aretha Franklin, the First Lady*

Philadelphia International cultivated a far less flamboyant image than Clinton did, but the label took a similarly unpredictable approach to Black identity, gesturing at different times toward universality and particularity. The O'Jays' breakthrough album, *Back Stabbers*, included "Love Train," a celebration of humanity that reached the top of both the R&B and the pop charts. They followed that album with *Ship Ahoy*, named for an immersive, nearly-ten-minute-long song that dramatizes the enslavement of Africans. Similarly, Billy Paul, after "Me and Mrs. Jones," his lovesick late-career smash, released a single called "Am I Black Enough for You," in 1972, which was a modest R&B hit and a failure at pop radio: it peaked at No. 79 on the Hot 100 chart. Paul never had another big crossover hit, and in the years afterward he blamed Gamble and other executives for using him to push a

Black-pride message and leaving him to pay the professional cost. "It damaged me," Paul remembered, "and I was bitter about it for a long time." Throughout the seventies, Gamble grew increasingly intent on making a statement: the label's new slogan was "The Message Is in the Music," and he sometimes wrote brief treatises on faith, love, and family, which he printed on his artists' record sleeves. Depending on your perspective, these messages might have seemed like refreshing displays of idealism or domineering examples of executive overreach, or perhaps both.

Like many successful music moguls, Gamble was a visionary, and he had strong opinions about how his vision should be realized. In 1979, the duo of McFadden & Whitehead had a hit with "Ain't No Stoppin' Us Now," an exuberant song that was often interpreted as an expression of Black pride and resolve. But John Whitehead, one of the singers, acknowledged that he and his partner, Gene McFadden, were thinking about a more personal struggle for self-determination: they had been working as songwriters for the label and were embroiled in a royalty dispute. "If anything," Whitehead recalled, "the song was a declaration of our independence from Gamble." The smooth sound of Philadelphia International was, in various ways, both conservative and radical, and the same was true of Gamble, who converted to Islam in 1976 and whose life was driven by a belief in the importance of Black economic independence. In 1993, he founded Universal Companies, which operates a network of schools in Philadelphia. And in 2000, he spoke at the Republican National Convention, delivering a characteristically hybrid message of Black empowerment and family values. "I'm putting my faith, *alhamdulillah*, I'm putting it on the line," he said, talking about his work in Philadelphia. "We've been rebuilding the family."

Compared to Gamble, who was in some ways his successor, Berry Gordy showed relatively little interest in sending a message through music. Gordy's main ambition was to be ambitious: Motown was inspired by his own dream of achieving the kind of success that would take him "way over there," in Smokey Robinson's words. Throughout the seventies, Gaye and

Wonder released astonishing records with little oversight. (Wonder's decade-long winning streak ended, abruptly, in 1979, when he followed *Songs in the Key of Life*, a classic, with *Stevie Wonder's Journey Through the Secret Life of Plants*, a double-album flop that has proved mainly immune to re-discovery and reappraisal.) Meanwhile, Gordy, having succeeded in establishing Diana Ross as a supper-club attraction, turned the considerable force of his attention to a trickier project: helping establish her in films. In 1972, Ross starred in *Lady Sings the Blues*, produced by Gordy, based on the life of Billie Holiday; in 1975, she starred in *Mahogany*, directed by Gordy, about an aspiring fashion designer. *Lady Sings the Blues* is often described as a disappointment, even though it was nominated for five Academy Awards and did indeed push Ross further into the mainstream; the director Lee Daniels has said that it inspired him to make movies. *Mahogany*, which had a smaller budget, performed modestly in theaters, but nevertheless came to be considered a cult classic, in part because of its theme song, which was sung by Ross and which became one of her signatures. What's striking about both films is the extent to which they reflect Gordy's ongoing preoccupation with mainstream success and its cost. This, of course, is precisely the preoccupation that compelled Gordy to try to move away from R&B, and away from Detroit, toward Las Vegas and Hollywood. These moves were sometimes interpreted as efforts to sever the company's ties to Black America. (After Berry left Detroit, some local radio DJs reportedly organized a boycott, refusing to play any Motown records—with the understandable exception of those made by Stevie Wonder.) But this urge to join the mainstream, coupled with misgivings about leaving one's own community behind, is precisely the thing that marks Gordy's story as a particularly African American story. The crossover narrative is by definition a narrative about what it feels like to be marginal, and what it might feel like to no longer be marginal. *Lady Sings the Blues* and *Mahogany* are crossover vehicles that are largely *about* crossing over; that may help explain, paradoxically, why each has found a loyal audience among Black viewers.

There was, though, one more Motown crossover act: the Jackson 5, a band of brothers that began making albums in 1969. The first one was called *Diana Ross Presents the Jackson 5*—the title may have been calculated to encourage the perception, which was widespread but apparently false, that she had discovered the group. Regardless, her endorsement was valuable, and *Diana Ross Presents* helped turn the Jacksons into instant pop stars; their first four singles all went to No. 1 on both the R&B and pop charts. Gordy remembered how excited one of his publicists was to get to work. "They're wholesome, clean, cute and black," the publicist said. "I can't wait to put together their press kit." Between 1969 and 1975, after which the Jackson 5 left Motown for Epic, a subsidiary of Columbia Records, Gordy released more than a dozen albums by the Jackson 5 and by the group's members, including Michael Jackson; one of the brothers, Jermaine, married Gordy's daughter, Hazel, in 1973. The Jacksons' pop success was the grandest fulfillment of Gordy's crossover dream, though a bittersweet one, since Michael Jackson was no longer a Motown recording artist by the time he conquered the world with *Thriller* in 1982. Even so, Gordy liked to claim the Jacksons as a personal triumph, and understandably so—the biggest pop success story of the 1980s was also the final triumph of sixties Motown. He said that the Jackson 5 were "the last big stars to come rolling off my assembly line."

Ain't Nothing to This Disco

On October 26, 1974, *Billboard* reported the release of a new compilation of funky R&B. It included hits by James Brown and Barry White alongside "Love Doctor," by the irreverent soul star Millie Jackson, and "Why Can't We Live Together," which had been a No. 1 R&B hit for an otherwise obscure singer named Timmy Thomas, and which paired Thomas's voice with an instrument that was then something of a novelty: a drum machine. The album, *Billboard* noted, was "an industry first," not because of the songs, none of which were new, but because of the way they were presented: non-stop, as a "continuous mix," which was "especially designed for use by discos." The album was called *Disco Par-r-r-ty*, and the elongated title was accompanied by a grid of snapshots of dance-floor revelry. In the same issue, a new chart made its debut: Disco Action, which listed the ten most popular tracks in New York's booming nightclub scene. This chart endured; these days, *Billboard* publishes a whole cluster of charts devoted to what is broadly known as dance music. But in 1974, that Top 10 list was the magazine's way of acknowledging the power of discos and the up-tempo R&B records that were played in them—disco records, as they were starting to be known.

Disco was in many ways an extension of R&B, and its sound wasn't so different from Philadelphia soul, with both the tempo and the hedonism turned up. Many of the singers who came to be known as disco stars emerged from the world of R&B, including Gloria Gaynor, who was listed at No. 1 on that first *Billboard* disco chart, with "Never Can Say Goodbye." Gaynor had begun her recording career in 1965, with a Motown-esque single called "She'll Be Sorry," and "Never Can Say Goodbye" really was a Motown single, once upon a time: her version was a cover of a 1971 hit by the Jackson 5. Gaynor's rendition, though, was thoroughly modern: more than half again as fast as the Jackson 5 original, sleek and smooth, with horns and strings and an insistent beat that created a feeling of constant motion. Dancers loved it: *Billboard* reported that "Never Can Say Goodbye" had been the biggest record in nightclubs for five weeks running. But R&B listeners evidently did not, and the song went no higher than No. 34 on the R&B chart. This is one way to track the emergence of a new genre: by paying attention to who is listening. In 1974, the industry was noticing that R&B singers could score big hits even without much support from R&B fans. A new market was emerging—and with it, perhaps, a new genre.

The rise of disco offered rewards that no R&B singer could afford to ignore, while also rearranging old R&B priorities, and sometimes alienating R&B veterans. Millie Jackson, who appeared on that trailblazing *Disco Par-r-r-ty* mix, was among the many great R&B singers who never found a comfortable home in the world of disco. In 1979, she released an album called *A Moment's Pleasure*, which included plenty of danceable tracks. (One of them, "We Got to Hit It Off," was repurposed, in 2010, to serve as the basis for "Use Me Again," an international nightclub favorite by a Dutch producer named Tom Trago.) The album also included a cheeky monologue in which Jackson played a heartbroken woman looking for distraction. "I'm gon' get fine, get dressed, go out and *disco*," she says, over a strutting beat. She shows up, shoos away some "nosy bitches" who are curious about her romantic life, learns some new dances, and finds herself pleasantly surprised. "Ain't nothing to this disco—*shucks*," she says brightly. But by the end of that year, she wasn't feeling quite so conciliatory. In an interview with *The New York Times*, in December 1979, she took a harder line. "I hate disco," she said. "Boom, boom, we dance, you dance. Disco music, the majority of it, just doesn't *say* anything. I'd rather listen to a good country-and-western song."

While Philadelphia International had been driven almost exclusively by male singers, the sound of disco was predominantly female. "Black male singers," Nelson George claimed, "were essentially shunned." (He was sure that this had something to do with the fact that many of the club DJs, who served as disco tastemakers, were "gay men.") Radio stations that played disco sometimes embraced a format called "urban contemporary," which was championed by Frankie Crocker, an influential DJ at WBLS, in New York. At WBLS and elsewhere, listeners expected to hear music that was danceable but lighthearted, rhythmic but not too bluesy. George reported that radio executives from "urban" stations believed that "many black artists were 'too black' for their format," and told record companies so. He mentioned two examples: Cameo, a funk band that was played almost exclusively on R&B stations, and Millie Jackson, whose skepticism of disco may have had something to do with the painful fact that, despite the danceable records she made, the world of disco was rather skeptical of *her*.

For R&B singers who were crafty enough to make room in their songs for thumping beats, the disco age was a new golden era. Thelma Houston had been recording for a decade when, in 1976, she released "Don't Leave Me This Way," a cover of a Harold Melvin & the Blue Notes song. She turned an R&B hit into a disco classic, with a gleaming beat and a surprisingly delicate vocal performance: her quiet, sighing verse is even more memorable than her forceful chorus. And disco provided the inspiration for the greatest triumph of Diana Ross's solo career: *diana*, her blockbuster 1980 album, written and produced by Bernard Edwards and Nile Rodgers, from the visionary disco group Chic. The album included two big hits, "Upside Down" and "I'm Coming Out." Ross had never sung with the power or grit of many of her R&B contemporaries; the cultural critic Gerald Early described her voice as "depthless" and "synthetic." But Rodgers understood that these qualities were precisely what made Ross such an effective pop singer. She delivered songs with poise and restraint, as if she were holding listeners at arm's length; throughout *diana*, she sounds like the only person in the nightclub who isn't breaking a sweat. For "Upside Down," Rodgers said that he and Edwards used "excessively polysyllabic words like 'instinctively' and 'respectfully,'" to add syncopation and to underscore Ross's sophistication. And "I'm Coming Out" was a deft cultural homage, inspired by some of the drag queens who impersonated—and worshipped—Ross. Rodgers said that he wanted to give Ross a chance to "talk to her gay fans in slightly coded language":

> *I'm coming out*
> *I want the world to know*
> *Got to let it show*

If the rise of disco was a challenge for the genre of R&B, so, too, was its inevitable and spectacular fall. By the end of the seventies, disco records were starting to drop out of the Top 40, and there was a growing belief that disco was silly and annoying—that disco *sucked*. George recalled that although the disco boom hadn't benefited all Black performers, the disco bust was less discerning. "All black dance music was for a time labeled 'disco,'" he wrote. "It was stupid. It was racist. It revealed again how powerful a force semantics can be in the reception of pop music." But the decline of disco also helped R&B regain its independence: it was, once more, a genre apart—"an *exclusive* music," as Amiri Baraka had put it. Its stars could justifiably proclaim to the world that they weren't merely disco acts, they were R&B singers. The only catch was that in the post-disco world, they had to figure out what "R&B" meant.

The Comforts of Crossover

When Smokey Robinson released his third solo album, the disco wave was still building. It was 1975; a few years before, he had left his group, the Miracles, and now he was easing into a new but familiar career as a purveyor of urbane, grown-up love songs. The album was called *A Quiet Storm*, and its cover depicted Robinson in front of some trees, on one knee, lost in thought, while a horse grazed meaningfully behind him. The first track was "Quiet Storm," and it sounded little like the concise Motown hits Robinson was known for: it was a jazzy ballad that lasted for nearly eight minutes, and although the radio edit was only half as long, it never climbed higher than No. 61 on the pop chart. There was, though, at least one radio station that loved it: WHUR, which was operated by Howard University, the historically Black college in Washington, DC. The name of the song became the name of a program hosted by a Howard junior named Melvin Lindsey, starting in 1976. And eventually Lindsey's show gave its name to a new radio format: "quiet storm" radio stations played a mellow mixture of R&B

ballads and so-called crossover jazz—the pop-friendly offshoot that came to be known, years later, as smooth jazz. "It's beautiful black music," Lindsey once said. "It's the counterpart of the easy-listening stations."

It might seem strange that one of the most influential radio DJs of the 1970s took inspiration from "easy listening," an old-fashioned format that was nearing the end of its life. (*Billboard* published an Easy Listening chart until 1979, when it was renamed Hot Adult Contemporary.) But in a way, Lindsey was continuing the work of Berry Gordy, who had yearned to see R&B singers given the same respect, and the same paychecks, as pop aristocrats like Frank Sinatra, who was a fixture on easy-listening playlists. Lindsey himself was a famously dignified figure: unlike the slang-talking motormouths who had traditionally defined R&B radio, he spoke quietly and solicitously, like the maître d' at an expensive restaurant; in 1979, Lindsey told an interviewer that he didn't much go to nightclubs and preferred to socialize with "intimate groups of people." Quiet storm was appealing to radio stations because it was appealing to advertisers, attracting a listenership that was middle-aged, middle-class, and racially mixed, though largely Black. In 1987, *The New York Times* noted that quiet storm stations reached listeners "with incomes of at least $30,000," and it quoted an advertising executive who gave the format his full endorsement. "When we find out there's a station with a 'Quiet Storm' format, we jump on it," the executive said.

Demographic research helped fuel the perception that quiet storm was the preferred soundtrack of an emergent Black middle class. And so did the music itself. The critic and cultural historian Mark Anthony Neal argued that quiet storm radio gratified Black middle-class listeners because it "affirmed their middle-class status and distanced them from the sonic rumblings of an urban underclass." And he argued that "in most cases," the music was "devoid of any significant political commentary," preferring to keep "a strict aesthetic and narrative distance from issues relating to black urban life." In practice, the divisions weren't quite so strict; Lindsey, in particular, had broad tastes, playing the smooth but streetwise R&B star Willie Hutch alongside the jazz singer Nancy Wilson. But it seems true that part of what quiet storm radio stations offered listeners was escape: a world of soothing love songs and upward mobility, as symbolized by a Black man from Detroit kneeling in a forest clearing, next to a horse.

This was one definition of R&B as the eighties began: "beautiful Black music"—an alternative to the thumping beats on the pop chart. The term "soul music," so closely linked to the sounds and hopes of the late sixties and early seventies, had begun to seem dated; this was surely one reason why, in 1982, *Billboard* ceased publishing a Soul Singles chart and began publishing a Black Singles chart instead. The change was a way of acknowledging that the country's listening habits were still largely segregated by race, although some worried that the change would perpetuate this segregation, by suggesting that Black music deserved to be kept separate from other genres. But the change was also a way of acknowledging stylistic diversity, sending a signal that Black radio stations and Black record stores could and often did embrace a range of styles. (There were, after all, many kinds of Black music.) The success of quiet storm helped establish R&B as a grown-up genre, older and more refined than the pop mainstream. At the same time, a renegade strand of R&B was evolving in the opposite direction, toward funk and toward the dance floor, seeking to outdo disco with harder, earthier grooves. One of the new funk heroes was a former Motown songwriter named Rick James, who understood, like George Clinton before him, the propulsive power of a gooey bassline. "Super Freak," James's definitive hit, is now revered as a club classic, as well as the source of one of the best-known basslines in the history of popular music, which MC Hammer borrowed for "U Can't Touch This," his 1990 blockbuster single. But when it was released, in 1981, "Super Freak" was just another in a string of Rick James hits that didn't quite go mainstream: No. 3 R&B, No. 16 pop.

At the time, James was one of the country's most popular entertainers;

his 1981 arena tour was, according to *Billboard*, the most lucrative tour to date by a Black performer. And yet MTV, which was launched in 1981, declined to add Rick James to its playlist, just as it had declined to add a number of other Black acts. In 1983, James told the *Los Angeles Times* that the network was "racist" for ignoring some of the country's most popular music. But an MTV executive, Buzz Brindle, replied that the decision was based not on race but on genre. "The rock audience, which is the audience we're after, isn't interested in hearing R&B or disco, which is how they define black music," he said. Decades later, in the oral history of MTV, a Black executive named Carolyn Baker argued that the "Super Freak" video, in particular, was simply unsuitable for broadcast. "It wasn't MTV that turned down 'Super Freak,'" she said. "*I* turned it down. You know why? Because there were half-naked women in it, and it was a piece of crap. As a black woman, I did not want that representing my people as the first black video on MTV."

In the 1980s, conversations about R&B tended to be conversations about the complicated question of crossing over. It is true that MTV, in its early years, played few videos by Black acts, partly because of its ostensible devotion to rock 'n' roll. But it is also true that in 1983, the network put "Billie Jean," by Michael Jackson, into heavy rotation; it was the first of a series of videos that made Jackson the most prominent artist on the network. When, in 1988, Nelson George titled his book *The Death of Rhythm & Blues*, he was not chiefly worried about exclusion. As he saw it, the existential threat to the genre was not its inability to go mainstream but its eagerness to compromise—to assimilate into the white mainstream—in search of success. Near the end of his book, he issued a grim warning. "Black America's assimilationist obsession is heading it straight toward cultural suicide," he wrote. And he urged Black musicians and executives to "free themselves from the comforts of crossover, to recapture their racial identity, and to fight for the right to exist on their own terms."

The story of R&B in the eighties is inseparable from the story of *Thriller*, the 1982 album by Michael Jackson, which is by some measures the most popular album ever made, and which spent thirty-seven weeks atop the *Billboard* album chart. (According to the Recording Industry Association of America, only a greatest-hits collection by the Eagles has sold and streamed more—but that is a compilation and not, strictly speaking, an album.) The "Billie Jean" video helped dispel the idea of MTV as an essentially rock-focused network, and two other videos from the album, "Beat It" and "Thriller," helped show how ambitious and effective music videos could be. Eventually, seven of the nine tracks on *Thriller* were released as singles, and all of them reached the Top 10. Because *Thriller* was so popular, and so dominant, it changed the general perception of what popular music should sound like. It was the first album by a Black artist to top the *Billboard* album chart in more than three years. After 1982, everyone knew that the sound of mainstream pop was the sound of Michael Jackson, a Motown veteran who epitomized the label's crossover dreams even though he had left the label behind. After 1982, in other words, the sound of mainstream pop was, more or less, the sound of R&B.

"More or less," because *Thriller* was hard to categorize. In 1979, Jackson had released *Off the Wall*, an extraordinarily elegant and infectious disco album. For *Thriller*, Jackson and his producer, Quincy Jones, modernized this disco template with machine-tooled beats and bursts of electronics. But the album also contained a duet with Paul McCartney (one of three Jackson-McCartney duets, in fact, from that era), and, on "Beat It," a quicksilver electric guitar solo by Eddie Van Halen, from the hard-rock band Van Halen, as well as a handful of slow jams that quiet storm DJs could play. *Thriller* was an exuberant jumble of styles, and also an unapologetic attempt to create a blockbuster. "Ever since I was a little boy," Jackson later recalled, "I had dreamed of creating the biggest-selling record of all time." But George was skeptical of Jackson's ambition, which he saw written on the star's body—a body that he viewed as distressingly inauthentic. "Michael Jackson's nose job, often ill-conceived makeup, and artificially curled hair is, in the eyes of many blacks, a denial of his color that constitutes an act of racial treason," George wrote. "Add to that a disquieting androgyny and you have an alarmingly unblack, unmasculine figure as the most popular black man in America."

George's alarm may seem puzzling in retrospect, and not merely because of his certainty that there was necessarily something wrong with Jackson's "androgyny." By the time Jackson died, in 2009, he was regarded as a towering music figure, but in no way a representative one; his body, however altered, marked him not as a Black man who had sold out for white popularity but as an anomaly, hugely successful and hugely strange. Recent revelations about his sexual behavior with children have only heightened the sense of Jackson as grotesque. But George, writing in the eighties, saw Jackson's success as an example of a broader trend: Black music becoming less distinctively Black. He wrote that Frankie Crocker, the WBLS DJ who pioneered the "urban contemporary" format, was "upwardly mobile to a fault," and quoted Crocker, saying he was interested in "artists where the music just transcends the color of the skin." He accused George Benson, the jazz singer and guitarist who became an unlikely pop star in the late seventies, of having undergone "facial alterations." And he criticized Janet Jackson, Whoopi Goldberg, and Oprah Winfrey for wearing "blue or green contact lenses" in pursuit of commercial success.

One of George's targets was a performer who now seems unimpeachable: Prince, who created his own astonishing form of R&B, starting in 1978, and who still seems uncannily modern, both for his wide-ranging music and for his provocative self-presentation. Prince was an R&B favorite long before he was a pop star—indeed, he never had a Top 10 hit until "Little Red Corvette," which came from his fifth album, *1999*, and which climbed the chart in 1983, the year after *Thriller*. MTV eventually realized that Prince was irresistible, and soon he became, like Jackson, an example of how an R&B singer could ascend to pop stardom. But in George's view, Prince achieved crossover success only by "running from" his "blackness."

He noted that in *Purple Rain*, the semi-autobiographical film, Prince's mother was played by a white actress, Olga Karlatos, even though in real life, his mother was a Black jazz singer, Mattie Della Shaw. And George faulted Prince for casting "mulatto and white leading ladies" in his music videos, implicitly promoting the idea that "dark-skinned black women are not as attractive." Rick James, who once took Prince on tour as his opening act, delivered a less nuanced version of this same critique, in an interview from 1994. "Prince is one of those kinds of Blacks who don't really want to be Black and don't want to be a man," James said.

This criticism was rooted in the fact that, by the eighties, the genre of R&B was linked to a kind of cultural conservatism. It had survived the rock 'n' roll upheaval, the soul insurgency, and the disco boom, and somewhere along the way it had become conventional. The long-dreamed-of era of musical integration had failed to arrive, and Black music still lived, in large part, in its own separate—and less remunerative—world. This meant that R&B was often treated as a second-class genre, neither popular enough nor hip enough to command respect. But it also meant that the genre maintained its identity and its independence: everyone knew that R&B was still alive, with its own stars and its own rules. R&B singers were expected to represent the Black community, reflecting both its pride and its prejudices. A number of singers built sturdy careers in this world. A graceful R&B band, Frankie Beverly and Maze, earned consistent airplay on R&B radio stations, and became one of the most popular touring acts in Black America, while remaining virtually unknown among white listeners. Anita Baker became a defining voice of quiet storm in the eighties, delivering smooth love songs while gently gesturing back toward jazz and the blues. And then there was Luther Vandross, a latter-day master of aching soul music and among the greatest singers R&B has ever produced. Beginning in 1981, with "Never Too Much," he released a series of albums that were so well made, and so consistent, that he earned a seemingly permanent place in the Black musical canon. (In a 2002 poll in *Ebony*, readers voted Vandross their favorite male singer of all time.) Throughout his career, Vandross was bothered by the fact that he never topped the Hot 100—he once admitted that he was "ravenous" for a No. 1 pop hit.

But in the wake of *Thriller*, a surprising number of R&B singers discovered that they, too, might cross over to the world of pop. Lionel Richie left his funk band, the Commodores, to become a deft purveyor of pop hits like "Hello" and "All Night Long (All Night)." Tina Turner, formerly half of the pioneering R&B duo Ike and Tina Turner, emerged as a solo hitmaker, drawing from rock and pop; so did Chaka Khan, formerly the lead singer of the funky R&B band Rufus. There was a spate of cross-racial duets: in addition to Jackson and McCartney, there was Diana Ross and the Spanish crooner Julio Iglesias ("All of You"); the R&B singer James Ingram with the pop balladeer Linda Ronstadt ("Somewhere Out There"); Dionne Warwick with Elton John and a couple of Motown legends, Stevie Wonder and Gladys Knight ("That's What Friends Are For"). In 1987, Aretha Franklin teamed with George Michael, the British pop star, for "I Knew You Were Waiting (for Me)," an electro-pop song with a gospel sensibility. If this was an effort to get pop radio play, it worked, giving Franklin her first No. 1 pop hit since "Respect," two decades earlier. In the eighties, it was still possible for an R&B immortal to conquer the pop charts—so long as she or he was willing to do what it took. Even Stevie Wonder, one of the most beloved musical figures of his era, reinvented himself in the 1980s. In 1982, he topped the pop chart with "Ebony and Ivory," a duet with Paul McCartney. And two years later, he released "I Just Called to Say I Love You," a rather un-funky love song, which became the bestselling single of his career and also one of the final hits from the original Motown. In 1988, Gordy sold Motown to MCA, a major label, which kept the brand alive but not the business model. The old, independent Motown had prospered back when R&B was a separate world. The new Motown was very much a part of the mainstream music industry—incorporated but not quite, for better and for worse, integrated.

The Other Black Music

In 1984, Teddy Pendergrass, the great R&B balladeer, released a single called "Hold Me." It was the start of a new era for Pendergrass: the first single from the first album he had recorded since a car accident, in 1982, that had left him paralyzed from the waist down. Pendergrass, who had been known for a voice that was frequently described as "muscular," sounded softer than before—after the accident, he was never the same. But he had some help: a duet partner with a rich and accurate voice who sang the second verse, and added some glorious high notes near the end. She was twenty years old and unknown then, but her name was Whitney Houston, and within a year she was one of the most popular singers in the country. Her first proper solo single was "You Give Good Love," in 1985, which went to the top of the R&B chart, and also—to the surprise of her record company—reached No. 3 on the pop chart. Clive Davis, the executive who helped guide Houston's career, told the *Los Angeles Times*, "We didn't think that it would cross over as strongly as it did." Houston was the daughter of a gospel singer, Cissy Houston; Dionne Warwick was her cousin, and Aretha Franklin was a family friend. But with her huge, clear voice, and her tendency, instilled in her by her mother, to enunciate clearly, Houston came across as a pop star, not an R&B star. *Time* called her "the prom queen of soul," a complicated compliment that acknowledged her popularity while also making her seem like a suburban teeny-bopper.

Because Houston was so technically adept and so photogenic (she had previously worked as a model), and because she did not write her own songs, she was sometimes viewed as a mere commercial product, not a serious artist. This kind of critical condescension is an occupational hazard for any musician who finds a home on the pop chart, but Houston faced additional scrutiny because her embrace of pop was sometimes viewed as an abandonment of R&B, or perhaps an abandonment of Black identity. The alternative-rock magazine *Spin* wrote that Houston's second album, *Whitney*, was "the aural equivalent of Michael [Jackson]'s nose-job." ("Calling it formulaic, or cross-over, or just too whitey would be an understatement," the review continued.) Cissy Houston remembered that a low point came at the 1989 Soul Train Awards, where Houston was nominated for Best Female R&B Single. "A few people started booing," Cissy Houston wrote in a book about her daughter. "And up in the balcony someone started yelling, 'White-ey! White-ey!'"

This criticism was cruel and unfair, but it seemed to resonate with Houston herself. For her third album, *I'm Your Baby Tonight*, in 1990, Houston worked with Luther Vandross, Stevie Wonder, and other collaborators with impeccable R&B credentials. Clive Davis, her mentor, explained in his memoir that these choices were strategic. "For a singer of Whitney's pedigree to be white-identified was unfortunate and wrong, and we set out to correct that impression," he wrote. "We'd enjoyed an unprecedented degree of pop success, and now we wanted to enhance her R&B credibility." He even talked about the importance of "crossing Whitney over to a very sizable African-American audience," a formulation that captured an emerging trend: by the start of the 1990s, the relationship between R&B and mainstream pop was shifting again. A pop-identified singer like Houston could seek a different kind of crossover success, not by leaving R&B behind but by embracing it.

For Houston, the desire for what Davis called "R&B credibility" wasn't driven purely by professional or artistic ambition. In her mother's telling, Houston had always been self-conscious about her background, which was middle-class, and about the suggestion that it made her less authentically Black. In high school, Cissy Houston recalled, Whitney Houston "started bragging"—falsely—"about being from the projects, or 'the bricks.'" And Cissy even speculated that this insecurity helped explain how her daughter's life came to be so intertwined with a very different sort of singer. "Maybe she got tired of that middle-class, churchgoing, good-girl image she had," she wrote. "She'd been telling everybody a few years earlier she was from 'the bricks'—well, here was somebody who really was from the bricks. And he had chosen her."

This somebody was Bobby Brown, who was married to Houston for fifteen years, and whom she liked to call "the King of R&B." The title was not universally recognized, but it underscored the perception that he had a closer connection to the genre than she did, even though she was far more successful. Brown really did grow up in the projects, and although he rose to fame as a member of a boy band, New Edition, he was also an early example of a new R&B archetype. He carried himself with swagger and truculence. One of his early solo hits was "My Prerogative," from 1988, which began not with love but with defiance: "Everybody's talking all this stuff about me / Why don't they just let me live?" From the eighties onward, R&B acquired a new definition: the genre's identity was increasingly shaped in opposition to hip-hop. Singers like Vandross and Baker were happy to supply the kind of "beautiful Black music" that rappers had little interest in, finding ways to take listeners away from the frustration and ugliness of daily life. Brown was one of the first major R&B stars to choose a different strategy: instead of offering his fans an alternative to hip-hop, he offered them his own version of it. He presented himself as, essentially, a rapper trapped in the body of an R&B singer, using the attitudes and rhythms of hip-hop to suggest that he was no mere purveyor of love songs. The same year, Gene Griffin, who produced "My Prerogative," and Teddy Riley, who played keyboards on it, teamed up to produce the self-titled debut album by an R&B trio called Guy, which also counted Riley as a member. The album, along with Brown's single, helped popularize a hybrid style known as new jack swing, which suggested that athletic beats, inspired by funk and hip-hop, could live in cheerful harmony with plaintive R&B vocals.

The era of new jack swing lasted only a few years, from the late eighties into the early nineties. But it spawned some memorable hits, none more indelible than "Poison," by Bell Biv DeVoe, a trio consisting of three of Brown's former fellow New Edition members. Riley soon left Guy and formed his own group, Blackstreet, while becoming one of the most influential producers in pop. New jack swing was both inventive and inevitable: as hip-hop grew, R&B had to keep up. The steady, stately pulse of disco had conjured up dance-floor bliss, but now R&B was rebuilding itself around sharper drum sounds, often electronic, and syncopated rhythms, both of which suggested a more rebellious mindset. One early adopter was Michael Jackson's beloved younger sister, Janet, a shy and seemingly mild-mannered pop star who reinvented her career with a pair of audacious, beat-driven albums: *Control*, in 1986, and *Rhythm Nation 1814*, in 1989.

Houston did eventually establish herself as an R&B presence—her voice was undeniable, even though she never quite managed to develop a musical identity that fit the genre's shifting sound. Her best singles were as powerful and expressive as anyone's, but by the 2000s, her albums had grown unsteady, and so had her life. (In 2012 she drowned in a bathtub, and the coroner found that her death was partly related to cocaine use.) Houston's musical heir was Mariah Carey, another balladeer with a glorious voice, who similarly began her career somewhere between R&B and pop; she has cited George Michael as one of her early inspirations. Critics accused Carey of "soullessness," and of peddling "NutraSweet soul," but she was craftier than her detractors realized. After a few years of pop success, she steered her career toward hip-hop, collaborating with the rapper Ol' Dirty Bastard and the producer Sean "Puffy" Combs, who built his name by finding connections between hip-hop and R&B. Carey was embraced by the hip-hop radio stations that were becoming a major musical force, and she helped teach a generation of pop and R&B singers to think of rappers as natural allies and potential collaborators. She also developed a slippery, syncopated singing style that helped her move away from grand ballads and toward more streamlined, club-friendly tracks. During the 1990s, hip-hop became the most popular and most influential Black music in America, seizing the dominant position that had belonged to R&B practically from its inception. Now R&B was the *other* Black music, and so singers had to adapt. *Billboard*'s R&B charts became, officially, R&B/Hip-Hop charts in 1999, in recognition of the genres' increasing symbiosis. (*Billboard* also maintained a separate "Hot Rap Singles" chart.) And the close relationship between rappers and singers inspired the American music industry's most important awards show, the Grammy Awards, to introduce, in 2001, a new category, "Best Rap/Sung Collaboration."

The challenge posed by hip-hop was not purely musical. Male R&B singers, in particular, had to contend with the perceived toughness of male rappers, who could make their R&B counterparts seem rather soft by comparison. One solution came from Combs, who ran an informal anti-charm school, which reversed the Motown approach: under his tutelage, R&B singers learned to be a little *less* clean-cut. Jodeci, an early-nineties R&B group with a gospel background, was encouraged by Combs to develop a rowdy, hip-hop-inspired image; this helped set them apart from courteous matching-suit R&B acts like Boyz II Men, which were starting to seem old-fashioned. The members of Jodeci wore baggy jeans and construction boots, and once showed up at an awards show with one of them wearing a ski mask and another wielding a machete. They specialized in passionate love songs that thrived on R&B radio and didn't generally cross over to pop, and Combs framed the group's lack of crossover success as a sign of musical and racial authenticity. "Boyz II Men have more of a mass appeal, but Jodeci is straight Black," he told *Vibe*, which was launched in 1993 and became the leading R&B magazine. "Straight chicken and grits." Combs provided a similar service to Usher, who was sent by the executive L. A. Reid from Atlanta to New York, to live under Combs's instruction. The goal was to give Usher some New York hip-hop attitude, even though he was only fifteen. The project was evidently a success, because Usher became one of R&B's biggest names. "Puffy had done exactly what I wanted him to do," Reid remembered. "He gave this little kid a hip-hop-infused R&B sound full of bad boy swagger." Combs worked, too, with Mary J. Blige, whose tough, bluesy music was sometimes categorized as "hip-hop soul." The first Mary J. Blige album, *What's the 411?*, began not with gentle keyboards but with a brusque message left on an answering machine: "Yo, Mary, it's Puff. Pick up the phone, nigga!" This was one way to tell listeners not to expect an hour of plush slow jams—and to insist that, even in a world that was starting to be transformed by hip-hop, R&B had nothing to be ashamed of.

Shame and Shamelessness

When Gordy talked about taking the Supremes from the R&B circuit to the supper clubs, he was talking about ambition—he wanted Motown to graduate to "the next level of show business," as he put it in his autobiography. One of the singers who shared this aspiration was Marvin Gaye, but his motivation was more complicated than Gordy's. Gaye spent years working, with the journalist David Ritz, on a book that was meant to be an autobiography. (Their conversations also produced one of Gaye's biggest hits, "Sexual Healing": Ritz is credited with having helped write the lyrics.) After Gaye's death, Ritz finished the book as a biography, *Divided Soul*, which is one of the best musical biographies ever written, full of memorable and unguarded quotes from Gaye. At one point, Gaye talks about an early single of his that did well on the R&B chart but failed to make the Top 40. He remembers that as the moment when he realized how difficult it would be for him to join the mainly white world of supper-club entertainers. "I knew I'd have to travel the same road as all black artists before me—establish a soul audience and then reach beyond that," he says. "Looking back, it was probably good for me. It kept me honest and forced me back to my roots, but it also frustrated me. It meant I'd have to get out there and shake my ass like everyone else."

Gaye spoke often of the connection he perceived between being a Black performer and being a sexual object, and he spent his life trying to figure out how he felt about it. He began performing as a boy, when the women at church encouraged him to sing. "They'd hug me and smother me in their huge breasts," he recalled. "I liked the way that felt—being able to please them with my voice, reaching to God, feeling their satisfaction." Years later, at his concerts, he developed a habit of wiping away his sweat with a handkerchief and then tossing it into the audience. "I loved watching the women fight over my sweat," he said. "It gave me a funny feeling, a thrill and a fear." Gaye dreamed of leaving this R&B world behind, graduating to a whiter, wealthier, less carnal form of celebrity. His secret ambition was "to sing for rich Republicans in tuxes and tails at the Copacabana." But he knew he couldn't afford to ignore the Black women who were his most loyal fans. He called them his "bread and butter," and explained that he felt compelled to give them a show. "There's integrity in the idea of pleasing your own people," he said, and indeed this is one ideal of musical integrity: never abandoning your fan base. (For this reason, R&B singers, like country singers, have traditionally paid close attention to the genre charts, which provide a rough accounting of who is best serving the core demographic.) But there is another definition of musical integrity: singing exactly what you feel like singing, with as few compromises as possible. Like many R&B singers, Gaye discovered that these two forms of integrity were not necessarily compatible. Later in his life, he ended his concerts by stripping down to his underwear; he insisted that this was what the fans demanded, although it could seem more like a voluntary ritual of self-degradation. In the liner notes to *Let's Get It On*, Gaye endorsed sexual liberation in terms that now sound decidedly contemporary. ("I can't see anything wrong with sex between consenting anybodies," he wrote.) But in his own life, he sometimes seemed more conflicted about sex and gender. He told Ritz that he was embarrassed by his father, whose gender expression could be "girlish," and that he felt "guilt and shame" about the fact that, like his father, he sometimes liked to wear women's clothes.

The title track to *Let's Get It On* was recorded around the same time that Gaye was falling in love with a girl named Janis Hunter, who became his lover at age seventeen and, a few years later, his wife. Gaye was, by his own account, an unpredictable and sometimes abusive husband; once, in Hawaii, he held a knife to Hunter's chest, resolving to kill her and then realizing that he couldn't do it. It is easy, nowadays, to hear the humor in a song like "Let's Get It On," which beautifully evokes a familiar and faintly ridiculous stock character: a man begging a woman for sex. But in the years after its release, Gaye's life became grim, roiled by his addiction to cocaine, and by his tumultuous relationship with his father. In 1984, on the day before his forty-fifth birthday, Gaye had a physical altercation with his father, who shot him to death.

Ritz's biography suggests that a number of Gaye's most important relationships were abusive—including, perhaps, his relationship with his fans. "After all these years," he said, near the end of his life, "I'm still out here on the rhythm-and-blues circuit." When James Brown had his announcer introduce him as "the hardest working man in show business," it sounded like a boast, a way of assuring crowds that he had the energy and stamina to entertain them all night. (This conceit was reflected in Brown's famous stage gimmick, in which he would collapse, suddenly an old man, only to spring back to his feet, rejuvenated, dancing once more.) But Gaye was wary of the expectation that R&B stars should wear themselves out for the delectation of fans, reenacting private passions for public consumption. In 1978, he released *Here, My Dear*, a resentful album dedicated to his ex-wife, Gordy's sister Anna, who was entitled to royalties from it. He sounded as if he were singing both to his ex and to his audience—singing under protest, addressing all the people who had pushed him into the recording studio. The music was often intoxicating, but there was no way to listen to it without being complicit in the alleged coercion.

Once you start viewing R&B this way, as a world of power dynamics that are often linked to sex, you start seeing complicity and coercion everywhere. Ohio Players were known for a series of albums with women's bodies prominently photographed on the cover; two of the earliest ones, both from 1972, were called *Pain* and *Pleasure*. Men as well as women faced pressure to present their bodies for the crowd. Once Teddy Pendergrass was wheelchair-bound, his huge audience never really returned. And Luther Vandross, who was self-conscious about his struggles to lose weight, tried with mixed success to resist the genre's obsession with anatomy. ("I want to be in the bag that includes the best singers of our time," he once said, "not in the bag with those who are bumping and grinding and talking about people's thighs and booties and stuff.") The story of Diana Ross, in particular, is full of compromises and obligations, not least because her musical mentor, Berry Gordy, was also the head of her record label and, for a time, her boyfriend. Her move from music to film was in part a fulfillment of Gordy's dream—he described filmmaking as "total artistic expression," by which he seemed to mean that Ross's films expressed *his* vision. Ross, in her memoir, says strikingly little about music, but there's a vivid passage in which she writes about putting on makeup and about the hard, nonoptional work of becoming, every night, the glamorous and attractive woman whom audiences expected to see. "This is what I have been doing since I was a child, putting this stuff on my face, then going onstage for two or two and a half hours, maybe three at the most, and then having to undergo the misery of taking it all off again," she writes. "It's not any fun, but there's no getting around it."

With the benefit of hindsight, it is easier to see how even Michael Jackson, the public face of Motown's most "wholesome" act, had to contend with the special voraciousness of R&B. Looking back at his time with the Jackson 5, he described his own panicked encounters with female fans. "They don't realize they might hurt you because they're acting out of love," he remembered in his autobiography. "They mean well, but I can testify that it *hurts* to be mobbed. You feel as if you're going to suffocate or be dismembered." (It is hard to read this description without thinking about the music video for "Thriller," in which Jackson's date is mobbed by a pack of zombies, while he himself toggles between roles: prey, protector, predator.) Jackson was only eleven when the group had its first hit, "I Want You Back," and precocity was central to his appeal. He borrowed grown-up dance moves from R&B stars like Jackie Wilson and James Brown, and although his appropriations were generally considered cute, the cultural critic Margo Jefferson challenged that perception in 2006, in a short but powerful book called *On Michael Jackson*. She reconsidered his early years, asking readers to entertain the possibility that Jackson, and the executives who encouraged him, were engaged in something that should trouble us. In her view, Jackson's twitches and poses were irreducibly sexual, and therefore sexualizing: a form of show-business "pedophilia" that encouraged "sexual desire" among his fans, many of whom were adults. And she suggested we listen again to "ABC," a puppy-love song in which Jackson either suggests or accedes to a classroom affair. "Tea-tea-tea-teacher's gonna show you / How to get an A," he yelps. Jefferson wrote, "These hits made Michael a national sex object—a sex toy, really."

By the time he became the biggest pop star in the world, Jackson was a different kind of sex object. In *The Closing of the American Mind*, a best-selling jeremiad about the decline of American culture, the philosopher Allan Bloom wrote, with evident distaste, about a White House ceremony in which President Reagan was seen "warmly grasping the daintily proffered gloved hand of Michael Jackson." In Bloom's view, Jackson was an example of how pop stars were competing to be "weirder" than one another; he also mentioned Prince in this regard. But Prince's various provocations— including a particularly transgressive song, "Sister," that was a sexual fantasy about a teenage boy and his grown-up sister—tended to be playful and knowing. I saw Prince onstage in 2002, by which time he was forty-three, no longer a hitmaker but still one of the most electrifying performers in the world: lithe and ferocious, less interested in pop futurism than in rummaging through sounds and styles from decades of R&B history. Where Prince radiated joy, Jackson's music was fueled by a combination of sentiment and paranoia. His love songs were often vague, but his diatribes were vivid, especially "Billie Jean," his MTV breakthrough, and its sequel, "Dirty Diana," both of which were about unscrupulous women who preyed on men. And more than any other sex symbol, before or since, Jackson was coy about what he himself wanted. One of his only convincing songs about sexual desire was "Muscles," which he wrote for Diana Ross. In it, she sighs, "I want muscles! / All, all over his body." The lyrics sound no less provocative when you learn that Muscles was the name of Jackson's pet python.

In 1993, police announced that they were investigating an allegation that Jackson had sexually abused a thirteen-year-old boy, one of a number of boys whom Jackson later said he considered close friends. He settled a civil suit filed by the boy's family for an undisclosed amount, reportedly more than $20 million, and his career was never the same. His first major single after the allegation was "Scream," a vituperative complaint about false allegations, which he paired with a gauzy and rather unpleasant ballad called "Childhood." This latter song, about a guy whose "painful youth" had rendered him eternally childlike, was presumably meant to explain why Jackson couldn't have done what he was accused of doing, although it also worked pretty well as an explanation of why he might have. A decade later, he was put on trial for multiple charges of child molestation, and while he was acquitted on all counts, he came to seem increasingly peripheral to the pop culture he had once ruled; with the release, in 2019, of a documentary about two men who said he had sexually abused them for years when they were boys, some listeners began to think that Jackson's music should be removed from contemporary playlists. Jackson, who died from a drug overdose in 2009, didn't live long enough to see himself widely shunned as a rapist. But he did live long enough to experience the complicated aftermath of crossover success. Like Gaye, Jackson never fully escaped the exhausting world of R&B. A few months after his death, his family authorized the release of *This Is It*, a concert movie that was actually a rehearsal movie, showing Jackson working hard, frail but precise, practicing songs and dance moves for a show that he didn't get to put on.

By the nineties, anyway, Jackson was still famous, but no longer so important. The era of pop crossover, which so alarmed Nelson George, had ended. A new era—the hip-hop era—was dawning. R&B singers were learning to work alongside rappers, and often the relationship was interpreted as a battle of the sexes. Hip-hop was associated with toughness and masculinity, and its audience was presumed to be largely male. R&B was associated with tenderness and femininity, and its audience was presumed to be largely female. (Dave Hollister, a former member of Teddy Riley's group Blackstreet, acknowledged this perception in a 1999 interview. "Guys always making albums for women," he said, "but nobody looks out for us.") These perceptions shifted the gender roles within R&B. In the eighties, stars like Jackson and, even more, Prince had inspired some male R&B acts to experiment with androgynous glamour, perhaps as a way to keep pace with the pop spectacle on MTV. In the nineties, the mood shifted, and it was often female R&B acts who adopted more androgynous images, as a way of acknowledging the increasing influence of hip-hop. In most of her early music videos, Mary J. Blige wore baggy jeans and sweats, or else rakishly tailored suits. The women of TLC, a trio from Atlanta, emerged wearing oversize overalls and T-shirts; the effect was playful, as if they had raided their older brothers' closets.

If the rise of hip-hop encouraged (or allowed) women in R&B to some-times deemphasize sex, it had the opposite effect on the men, who seemed to be working harder than ever before. They may have wanted to be guys' guys, and yet they were widely perceived as ladies' men, performing for— and at—the pleasure of the women who bought most of their tickets and albums. Jodeci tried to resolve this paradox by looking extra-tough, despite singing love songs that were relatively courteous. (The members of Jodeci also had a reputation for disturbing behavior: a stylist told *Vibe* that they had sexually harassed models and interns during a video shoot, and after a different woman accused two of them of fondling her at gunpoint, one pleaded guilty to sexual contact, and another pleaded guilty to gun charges.) A male quintet called DRS, or Dirty Rotten Scoundrels, had a big R&B hit, in 1993, called "Gangsta Lean," which sounded like a romantic slow jam but was actually homosocial, an elegy for "homies" who were dead or incarcerated. The most effective way for male R&B singers to borrow a little bit of hip-hop swagger was simply to turn their love songs into sex songs: by making their lyrics more explicit, they could flout the demands of decorum while simultaneously advertising their commitment to their fe-male fans. "I Wanna Sex You Up," by a lightweight R&B group called Color Me Badd, might have sounded like a novelty in 1991, when it became a big hit. But over the next few years, as so-called gangsta rap exploded, the R&B charts grew more sexually frank. One of the biggest R&B hits of 1994 was

"I'll Make Love to You," a forthright ballad by the generally gentlemanly group Boyz II Men; another was "Any Time, Any Place," by Janet Jackson. A few years later, a group called Next released "Too Close," a deadpan ballad about a dance-floor erection that topped both the R&B and the pop charts. (The members sang the lyrics plaintively, which was part of the fun: "Oh, you're dancing real close / Plus it's real, real slow / You're making it hard for me.") In 2006, on *Saturday Night Live*, Justin Timberlake and Andy Samberg sang a song called "Dick in a Box," which was meant to parody the absurd sex songs of the nineties; their version was funny, but it wasn't much more outlandish than the real thing.

Guilty

In the 1990s and the 2000s, there was one R&B singer who appropriated hip-hop swagger more effectively than anyone else, a singer who was often described, in those days, with the honorific that Houston thought Bobby Brown deserved: the king of R&B. His name is R. Kelly, and he emerged in 1991 as part of a group called Public Announcement. Although he drew from new jack swing, he soon developed a reputation as a versatile pop hitmaker (collaborating with Michael Jackson and Celine Dion, the Canadian balladeer) and an honorary member of the hip-hop A-list. His music videos resembled rap videos, full of gleaming cars, writhing women, and stone-faced men. He was also, from near the beginning of his career, a notorious figure. In late 1994, the journalist Danyel Smith published an article in *Vibe* about Kelly's life and burgeoning career. In the article, which was called "Superfreak," Smith wrote about the rumors that Kelly was carrying on a sexual relationship with his teenage protégée, Aaliyah. The magazine published a marriage certificate from earlier in the year, which listed Aaliyah's age as eighteen, although she was actually fifteen at the time;

Kelly was twenty-seven. (Earlier that year, Aaliyah had released an album called "Age Ain't Nothing but a Number"; almost all of it was written by Kelly, including the title track.) The marriage was soon annulled, and Aaliyah went on, without R. Kelly, to create a pair of futuristic—and highly influential—albums of electronic R&B before her death at the age of twenty-two, in a plane crash, in 2001.

But Kelly went on, too. From the early 1990s until the late 2000s, he was a dominant presence, inventing a form of R&B that was smooth but slangy and heavily rhythmic. Many of his best-loved songs were about sex: "Bump n' Grind," from 1993, became a nightclub perennial, synonymous with raunchy slow dancing; a few years later, he collaborated with the Notorious B.I.G. on "#!*@ You Tonight," singing, "You must be used to me spending / All that sweet wining and dining / Well, I'm fuckin' you tonight!" Like virtually all of his male peers, he conceived of himself as a man whose chief job was to entertain women, and he delivered these licentious lyrics with a wink, and often balanced them with earnest relationship songs like "When a Woman's Fed Up," a bluesy lament about a man who realizes it's too late for him to apologize to the partner he has wronged.

Kelly's notoriety increased in 2002, after a video started circulating that showed him with an underage girl, having intercourse with her and peeing on her. He was indicted on twenty-one counts of making child pornography, and eventually acquitted; he was arrested on charges of possessing child pornography, although those charges were dropped; and he settled at least three lawsuits filed by women who alleged that he had preyed on them. Through all this, though, he kept making hits, including "Ignition (Remix)," a lighthearted sex song that became one of those hits that everyone seemed to like. (Adam Levine, from the pop group Maroon 5, played it live; the rapper Lil Wayne recorded his own version; footage emerged of Michael Jackson dancing to it; in 2013, the French indie band Phoenix brought out Kelly to help them perform it at Coachella.) Kelly also had a big and loyal core fan base, and I was part of it: I thought his music was extraordinary, and as a critic, I often said so. I never suggested that Kelly was innocent, but neither did I imagine what now seems clear: that his abusive conduct was still ongoing, and that the totality of it was even more disturbing than what prosecutors were alleging. I wish I had thought more about that, and that I had dug deeper into the many allegations against him. Certainly I would cover him very differently today.

It was only in 2017, within the context of the #MeToo movement, and after the journalist Jim DeRogatis reported that Kelly was keeping young women in what their parents described as a "cult," that he was brought down. In 2018, his ex-wife accused him of domestic violence. In 2019, after the release of a damning television documentary, *Surviving R. Kelly*, he was dropped by his record label, RCA. Later that year he was charged with multiple crimes in multiple jurisdictions, and as I write, he is currently in prison, awaiting trial on charges that could keep him behind bars for the rest of his life. Kelly is a pariah now, and most people will, I suspect, find it increasingly easy to avoid his music, which was once inescapable. But still the music exists. And it goes a long way toward explaining why he was so dominant—and perhaps so untouchable—for so long. Even with Kelly's songs banished from many playlists, both broadcast and streaming, his influence endures in the work of countless performers who may not even realize how different R&B sounded in the pre-Kelly era. One of the many singers who expanded upon Kelly's musical innovations was Chris Brown, who was a rising mainstream star until the day, in 2009, when he brutally attacked his fellow singer Rihanna, whom he was then dating. Brown's reputation never recovered, but his career didn't end: he kept singing, often brilliantly, and kept making hits, especially in the world of R&B, where some fans seemed to take a perverse pride in loving a man who was so reviled by polite society. To me, Kelly is not an R&B anomaly, but is instead an extreme example of many of the genre's most confounding tendencies, including its abiding obsession with sex. Throughout its history, R&B has often been a guilty pleasure—not because the music hasn't been great, but because it has often revolved around complicated questions of gratification and complicity.

Deplorable

*NSYNC was the most popular boy band in the world—maybe the most popular boy band in the history of the world, depending on whether you count the Beatles—in 2000, when *No Strings Attached* arrived in record shops. It sold 2.4 million copies in its first week, setting a new record; it seems likely that no one will ever again sell that many physical albums in seven days. (Adele, the British balladeer, sold 3.4 million copies of her album *25* during the first week of its release in 2015. But about half of those were digital downloads.) That kind of popularity is impossible to sustain, especially for a boy band, whose fans tend to be young and growing up quickly. But that kind of popularity is also impossible to ignore—indeed, the follow-up *NSYNC album, released the next year, was called *Celebrity*. It is often a sign of trouble, or of exhaustion, when a pop group starts singing about its own popularity. And the album's first single, "Pop," was a rather tetchy dance track, written in defense of the group's chosen genre. But the second single pointed the group in a different direction. It was simpler and prettier: a fluttery breakup song called "Gone." Justin Timberlake sang the falsetto lead, and the video was filmed in black and white, starting with Timberlake alone in a bedroom, barefoot and pensive. "Gone" went to No. 11 on the pop chart; by the group's high standards, it was a modest hit. But in another sense it was a breakthrough. The video made it into rotation on Black Entertainment Television, a network that had mainly ignored the group. And the song was popular enough on R&B radio stations that it rose to No. 14 on the R&B chart, giving the group its first official R&B hit.

Did *NSYNC belong on the R&B chart? Certainly "Gone" sounded, more or less, like a slow jam. It featured a guitar playing broken chords, in the tradition of Babyface, the R&B singer and executive who was known for R&B ballads driven by acoustic guitar. And in the chorus, while the group members intoned the song's one-word refrain, Timberlake improvised a series of bluesy falsetto ad-libs, in the tradition of classic R&B. On the other hand, there was the obvious fact that the five members of *NSYNC were white, whereas R&B singers were, even then—and are, even now—expected to be Black. In the sixties, white R&B singers were common enough to inspire a term: "blue-eyed soul." In the seventies, this term was sometimes affixed to rock stars like Elton John and David Bowie, both of whom traveled to Philadelphia to make soul-inspired albums; in the eighties, Hall and Oates, who had a series of R&B-inspired hits, were sometimes called blue-eyed soul. But R&B radio stations often didn't play these singers, and in many cases the exponents of blue-eyed soul were thought of as rock stars or pop stars, not R&B stars. There have been some exceptions, although surprisingly few. Rick James had a white protégée named Teena Marie, who recorded for Motown and had a string of R&B hits in the eighties. And in the nineties, a white R&B singer named Jon B. had some success, with assistance from Babyface, who produced his first album. (Jon B. was careful to assure R&B listeners that he was committed to the genre and conscientious about race. "I always use Black girls in my videos," he once said, "because there aren't enough interracial relationships on television.") White rappers have always been figures of fascination, but they have also enjoyed outsize success, from Debbie Harry, of Blondie, to the Beastie Boys, from Eminem to Macklemore. By contrast, white R&B singers have been rarer, and less successful.

The reason for this has something to do with the nebulous musical identity of R&B itself. There are some general guidelines: R&B songs tend to emphasize the backbeat more than pop songs do, with more bent notes and bluesy ad-libs, and lyrics drawing more deeply from the grammar and vocabulary of African American vernacular English. But compared to hip-hop, R&B can be hard to identify. You can tell immediately when someone is rapping, but you can't always tell when someone is singing R&B, as opposed to singing pop. In practice, R&B, like most genres, has been primarily defined by its listeners, or by radio programmers' ideas of what those listeners want to hear. Which means that R&B has continued to be defined by race. Even after attending anti-charm school with Sean "Puffy" Combs, Usher specialized in what was essentially teen pop, but because he is Black, he was viewed from the beginning as an R&B singer and embraced by R&B radio stations and their listeners. By contrast, Christina Aguilera had a big voice that evoked Whitney Houston, and she loved to do the kind of bluesy ad-libs that R&B singers use to show off. But she has never been viewed as an R&B singer and never received real airplay on R&B radio; she was always considered a pop singer, partly because she was seen as white. (She is also Latina, through her father, who was born in Ecuador.) This racial division was self-perpetuating, because singers gravitated toward the formats that embraced them. The white singer known as P!nk emerged, in 2000, with a sassy song called "There You Go," which was thoroughly R&B: it was cowritten by Kandi Burruss, from the R&B group Xscape (and, more recently, from the reality show *The Real Housewives of Atlanta*), and produced by Kevin "She'kspere" Briggs, who had made hits for TLC and Destiny's Child. The song reached No. 7 on the Hot 100, and No. 15 on the R&B chart. P!nk became one of the most successful pop stars of the 2000s, but she never had another R&B hit.

This ongoing system of musical segregation did not affect Black and white singers equally, of course. As Eddie Levert, from the O'Jays, once put it, "Doing Black music does not always pay as well as doing pop." Luther Vandross's inability to establish himself on the pop chart circumscribed his career, as he well knew. By contrast, Madonna's failure to conquer the R&B chart scarcely hampered hers. In the case of Timberlake, "Gone" was a strategic triumph, even though it didn't crack the Top 10. The song gave him a dash of R&B credibility, which eased his transition from boy-band phenomenon to grown-up singer. In 2002, he released *Justified*, his debut solo album, a pop blockbuster that also sent one song, "Cry Me a River," to No. 11 on the R&B chart. To celebrate his new solo career, Timberlake appeared at the 2004 Super Bowl, alongside a singer from the other side of the pop/R&B divide: Janet Jackson, whose electronic pop music was an influence on Timberlake and his frequent collaborator, the producer known as Timbaland. Of course, the performance was not remembered as a triumph, because it included a dance sequence in which Timberlake removed part of Jackson's bra, exposing her right breast. The incident, known as Nipplegate, became one of the biggest pop-culture stories of the year: Michael Powell, the chairman of the Federal Communications Commission, called it "deplorable," and the FCC fined CBS, the network that broadcast the Super Bowl, more than half a million dollars, although the fine was eventually overturned in court. The uproar effectively ended Jackson's career as a hitmaker: before Nipplegate, every Janet Jackson album since *Control* had spun off at least two Top 10 singles; after Nipplegate, she never had another big hit. And yet Timberlake escaped punishment—he even performed at the Grammys, also on CBS, a week later, and he continued to be one of the most popular singers in the country. (He was invited back to be the Super Bowl halftime performer in 2018.) It was a clarifying moment: Jackson, for all her success, was viewed as an R&B singer, and suddenly she was marginal again. Meanwhile, Timberlake could continue on as a clean-scrubbed pop star—inspired by R&B, to be sure, but not limited by it.

Is it possible that the longevity of R&B is related, somehow, to its brazenness? Two of its forebears, jazz and the blues, grew more respectable as they grew more estranged from contemporary popular culture. By the 1980s, for instance, jazz was one of the most universally esteemed artistic traditions in the country, although it thrived not on the radio but, increasingly, in conservatories and nonprofit institutions, such as Jazz at Lincoln Center, which was founded in 1987. (The exception was smooth jazz, which was, for a time, a modestly popular radio format—and which was also, tellingly, the one form of jazz that did not tend to command respect.) Perhaps it is easier to put a genre into a museum, or a curriculum, if it seems in danger of going extinct; perhaps R&B's rude health made it easier to take for granted. But maybe the process works in reverse, too: sometimes, the genres that thrive for decades are the ones that are ruthlessly, shamelessly devoted to pleasing their audiences. "So Gone," by Monica, was in many respects a typical—and typically excellent—early-2000s R&B hit. It was produced by the hip-hop pioneer Missy Elliott, who used horns and strings from a seventies slow jam to create a languorous club track. Monica's voice was luxuriously multitracked, but the lyrics were prosaic, reflecting the workaday frustration of a lousy relationship: "I ask myself over again, what am I doing wrong / To make you stay out all night and not think to call?" The song spent five weeks atop the R&B chart, although it was less dominant—No. 10—on the Hot 100. Then, in 2016, the song was revived, in the form of a social media phenomenon called #sogonechallenge, where users recorded themselves rapping over the beat. There was no particular reason why that song should have reappeared at exactly that moment, but the challenge mined a specific form of nostalgia. In its moment, "So Gone" had been a big deal in the world of R&B, but less so outside that world. People who loved it, back then, could feel as if they owned it, as if it were "*exclusive* music," as R&B often has been, even after all these years.

A Rebirthing Process

There was another way, though, to look at late-period R&B: not as a shapeshifting genre, finding new ways to please its traditional audience, but as a degraded shell of its former self. In this version of R&B history, the "death" of the genre came not with the rise of "crossover" pop in the eighties, but with the rise of flashy and sexy hip-hop-inspired club tracks in the nineties. This music, so the story went, had once been the realm of thoughtful, politically conscious singers like Marvin Gaye and Aretha Franklin. Somehow, a venerable tradition had been hijacked by sleazy lotharios singing songs that all seemed to be about the same thing: "Freak Me" (Silk, 1993), "Freak Like Me" (Adina Howard, 1995), and "Freek'n You" (Jodeci, 1995). In this view, R&B's bad reputation was well deserved. Now it was time for an R&B reformation.

The name of this reformational movement was neo-soul, which was coined by a record executive named Kedar Massenburg. He used the term to describe two singers in particular: D'Angelo, whom he managed, and Erykah Badu, whom he signed to his record label, which was distributed by Universal Records. (Badu made her debut in 1997, and the next year, Massenburg was appointed the president of another label in the Universal family: Motown.) Neo-soul aimed to provide an alternative to contemporary R&B by looking back to the soul music of the 1970s. "It wasn't a new sound," Massenburg told me, years later. "It was just an old sound, reintroduced." During a BET special, early in her career, Badu took the stage holding an incense stick and performed what looked like a healing ritual. "Music is kind of sick," she said. "It's going through a rebirthing process, and I found myself being one of the midwives."

It was true that many neo-soul performers looked back fondly to moody seventies soul singers like Ann Peebles and Donny Hathaway. Massenburg embraced the word "soul" for the same reason that many performers and executives had abandoned it after the seventies: because it conjured up an older, more respectable version of R&B. But neo-soul was not simply retro; it also represented a new attempt to merge R&B and hip-hop. Both D'Angelo and Erykah Badu started their careers as members of hip-hop groups, but they showed R&B singers a counterintuitive way to acknowledge hip-hop: not by amping up the energy, but by tamping it down. D'Angelo's debut album, *Brown Sugar*, appeared in 1995, and its sensibility was jazzy and slightly stoned; the beats slouched and thumped, and he murmured the lyrics, as if he were too cool for enunciation. The first Erykah Badu album, *Baduizm*, showcased both her willowy voice, which was often compared to Billie Holiday's, and her tricky sense of rhythm. The album's lead single, "On & On," was the first neo-soul song to reach the top of the R&B chart, and its chorus was a bit of old-fashioned hip-hop doggerel: "On and on, and on and on / My cipher keeps moving like a rolling stone." Badu exhaled the words as softly as pillow talk, as if to remind all those rappers that there was something she could do that they couldn't: sing.

In the years that followed, the term "neo-soul" was applied to a wide range of singers. Maxwell was a broad-minded balladeer; Jill Scott was both a singer-songwriter and a poet; Lauryn Hill sometimes rapped and sometimes sang, which made her both a hip-hop pioneer and a neo-soul exemplar. Neo-soul was typically a negative category, which is to say that it defined itself in opposition to the mainstream: the music on the radio was full of samples and electronic sounds, so neo-soul often relied on live musicians playing traditional instruments; the people on the radio were chronicling one-night stands, so the paragons of neo-soul emphasized timeless love, in hopes that their music would come to seem timeless, too, rather than merely trendy. You can hear this attitude in the song "Video," from 2001, by India Arie, a modest hit (it peaked at No. 14 on the R&B chart and never made the Top 40) that had an outsize impact because its message was so forthright, so unusual—and so oppositional. In the music video, Arie wielded an acoustic guitar while delivering a message of self-celebration that would not become common in popular music for another decade or two:

> *I'm not the average girl from your video*
> *And I ain't built like a supermodel*
> *But I learned to love myself unconditionally*
> *Because I am a queen*

When Marvin Gaye judged that there was "integrity in the idea of pleasing your own people," he was consoling himself, looking for a reason to conclude that there was something noble about giving listeners what they seemed to want, even if it wasn't exactly what *he* wanted. For the neo-soul singers, though, the other definition of integrity was more important. They vowed to follow their own consciences—indeed, the neo-soul singers were closely linked to the so-called conscious rappers, who were waging a similar campaign within hip-hop. In the neo-soul movement, integrity meant resisting the dictates of R&B radio, and refusing to be "the average girl from your video."

And yet neo-soul was never as simple, or as pure, as it seemed. The movement's most popular records were played on the same radio stations that played mainstream contemporary R&B; most listeners, no doubt, enjoyed both. And while Arie never had another major hit, many of the most popular neo-soul singers had careers that made them hard to categorize. One of Maxwell's most popular songs, "Fortunate," was written by a different sort of soul singer: R. Kelly. After *Brown Sugar*, D'Angelo released an album called *Voodoo*, a masterpiece of insinuative funk that transformed its maker into a mainstream sex symbol: D'Angelo was shirtless on the cover, and quivering with anticipation in the video for "Untitled (How Does It Feel)." Some of D'Angelo's collaborators described him as being unnerved, like Gaye before him, by the perception that his popularity was linked to his sexual appeal; D'Angelo took fourteen years to release the follow-up, a somber and diffident album that contained nothing like a radio hit. Erykah Badu took particular pleasure in upending listeners' expectations of neo-soul. She collaborated with rappers, experimented with electronic sounds, and released a series of excellent and unpredictable records: one had an eleven-minute track that sounded like minimalist techno; another was a lighthearted mixtape full of songs about telephones. She seemed intent on showing the world that a so-called neo-soul singer need not be a nostalgic revivalist, and she was proud of the easy rapport she had developed with younger singers and rappers. "I'm the OG," she told me. "Godmother. Auntie. They keep aging and getting old—and I just stay the same."

Musicians tend not to like labels, especially successful musicians, who prefer to think of themselves as singular talents, rather than exponents of some spurious subgenre. Neo-soul was no exception: none of the singers from the original neo-soul cohort embraced the term. And yet "neo-soul," both the term and the tendency, helped change and enrich the perception of R&B, which explains why it outlived Massenburg's initial marketing push. In 2001, *Rolling Stone* told its readers about an emerging singer whom they called "neo-soul's newest princess," one who had served as an opening act for Maxwell. At a time when most mainstream R&B was computer music, she was devoted to an old-fashioned instrument—so devoted, in fact, that she named herself after it. She called herself Alicia Keys, and she was a pianist and singer who was also an eager student of R&B history. (At a concert I saw at Radio City Music Hall in 2002, she interpolated bits and pieces of Marvin Gaye, Prince, Michael Jackson, and Roy Ayers, the vibraphonist and bandleader.) Her breakout hit, "Fallin'," was a gentle but bluesy ballad that was proudly unlike everything else on the radio. But Keys had a champion who knew how to navigate the world of R&B: Clive Davis, the same executive who had guided the career of Whitney Houston years earlier. With some help from Davis, Keys transcended not only neo-soul but R&B in general, becoming first a hitmaker and then an all-purpose celebrity; in 2019, she served as host of the Grammy Awards, a ceremony that is most useful as a gauge of how the American music industry wants to be viewed. A substantial part of Keys's appeal, both to listeners and to the organizers of the Grammys, was that she represented a bygone ideal of "real" musicianship: a skillful and poised singer-pianist, providing a brief respite from the chaos that was—and is—contemporary popular music.

Maybe it was fitting that the rebellious, reformational spirit of neo-soul would culminate in the rise of a widely accessible star like Alicia Keys. Despite the experiments of singers like Badu, the neo-soul impulse was a rather reactionary one, seeking to take R&B back to an earlier and perhaps simpler time. Neo-soul was sometimes celebrated as if it were a more authentically Black strain of R&B, but in the 1990s, as in the 1970s, musical Blackness was hard to quantify. It certainly wasn't clear, from either the concerts or the radio playlists, that neo-soul served Black listeners more faithfully, or more *exclusively*, than the mainstream alternative. The neo-soul era was also a time of extraordinary innovation for mainstream R&B, which was embracing a futuristic sound that combined electronic instrumentation with tricky syncopation. A number of listeners (and perhaps a few singers) didn't seem to notice this innovative spirit at the time. This could be because the music itself was generally unpretentious—the people behind the latest R&B hits typically didn't issue manifestos, or give interviews explaining how they settled on a particular drumbeat. It could be, too, because many listeners were paying attention to the lyrics, which tended to be plain, rather than to the timbres and rhythms, which tended to be exotic.

No song embodied the innovative spirit of post-hip-hop R&B better than "Are You That Somebody?," by Aaliyah, who had rebuilt her career in collaboration with Timbaland, a visionary producer who took pride in making beats that weren't easy to sing (or rap) over. For "Are You That Somebody?," which was released in 1998, he composed a track that was both minimalist, with daring eruptions of silence, and artfully jumbled. (The arrival of the chorus was announced by the sound of a baby's gurgle.) Aaliyah's voice was never particularly powerful, but like Diana Ross before her, she knew how to sound cool, or even icy, playfully shirking the traditional responsibility of R&B singers to sing with heat. It might be hard to convey, now, just how startling it was to hear a record like "Are You That Somebody?" on the radio in 1998. I was living in Cambridge, Massachusetts, then, and learning to love the local R&B station, JAM'N 94.5, which was trying, rather quaintly, to resist the hip-hop tide: on its airwaves, singers were the stars, and rappers were featured only sparingly. "Are You That Somebody?" captured my imagination because it sounded as if it came from the future—it made me wonder whether R&B might actually be more imaginative than its younger cousin hip-hop. I loved the idea that the local R&B

station could be as musically adventurous as any cacophonous basement band or obscure noise record, if not more so. A few months later, TLC released a startling single called "Silly Ho!," which I also loved: a violent buzzing sound interrupted every few lines, as if the producer, Dallas Austin, were playing a prank.

These records were sneaky: radical electronic experiments disguised as innocent pop songs. This, too, was an R&B tradition: from Stevie Wonder to Donna Summer, the genre's history includes plenty of singers who helped bring electronic sounds into the musical mainstream. But these records were also a reminder of how unreliable, and unstable, musical categories can be. Throughout its history, R&B has been defined by its twin impulses: one outward, toward the mainstream and toward crossover success; the other inward, toward a deeper connection with the Black listeners who give the genre its identity. The story of neo-soul and mainstream R&B, in the late nineties, is the story of these two impulses—and of how hard it can be, sometimes, to tell one from the other.

Mea Culpa

On July 6, 2003, *The New York Times* published a six-word headline that has lived in infamy ever since: THE SOLO BEYONCÉ: SHE'S NO ASHANTI. On Twitter, that headline tends to resurface whenever Beyoncé is in the news, which is often, or whenever people need a good laugh, which is just about all the time. Often on social media, headlines circulate with no context, not even a byline. But in this case, the byline beneath the headline is usually clearly visible. I know, because the byline is mine.

Suffice it to say that being wrong in public is far less pleasant than being wrong in private, and that a *New York Times* headline that goes viral is pretty close to maximally public. I can't defend that judgment, so I won't try. *Mea culpa.* But I think I can explain.

Long before Beyoncé secured her place as one of the great R&B singers of all time, she was merely the most important member of the most impressive girl group of the moment. Her group, Destiny's Child, was featured on the cover of a 1999 issue of *Jet*, with a headline that offered a notably mild compliment. It read, DESTINY'S CHILD: AMONG HOTTEST NEW FEMALE GROUPS. (The accompanying story also included a number of groups that subsequently failed to find sustained success beyond the R&B world, or in some cases within it: Total, 702, Blaque, Divine, Before Dark.) From the beginning, Beyoncé was the designated star, not least because her father, Mathew Knowles, was the manager. Knowles saw himself as a latter-day Berry Gordy, nurturing a latter-day Supremes, and he encouraged the perception that Destiny's Child was primarily a commercial venture. "Success is having a great product and maximizing on the needs of the consumer," he said in one interview; in another, after he expelled two of the four members, he reassured fans that Destiny's Child was a brand, as reliable as Coca-Cola. Beyoncé was known—and sometimes criticized—for playing the role of the cautious and wholesome pop star, disinclined to cause trouble. In 2001, Destiny's Child took part in a concert in Washington, DC, to celebrate the inauguration of President George W. Bush. MTV reported that Beyoncé fired up the crowd by calling out, "I wanna hear you say 'Bush!'"

Between 1997 and 2001, the group released three albums of state-of-the-art R&B, sleek and staccato, powered by precise harmonies and an attitude that was typically described, not always approvingly, as "sassy." The group was known, in the early years, for "Bills, Bills, Bills," which had a monstrously catchy chorus that expressed an unsentimental view of love:

> *Can you pay my bills?*
> *Can you pay my telephone bills?*
> *Do you pay my automo-bills?*
> *If you did, then maybe we could chill*
> *I don't think you do*
> *So you and me are through*

In 2001, in *The New York Times*, Ann Powers celebrated Destiny Child's "no-nonsense" message, praising the group for using a "fractured female identity" as a "source of strength." (Powers was writing partly about "Survivor," in which Beyoncé and her fellow members taunted the two singers who had been expelled: "You thought I wouldn't sell without you—sold nine million.") But a couple of weeks later, the paper printed a letter from a reader who compared the members of Destiny's Child unfavorably to rock-oriented singer-songwriters such as Liz Phair and Ani DiFranco, who represented "a truer musical ideal of feminism." Many music critics were similarly unimpressed: *Rolling Stone* diagnosed the group as having a "case of the blahs"; Nick Hornby, in *The New Yorker*, called the music "utterly derivative" and "almost perversely unmemorable." None of those three Destiny's Child albums found a place on the *Village Voice*'s year-end Pazz & Jop list, which tallied critics' favorite albums. And in the course of a career that lasted more than a decade, with four No. 1 hits (and five more singles that went Top 5), Destiny's Child won only three Grammy Awards, all of them in R&B categories, as opposed to general categories, which are more prestigious. The group was under-celebrated.

I remember thinking that Beyoncé's debut solo album would change all that, especially after the blockbuster success of "Crazy in Love," the first single. But the rest of the album was grand and slightly old-fashioned compared to the Destiny's Child catalog—at least, that's how it sounded to me then. And I remember being pleasantly surprised, too, by the second album from Ashanti, an R&B singer with a rather wispy voice who was best known (and remains best known) for her breezy duets with the rapper Ja Rule. Nowadays, of course, this seems nuts; no doubt it seemed nuts then, too. I was guided too much by my own expectations, and not enough by the songs on Beyoncé's and Ashanti's albums, which sound, respectively, more and less exciting to me now than they did then. Perhaps I was guided too much, as well, by the desire to say something interesting. Music critics who hew too closely to conventional wisdom can seem boring, or superfluous. But those who veer too sharply away from conventional wisdom can seem batshit crazy.

Happily, one batshit crazy review was not sufficient to derail Beyoncé's solo career. (I have said hello to Beyoncé a few times, but we have never had a conversation; if ever we do, perhaps I'll get a chance to find out whether she has been saving an insult for me, or whether, as seems more likely, she has been far too busy to care.) When she first went solo, Beyoncé was constantly compared to Diana Ross leaving the Supremes. But a better comparison would have been Stevie Wonder, another teen-pop phenomenon who grew up and branched out and got the whole world to sing along with his musical experiments. Beyoncé's second solo album, *B'Day*, was short and astonishingly fierce, full of pummeling rhythmic assaults in the tradition of James Brown and Janet Jackson. Even the most radio-friendly song, "Irreplaceable," was a brutally dismissive sing-along: "You must not know 'bout me / I can have another you by tomorrow." The release of *B'Day* marked the beginning of a series of albums in which Beyoncé remade herself to match a new cultural moment. Years earlier, one writer had described the members of Destiny's Child, sarcastically, as "budding theoretical feminists." But in her solo career, Beyoncé was increasingly explicit about her commitment to feminism; her 2013 self-titled album included a feminist interlude by Chimamanda Ngozi Adichie, the Nigerian writer. She aligned herself with the Black Lives Matter movement and with the distinctive hip-hop culture of her hometown, Houston—she was, she sang, a "Texas bama."

Pop stars run the risk of seeming inauthentic, or desperate, when they try to reinvent themselves by embracing the political moment, like Diana Ross singing "Love Child." But Beyoncé's reinvention was unusually well judged, and it elevated her from mere pop star to something else: a cross between a folk hero, a cult leader, and a royal eminence; she was celebrated with the kind of enthusiasm and unanimity that is typically reserved for musicians who are dead, or getting there. Michelle Obama, who was by some measures the most beloved woman in America, said that if she could have any other job in the world she would like to be Beyoncé. And when the British singer Adele, who is vastly popular in her own right (and in some broad sense an R&B singer, despite being white), won the Grammy for Album of the Year in 2017, she seemed mortified to have beaten Beyoncé's latest, *Lemonade*. In a deft act of cultural diplomacy, Adele used her speech to pay tribute. "My artist of my life is Beyoncé," she said weepily, looking down at Beyoncé in the audience. "All us artists here, we fucking *adore* you. You are our light."

The beatification of the living Beyoncé came at a time when something odd was happening: R&B was becoming prestigious. One turning point came on March 11, 2011, which was the day an up-and-coming singer posted a picture of himself in the studio with Beyoncé. The singer added a brief caption: "This is the room i'm working in this day. not to brag but man, this is surreal." His name was Frank Ocean, and at the time he was best known as a soft-spoken member of an otherwise rowdy Los Angeles hip-hop collective called Odd Future. A few weeks after that photograph was posted, I met up with Frank Ocean at a restaurant in Beverly Hills, and he talked about how he had learned the importance of patience—a quality that did not, he said, come naturally to him. He was twenty-three then, older than the rappers in the crew, and although he already had a record deal, he had decided, on his own, to introduce himself to the world with a free, downloadable mixtape, *nostalgia, ULTRA*. It was full of sweet, melancholy R&B songs that flaunted their influences: one track recycled bits of "Hotel California," the seventies soft-rock staple by the Eagles; another repurposed "Electric Feel," an indie-rock hit by MGMT. Frank Ocean quickly attracted a cult audience, separate from Odd Future; the selfie with Beyoncé was an early sign that he was going to join the R&B mainstream and help redefine it. That summer, when Beyoncé's fourth album appeared, it included a song cowritten by Ocean. The next year, he posted a story, on the social media platform Tumblr, about having been in love with a man; it was effectively a coming-out story, and it made him an LGBTQ+ pioneer in the world of R&B.

Around the same time, a mysterious entity known only as the Weeknd was creating dark and eerie electronic slow jams—a ghostly digital echo of the old quiet storm era. Soon the Weeknd was revealed to be Abel Tesfaye, a Canadian whose parents were Ethiopian immigrants; like Frank Ocean, he made his way onto the R&B A-list. The Weeknd figured out how to conquer the R&B and pop charts, while Frank Ocean created a sensation, and a mystique, by releasing beguiling albums on his own schedule, seemingly unconcerned with hitmaking. Simultaneously, another pair of R&B singers was finding different ways to summon the adventurous spirit of eighties Prince: Janelle Monáe built an enthusiastic fan base with stylized, exuberant tracks, and Miguel was getting his dreamy love songs onto the radio. Together, these four singers transformed the genre's reputation. Only a few years earlier, R&B had been considered, by the mainstream, a bit of a joke—"Dick in a Box" music, more or less. But in the early 2010s, it was widely recognized as the coolest, most creative genre in the country: the home of Beyoncé, our American idol, and also a handful of cool and musically ambitious young stars. In the world of indie rock, where musicians and listeners might once have chuckled at R&B, now they looked for ways to embrace it. Justin Vernon, leader of an indie group called Bon Iver, created a modern form of blue-eyed soul. The producer and singer known as Grimes created unearthly electronic pop songs that drew inspiration from Mariah Carey. In one interview, A. C. Newman, founder of an old-fashioned indie-rock band called the New Pornographers, registered a generic shift. "A lot of what is considered hugely cool, popular indie rock these days sounds like nineties R&B," he said. "Like, it doesn't even sound like indie rock."

No one ever found a good name for this moment in the early 2010s, when R&B culture collided with so-called hipster culture. (One term that didn't stick was "PBR&B," named after white hipsters' putative fondness for Pabst Blue Ribbon beer.) In some ways, the rise of hipster R&B was a true cultural exchange. Beyoncé recorded a song partly written and produced by Caroline Polachek, from the indie band Chairlift. White indie fans embraced uncategorizable Black singers who drew from R&B, including Blood Orange and FKA twigs. But some listeners and critics took exception to the idea that R&B was suddenly hip—as if, for all those decades before, it had been unhip, and therefore uninteresting. One R&B singer who tried to wrestle with this conundrum was Solange, a restless singer and songwriter who also happened to be Beyoncé's younger sister. Solange began her career singing playful pop but soon set out in different directions, and she eventually found an artistic home at the intersection of R&B and indie music. She worked with Blood Orange and recorded a much-praised cover version of "Stillness Is the Move," by the indie band Dirty Projectors. By drawing out the R&B spirit lurking within an indie favorite (she fortified the song with a beat made famous by Erykah Badu), Solange made both herself and the band seem cooler. In 2016, she released a remarkable album called *A Seat at the Table*, which was widely and accurately celebrated as an R&B landmark: a barbed but graceful collection of R&B songs that reflected an anxious and angry moment, and that earned nearly universal praise from critics.

Solange was suspicious of critics' newfound enthusiasm for R&B, especially the ones who seemed like recent converts to the genre she called home. One of Solange's favorites was Brandy, the singer and actress who made R&B hits in the nineties, and (more quietly) made some adventurous R&B records in the 2000s. In 2013, after having apparently read some mixed reviews of Brandy's latest album, Solange posted a kind of R&B manifesto on Twitter. "Some of these music blogs could actually benefit from hiring people who REALLY understand the culture of R&B to write about R&B," she wrote. This was an unusual provocation: people have been praising and bemoaning hip-hop culture for decades, but R&B culture is less commonly discussed—some people might have been surprised by the notion that R&B even has a culture. She asked journalists to "stop acting like it just popped off last year for R&B," as if the genre had only recently become "interesting and experimental." She also proposed a credential system: "You really should know about deep Brandy album cuts before you are giving a 'grade' or a 'score' to any R&B artist." This last claim was the one that earned Solange the most attention, not all of it positive: some people thought it was hilarious that she was using the language of rock snobbery (championing "deep" album cuts, as opposed to hit singles) to praise a singer like Brandy, who in the nineties was not only a pop hitmaker but also a sitcom star. But that was precisely the point: Solange was using Brandy as a symbol of R&B authenticity not just because she loved Brandy's music but because Brandy was considered so unhip, so lightweight, so pop. In the early 2010s, the same qualities that once made Brandy a crossover sensation now made it possible to think of her as a gatekeeper, the person you needed to know about if you wanted to be judged a true R&B connoisseur.

It would be easy to say that Brandy's fluctuating reputation shows how inane the conversation about R&B authenticity really is. With the passage of time, the distinction between R&B radio hits and R&B deep cuts sometimes fades. And so, often, do seemingly crucial arguments about soul and selling out. But in the years since Berry Gordy made his bold proclamation, there has generally been something self-correcting in the nature of R&B, a genre that can never quite decide whether it wants to be the universal sound of young (and not-so-young) America, or Black people's best-kept secret, or—somehow—both at once. That indecision may help explain why fans like Solange can sometimes sound defensive about the genre's changing fortunes. Maybe it helps explain, too, why a critic like me might have been so eager to establish the bona fides of someone like Ashanti, whom I think I viewed as a stand-in for all the singers over the decades who were unfairly dismissed as merely the latest semi-forgettable acts to top the R&B charts; who didn't get the attention or respect they deserved. Nelson George, in the eighties, worried that the rise of crossover artists might pose a mortal threat to the genre. But the bittersweet truth is that R&B, as a whole, never crossed over comprehensively enough to disappear. Ever since *Billboard* renamed its Race Records chart, there have been good and often great Black singers whom Black audiences loved, and whom white audiences did not love as much. And for as long as that remains true, people may turn to a term that was once a euphemism for musical segregation, and that sometimes still functions that way today: R&B.

3.

COUNTRY

At Its Purest

IKE MANY COUNTRY MUSIC FANS, Paul Hemphill was looking for *real* country music when he went to Nashville. He was a columnist for *The Atlanta Journal*, curious about the industry that was remaking a formerly sleepy town in the middle of Tennessee. He compiled his impressions into a witty and insightful book, *The Nashville Sound*, which was published in 1970 and which captured an industry, and a genre, that was wrestling with an enviable problem: popularity. Hemphill talked to Wesley Rose, a second-generation country music executive, who turned out to be something of a purist. "You can't be country and be on the pop charts at the same time," Rose told him, issuing a judgment that sounded antique even then. But Rose was prescient, too, in seeing that the mishmash of styles on late-sixties charts did not portend a genreless future of universal pop. "Anybody who believes there'll be one music has lost his head," he said. Hemphill wasn't sure. In his view, grizzled country singers like Johnny Cash and Merle Haggard—"only half a step removed from the hard life of the soil," in sensibility if not in fact—were destined to be replaced by ambitious, pop-minded upstarts. But one night, at the Grand Ole Opry, the long-running country revue that made Nashville the genre's hometown in the first place, Hemphill saw reason for hope. He witnessed "a petite blonde of incredible vanilla-ice-cream beauty," equipped with "a quavering Appalachian soprano." This singer and her band, he declared, represented "gut-country music at its purest." Her name was Dolly Parton.

In the decades that followed, Parton grew to be one of the most beloved entertainers in America, although of course her name has not been associated exclusively with purity. She grew up in a small mountain town in eastern Tennessee. As a girl, she sang in church, on the radio, and, in 1959, at the age of thirteen, at the Grand Ole Opry. "I thought of myself as a country singer, and that was all I had ever wanted to be," she later recalled. But it turned out to be a complicated business. After high school, she moved to Nashville and got herself a songwriting contract and then, more important, a role on *The Porter Wagoner Show*, a televised revue; Wagoner, a reliable hitmaker, became Parton's mentor and her frequent duet partner. Parton was invariably introduced as the "pretty little gal" or the "beautiful little lady," but she was a disruptive presence, with a high, bright voice that could evoke the music's rural history, as Hemphill noticed. In an episode from 1973, she introduced a new composition of hers, saying it sounded like "an old folk song that's kind of got a little heavier, up-to-date beat." And then she sang "Jolene," an evocation of modern romantic anxiety that somehow seemed as old as the hills. It went to No. 1 on the *Billboard* Hot Country chart, and so did her next single, "I Will Always Love You," a classic torch song, which was her fond farewell to Wagoner and his show. It, too, became a No. 1 country hit—twice, in fact, because Parton recorded another version in 1982, which also topped the chart. It is a tribute to the song's versatility that plenty of people don't even think of it as a country song nowadays: they associate it with Whitney Houston, whose grand version of it became, in 1992, the longest-reigning No. 1 hit in the history of the pop chart.

If Parton's voice was in some sense a reflection of her Tennessee girlhood, then so was her unapologetic ambition. In her 1994 autobiography, which was characteristically witty, she remembered buying a Cadillac with one of her first big checks, just like the stereotype of the "hick who strikes it rich"; she also described herself as a "trashy-looking blond country singer," which was a sly way of acknowledging that her campy, glamorous appearance only made her seem more authentic. And she explained how, after leaving *The Porter Wagoner Show*, she met with Sandy Gallin, a Los Angeles talent manager, telling him, "I'm going to be a superstar, and whoever helps me will also be rich and famous." Parton convinced him, and in return he convinced her not to worry about alienating the Nashville establishment. The result was "Here You Come Again," a piano-driven pop song, with a few strains of steel guitar added, at Parton's request, as a conciliatory message to her country fans. The song was a hit—No. 3 pop, No. 1 country—and it marked the beginning of Parton's new career as an all-American pop star, serving as an ambassador for the culture of country music even as she made some very un-"gut-country" musical choices. In 1980, her prediction to Gallin came stupendously true with *9 to 5*, which was both a blockbuster comedy, costarring Parton, and a blockbuster pop single, with a danceable beat that was practically disco. Country radio stations played it, too (no steel guitar necessary), perhaps because Parton's country credentials were so unimpeachable: precisely because she was a self-described hillbilly, she could go Hollywood without losing her country identity. Just as hair-metal bands could record power ballads and still seem rock 'n' roll, Parton could sing just about whatever she wanted—she was always going to be Dolly Parton. When she was accused of leaving country music, she just shrugged. "I'm not leaving it," she liked to say. "I'm taking it with me to new places."

What Is Country Music?

Just about everyone can agree on Dolly Parton. But when it comes to country music, people seem to disagree on just about everything else. From the start, it was marketed as unusually honest music, linked to the perceived simplicity of rural life in America. Country music is more old-fashioned than rock 'n' roll, but less traditional—or, rather, more ambivalent about tradition. The basic template for a rock 'n' roll band has remained remarkably stable ever since the seventies: drums, electric bass, and, above all, electric guitar. But in country music, traditional instruments like the banjo and the pedal steel guitar tend to fall in and out of favor, as country singers try to figure out precisely how "country" they really want to be. Music historians sometimes trace the birth of country music as a recorded genre to the 1920s, when the Victor Talking Machine Company—not primarily a record label, but a manufacturer of record players—sent Ralph Peer south in search of singers. Some of the Black performers he recorded, including Will Shade, leader of the Memphis Jug Band, later came to be viewed as R&B pioneers. And some of the white performers were later regarded as forefathers of country music. Peer recorded Fiddlin' John Carson, a former cotton-mill worker from Georgia, singing a nineteenth-century minstrel song, "The Little Old Log Cabin in the Lane," that had originally been written by Will S. Hays, a white songwriter, using Negro dialect, or an approximation of it. Peer recorded Jimmie Rodgers, a former railroad brakeman from Mississippi, whose playful, yodeling songs made him one of the first country stars. (In 1970, Dolly Parton took a forty-year-old Jimmie Rodgers song to No. 3 on the country chart, yodeling all the way.) And Peer recorded the Carter Family, from the Appalachian Mountains in western Virginia. "Mother" Maybelle Carter, a virtuoso on the guitar and the autoharp, popularized the pick-and-strum style that may still be what you hear in your head when you think of country music.

For a time, all this music was considered folk music, a term that made it seem rural and traditional, and possibly unchanging, as if the songs were passing endlessly from one generation to the next. *Billboard* began publishing a chart of Most Played Juke Box Folk Records in 1944; five years later, the magazine introduced another chart, focusing on radio stations, which were booming: Country & Western Records Most Played by Folk Disk Jockeys. The two halves of the name evoked the hybrid nature of the music itself.

"Country" denoted the Appalachian legacy of acts like the Carter Family—hillbilly music, as it was sometimes called, not always kindly. And "Western" acknowledged the influence of Texas and the Southwest, and the increasing popularity of cowboy music and imagery. Hank Williams was the paradigmatic modern country star, and his rural Southern credibility was part of his appeal. In 1947, his record company promised listeners that his latest single was "as hillbilly as korn likker." He called his backing band the Drifting Cowboys, in tribute to the cowboy movies he loved, and in accord with the genre's quasi-Western identity. (Williams died, possibly from drugs and alcohol, in 1953, at the age of twenty-nine. He has been country music's patron saint ever since.) In time, "& Western" faded out of the genre's name—Billboard renamed its chart Hot Country Singles in 1962. But the Western influence stuck around, and nowadays hardly anyone stops to wonder why Nashville, a city not known for ranching, is synonymous with cowboy hats and boots.

At the start of the 1970s, when Hemphill published *The Nashville Sound*, country music was still widely viewed as a regional phenomenon. By the end of the seventies, thanks in part to Parton's success, country music was a national craze, with radio stations proliferating and record sales booming. "If 1978 went down as the Year of Disco," an article in *Billboard* declared, "then 1979 will definitely be remembered as the year that saw country breaking loose everywhere." *Esquire* had recently published an article about country music fans in Houston: they weren't ranchers, but they were enthralled by cowboy mythology, and they spent their nights at a supersize honky-tonk called Gilley's. In 1980, this article was turned into a movie, *Urban Cowboy*, about a man in a cowboy hat, played by John Travolta, who was struggling to tame a mechanical bull in a local bar. (The film was not, despite its plot, a comedy.) Just as an earlier Travolta film, *Saturday Night Fever*, pushed disco into the mainstream, *Urban Cowboy* did something similar for country music, with similarly confusing results. For a time, lots of people wanted to be country, even if they weren't quite sure what "country" meant. The next year, a perennial country hitmaker named Barbara Mandrell took note of this situation with a song called "I Was Country When Country Wasn't Cool." The title was a humblebrag, and maybe a message to post-Travolta converts, while the verses paid charming tribute to country authenticity: flannel shirts, the Grand Ole Opry, "puttin' peanuts in my Coke." But the song's piano-driven arrangement was practically soft rock. The song raised—but didn't quite settle—a question that has been asked ever since country music stopped being folk music and started being something else. What does country music even mean in the age of rock 'n' roll? Or the age of disco? Or the age of hip-hop? What *is* country music?

One answer, provided by a small but insistent minority, is that country music is and ought to be what it used to be: fiddles and banjos and pedal steel, twangy guitars and twangy accents, stylized lyrics and lonesome harmonies. To these traditionalists, country music is an endangered species, at risk of going extinct, if it hasn't already. In just about every phase of the genre's evolution, there have been people lamenting that the older, truer country music is being left behind, and often these killjoys have been right, or half-right. The rise of radio, which created a national audience for country music, also helped extinguish the regional musical traditions that were the genre's original source. And many people since then have worried that country music is growing less distinctive and more similar to every other kind of music. "I think we've strayed away from country and got more into pop," observed one disappointed country listener in 1990. It turned out, though, that this disappointed country listener was also a successful country singer: Garth Brooks, a tradition-minded fellow who also, over the following five years, did as much as anyone to push the genre toward mainstream pop. These days, Brooks remains one of the genre's biggest attractions, and if he now seems like a rather old-fashioned figure, that says something about how many country stars followed his example over the past few decades, and kept pushing.

A second answer to the question of country identity is the Parton answer: that country music is a cultural identity, something that lives deep within anyone lucky enough to have grown up that way. Not long ago I interviewed Morgan Wallen, a country star who emerged at the end of the 2010s, and who grew up listening to radio-friendly rock bands like Breaking Benjamin and Nickelback. "It may not have been the biggest influence in my life, as far as musically," he told me, when I asked him about country music. "But once I started writing songs, it just *sounded* country. And I was, like, well, I guess I'll sing country music, because this is the life I know." Country music has remained distinctive partly because "country" refers to something more than music: the genre's name is also a demographic, a group of people who tend to be white and tend to think of themselves as not quite at home in the city, even if that is where they happen to live. (Wallen grew up in tiny Sneedville, Tennessee, although his family later moved to Knoxville, a midsize city.) Often, "country" has been treated as a rough synonym for a handful of terms that are often pejorative: "hillbilly," "redneck," "hick." And often, this social identity has given singers like Parton—and, for that matter, Wallen—freedom to cross musical boundaries. If country is a culture that you have to be born into, that means outsiders will not necessarily be welcome. But it also means that insiders have room to experiment, as long as they don't forget where they come from. As hair-metal bands discovered in the eighties, fans will let you get away with murder, as long as you look and act the part.

The third answer to this question is the least idealistic, and perhaps the most plausible. Barbara Mandrell, the singer who put peanuts in her Coke, had all the country credibility a singer might want: she was raised on the old "hillbilly" records, and she was an accomplished steel guitar player before she was a teenager. But she succeeded, in the seventies and eighties, with a series of soft-rock ballads and came to seem like the epitome of pop country. She represented Nashville at its most ingratiating. But she also represented Nashville at its most resourceful and flexible, finding ways to incorporate the sounds of other genres: saxophone solos and synthesizer parts on record; choreography and cabaret-style monologues onstage. Mandrell knew that some audiences considered her music inauthentic—she remembered getting a "decidedly distant" reception at a country music festival in London, where concertgoers were apparently expecting a more old-fashioned performance. In her autobiography, though, she wrote that she was proud to have played a part in the genre's evolution. "To some degree," she wrote, "country music is whoever happens to be hot in Nashville and on country stations at the time."

Even more than most genres, country music aims to please its fans—not for nothing is the industry's most coveted award called Entertainer of the Year. This is why Mandrell, like most mainstream country singers of the past half century, paid close attention to radio playlists and *Billboard* charts. This is why, too, her own country hits often gestured toward mainstream pop. And yet this eagerness to please never eroded her strong sense of identity—or the genre's. On the contrary, by paying unusually close attention to their fans, country singers and executives have encouraged listeners to be not only loyal but tribal, thinking of themselves as forming a country community. Just as "R&B" has historically referred to music made by and for Black people, "country" has historically referred to music made by and for white people—indeed, over the years, this commitment to whiteness has often been an implicit theme in the music, and occasionally an explicit one. Not all white people, of course: the genre has often claimed to speak to, and for, a specific kind of white people. Some country songs make the genre seem like the voice of the respectable American mainstream; others make it seem like a rebellion against mainstream respectability; most great country singers have songs of both types. But all successful country singers realize that there is an identifiable and influential country music audience. And many of them acknowledge that country music is whatever those people want it to be.

Over the years, this third answer has mainly won out: country music endures and thrives today because "country" listeners say it does. But the argument over who belongs in country music, and how it should sound, never died down. Often, the most popular country acts have defined themselves in opposition to one or another perception of the genre's mainstream, like Garth Brooks, disdaining pop country even while he perfected his own state-of-the-art version of it. For a while, the Dixie Chicks redefined country stardom, although they were eventually pushed out of the genre—thereby reminding country singers everywhere that plenty of limits still remained. Taylor Swift was one of the greatest country success stories of all time, although her trajectory eventually propelled her up and away from Nashville and from country radio. And in 2019, an unknown Black singer called Lil Nas X conquered the world with "Old Town Road," a twangy, danceable delight that became one of the biggest hits in pop history, inspiring a debate over whether it should be considered a country song at all.

Unlike Dolly Parton, or Morgan Wallen, I did not grow up "country," by any possible definition. Neither my parents nor my peers paid any attention to country music, beyond the occasional big hit. And so when I first started spending time with the genre, as a full-time critic and therefore a full-time concertgoer, it might as well have been a species of world music, exotic and sublime. I already knew a few of the classics—even as a teenage punk rocker, I had grasped the countercultural appeal of Johnny Cash, alternately stern and silly, entertaining a rowdy audience at Folsom Prison. But I was increasingly drawn to what some people were dismissively calling "new country": the sweet, hybrid concoctions that filled country radio playlists. Nashville seemed like a city of perfectionists, stuffed with great players and great writers, working within the same narrow parameters, all trying to solve the same puzzle: how to write the perfect song. I loved the idea that a chorus might double as a punch line. ("I may hate myself in the morning / But I'm gonna love you tonight," as Lee Ann Womack sang.) I loved the way the pedal steel could make even the goofiest song sound a little bit wistful. And I thought there was something brave and audacious about the genre's insistence on big hooks and unambiguous words: no squalls of noise, no impressionistic lyrics, nowhere to hide. Those songs became a permanent part of my musical diet, and of my life; when I got married, in 2009, my wife, Sarah, and I had our first dance to a country song, "It Just Comes Natural," a sturdy and warmhearted 2006 hit by

George Strait. And part of the fun of going to country shows in and around New York City was that it felt like leaving town: the crowds were full of transplants from other parts of the country, interacting with the easy conviviality of expatriates abroad. Often, tributes to the military, rarely emphasized at other New York concerts, inspired huge, stirring ovations. At least once, in response to nothing in particular, a crowd started chanting, "USA! USA!"

By then, in the 2000s, the genre was figuring out how to emphasize rock 'n' roll guitars and, more and more, hip-hop beats; it was sometimes grappling, too, with the meaning of its long-standing identity as white music. Through it all, country music still mattered, not least because the audience did: the question of who deserved to be considered a country singer was related to the question of who would get access to the country market, which remains distinct, and which has grown vastly bigger and more lucrative since Hemphill went to Nashville. This is one of the most surprising things about country music: how it has remained a genre worth fighting over and still remains one.

Absolutely No Hollering

One way to tell the story of modern country music is to say that the genre still hasn't recovered from the shock of Elvis Presley. "The sound went straight up your spine," Waylon Jennings wrote in his 1996 autobiography, about the first time he heard Presley on the radio. "The way he sang, the singer sounded black, but something about the songs was really country." In 1956, the year Presley exploded, an article in *Billboard* cited him as the most important example of a new trend: "the diskeries"—that is, record companies—"are pushing out an increasing number of disks which are cut by country artists, but which have a definite r.&b. quality about them." Some people called this music "rockabilly," to suggest that it was rock 'n' roll made by hillbillies. Presley had grown up in Tupelo, Mississippi, and then in Memphis, listening to gospel music, country music, and the blues. And his first hits were so dominant that they posed an existential threat to *Billboard*'s classification system: "Don't Be Cruel" and "Hound Dog" were No. 1 hits on the pop, R&B, and country charts, which not all country fans appreciated. *Billboard* acknowledged the backlash with a reproachful editorial. "It has already been suggested that country artists with r.&b.-styled material, or r.&b.-styled delivery, be excluded from the best-selling country chart," the magazine wrote. "These suggestions are ill-advised." (The next year, in 1957, Jerry Lee Lewis also had triple-chart success with an incendiary pair of singles, "Whole Lotta Shakin' Goin' On" and "Great Balls of Fire.") Presley's presence on the country charts both reflected and encouraged the growing popularity of rock 'n' roll among listeners who loved country music, one of whom was Jennings, who was then a young disc jockey in Lubbock, Texas, and who suddenly found himself rethinking his musical priorities.

Part of what made Presley such a shock was the fact that, while he may have "sounded black," as Jennings put it, he was actually white, which helped set him apart from the many R&B pioneers he drew from, and which surely made him more appealing to many white listeners. Presley's movement, the rock 'n' roll movement, was a youth movement, and so it made country music seem like old folks' music, a reputation that the genre retained for decades. Some country singers responded to the shock by embracing the sound or spirit of rock 'n' roll. Jennings was fired from his radio station, he said, for playing two Little Richard records in a row, and he joined the touring band of a friend of his from Lubbock: Buddy Holly. (Jennings was traveling with Holly on the night, in 1959, when Holly chartered a flight to get to his next concert; Jennings ceded his seat on the airplane to J. P. Richardson, known as the Big Bopper, who was killed, along with Ritchie Valens and Holly, when the airplane crashed.) In Bakersfield, California, a rock 'n' roll fan named Buck Owens honed a lean, guitar-driven version of country music— the Bakersfield sound, they called it. And then there was Johnny Cash, who was briefly Presley's labelmate at Sun Records, and who made unpredictable country hits for decades while remaining somehow unclassifiable; no one ever had more success in country music while taking the industry less seriously.

On the whole, though, the response of country music to rock 'n' roll was not to compete but to counterprogram. A group of canny producers, led by Owen Bradley and Chet Atkins, created what came to be known as the Nashville sound. The idea was to market country as urbane music for grown-ups, with hardly any fiddling, unless it came from a string section, and absolutely no hollering. Listeners uninterested in the manic energy of rock 'n' roll could turn, instead, to sophisticated singers like Patsy Cline and Jim Reeves, both of whom were in their prime when they died in airplane crashes in 1963 and 1964, respectively. The Nashville sound was succeeded by the so-called countrypolitan sound, which was even plusher and smoother; both were paradoxical efforts to modernize and popularize country music by making it synonymous with old-fashioned musical values. Many critics described these stratagems less glowingly. In a front-page *New York Times* article, in 1985, the critic Robert Palmer bemoaned the continuing influence of the Nashville sound, which he described as "sticky-sweet orchestral arrangements and mooing vocal choruses." Like many critics, Palmer found the Nashville sound unforgivably bland and conservative, "too slick and pop oriented to appeal to frontier nostalgia"—basically, not country enough. This critique became the conventional wisdom, a common explanation for what went wrong with the genre in the sixties and seventies. Threatened by a cultural uprising, country music retreated, devolving into a procession of men in suits and women in ball gowns, singing (softly!) for the parents and grandparents of the rock 'n' roll generation.

Charles L. Hughes, a historian of Southern music, has argued that this smooth country sound was more sophisticated than many critics realized, because it reflected a process of cultural and racial crossover: soft country, much like soft rock, encouraged singers to explore a wide range of styles, including contemporary Black styles. Billy Sherrill, the producer who helped invent the countrypolitan sound, came from the world of R&B: in 1959, he had cofounded the FAME Recording Studio in Muscle Shoals, Alabama, which nurtured the sound of Southern soul music. In Nashville, Sherrill made hits with Tammy Wynette and George Jones, who helped define the sound of post-Elvis country music. (One of Jones's hits with Sherrill was a cover of "Hallelujah, I Love You So," by Ray Charles, complete with saxophone, an instrument that was generally taboo on country radio stations.) Another of Sherrill's most successful clients was Charlie Rich, who had a string of top singles in the seventies that were, essentially, the country equivalent of slow jams; Rich's manager once bragged that his touring band included "three Black singers—the Treasures, all girls, who come out of Memphis—and four horns." Ronnie Milsap, one of the most consistent country hitmakers of the seventies and eighties, got his start in the worlds of blues and R&B, and once opened for James Brown before reinventing himself as a country singer, albeit one known for gently swinging love songs. "Nearly every major countrypolitan star of the 1970s," Hughes writes, used "a soul-influenced sound to demonstrate crossover potential." For country singers, going pop sometimes meant engaging more fully with Black music.

This subtle, hybrid strategy expanded the genre's palette while also helping to ensure that country music remained distinct and easy to recognize—set apart, sometimes sharply, from the rock 'n' roll movement that once threatened to swallow it up. Nashville's expert counterprogramming also enabled some great singers to thrive there, including Glen Campbell, whose gentle delivery and arrangements sometimes added to the sneaky power of the songs he sang. One of Campbell's first big hits, in 1968, was "Wichita Lineman," written by the pop songwriter Jimmy Webb, who imagined the life of a worker up on the telephone poles, somewhere in Kansas, daydreaming about his woman. "I hear you singing in the wire," Campbell sang, softly, beckoning listeners to lean in and hear her, too.

Campbell crossed over not just to the pop charts but to network television, as the host of *The Glen Campbell Goodtime Hour*, which made its debut on CBS in 1969, the same year as two other programs: *The Johnny Cash Show*, which lasted for two seasons, and *Hee Haw*, a countrified variety program, which somehow survived all the way into the 1990s. But not every country singer aspired to a life of gentle balladry. Jennings, having returned to country music after a few years playing rock 'n' roll, seemed for a time as if he might follow Campbell's path. He teamed up with Chet Atkins, adopted an easygoing style, and even found success with his own version of a Jimmy Webb song—in his case, "MacArthur Park," a strange and sentimental lament, for which Jennings won a Grammy. (The song had previously been a hit for the actor Richard Harris, although the most popular version was recorded in the late seventies by Donna Summer, the disco queen.) But the Nashville sound never took Jennings to the top of the country chart, and eventually he split with Atkins; starting in 1972, Jennings released a series of albums that were not quite so gentle. The first of these was *Good Hearted Woman*, about a couple that was in love but not entirely happy: "She's a good hearted woman in love with a good-timin' man / She loves him in spite of his ways she don't understand."

Jennings had written the song with a friend, a fellow Texan who had grown similarly frustrated with Nashville's approach to country music. The friend's name was Willie Nelson, and in some ways he should have been a great match for the post-Elvis country music industry. Nelson had a knack for writing easeful, jazzy-influenced tunes that slipped between genres, including "Crazy," which had been Patsy Cline's signature song and which is now so firmly installed in the American songbook that many listeners probably don't even think of it as a country song. But he initially struggled on the charts as a singer, perhaps because his delivery was quirky and informal: in the sixties, and throughout his career, Nelson loved to sing far behind the beat, sometimes waiting to deliver a phrase until listeners might have thought he had given up on it.

Nelson did give up, in the end, on Nashville. In 1972, he settled in Texas—not in Abbott, the small town where he had grown up, but a couple of hours away in Austin, where a freewheeling hybrid of country and rock music was growing. The galvanizing event there was a debacle: the Dripping Springs Reunion, a 1972 festival that was modeled after Woodstock and that suffered the opposite problem—not too many attendees but too few. Even so, Nelson, one of the headliners, was inspired by the vibe, which was druggy and convivial, and the next year he began organizing an annual festival, Willie Nelson's Fourth of July Picnic, a tradition that he continued nearly every year until 2019. One of Nelson's fellow headliners at Dripping Springs was Kris Kristofferson, who was then emerging as a celebrated Nashville songwriter, as well as a cult-favorite singer and a budding actor. Another was Jennings, who began traveling regularly to Austin, playing for crowds that didn't always look as if they would be receptive to his music. He remembered once encountering a roomful of "longhairs," and summoning Nelson backstage. Jennings asked, "What the hell have you got me into?" But it turned out that the longhairs loved Jennings's music, which was growing more sullen and more mysterious. In 1973, he released an album called *Lonesome, On'ry & Mean*, which encouraged fans to think of Jennings not as an old Nashville pro but as a new kind of country antihero—as much a part of the counterculture, in his own way, as the hippies in Austin.

A Revolt, a Revival, and a Sales Pitch

It wasn't just Nelson and Jennings. Starting in the sixties, a number of rock bands and fans had been discovering country music, treating the genre as a kind of musical thrift shop, full of extraordinary styles and songs that seemed cool precisely because they were a bit old-fashioned, or more than a bit. In 1968, the Byrds, a venturesome California rock band, released *Sweetheart of the Rodeo*, an album adorned with plenty of banjo, fiddle, and pedal steel. Country radio paid no attention, but the album helped spark a new subgenre, country rock. Gram Parsons, a country-loving hipster who played on the record, became a country-rock cult hero, releasing a handful of albums, on his own and with the Flying Burrito Brothers, before his death from an overdose of alcohol and morphine, in 1973. Parsons was close with the Rolling Stones, who had been experimenting with country rock during these years. (One of those experiments was "Wild Horses," a Rolling Stones song with a complicated history: it first appeared on a Flying Burrito Brothers album, because Parsons had received permission from the band to record his own version.) Janis Joplin is considered a defining voice of the rock 'n' roll explosion, but her lone pop hit was her volcanic version of "Me and Bobby McGee," a Kristofferson song. The most important of these emissaries from the rock world was Bob Dylan, who recorded a series of albums in Nashville; one of them, *Nashville Skyline*, arrived in 1969, with its back cover given over to a long and mainly indecipherable poem of praise by Johnny Cash. The first track was a new version of an older Dylan favorite, "Girl from the North Country," sung as a duet with Cash, and a number of fans noticed that Dylan's wheezing, braying voice sounded smoother than it once had, as if he were trying to make himself croon—paying hip tribute to the unhip Nashville sound.

While Nelson built his following in Austin, Jennings found a congenial home in Nashville. Tompall Glaser, a like-minded singer, owned a studio there, which became known as Hillbilly Central, an anti-Nashville clubhouse in the heart of the city—just around the corner from RCA Studios, where Chet Atkins was the boss. Some radio stations and journalists were using the term "progressive country" to refer to Willie Nelson's picnic and all the music associated with it. But in those years, the modifier "progressive" was being claimed by a cohort of rock bands, whose albums tended, as Jennings's and Nelson's did not, to celebrate novelty and complexity. These country singers were united by their conviction that the Nashville sound had grown cluttered and fussy, and that the songs would be more powerful if they were stripped down. This was a revivalist movement, even if it was not quite clear what, exactly, these singers hoped to revive. Unlike some of the singers who came later, this cohort was not single-mindedly trying to re-create the look and sound of the pre–rock 'n' roll pioneers. And despite the deviations from Nashville orthodoxy—fewer string sections, somewhat gloomier lyrics—this music remained recognizably country, even though it represented a cultural shift.

In 1973, Hazel Smith, a canny Nashville publicist, proposed a name that stuck: "outlaw country." The word "outlaw" evoked the mythology of the Old West, as well as films like *Bonnie and Clyde* and *Easy Rider*, and also one of Bob Dylan's most quotable lyrics: "To live outside the law, you must be honest." The outlaw movement spawned a surprise hit two years later, when Nelson released *Red Headed Stranger*, a mesmerizing cowboy concept album that was so sparse in its arrangement that label executives originally mistook it for a demo tape. The next year, RCA Records assembled a cash-in compilation called *Wanted! The Outlaws*, featuring Jennings, Nelson, Glaser, and Jessi Colter, a country veteran who also happened to be Jennings's wife. *Wanted!* turned out to be another surprise, the first album in the history of country music to be certified platinum, for sales of over a million copies. *Wanted!* turned "outlaw country" into the genre's most marketable brand, and challenged the industry's view of country fans—the conventional wisdom was that they mainly bought singles, not albums, or just listened to the radio. Plenty of the people who bought the compilation, though, probably weren't country fans. On the back cover, Chet Flippo, a *Rolling Stone* critic, sought to reassure skeptical listeners that these country singers weren't actually country singers. "It's not country and it's not country-rock," he wrote. "It's just damned good music that's true and"—as Dylan might have put it—"honest."

Like many musical movements, outlaw country was in part a marketing strategy, giving a new name to a not-so-new cultural phenomenon. Outlaw country was a revolt, a revival, and a sales pitch; it has that in common with punk rock, which arose around the same time, and with reformational movements that came along later, like conscious hip-hop and neo-soul. Merle

Haggard, from California, was an outlaw before there was a movement—he had served time in prison for attempted robbery and jailbreak. Since the midsixties, long before "outlaw country" was coined, he had been topping the country charts with sharply observed songs that were often about desperate men. And in 1983, Haggard and Nelson released *Pancho & Lefty*, a charming album of duets that became a latter-day classic of outlaw country. Kristofferson was also an outlaw, and Shel Silverstein, who was a country songwriter in addition to being a cartoonist and author, was an "honorary outlaw," according to Jennings. Johnny Cash was in some sense the original outlaw: he and Jennings were housemates for a time, and in the eighties he joined with Nelson, Jennings, and Kristofferson to form the Highwaymen, an outlaw supergroup.

Not all the outlaws were great songwriters, but the outlaw movement was driven by a conviction that great songs were more important than great musicianship. Kristofferson, in particular, had a rickety voice, and he helped a generation of Nashville songwriters realize that they, too, might be welcome behind a microphone. The seventies was also the golden era of Southern rock, a bluesy hybrid that embraced some of the same "outlaw" imagery. Southern rock occasionally snuck onto country radio playlists through cover versions: Jennings's version of "Can't You See," by the Marshall Tucker Band, went to No. 4; Nelson took "Midnight Rider," by the Allman Brothers Band, to No. 6. But country radio stations ignored the Byrds and Parsons; even the Eagles, whose agreeable version of country rock made them one of the biggest bands of the seventies, never had much success on country radio.

The outlaw movement was a musical hybrid, but to casual listeners it probably seemed more like a caricature. Cash's struggles with addiction and the law lent his songs a voyeuristic appeal, especially on the live albums he recorded in Folsom and San Quentin state prisons. ("We've been in several prisons," he said, between bursts of applause in San Quentin—although, despite a number of arrests, Cash never actually served a prison sentence.)

A singer with a similar stage name, Johnny Paycheck, had been known for romantic ballads, but in the seventies, he successfully remade himself as an outlaw. This transformation was enabled by his biography: Paycheck was a long-term addict who once shot a man during a bar fight. And it was enabled, too, by a big country hit, which was built around a defiant chorus that still sounds like a punch in the mouth. "Take this job and shove it," Paycheck snarled. "I ain't workin' here no more." Like many country songs, this one was more equivocal than it first sounded, and a good deal funnier. (The joke is that the narrator, for all his tough talk, is a daydreamer and perhaps a wimp. Right before he gets to the refrain, he sings, "Lord, I can't wait to see their faces / When I get the nerve to say...") The song was written by a different outlaw, David Allan Coe, a wild and quarrelsome figure who claimed to live even further outside the law than the official outlaws.

The outlaws often linked creativity to misbehavior, creating the impression that they were both too daring and too disorderly for the country establishment. Long before Nelson emerged as one of America's leading marijuana advocates, his picnic was famous for uniting pot-smoking hippies with more traditional country fans—in 1976, an article in *Texas Monthly* praised Nelson for "bringing together the ropers and the dopers." And in Nashville, Jennings developed a reputation for raising hell in service of his addictions, which included, at various times, cocaine, amphetamines, and pinball. (At one point, Jennings recalled, he and his friends were going through a thousand dollars' worth of quarters every night, which raises the question of how a pinball obsessive could be such a lousy player.) Rumors about the outlaws' wild behavior became hard news when, in 1977, Jennings was arrested and charged with possession of cocaine with intent to distribute. The charges were dropped, and Jennings wrote a suitably up-tempo song about the incident, which went to No. 5, despite its coded reference to cocaine:

> *What started out to be a joke, the law don't understand*
> *Was it singing through my nose that got me busted by the man?*

The song was called "Don't You Think This Outlaw Bit's Done Got Out of Hand," and the message seemed to be directed as much to fans as to "the man." Nelson was sly and versatile enough to slip out of his "outlaw" costume whenever it no longer suited him. (In 1978, he released *Stardust*, a collection of standards, and it became an unlikely bestseller.) But Jennings—who said he stopped using cocaine in 1984, nearly two decades before his death, in 2002—never shed his outlaw image. In a way, the genre didn't, either. The outlaw era created an ideal of feisty independence against which country singers have been measured ever since. The legend of Johnny Cash reached a new generation of fans in the 1990s and the 2000s, when he teamed with the rock producer Rick Rubin to make a series of funereal albums full of songs by younger songwriters from well beyond the world of country. Among younger listeners, the most popular Johnny Cash song is surely his 2002 version of "Hurt," by Nine Inch Nails, from the Rubin sessions. Even now, when someone complains about the dearth of "real" country music, or claims to only like "the old stuff," they may well be talking about the outlaws, a small and rather motley group of singers who set themselves against the country mainstream, and thereby helped redefine it.

The outlaws may now be regarded as symbols of authenticity, but they tended to be self-conscious about their own authenticity, or lack of it. In 1975, Waylon Jennings anxiously compared himself to Hank Williams, the country pioneer who might have been the original outlaw. He sang, "Are you sure Hank done it this way?" In 2009, an emerging country star named Eric Church updated the sentiment in a song called "Lotta Boot Left to Fill." He sneered at younger country singers who used the outlaws' names to bolster their own credibility: "You sing about Johnny Cash / The Man in Black would have whipped your ass!" But of course, Church was doing it, too. "I don't think Waylon done it that way," he sang, over snarling electric guitars that sounded nothing at all like those classic Jennings albums. The song was a mixed-up hybrid, and in that sense it was a fitting tribute to the outlaw sound of the seventies.

Make Country Country Again

Despite its permanent scowl, so-called outlaw country turned out to have surprisingly broad appeal. People who never would have bought a Waylon Jennings album nevertheless enjoyed the ornery attitude he brought weekly to *The Dukes of Hazzard*, the television show, which ran from 1979 to 1985; like many kids who grew up in the eighties, I knew all the words to that theme song long before I had any idea who Jennings was. And the cowboy imagery of the outlaws found an echo in Travolta's *Urban Cowboy*, which created, in turn, an opening for a genuine cowboy named George Strait, a full-time singer and part-time rancher from Texas who, in 1981, sent a brisk, fiddle-driven record called "Unwound" up the country chart, all the way to No. 6. Where Travolta was doubly fake—an actor playing a guy playing at being a cowboy—Strait was marketed as a "real, live cowboy" singing real, live country music. (Headline writers didn't always resist the urge to connect the name to the style: SOME REAL STRAIT-FORWARD COUNTRY; PLAYING IT STRAIT; COUNTRY MUSIC SERVED STRAIT UP.) A few years ago, on a tour bus parked just outside an arena in Las Vegas, I asked Strait what he made of the pop-country sound that was dominant in Nashville when he first emerged. Strait is known for his reticence: he doesn't talk much to reporters, and when he does, he doesn't say a lot. But on this topic he grew expansive, relatively speaking. "I didn't want to really have anything to do with that," he told me. "I wanted to be country. I *was* country."

In the decades after 1981, Strait became, by some measures, the most popular country singer of all time, which explains why he was still filling arenas in Las Vegas when I talked to him. After "Unwound," he sent eighty-five more singles into the country Top 10, and forty-four of them hit No. 1—an all-time record. In 1992, he starred in a feature film, *Pure Country*, which performed poorly at the box office but impressively on home video and, in the decades to come, on cable television. Strait was one of the first of the so-called new traditionalists, a cohort of young singers who were eager to help make country country again. This was a relatively modest movement, but an impressive one, producing few crossover hits and no manifestos, but a steady procession of accomplished singers. Randy Travis, like Strait, specialized in marvelously plain and well-turned songs that were everywhere on country radio stations, and nowhere on non-country radio stations; Alan Jackson, a few years later, had a wry sense of humor that helped him endure as a hitmaker for decades. (Jackson's discography includes "The Talkin' Song Repair Blues," in which a songwriter and a mechanic exchange technical diagnoses.) And Reba McEntire, one of the most successful new traditionalists, showed how porous these boundaries could be. Early in her career, she made a point of avoiding what she called "contemporary, crossover stuff"; she was inspired by classic country records by Dolly Parton and Merle Haggard. But one of her biggest successes came when she decided to depart from this austere approach. "Whoever's in New England," a chart-topping ballad from 1986, had tinkling keyboards and a music video, McEntire's first, that resembled a made-for-TV movie, with the singer playing a desperate wife whose husband was taking suspicious business trips. The song helped establish McEntire as one of country music's biggest names, and the video marked the beginning of an acting career that put her in films, on Broadway, and, for six seasons, at the center of her own sitcom, *Reba*. And yet "Whoever's in New England" earned no significant airplay on pop radio stations and never appeared on the Top 40—it may have looked and sounded like a crossover hit, but it lived entirely within the world of country music.

What's most startling, in retrospect, about mainstream country music in the eighties is how isolated it was. As the *Urban Cowboy* frenzy died down, the genre came to seem painfully unhip—a bit like disco after its own encounter with Travolta. The difference was that, unlike disco, which was a new hybrid, country music was relatively old. The genre had spent decades teaching its listeners to think of themselves as country fans and building an infrastructure to encourage and monetize that sense of identity.

In this way, the genre had more in common with R&B, except that country singers, in the eighties, were further from the mainstream than R&B singers were, and consequently less likely to find themselves on Top 40 radio, let alone MTV. It is mystifying that Luther Vandross, despite countless great R&B hits, never topped the pop chart. But it may be even more mystifying that the Judds—the extraordinary and musically adventurous duo of Wynonna Judd and her mother, Naomi—sent fourteen songs to the top of the country chart in the eighties without ever making an appearance on *Billboard*'s pop chart, the Hot 100. The Judds were new traditionalists, of a sort, using close harmonies and a prominent acoustic guitar to evoke the long-ago days when country music was folk music. But their rhythms suggested rock 'n' roll, and so did Wynonna Judd's ability to go from a murmur to a snarl within a single phrase. In theory, many genres might have claimed the Judds. In practice, country fans were lucky enough to have the duo all to themselves.

Reasonable people tend to disagree, of course, about what it might mean to be, as the title of Strait's feature film put it, "pure country." That soundtrack turned out to be the bestselling album of Strait's career, and it spawned a No. 1 hit called "Heartland," which was not, in fact, "pure country." ("It's about as rocked up and popped up as you can get and still pass it along to the country market," Strait said at the time.) Listeners who wanted something more traditional than the new traditionalists might have opted, instead, for bluegrass. The term emerged in the 1950s to describe a sound that had solidified in the 1930s: up-tempo Appalachian music, acoustic and drumless, which rarely produced big hits, unless you count the theme from *The Beverly Hillbillies*. But bluegrass endured, much the way the blues and the Great American Songbook and numerous forms of jazz did: as a kind of American repertory music. It was continually being rediscovered, as in 1972, when a country-rock group called Nitty Gritty Dirt Band released *Will the Circle Be Unbroken*, a triple album featuring many of the bluegrass pioneers, including "Mother" Maybelle Carter. Where popular music, broadly defined, was driven by hit records and mediagenic personas and shifting fashions, styles like bluegrass were defined more by their rich histories, and by the extraordinary technique and interpretive expression of the musicians who were devoted to them. Bluegrass fans created their own festivals and institutions, and revered their own pantheon of heroes, like the guitar-and-banjo duo Flatt and Scruggs, which recorded that *Beverly Hillbillies* theme, and Ralph Stanley, the banjo virtuoso, who stopped playing only shortly before his death, in 2016, at the age of eighty-nine.

To a bluegrass singer, "crossing over" might have meant not fleeing the world of country music but finding a place in it. In the eighties, Ricky Skaggs and Keith Whitley went from the bluegrass circuit to the top of the country chart, again and again. Alison Krauss, a bluegrass fiddler and singer, made a similar journey, earning both country success and outsize recognition from the wider music industry. By 2011, Krauss had won twenty-seven Grammy Awards, setting a record for the most won by any singer until 2021, when Beyoncé surpassed her. Krauss's accolades, along with her wonderfully soft singing voice, eventually made her an honorary member of the Nashville elite. She had a big radio hit with "Whiskey Lullaby," a doleful duet with the country star Brad Paisley. And in 2006, Krauss produced *Like Red on a Rose*, a mellow but imaginative Alan Jackson album, full of rootsy slow jams. The next year, at the inaugural edition of the California country festival Stagecoach, Jackson was one of the headliners, and his performance of the title track—a laid-back, grown-up love song—was the most memorable thing I heard all weekend. Jackson's album was exceptional, but his strategy was not: mainstream country stars are expected to acknowledge, every now and then, their connections to older versions of country music. An occasional cover song or collaboration confers authenticity, and perhaps it inspires a certain amount of secondhand nostalgia in fans, who may feel wistful about the old days of country music, even if they never actually experienced them. Just about everyone claims to love the old stuff, even if radio programmers know that most people actually prefer to listen to the new stuff.

The Horseshit Rebellion

Over the decades, the tight playlists and evolving tastes of country radio have frustrated more than a few musicians and listeners: even more, perhaps, than record executives, radio programmers make great villains for anyone who worries that there is something wrong with the listening habits of the general public. The outlaw movement helped show a generation of listeners that there was plenty of country music that wasn't on the radio, boosting eloquent singer-songwriters like Guy Clark and Billy Joe Shaver. (Waylon Jennings once said, "Billy Joe talked the way a modern cowboy would speak, if he stepped out of the West and lived today.") John Prine emerged in 1971, with the support of Kris Kristofferson, as an obdurate and sometimes acerbic singer-songwriter; he was celebrated in the press as a brilliant new country singer, even though he drew just as much from Dylan's version of folk music. Emmylou Harris was a folk singer, too, a veteran of the late-sixties New York scene who rose to prominence by singing with Gram Parsons, and who became, for decades after his death, an unlikely hitmaker. She sometimes seemed to have two careers at once, being both a countercultural country pioneer and, for a time, a consistent presence on country radio, bringing a gentle echo of country rock to many listeners who had probably never heard of Gram Parsons. In 1995, when she had mainly disappeared from country radio playlists, Harris released *Wrecking Ball*, a warm, glowing album consisting mainly of cover versions, which generated no hits but became a touchstone for listeners and singers in search of a new kind of country. Harris later remembered that the album was in part her response to being shunned by country radio. She said, "Basically I was told, 'You're just not invited to this party anymore.'"

By the time *Wrecking Ball* appeared, a growing number of country singers were pushing back against Nashville. Often their music was rootsy in sound and reformational in spirit, sometimes confrontationally so: the idea was to journey back to a time before country music had become degraded, rewriting the genre's history the way it should have gone. Dwight Yoakam wasn't just neotraditional, he was fully retro—devoted to Buck Owens—and contemptuous of all the modern country acts that sounded nothing like Owens; he once described the Oak Ridge Boys, a long-running and easy-going vocal group, as "B-grade pop-schlock horseshit." Yoakam managed to get a string of hit singles onto country radio, and in 1986 he also became the first country singer to get a video into rotation on MTV, where his anti-Nashville attitude helped him fit in. (He and his band might have reminded some viewers of the Stray Cats, a punkish rockabilly-revival trio that briefly conquered the network in the early eighties.) Steve Earle and Lyle Lovett, two of the decade's most celebrated country singer-songwriters, built successful careers without much help from country radio, which was partly the point; "I'm not trying to be George Strait," Lovett once said. Those same radio stations mainly ignored k.d. lang, a former performance artist from Canada who created a stylized version of country music inspired by her idol, Patsy Cline. For her debut album, in 1988, lang convinced Cline's former producer, Owen Bradley, cocreator of the Nashville sound, to temporarily unretire. While she won a pair of Grammy Awards in the country category, she has never been nominated for a Country Music Association Award. When lang took part in a pro-vegetarian ad campaign, in 1990, a handful of country stations banned her records; one accused her of espousing a "fanatic anti-meat philosophy." In 1992, she came out as lesbian, which had no effect on her career as a country hitmaker—because by then, she was no longer making country hits anyway. In a 1995 interview with *The Boston Globe*, lang cast her estrangement from Nashville as a matter of choice. "I didn't want to be Reba McEntire or Randy Travis because that would have meant I was doing something too accessible," she said. "I wanted to be a rebel."

Country music is full of self-styled rebels who tend to claim, at the same time, to be staying true to the genre's essence. Lyle Lovett didn't want to be George Strait, and k.d. lang didn't want to be Reba McEntire. But then again, Strait and McEntire also began their careers by swimming against the Nashville mainstream, or their interpretation of it. Sometimes when country singers talk about Nashville, they resemble American politicians, railing against the corruption and incompetence of Washington while eagerly seeking to get there and stay there. But there is also a less cynical way to think about this phenomenon. Just about every major country star has found a way to change the Nashville status quo. Often, the way to join the Nashville elite is to challenge it. Country singers weren't typically supposed to sing smooth seventies slow jams before Charlie Rich and Ronnie Milsap came along, just as Strait's "pure country" was unfashionable in Nashville— right up until he made it cool.

We know, now, that most of the eighties country rebels like Lovett and lang were not destined to conquer Nashville, so it is easier to see what they were really doing: building an alternative to it, turning the anti-Nashville sensibility into a viable business model. In the eighties and nineties, critics and executives—and, to a much lesser extent, musicians—began using terms like "alternative country" (this was how *The New York Times* had described Harris's *Wrecking Ball*) or "alt-country," and "Americana." These were unsatisfying labels that nevertheless served a purpose, denoting countryish acts that engaged with the genre's history while sometimes drawing inspiration from the spirit of punk; many attracted fans from outside the core country demographic. The labels were affixed to a wide range of performers, ranging from Iris DeMent, a transfixing singer-songwriter whom Ralph Peer would have loved, to Uncle Tupelo, a post-punk band that evoked premodern country. These acts never took over country radio, but they sometimes prospered without it. Jeff Tweedy, from Uncle Tupelo, founded Wilco, one of the most popular alternative-rock bands of the 2000s. And in 2000, alt-country even produced a multiplatinum album: the soundtrack to *O Brother, Where Art Thou?*, the Coen brothers film, which mixed old recordings with new work by tradition-minded country and bluegrass singers like Krauss and Gillian Welch, and which sold more than eight million copies—it became by a large margin the bestselling country album in America, with scarcely any help from country radio stations. In *The New*

York Times, Neil Strauss wondered whether the soundtrack would inspire country radio to "start playing traditional country music." He quoted Paul Allen, from the trade group representing country radio, who told him, "Country radio is purely about mass appeal music, and it has some very defined limits." Those "very defined limits" were linked to a very defined audience, one that evidently was not eager to hear Gillian Welch alongside, say, George Strait. But the soundtrack's success was a useful reminder that there are many different kinds of musical popularity—and many people with a taste for country music who don't have any particular interest in country radio.

The funny thing about the alt-country movement, though, is that it endured and grew much the way mainstream country music did, drawing in new listeners by updating and sometimes downplaying its identity. By the 2000s, a movement that once kicked against Nashville stood increasingly on its own, as a kind of modern folk music, crafting literary-minded songs for an audience that tended to be grown-up and sophisticated. Fans of Dylan and Prine could hear a similar spirit in Lucinda Williams, who released *Car Wheels on a Gravel Road*, an alt-country landmark that was not really all that country; it could just as easily have been considered alt-blues—or alt-rock, if that term hadn't already been claimed by a different movement. The Americana Honors and Awards, founded in 2002, have honored alt-country singers like Gillian Welch alongside country pioneers like Willie Nelson and classic-rock heroes like Van Morrison. And just as mainstream country singers in the 2010s grew more determined to demonstrate their hip-hop fluency, so did some figures in the alt-country movement grow more determined to highlight Black contributions to a genre that has generally been thought of as white. In 2017, the MacArthur Foundation awarded a "genius grant" to Rhiannon Giddens, formerly of a group called the Carolina Chocolate Drops, for "reclaiming African American contributions to folk and country genres."

Suffice it to say that non-alt-country singers tend not to receive MacArthur fellowships: in contemporary country music, as elsewhere, the relationship between the mainstream and the self-identified alternative can be rather polarized, with big audiences and big money on one side, and critical acclaim and social prestige on the other. Even so, the two worlds live much closer together today than they did in the nineties, when it seemed likely that the average country hitmaker had never even heard of Uncle Tupelo. Miranda Lambert was a mainstream star who emerged in 2004, after finishing third on a reality-television show called *Nashville Star*, and became one of the most influential figures in the genre, known for playful and sometimes caustic songs that evoked both Dolly Parton and the seventies outlaws; in her wake, a new generation of singers found ways to smuggle a spirit of defiance onto country radio. Dave Cobb, a visionary producer who arrived in Nashville in 2011, helped this process along, precisely because he had no particular allegiance to any vision of country music: he once said that he aspired to make records that sounded as if they were "from outer space," and his list of clients has ranged from John Prine, who recorded his final studio album with Cobb, to Jason Isbell, one of the most acclaimed figures in the modern Americana movement, to the Oak Ridge Boys, the vocal group whom Yoakam had deplored, back in the eighties, as "horseshit." Starting in 2015, Cobb helped turn a singer-songwriter named Chris Stapleton into a mainstream star: an austere figure with a raspy voice and a biblical beard, pleasingly anomalous amid the clean-cut hunks then dominant on country radio.

By the end of the 2010s, a new crossover act had emerged: Kacey Musgraves, who deployed cowgirl imagery with a wink, attracting pop fans and country fans alike. (She once toured with the pop star Katy Perry, but I first met her backstage in a Las Vegas arena, where she was the opening act for George Strait. "I've gotten to hang out with him a little," she told me. "We mainly just talk about horses.") In 2018, Musgraves released *Golden Hour*, which was less kitschy than her earlier recordings and more affecting—it was one of the decade's best country albums, although Musgraves wore her country identity lightly, incorporating disco beats and electronic accents as effectively as she incorporated banjos and pedal steel.

Country radio essentially ignored the album, but she was justifiably proud of being able to fill big theaters without much help from country radio, and she was happy to have a fan base full of listeners who weren't necessarily country fans. Of course, the further she got from the sound and industry of country music, the less she seemed like a Nashville rebel, and the more she seemed like nothing more or less than an extraordinary singer and songwriter. A performer like Musgraves is a credit to the deep and broad musical heritage of country music. But it is no criticism of Musgraves, or of country music, to say that by the time *Golden Hour* appeared, she seemed to be in her own world.

Lots of this anti-Nashville music sounds great to me, but then, country radio sounds pretty great to me, too. In fact, I think that the alt-country and Americana scenes can be too precious in their efforts to resist the polluting influence of the country industry, and in their attempts to evoke a simpler world through archaic slang and ostentatious hats. Maybe this judgment is simply a kind of reverse snobbery, a way for me to feel superior to the kind of people who feel superior to the kind of people who love "commercial" country music. (Snobbery, I've learned, is hard to define, and even harder to avoid; there is virtually no way to judge popular music without making some judgment about the people who listen to it.) This judgment surely reflects, too, my general allergy to any music that strains to be "retro," even though I realize that a current of nostalgia runs through all popular culture. (It sometimes seems that popular music is more nostalgic than it used to be, which could mean that my distaste for nostalgia is itself a form of nostalgia for a pre-nostalgic past.) Mainly, though, I reject the dissidents' view of mainstream country, even while loving some of their music. I think that contemporary country radio, with all its strict rules and silly fads, is a delightful institution, a cavalcade of exceptionally singable songs, organized around a common culture that is hard to define and easy, once you hear it, to recognize. It is the kind of thing future historians will study—and if they have any sense, sing along with, too.

Suburbs and Sippy Cups

In his 1985 *New York Times* report on the allegedly moribund state of country music, Robert Palmer provided a few reasons to be optimistic about a Nashville revival. Country music fans were "dwindling," he wrote, but there was hope: "A new crop of outstanding young rock bands has brought excitement to Nashville." He mentioned Jason and the Scorchers, Walk the West, and a few other bands, none of which proved nearly popular enough to alter the town's musical identity, or its signature industry. When a new act finally did arrive to redefine and revivify the genre, it was not a brash rock 'n' roll band but a friendly new traditionalist from Oklahoma, armed with a single called "Much Too Young (to Feel This Damn Old)." The lyrics presented the testimony of an old rodeo pro, tired and lonely. But the singer's voice was surprisingly soft and quavering, emphasizing not the character's toughness but his neediness, instead.

This was the debut single from Garth Brooks, an unusually ambitious country star who eventually grew so successful—he is, by some measures, the bestselling singer in American history—that he had to develop new ambitions, with mixed results. At first, he seemed content to join the ranks of the new traditionalists. But soon he found his own way to dissent from the Nashville consensus. Although he was critical of country music that was too pop, he was also critical of country music that was too old-fashioned. "What interests the country music listener today isn't what interests the country music listener in the sixties and seventies," he said. "Songs like, 'I Lost My Wife at the Truck Stop and My Dog Got Ran Over Today.'" (There is an old joke that country singers are always mourning their lost dogs, but there have been relatively few popular country songs about dogs; "Dirty Old Egg-Sucking Dog," by Johnny Cash, is one exception, although it is hardly an elegy.) "Today's country music," Brooks continued, "is enjoying its glory days, because it's back to traditional country, about real life." True, Brooks was not, in real life, an old rodeo pro; he was a singer with a degree in advertising from Oklahoma State University. But in the years after his debut single, Brooks largely set aside cowboy mythology to cast himself as a bard of "real life." One of his first big hits, "The Dance," was about a man thinking about the woman he had lost and finding reason for gratitude. Another, "Unanswered Prayers," was about a man seeing a woman he used to love and realizing how lucky he was that she hadn't loved him back:

> As she walked away, I looked at my wife
> And then and there
> I thanked the good Lord for the gifts in my life

Accounts of Brooks's rise to stardom sometimes stress his spectacular live show: as he graduated to arenas and then stadiums, he learned to enliven his concerts with pyrotechnics and screaming electric guitar solos. Using a wireless microphone, he roamed the stage like a TV preacher— although it seems possible, too, that some modern TV preachers actually learned their technique from Brooks. On records, though, Brooks had a knack for creating a sense of intimacy, singing not about mythical outlaws but about normal people with normal problems. His second album, *No Fences*, included a bluesy song called "The Thunder Rolls," about a woman whose man comes home late, smelling like "a strange new perfume." But in the music video, from 1991, Brooks expanded the narrative: the man, played by Brooks himself, is physically abusive; during the final chorus, the woman picks up a gun and pulls the trigger. The video was banned by the two leading country music television networks, TNN and CMT, and the controversy helped establish Brooks as the new king of country, especially because the message in the video was not especially controversial. This was a crime-and-punishment story, transplanted from the Old West to a modern suburban home.

In *Dreaming Out Loud*, a perceptive book about Brooks and the evolution of country music, Bruce Feiler explained how country music in the nineties finally shed its backwoods identity. Brooks, he wrote, "created a new icon in American life: the suburban cowboy." As Feiler notes, Brooks was hardly the first country singer to address himself to the suburbs. Part of the idea behind "countrypolitan" music, after all, was a recognition that the genre's audience no longer needed or wanted to hear music that sounded like rural America. And the rise of music videos, in the eighties, helped spur country stars to tell stories set in the modern world. (Reba McEntire's "Whoever's in New England" video was striking partly because it avoided traditional country imagery—with the sole, subtle exception of an airport scene where McEntire appeared to be wearing Wrangler jeans and cowboy boots.) But Brooks was so popular that even noncountry fans paid attention, and so he helped a generation of listeners realize that their perceptions of the genre were outdated.

Part of Brooks's secret was great timing. In 1991, just as Brooks was rising, *Billboard* updated its main album chart, the *Billboard* 200: instead of relying on "rankings of best-selling records obtained from stores, over the telephone or by messenger service," the magazine began a partnership with a company called SoundScan, which monitored bar-code scans to track sales nationwide. It turned out that the old method had overestimated the popularity of the sort of rock acts that industry executives tended to like and underestimated the popularity of genres viewed as more marginal, particularly hip-hop and country music. A few months after this new system was instituted, Brooks's third album, *Ropin' the Wind*, became the first country album ever to make its debut at No. 1 on the album chart. Brooks may have benefited, too, from the changing sound of American music. Bud Wendell, an executive at the Grand Ole Opry, told Peter Applebome, a *New York Times* reporter, that other genres had grown too extreme. "Heavy metal drove away as many people as it attracted," he said. "Rap drove away people. You had to listen to something. And here we are!" A cover story in *Time* quoted Jimmy Bowen, one of the most successful country music producers of recent decades. "Thank God for rap," Bowen said. "Every morning when they play that stuff, some people come running to us." For most of its history, country music defined itself by measuring its distance from the American mainstream. But in the Garth Brooks era, it sometimes seemed that country music *was* the mainstream. Tim DuBois, a Nashville executive, told Applebome that the genre was thriving because, in its nineties suburban incarnation, it reminded baby boomers of the music they already loved: it was "more like the rock 'n' roll they were comfortable with than anything else out there."

Brooks, it turned out, was not content to remain merely the new voice of mainstream America. At the peak of his popularity, he feuded with his record company, tried to establish himself as a figurehead for social change, and—infamously—recorded an album in the persona of a brooding, dark-haired singer-songwriter named Chris Gaines. By the 2000s, he was no longer a dominant presence on the country charts, although he never stopped drawing huge crowds to his concerts. But the idea of country music as suburban music never went away, and in some ways it intensified. By the early 2000s, the popularity of country songs extolling suburban bliss had become, to some fans, a running joke. In 2003, a group called Lonestar, once known for songs about Cadillacs and tequila, went to No. 1 with "My Front Porch Looking In," about a dad who loves his family home: "The view I love the most is my front porch looking in." One lyric described "a carrot-top who can barely walk, with a sippy cup of milk," and some critics turned this line into an indictment of an entire subgenre. "Sippy-cup country," they called it—the term was meant as a derisive comment on the distance the genre had traveled from its badass past to its soft-ass present.

There is nothing wrong, of course, with songs about suburban bliss. And one of the most distinctive things about country music in the 2000s was that, unlike other genres, it didn't oblige its stars to pretend to be more reckless or more radical than they really were. No singer was shrewder at exploiting this state of affairs than Brad Paisley, who reeled off a string of

No. 1 hits that were, alternately, sentimental and mischievous. (Paisley's breakthrough song was "He Didn't Have to Be," in which a boy pays heart-felt tribute to his mother's new husband, but he also once built a hit around a helpful proposal: "I'd like to check you for ticks.") "I try to be careful how much I sing about the suburban house, or whatever," he told me. Neverthe-less, some of his most effective songs resembled romantic comedies. "Waitin' on a Woman," for instance, begins with familiar jokes about how women are always late; by the end, it's about a husband promising to stay faithful to his wife in the afterlife. Paisley cowrote most of his hits, and he said he was proud to be able to describe the sorts of everyday scenes that other kinds of singers ignore. "That's where country music has found its place in modern society, is those stories," he said. "You're not going to tell that story in a pop song."

Good Luck on Your New Venture

Back in the nineties, Brooks, with his bombastic performances and sensitive-guy lyrics, changed country music forever. But that was possible only because he was devoted to country music—so devoted, in fact, that when he wanted to experiment with a slightly different musical style, he felt compelled to adopt a new look, and a new name. Some of his most successful contemporaries, especially the women, had a more ambivalent relationship to the genre. Brooks, like Paisley, wore a cowboy hat, a prop that functioned as a symbol of commitment to the music and to its fans: you put on a hat and you step into character as a country star, no matter how newfangled your idea of country may be. But in modern country music, women typically have not worn cowboy hats. And often, it has seemed that women stars, either by choice or by necessity, have had a more complicated relationship to the genre than men.

One of Garth Brooks's few peers in the nineties country stratosphere was Shania Twain, whose state-of-the-art records made even Brooks seem rather antiquated. Her breakthrough album, *The Woman in Me*, from 1995, sounded like a transmission from the genre's imaginary future. There was plenty that signified country: mournful pedal steel guitar, fluttering mandolin, frisky fiddle. But the songs were slick and streamlined, sung with superhuman precision by Twain, whose voice bore traces of neither a genuine Canadian accent nor a fake Southern one. *Come On Over*, from 1997, was even bigger and bolder, a futuristic hybrid of pop country and bubblegum rock that seemed to exist in a subgenre unto itself. Twain's producer was Robert "Mutt" Lange, who was also her husband, and who had helped create the sound of eighties rock by producing AC/DC and Def Leppard. The album included "Man! I Feel Like a Woman!" a giddy declaration with an opening riff that seems to emanate simultaneously from an electric guitar and a synthesizer. *Come On Over* became the bestselling country album of all time, a distinction it still holds, unless the Eagles are considered country—and back in 1976, when they released twin blockbusters, their first greatest-hits compilation and *Hotel California*, they generally weren't. Twain's follow-up, *Up!*, was less successful but even more postmodern: it was released in three different versions simultaneously, as a country album, a pop album, and a Bollywood-inspired world-music album. Perhaps the strategy was a way of demonstrating Twain's all-purpose mastery, or perhaps it was a way of dramatizing the conflicting demands she faced. Either way, it marked the end of her extraordinary period of dominance: after *Up!* she split with Lange, both professionally and personally, and she didn't release another album for fifteen years.

In country music, crossover success can be dangerous, because the genre's listeners, and perhaps its executives, expect dedication and gratitude from the singers whom they turn into stars. This danger has been especially pronounced for women, who have typically been asked to be glamorous—but not too glamorous, lest they create the impression that they have forsaken Nashville for Hollywood. Faith Hill was one of the brightest country stars of the nineties; in 1998, "This Kiss," an ecstatic love song, crossed over from the country chart (No. 1) to the pop chart (No. 7), despite its prominent steel guitar. But in 2002, Hill released *Cry*, which was perceived as a pop album—it began with a snarling dance beat—and which was a relative commercial failure. Hill responded by returning decisively and permanently to country music. On *Fireflies*, her 2005 album, the first sound you heard was a banjo, and the album's first single was "Mississippi Girl," a tribute to the state where Hill was born and a promise that she hadn't forgotten it. "They might know me all around the world," Hill sang. "But, y'all, I'm still a Mississippi girl." She was simultaneously pandering and groveling, but it worked: the song was a No. 1 country hit.

It's not clear how much the rules of pop country have changed since then. The singer who did the most to challenge them was Taylor Swift, who began her career, at sixteen, with a meta-country hit: "Tim McGraw," about falling in love while listening to McGraw, who was then one of country's biggest names, as well as Faith Hill's husband. For a time, Swift's extraordinary popularity made her the pride of Nashville—the biggest country music star since Garth Brooks, and maybe since before him, too. Her broad appeal and her brilliantly conversational lyrics made country seem like a modern genre, as forthright and as sardonic as emo or hip-hop. She captured not only the exuberance of young infatuation but its meanness, too:

> *I'm in the room, it's a typical Tuesday night*
> *I'm listening to the kind of music she doesn't like*
> *And she'll never know your story like I do*

Like Dolly Parton before her, Swift changed the image of country music, and executives have credited her with helping to convert a new generation of young listeners to the genre. But Swift's persona, unlike Parton's, was not especially country: she was from Reading, Pennsylvania, and had been drawn into the genre by pop-friendly singers like Twain;

unlike Parton, she could not claim to have been born country. So Swift's massive success did not earn her the right to go pop without facing the consequences. In 2014, she released an upbeat dance track called "Shake It Off," which seemed inspired by pop songs like "Hey Ya!," by OutKast, and "Hollaback Girl," by Gwen Stefani. Swift's fans loved it, and the song duly made its way to the top of the pop charts. But country music executives were not impressed. The Country Music Academy sent out a tweet that was widely interpreted as a farewell message: "Good luck on your new venture @taylorswift13! We've LOVED watching you grow!" (The CMA deleted the tweet within hours and issued a follow-up statement that paraphrased one of Swift's country hits: "We will never, ever, ever say goodbye to @taylor swift13.") And in *USA Today*, a country radio programmer suggested that Swift should not expect to hear her new music on country radio stations. "I hope she gets the country muse again soon," he said, "and we'll gladly welcome her back whenever that is." These verdicts may have been harsh, but they proved correct: over the next five years, Swift remained one of the most popular entertainers in the world, but none of her singles received significant airplay on country radio.

No mainstream country career has ever ended more suddenly, or more traumatically, than that of the Dixie Chicks, who for a few years seemed like the successors to Brooks and Twain as the biggest act in pop-friendly country music. The group began, in the early nineties, as a folky throwback act from Texas, making the kind of music that critics tend to extol and country radio programmers tend to ignore. But they evolved toward a sound that was less quaint and more forceful, especially after replacing their lead singer with Natalie Maines, a fellow Texan whose voice contained just enough bitterness to suggest a musical kinship, however distant, with alternative rock. The group's first two albums with Maines, *Wide Open Spaces* and *Fly*, were extraordinarily successful: they generated eleven Top 10 country hits, rejuvenating country radio with old-fashioned instrumentation—Martie Maguire, a cofounder of the group, is a fiddle player—and a mischievous sense of fun. One of their most popular songs was "Goodbye Earl," which had roughly the same plot as Garth Brooks's melodramatic video for "The Thunder Rolls," except it was a high-spirited comedy. (Maines asks, "Ain't it dark / Wrapped up in that tarp, Earl?") The group released the song as a single, backed with a cover of a country classic: "Stand by Your Man," Tammy Wynette's ode to romantic perseverance. At the CMA Awards in 2000, "Goodbye Earl" was named Video of the Year, and the Dixie Chicks were named Entertainer of the Year.

The Dixie Chicks' downfall began at a concert in London on March 10, 2003. "Just so you know, we're on the good side with y'all," Maines told the crowd. "We do not want this war, this violence, and we're ashamed that the president of the United States is from Texas." This was Maines's way of expressing her opposition to President George W. Bush and to America's looming invasion of Iraq, which began ten days later. Her comments sparked a backlash that soon grew into a surreal national campaign: country radio stations pulled the Dixie Chicks off the air, and some hosted rallies where fans could throw out their Dixie Chicks CDs or have them smashed by a bulldozer; the group's appearance, via satellite, was booed at the Academy of Country Music Awards, which is a less prestigious (but nevertheless grand) competitor to the CMA Awards.

At first, it seemed likely that the backlash would soon die down. The Dixie Chicks were the top-selling country group in recent history; surely listeners would be happy to welcome them back. But Maines's faint apologies didn't quell the anger. Toby Keith, one of the era's most popular singers, became the group's chief antagonist: at concerts, he displayed a doctored image of Maines getting cozy with Saddam Hussein, the dictator of Iraq. Chet Flippo, the former *Rolling Stone* journalist who wrote the liner notes for the *Wanted! The Outlaws* compilation, was then editorial director of CMT, Country Music Television; he wrote a column criticizing the group's response to the controversy, and telling Maines to "shut up and sing." (That phrase became the title of a documentary about the group.) And the band members—quite understandably—began criticizing the genre that had once been their home. In a *Time* magazine cover story, a few years later, Maguire said the group was glad to have shed some of its country following. A musician responsible for some of the most popular country music of all time now sounded more like k.d. lang. "I'd rather have a smaller following of really cool people who get it," she said, "who will grow with us as we grow and are fans for life, than people that have us in their five-disc changer with Reba McEntire and Toby Keith. We don't want those kinds of fans. They limit what you can do."

In 2006, the group returned with an album called *Taking the Long Way*, which was a success but not a reconciliation. The first single was a defiant song called "Not Ready to Make Nice," which went to No. 4 on the Hot 100 and won three awards, including Record of the Year, at the Grammys. But it only reached No. 36 on the country chart. The Dixie Chicks had made their break with country music, and it was hard to blame them. They had been kicked off the radio—censored, in effect—for voicing a thoroughly mainstream (though contentious) political opinion. Without them, country radio seemed less interesting. But it turned out that once they no longer had to worry about pleasing country fans, the Dixie Chicks became a bit less interesting, too. I remember finding the whole affair somewhat depressing, because it made it easier for smug partisans on both sides to feel vindicated. Some country fans felt that their suspicions had been validated: the Dixie Chicks seemed to think they were too good for the genre, too interesting to be heard alongside singers like McEntire and Keith. And some Dixie Chicks fans felt that their suspicions had been validated, too: Nashville was too corporate, and too partisan, to accept a group as independent-minded as the Dixie Chicks. Modern country music, they figured, had no tolerance for political protest.

Where Are Your Guts?

During one spring week in 1966, the most popular country song in America was "Waitin' in Your Welfare Line," by Buck Owens. Despite the title, it was not a protest song, or even an evocation of the hardships of poverty. It was a love song, and a bit of a joke. Owens howled the titular phrase as if it were a pretty good punch line, and in fact it was:

> *I'm-a gonna be the richest guy around, the day you say you're*
> * mine*
> *I got the hu-u-ungries for your love, and I'm waitin' in your*
> * welfare line*

That same week, the No. 2 country song in America was a good deal more political: "The Ballad of the Green Berets," an ode to the military that had become a novelty hit. The singer was Staff Sergeant Barry Sadler, who had served as a medic in the Army Special Forces, known as the Green Berets, and who delivered an ode to the bravery of America's military. "These are men, America's best," he sang, accompanied by little more than a martial snare drum. The song was not pro-war—not explicitly, anyway. But it was pro-military, and it helped create the impression that country music should be explicitly patriotic, and perhaps implicitly anti-anti-war.

In the sixties, the political identity of country music was linked to its demographic identity. The genre's sensibility was Southern, white, and middle-aged, or more-than-middle-aged. The world of mainstream country music was a conservative place, as much by temperament as by philosophy; the genre's stars were expected to avoid political provocation. In 1966, Loretta Lynn had a hit called "Dear Uncle Sam," an affecting but nonideological ballad about a lonely military bride: "He proudly wears the colors of the old red, white, and blue / While I wear a heartache, since he left me for you." In 1971, a singer named Terry Nelson released a country single that functioned as a provocative sequel to Sadler's "Ballad of the Green Berets." It was called "Battle Hymn of Lt. Calley," and it was an exculpatory monologue delivered in the voice of William Calley, the platoon leader who was convicted that year for helping to carry out the My Lai massacre. "I followed all my orders, and I did the best I could," he says. The song was a sensation, reportedly selling more than a million copies, and making a memorable appearance in Hunter S. Thompson's *Fear and Loathing in Las Vegas*, emanating from his car radio. (Thompson's review: "Great God! What is this terrible music? ... No! I *can't* be hearing this! It must be the drug.") But despite its popularity in record shops, Nelson's single was not a hit on country radio. It climbed no higher than No. 49 on the chart, and *Billboard* reported that executives were wary of it. Capitol Records considered but scrapped a plan to have the actor and country singer Tex Ritter record his own version. In 1971, as in 2003, the genre seemed keen to avoid political trouble.

Not every country singer was willing to follow this unwritten rule. In 1969 and 1970, Merle Haggard released two singles designed to start fights. The first was "Okie from Muskogee," a teasing critique of hippies, sung in the voice of a small-town square: "We don't burn no draft cards down on Main Street / 'Cause we like living right, and being free." The other, less good-humored, was "The Fightin' Side of Me," which took aim at everyone who was "harpin' on the wars we fight," and which had a refrain that took the form of a threat: "If you don't love it, leave it / Let this song that I'm singin' be a warnin'." In later years, Haggard sometimes claimed that he never meant for these songs to be interpreted as anti-anti-war statements. He was writing character studies about small-town Americans, he said, or maybe he was just kidding around. But these two songs helped give country music a sharply political reputation, even a tribal reputation—it was the genre for everybody who was sick of the hippies. This reputation has endured, even though Haggard himself turned out not to be quite as anti-anti-war as many listeners assumed. (In 2005, long after country radio had stopped playing him, Haggard released a resolute but rather dull single called

"America First," which included a call for America to "get out of Iraq.") It was significant, too, that Haggard himself, author of these classic anti-hippie songs, was loosely allied with what would become known as the outlaw movement, which was countercultural but ideologically undefined. Michael Streissguth, a country historian, described the outlaw movement as "vacuous politically," though this was not necessarily a weakness: Willie Nelson could unite "the ropers and the dopers" precisely because he didn't ask them to join him in any particular political struggle. Nelson later revealed himself to be a political liberal, but he tended to gravitate toward causes—support for American farmers, marijuana legalization—that could unite liberals and conservatives.

Johnny Cash, the ultimate outlaw, was more outspoken, and more complicated. In 1964, he released *Bitter Tears*, an album full of songs about the mistreatment of Native Americans. When radio stations were slow to embrace the lead single, "The Ballad of Ira Hayes," about a marine from the Akimel O'odham people, Cash took out a full-page advertisement in *Billboard*, asking, "D.J.'s—station managers—owners, etc., where are your guts?" (The song eventually made it to No. 3.) But Cash, who supported President Richard Nixon, conspicuously declined to join the movement against the Vietnam War. After Nixon's famous "Silent Majority" speech, in 1969, Cash said, on his television show, "My family here and I stand behind the president of the United States in his quest for a just and lasting peace." Cash was summoned to the White House to perform for Nixon in 1970, and Nixon made some requests, including Haggard's "Okie from Muskogee," as well as "Welfare Cadillac," by Guy Drake, a novelty country hit (No. 6) about a man who gleefully takes advantage of government benefits. Cash declined to sing either of these, and his White House set included, instead, "What Is Truth," a passionate though rather vague treatise on social turmoil. Cash liked the idea of being a truth teller, but he didn't always like having to pick a side. In "Man in Black," a 1971 song that functioned as a statement of purpose, he sternly avowed that "things need changin' everywhere you go"—he sang it less as a protest than as a lament, and perhaps an eternal truth.

President Nixon, a Republican, attracted plenty of support among country singers. In 1974, when the Grand Ole Opry moved to a new theater, Nixon made an appearance on opening weekend. "He's a real trouper as well as one of our best presidents," said Roy Acuff, a country pioneer who was one of the hosts. But in those days, the genre had no fixed partisan identity. George Wallace, the longtime governor of Alabama, was a Democrat and had been an avowed segregationist; in 1972, George Jones and Tammy Wynette, then the reigning king and queen of country, held a fundraiser for him. (Wallace was essentially part of the country music community: he used country musicians as his campaign warm-up acts, and his second wife, his third wife, and his son were all, at various times, aspiring country stars.) Jimmy Carter, a moderate Democrat and the former governor of Georgia, was a country fan, too, and some singers viewed him as a kindred spirit. Loretta Lynn sang at his inauguration eve concert in 1977. "Maybe people will quit laughin' about the way I talk, now since the president of the United States talks the same way," she said. By then, the idea of political candidates seeking support from country singers had become something of a cliché; *Nashville*, the 1975 Robert Altman satire, is all about the planning of a political fundraiser in town, which turns out to be a very bad idea.

Only in America

As America's political divisions grew more predictable, so too did the politics of mainstream country music. The genre's tradition of patriotism and respect for the military made it particularly compatible with the Republican Party, and so did its popularity in the South and in growing suburbs and exurbs, where the party was increasingly strong. President George H. W. Bush appeared at the 1991 CMAs, paying tribute to the genre. "One reason I've liked country music for so many years has been its unwavering support of our country, our flag, and the ideals for which this country was founded," he said, introducing a montage of patriotic CMA performances from previous years. (When Bush died, in 2018, Reba McEntire sang at his funeral.) Garth Brooks was one star who seemed to push against the genre's political consensus. In a 1993 Barbara Walters interview, he mentioned that his sister was gay and said, "I'm sorry, I just can't condemn somebody for being happy and loving someone else." But often, the genre's politics were implicit, not explicit. Where Haggard made country music seem like a factional genre, defined in opposition to the hippie counterculture, eighties and nineties country music often positioned itself as merely and firmly mainstream, representing that patriotic faction of the country that liked to think of itself as belonging to no faction at all. In June 2001, Brooks & Dunn, a duo that created its own rousing form of country rock, released an infectious single called "Only in America," with guitars that rang as loud as the message of pride: "Only in America! Where we dream as big as we want to!" But by the time the song reached the top of the country charts, in late October, the context had changed, and so perhaps had the message.

No genre responded more decisively to the terrorist attacks of September 11, 2001, than country music, which had a ready supply of patriotic material, a fondness for topical songwriting, and a preexisting tendency to support Republicans, like President George W. Bush. After the attacks, "God Bless the USA," a 1980s country hit by Lee Greenwood, was put back on the radio, and even crossed over onto the pop chart. Alan Jackson released "Where Were You (When the World Stopped Turning)," a lament that was memorable because it was so restrained, as if Jackson couldn't bring himself to do much more than sigh and pray. "Have You Forgotten?" by Darryl Worley, reached No. 1 in 2003, by which time simple sorrow had given way to a political debate; the song suggested that no one who remembered 9/11 could sensibly oppose President Bush's foreign policy. (The song was released as Bush prepared America to invade Iraq.) Most of all, there was Toby Keith, who in 2002 released one of the most controversial songs in the history of country music. It was called "Courtesy of the Red, White, and Blue (the Angry American)," and the lyrics were as unwieldy as the title: "You'll be sorry that you messed with the U. S. of A. / 'Cause we'll put a boot in your ass—it's the American way." I saw Keith in concert in the summer of 2005, three years after the song was released, and it was still the pinnacle of his show: not the best song he played all night, but by far the most galvanizing, inciting the crowd to roar as one. This was a moment of unity—and, like many moments of unity, also a moment of division. The concert was in suburban New Jersey, close enough to the site of the 9/11 attacks, but also right in the middle of a state that had recently voted against reelecting President Bush, 53 percent to 46 percent. Keith's song was powerful partly because it was pointed. It was a roaring endorsement of the troops and the wars they were fighting, and a roaring indictment of everyone who disagreed. It was a tribal moment.

It turned out that Keith, like Haggard before him, was a more complicated figure than he first seemed. Like Haggard, he was something of an outlaw: he recorded largely for independent labels from his home base of Oklahoma, and declined to move to Nashville. Even as "Courtesy of the Red, White, and Blue" was becoming a country classic, Keith was trying to explain that he was a longtime Democrat, and that he had mixed feelings about America's wars. ("I was for Afghanistan, 100%," he told the *Los Angeles Times*, in the fall of 2003. "But this war here, in Iraq, I didn't necessarily have it all worked out.") The song earned him lots of critics, which in turn earned him lots more fans. One of those critics was Natalie Maines, from the Dixie Chicks. "It makes country music sound ignorant," she said, in an interview with the *Los Angeles Daily News*. "Anybody can write, 'We'll put a boot in your ass.'" This was the origin of the dispute between Maines and Keith, which was a dispute over the identity of country music. Keith won that dispute, not really because his song was better but because at that moment, his sensibility was closer to the sensibility of the people who considered themselves country fans. "I'm embarrassed about the way I let myself get sucked into all of that," Keith said the following year, not long after the controversy. But the effect on his career was permanent: even as Keith's new singles became scarce on country radio, in the 2010s, he remained a popular live act. His catalog of hits includes "Beer for My Horses," a startling duet with Willie Nelson that endorses lynching. ("Take all the rope in Texas, find a tall oak tree / Round up all of them bad boys, hang 'em high in the street," Nelson sings.) But many of Keith's best-loved songs are cheerful and sly, like "As Good as I Once Was," in which he warns friendly women and unfriendly men that he's not quite as old as he looks. Through it all, he remained a roguish and charismatic singer, and also an emblem of country music at its most unapologetic.

As Keith moved on, and the Dixie Chicks bowed out, their encounter reverberated, teaching a generation of singers that political provocation could be enormously profitable or enormously costly, depending on the type. (In 2019, Taylor Swift said that she had thought of the Dixie Chicks' fate when she decided not to endorse Hillary Clinton during the 2016 presidential campaign. She said, "The number one thing they absolutely drill into you as a country artist, and you can ask any other country artist this, is 'Don't be like the Dixie Chicks!'") One singer determined to try his luck was Brad Paisley, who released a single called "Welcome to the Future" in 2009. It begins cheerfully, with a celebration of cell phone video games, but in the third verse the band drops out so that Paisley, guided by an acoustic guitar, can address weightier matters. He sings about a boy, presumably Black, whose home is the target of a cross burning. And then he adds a bit of history, and a bit of hope: "I thought about him today, and everybody who'd seen what he'd seen / From a woman on a bus to a man with a dream."

In the music video, Paisley sings these words in front of the Lincoln Memorial, and for many listeners the clear reference to the Ku Klux Klan was probably less unexpected than the coded salute to a liberal Democrat, President Barack Obama—the song was, implicitly, a celebration of the fact that he had just become America's first Black president. Paisley told me that to help the record's chances on the country chart, he called country radio stations coast-to-coast. He knew many country listeners had voted against Obama, and he wanted to reassure DJs that no partisan message was intended. (A 2009 survey of country radio listeners found that only 17 percent described themselves as "somewhat" or "very" liberal, while 37 percent described themselves as "somewhat" or "very" conservative; 46 percent called themselves "moderate.") Paisley explained to the DJs that he would have written the same song if Colin Powell, the Black secretary of state under George W. Bush, had been elected instead. "That was harder work than I've ever had to do," Paisley told me, but it succeeded, sort of. "Welcome to the Future" traveled all the way up the chart—to No. 2, breaking Paisley's streak of ten No. 1 singles in a row. Paisley had proved that it was possible to get a song with a pro-liberal message onto country radio, but he had also proved that it wasn't easy.

The White Experience

A few years after "Welcome to the Future," Paisley tried again to test the boundaries of country music—and this time, he failed. He told *The Tennessean* that he was inspired by a T-shirt he once wore featuring Alabama, the long-running country band; the design included a Confederate flag, which some people objected to, which in turn got Paisley thinking about why that flag was on his chest in the first place. The result of all this rumination was "Accidental Racist," an earnest and awkward collaboration with the rapper LL Cool J, which was released in 2013, to much Internet mockery and virtually no radio play. "Just a proud rebel son with an old can of worms / Looking like I got a lot to learn," Paisley sang, although in truth he is a son of West Virginia, the state that was formed by counties from Virginia that did not want to join the Confederate rebellion. In the song, Paisley sings about being "caught between Southern pride and Southern blame," but here, as is often the case in country music, "Southern pride" seems to mean *white* Southern pride. The genre's whiteness has been central to its identity for decades, and to its continuing tribal appeal: it has often been music made by "proud rebel" sons and daughters, celebrating and helping to define whiteness in America. In the fifties, when country music and R&B were briefly coming together, *Billboard* explained that the genres were divided by small but significant musical details. "Often," the magazine observed, "the difference between a country side and an r.&b. side is merely the use of strings as against the use of horns." Another difference, of course, was that R&B singers were often Black, and country singers were generally not—indeed, this was one reason why Presley, who "sounded black," as Waylon Jennings put it, was so confounding to some executives, and maybe to some listeners. With the rise of the Nashville sound, country maintained its reputation as a determinedly white genre, although there were a few exceptions. In 1962, Ray Charles, a titan of Black music, released *Modern Sounds in Country and Western Music*, volumes one and two, a pair of hybrid albums (with both strings and horns) that succeeded in just about every way except one: country radio stations ignored them. Starting in 1966, Charley Pride, a Black singer from Mississippi, began a decades-long run of smooth and straightforward country hits, becoming by far the most successful Black performer in the genre's history. But virtually all the rest of the genre's hitmakers were white.

Country music was not unique in this. By the end of the sixties, rock 'n' roll, too, was increasingly dominated by white acts, while Black performers in the rock tradition were often categorized as R&B. But early rock stars like the Rolling Stones tended to be self-conscious about their whiteness, because it set them apart from the pioneering Black musicians who represented authenticity. In country music, by contrast, it was *whiteness* that was linked to authenticity—to "the hard life of the soil," as Paul Hemphill put it. Often this whiteness was implicit, although Haggard made it memorably explicit in a song called "I'm a White Boy," in which he derided "handout livin'" and declared, "I'm a white boy, lookin' for a place to do my thing." The hillbilly, the cowboy, the outlaw: the genre's stock characters were all thought of as white. There was also another character: the good ol' boy, which usually meant a white guy from the South who upheld traditional regional values, often in defiance of legal authority. In his *Dukes of Hazzard* theme, Jennings paid tribute to the show's pair of archetypes: "Just two good ol' boys / Never meaning no harm." *The Dukes of Hazzard* was a car-chase show, but it was also an exercise in Confederate nostalgia. The main character was neither of the two lead actors but the Dodge Charger they drove, which had a Confederate flag painted on the roof and which was named the General Lee, in honor of the Confederate States Army commander. The show was unremittingly upbeat, but each episode served as a reminder of the link between outlaw mythology and Southern history. In the world of country music, the word "rebel" tended to come with lots of history attached.

Some of the most vivid expressions of white Southern identity came not from country singers but from their musical cousins in Southern rock bands. (Most of the Southern rock bands were white, although there were some exceptions, including the Black drummer known as Jaimoe, from the Allman Brothers Band.) Lynyrd Skynyrd often used the Confederate flag in its imagery—in fact, in "Accidental Racist," Paisley sings about a Lynyrd Skynyrd T-shirt, not an Alabama T-shirt. And "Sweet Home Alabama," the band's defining song, from 1974, was inspired by Neil Young, who had previously released two songs, "Southern Man" and "Alabama," targeting Southern racism. The band's response was defiant: "I hope Neil Young will remember / A Southern man don't need him around, anyhow." And the lyrics included an explicitly political message: a declaration of support for George Wallace. "Sweet Home Alabama," went the final chorus. "Where the skies are so blue / And the governor's true."

One of the country singers who did the most to bring Southern rock into country music was Hank Williams Jr., son of the genre's ultimate hero, who cultivated a reputation as both a hell-raiser and a traditionalist—in other words, perhaps, a good ol' boy. "I'm tired of being Johnny B. Goode, and I'm gonna be Johnny Reb," Williams once sang, drawing a contrast between two very different characters, one an icon of Black rock 'n' roll and the other the personification of the Confederacy. Williams's approach could be heavy-handed, but starting in the late seventies he emerged as the defining voice of country music as an identity, not merely a musical genre. "A Country Boy Can Survive," one of the songs he's known for, celebrates the pleasures and virtues of rural life, "good ole tomatoes and homemade wine." But like many of Williams's songs, it is implacably defiant: he is less interested in praising nature than he is in drawing distinctions between the self-reliant people of the country and the untrustworthy people in the big cities, where "you only get mugged if you go downtown." Williams, who is known as Bocephus, is a culture warrior, among other things, and his "country" identity was bolstered by a conviction that in the rest of America, things had gone wrong. In 1988, Williams went to No. 8 with "If the South Woulda Won," a counterfactual daydream that imagined a modern Confederacy, with convicted killers swiftly hanged to death, and his own father memorialized on the hundred-dollar bills.

The spirit of Bocephus lived on in groups like Confederate Railroad, a country-rock band that had a handful of country hits in the nineties, and that used the flag in its logo and on some of its merchandise. (In 2019, after a couple of the group's concerts were canceled because of the name and logo, Danny Shirley, the lead singer, told *Rolling Stone* that he had grown up around the flag in Chattanooga, Tennessee. "We were taught that flag means you like the part of the country you come from," he said.) Some rock acts treated the Confederate flag as a symbol of rebellion: Tom Petty, from Gainesville, Florida, used it during his *Southern Accents* tour, in 1985, though he later renounced it; the metal band Pantera, from Texas, displayed it during a 2001 tour. But in country music, Confederate imagery was not always intended as a provocation. Nostalgia for a time before the Civil War is inscribed in the name "Lady Antebellum," which was chosen by a trio of singers who topped country charts, starting in the late 2000s, with bittersweet love songs and warm vocal harmonies. Even the Dixie Chicks, now famous for criticizing the parochialism of country music, were named after "Dixie Chicken," a funky Southern rock song by the band Little Feat, which evoked late nights in "Dixieland"—a term for the old South. In 2020, amid nationwide protests for racial justice, Lady Antebellum shortened its name to Lady A, thereby affronting a Black blues singer who was already using that name. And the Dixie Chicks became the Chicks. There is no way to separate Southern pride from the politics and the history that helped to make Southern identity so powerful. (People don't tend to sing about—or fight over—New England or the Midwest, in large part because neither of those regions waged a bloody war of secession against the US government.) But there are different ways to sing about the South. "Southern Voice," a No. 1 hit from 2009 by Tim McGraw, expounded a pointedly inclusive form of Southern pride, celebrating a tradition that included Dolly Parton and Rosa Parks, Hank Williams and Hank Aaron. This was one way to think about country music: as an expression of a multiracial Southern identity.

In the years since Ralph Peer's 1920s recordings, though, country music has grown both less rural and less Southern; its contemporary musicians and listeners tend to share neither an agrarian culture nor a regional identity. What they still have in common, often, is being white. Surveys suggest that the genre's audience remains disproportionately white, and the charts show that its most popular performers are almost always white, too. (African American hitmakers remain so rare in country music that they can be enumerated, and they often are: Darius Rucker, from the rock group Hootie and the Blowfish, made a successful transition to country music in the late 2000s; Kane Brown, the son of a Black and Cherokee father, who describes himself as biracial, emerged as a country star in the late 2010s.) This is not necessarily an anomalous state of affairs: in New York in the 2000s, I noticed that country concerts tended to have white people onstage and in the audience, but the same was largely true at indie-rock concerts, and heavy-metal concerts, and even techno clubs. Country music, though, has remained unusually unapologetic about its white identity. Ralph Emery, who was for decades the genre's most prominent radio personality, told *Time* magazine in 1992 that country music provided a form of racial balance in the musical landscape. "Rap music speaks only to black issues," he said, "and has turned a lot of white people off." In his book about Garth Brooks and the evolution of country, Bruce Feiler talked to Ed Morris, formerly the country editor for *Billboard*. "Country is fundamentally based on the white experience," Morris told him. "It's about where whites live, what they read, what they see."

In earlier decades, it seemed obvious that country music reflected not white people in general but a particular kind of white people—the ones who might be referred to with slurs like "hillbilly" or "redneck." This is what gave the music its countercultural identity, allowing Hank Williams Jr. to mythologize himself as a stubborn "country boy," fighting to survive in an un-country world. But in the decades since Garth Brooks, especially, country singers have often strained, instead, to present themselves as normal: everyday Americans, generally but not necessarily white; the kind of people politicians are always talking about representing. The idea of a predominantly white genre can sound offensive; all-white places in America have historically been restricted places, segregated places. But no genre truly appeals to *everyone*. Perhaps country music is merely more honest than rock 'n' roll about the identity of its audience. Certainly the whiteness of country music has never seemed like a barrier to me. I am half-white, which means not white, according to the rules I learned soon after I arrived in America as a five-year-old. I became an American citizen in 1995, but my preoccupation with the many forms of American identity probably marks me as an immigrant. And so I can't help but hear country music, still, as ethnic music: the sound of white America, or at any rate *a* sound of white America. Like all the music I love, country music gives me a way to peer into lives that are different from mine—in some ways, though not all ways. It presents a vision of a "normal" America, sometimes stylized well past the point of normalcy.

What Makes You Country

In 1970, an unknown singer and songwriter released an unnoticed album called *Down to Earth*. He was an aspiring country star, but radio stations showed little interest in his folk-inspired songs, and by the time he finally did find success, in the late seventies, he wasn't exactly a country singer any more: he was Jimmy Buffett, and he was building a mainstream musical empire by singing easygoing songs about long days and longer nights in warm places. In the 2000s, a number of country singers rediscovered the appeal of Buffett and his escapist approach, and the genre grew more lighthearted—less about work, perhaps, and more about play. Buffett himself collaborated with Alan Jackson on "It's Five O'Clock Somewhere," which gave Buffett his first No. 1 country hit, at the age of fifty-six. (Buffett topped the country chart for a second time eight years later, singing a duet with a different country singer, Zac Brown.) And a Buffett-influenced singer named Kenny Chesney emerged as one of the genre's biggest and most dependable stars, with a way of sounding wistful even when the topic was "Beer in Mexico," which was also the title of one of Chesney's innumerable hits.

The party continued into the 2010s, with the rise of a style known as bro-country, which was dominated by hunky and cheerful men who sang about flirting and drinking—topics that were meant to be universally appealing. The irony was that these concertedly all-American songs were not, it transpired, irresistible to all of America. Music critics and other outsiders tended to deride bro-country, which seemed to them painfully unhip, and objectionably old-fashioned. Luke Bryan became a star with a series of jovial albums like *Tailgates & Tanlines*, from 2011. (This title reflected the genre's upbeat and inclusive mood, although of course both tailgate parties and tan lines are traditionally associated with white people, for cultural and phenotypical reasons, respectively.) And yet Luke Bryan was not particularly successful as a crossover act, precisely because his inveterate normalcy—his tendency to extol the simple pleasures of, say, a "goodnight kiss"—made his music seem, in the druggy and louche context of popular music, rather alien. "Just be proud of what makes you country," Bryan once sang, listing his own rural bona fides while also reassuring listeners that their own country identities were equally valid, no matter what they were. "We're all a little different, but we're all the same / Everybody doin' their own thing," he sang, wisely declining to define that "we": it was a word meant to include all the people who might ever be inclined to listen.

In recent years, a lot of criticism of country music has focused on bro-country—which seemed, to some critics, like a sinister plot launched by radio executives on a mission to homogenize the genre. The discussion became more heated in 2015, when a country radio consultant named Keith Hill gave an interview to *Country Aircheck*, an industry magazine, in which he said that programmers should be careful not to play too many women singers. "If you want to make ratings in country radio, take females out," he said. (Looking through some playlists, he noted with approval that none were more than 19 percent women.) Hill explained, rather cryptically, that men were "the lettuce in our salad," and that women were the tomatoes. The resulting outrage spawned a controversy that came to be known as Tomato-gate—Hill's comments resonated widely, in large part because there were lots of listeners and singers who were bothered by the relative paucity of women on country radio. Country veterans knew that, far from being an outlier, Hill was merely echoing decades of conventional wisdom. In her autobiography, which was published in 1994, Reba McEntire suggested that it was harder for women than for men to become top country live acts, and she offered a possible explanation. "Women are usually the ones who buy the concert tickets," she wrote, "and women naturally want to see men—who can blame them?" Similarly, Hill claimed that women country listeners mainly wanted to hear men singing, and though many executives rushed to denounce his remarks, no major country station found a way, in the years immediately after Tomato-gate, to significantly increase the number of women on country radio.

Country radio, which has so far withstood the rise of streaming music services, is valuable for the same reason that it is infuriating: it represents an unapologetic effort to give listeners nothing other than what they demonstrably want to hear. This effort is imperfect, to be sure, and it is always influenced by business considerations, although not always in the way you might think. (Historically, for instance, country radio has paid particular attention to women listeners, who are considered the format's base.) Despite the dominance of country radio, and in some ways because of it, country music in the new century has mutated in ways that neither fans nor detractors might have predicted, drawing in outside genres and styles.

One person who might have predicted it was Hank Williams Jr., who saw early on that country music and Southern rock were kindred spirits. By the early 2000s, bands like Lynyrd Skynyrd had been retroactively welcomed into the country canon; alongside the beach songs, a kind of retrofitted Southern rock was spreading. The genre produced its own rock stars: Brooks & Dunn and Montgomery Gentry, a pair of revved-up duos; Keith Urban, an arena-rock guitar hero; Carrie Underwood, a grand balladeer who had some of her greatest success with bluesy rock songs; Eric Church, who made snarling rock 'n' roll sound like a pure expression of country identity. (Church even had a big hit called "Springsteen," a lovely country song about listening to Bruce.) In a way, this was a new version of the Nashville sound: hip-hop was dominating the Top 40, and so country music looked back a few decades, finding ways to draw in listeners who missed the loud but cheerful roar of 1980s hard rock. Noticing this, the members of Bon Jovi, hard-rock favorites from the MTV era, recorded a song with Jennifer Nettles, from the rock-influenced country group Sugarland, which became a No. 1 country hit, and which sounded not at all out of place on country radio.

Another thing Williams might have predicted was the crossover success of one of the most unlikely country stars of the modern era: Kid Rock, a famously debaucherous white rapper from outside Detroit who became increasingly obsessed with the culture of country music. He took to covering

"A Country Boy Can Survive" in his concerts, which led to a friendship with Williams, and also a mutually advantageous professional relationship. They recorded a concert together for *CMT Crossroads*, a series that paired country acts with noncountry acts. (Williams called him "My rebel son, Mr. Rock.") In 2002, Kid Rock released an uncharacteristically tender ballad called "Picture," with Sheryl Crow, which got enough airplay on country stations to rise to No. 21 on the chart. A few years later, he went to No. 4 with "All Summer Long," a country hit borrowed from both "Werewolves of London," the rock 'n' roll hit by Warren Zevon, and "Sweet Home Alabama," by Lynyrd Skynyrd, which earned a shout-out in the refrain: "Singin' 'Sweet Home Alabama' all summer long." I talked to Kid Rock about his evolution, and he told me that he might never have been accepted in Nashville if it hadn't been for Williams's endorsement. "That kind of gave me a lot of credibility," he said.

Thanks in part to Kid Rock, country music in those years was slowly growing more open to hip-hop, perhaps because the genre was by then old enough to seem like part of America's cultural heritage. In 2004, a duo called Big & Rich had a hit with "Save a Horse (Ride a Cowboy)," a hip-hop-inspired party song that was daft and charming and that seemed, accordingly, like a one-off novelty. But the novelty of country mixed with hip-hop never seemed to wear off. Big & Rich had a protégé named Cowboy Troy, an African American rapper who had a minor country hit of his own. Tim McGraw collaborated with the hip-hop star Nelly for "Over and Over," which became a big hit—although not, notably, on country radio, which mainly declined to play it. At the same time, a genre known as country rap was emerging, led largely by white rappers who embraced an avowedly "country" sensibility. One of them was Colt Ford, who had a track called "Dirt Road Anthem"; in 2010, the country singer Jason Aldean released his own version, singing the choruses and rapping the verses, and it went to No. 1 on the country chart, proving that country radio listeners no longer minded a little bit of rapping.

What's Right with the Format

The most popular track of 2019, in any genre, was a country song. Except perhaps it wasn't. "Old Town Road" spent nineteen weeks at No. 1 on *Billboard*'s Hot 100 chart, a new record. One version featured Billy Ray Cyrus, a country veteran, and the lyrics were all about riding horses. But then again, it had a hip-hop beat and a hip-hop identity: it was the work of Lil Nas X, a Black singer and rapper who was previously unknown. But "Old Town Road" was not very dominant on the country chart, for a simple reason: after its debut at No. 19, *Billboard* removed it. To explain this decision, *Billboard* issued a statement that instantly became one of the most controversial sentences in the publication's history. "While 'Old Town Road' incorporates references to country and cowboy imagery," the editors explained, "it does not embrace enough elements of today's country music to chart in its current version." This was a puzzling statement, and a circular one: the idea seemed to be that "Old Town Road" couldn't possibly reflect "today's country music," because it didn't contain "enough elements of today's country music." How could we know for sure?

It would have been more accurate—and, surely, less controversial—for *Billboard* to make a simpler declaration. Perhaps "Old Town Road" didn't belong on the country chart because its listeners were generally not country music fans. The song never earned much airplay on country radio stations. And the algorithms of streaming services like Spotify seemed to suggest that people who listened to "Old Town Road" were also listening to hip-hop and pop, not country music. The argument over how to classify the song was partly an argument over the way technology was changing musical consumption. In 2019, country radio was still a mighty force, but an increasing number of listeners, especially younger ones, were spending time on streaming services like Spotify and Apple Music, where they played the songs they wanted, or else listened to curated playlists. In 2012, *Billboard* had modernized the formula for its Hot Country Songs chart, factoring in downloads and online streams, and measuring radio airplay across all formats, not only at country stations. While country radio program directors like to keep songs rotating in and out of the chart's top positions, streaming services sometimes show songs remaining at No. 1 for weeks or months, perhaps because new listeners keep discovering them, or because the most devoted fans are slow to move on. "Meant to Be," a collaboration between the country duo Florida Georgia Line and the pop star Bebe Rexha, went to the top of the Hot Country chart in December 2017 and remained there until the following November: an impressive feat, but also a sign that the chart was essentially broken, or at least that it no longer measured what it used to. Anyone curious about what was actually playing on country radio now had to look, instead, at the separate Billboard Country Airplay chart, where "Meant to Be" was No. 1 for only one week, in April. The rise of streaming services introduced a subtle but consequential change in the way people think about music genres. The old, radio-driven country chart measured which songs were most popular among people who listened to country radio. The new, streaming-driven country chart measured which country songs were most popular among listeners in general—which meant that it was up to the chart compilers, not the radio programmers, to decide what "country" meant. In the Spotify era, the Barbara Mandrell rule may come under threat: it may grow harder to figure out what the country audience likes, because it may grow harder to figure out who the country audience is.

If the country sensibility grows less distinctive, then perhaps more people will look back fondly at bro-country, which actually did a lot to expand the genre's music palette. Many of the movement's biggest names used hip-hop to create the convivial atmosphere that made their songs so effective—often while insisting, at the same time, on their own country credentials. One of the first songs to be widely described as "bro-country," in 2013, was "Boys 'Round Here," by Blake Shelton, which begins with a declaration of country fealty:

Well, the boys 'round here don't listen to the Beatles
Run old Bocephus through a jukebox needle
At the honky-tonk,
Where their boots stomp
All night

It sounded pretty orthodox, except for the fact that Shelton was rapping, not singing, more or less keeping time to a hip-hop beat, and waiting for the electric guitars to come in for the chorus. Florida Georgia Line, the gregarious bro-country duo, brought Nelly back into country music with "Cruise," an addictive hit single that went to the top of *Billboard*'s country airplay chart. And Sam Hunt, a hunky former college quarterback, released his debut album in 2014; it was full of nods to hip-hop and R&B, especially in the nimble syncopation of Hunt's delivery. (His concerts sometimes included an effective interpolation of "Marvin's Room," the moody hip-hop hit by Drake.) I asked John Dickey, an executive from the country radio conglomerate Cumulus Media, about Hunt's success—the album sent five songs to No. 1 or No. 2 on *Billboard*'s Country Airplay chart. Dickey said that Hunt was an example of how country music was evolving. "What would have been a very difficult business proposition five, six, seven years ago with an artist like Sam Hunt—today, he's a poster child for what's right with the format," Dickey told me. In the wake of Hunt's success, the charts filled up with country singers using the tools of hip-hop: electronic beats in addition to live drummers, auto-tune to make vocals sound slightly robotic, and slangy and slippery vocal lines.

As always, Nashville's latest version of country music annoyed some listeners and some musicians. In 2017, Steve Earle, who long ago embraced his role as a country dissident, suggested that modern country music was essentially "hip-hop for people who are afraid of Black people." It seems unfair, though, to suggest that listeners' enthusiasm for hip-hop/country hybrids merely shows that they are "afraid of Black people." (What would it show if they *rejected* those hybrids?) Now, just as during the "countrypolitan" seventies, the sound of country going "pop" is often the sound of country music embracing elements borrowed from Black genres—while insisting, all the while, that its cultural identity is as "gut-country" pure as it ever was. Morgan Wallen, who succeeded Sam Hunt as the genre's leading heartthrob, liked to play with hip-hop phrasing and even hip-hop beats, while also distancing himself from hip-hop culture. "Beer don't taste half as good in the city," he sang. "Beer don't buzz with that hip-hop, cuz / But it damn sure does with a little Nitty Gritty." He was wrong about beer, but he was surely right that many of his listeners liked to think of him as one of their own—loyal to a country community that continued to harbor mixed feelings about the cultural dominance of hip-hop. Early in 2021, not long after the album was released, Wallen was caught on video using the n-word, while bidding a bleary goodnight to one of his friends. (He sounded as if he was trying to use the word the way a Black person might.) The reaction was immediate: Wallen became the first country act since the Dixie Chicks to be pulled from country radio stations nationwide, and his record label said that it would "suspend" his contract. Wallen himself issued a brief apology, and then a more fulsome one, and announced that he would take some time away from music. But his fans didn't seem to mind: they kept listening to his new album, which spent its first ten weeks atop the *Billboard* album chart. (This had been done only twice before: by Stevie Wonder, in 1976, and by Whitney Houston, in 1987.) Perhaps his future as a crossover act was in doubt, but his status as country's biggest star never wavered.

This is the strange and remarkable thing about country music: that, despite all the decades and all the change, it still functions as a genre, a community with its own tastes and tolerances, for better and for worse. It still has fans who want to claim it and critics who want to fight over it; radio stations that play it and record companies that sell it. No one quite knows the rules, but everyone knows that there *are* some rules: like every genre, country music is defined in large part by what it rules out. Even more than most genres, country music attracts detractors—ever since the sixties, it has remained among the most despised forms of music in America, sneered at for being too country, or perhaps not country enough. And yet country music has managed to do the two most important things a musical genre can do: it has changed, and it has endured.

4.

PUNK

Converted

D ID I LIKE MUSIC? Sure I did—doesn't everyone? In second or third grade, I taped pop songs from the radio. A few years after that, I memorized a small handful of hip-hop cassettes. A few years after *that*, I acquired and studied a common-core curriculum of greatest-hits compilations by the Beatles, Bob Marley, and the Rolling Stones. But I didn't start obsessing over music until my fourteenth birthday, in 1990, when my best friend, Matt, gave me a mixtape.

Matt had been watching my progress over the previous year, and he had noticed a few things about me. I was listening to *Mother's Milk*, the 1989 album by the Red Hot Chili Peppers, a punk-rock party band that was mugging and wriggling toward mainstream-rock stardom. I was also listening to an album by the rapper Ice-T that had a strange spoken-word introduction, a creepy bulletin announcing America's descent into "martial law." I didn't think to wonder about the provenance of this speech, delivered by an ominous man with a nasal voice, but Matt knew: it was taken from a spoken-word record by Jello Biafra, who had been the lead singer of an acerbic left-wing punk band called Dead Kennedys. From those two data points, Matt deduced that I was getting my musical education from MTV and that I might be ready for some more esoteric teachings. And so he gave me a punk-rock mixtape, carefully compiled from his own burgeoning punk-rock collection. He wanted to convert me, and he succeeded: within a few weeks, I was intensely interested in everything that was punk rock, and intensely uninterested in just about everything that wasn't. I seem to remember pushing aside an old shoebox full of cassettes and thinking, "I will never listen to the Rolling Stones again."

I was wrong, of course. But for a few formative years, I was gloriously and furiously right. I was a punk—whatever that meant. Probably I still am.

Incoherent and Inescapable

Once upon a time, a "punk" was a person, and generally a disreputable one. The word connoted impudence or decadence; punks were disrespectful upstarts, petty criminals, male hustlers. In the seventies, "punk" was used first to describe a grimy approach to rock 'n' roll, and then, more specifically, to denote a rock 'n' roll movement. "Punk rock" was one of those genre names that swiftly became a rallying cry, taken up by musicians and fans who wanted to remind the mainstream world that they wanted no part of it. One of the bands on that mixtape was the Sex Pistols, who popularized the basic punk template in 1977, with the release of *Never Mind the Bollocks: Here's the Sex Pistols*, their first and only proper album. The band was considered a commercial failure in America, but in their native United Kingdom, the Sex Pistols were front-page news. During an appearance on a British television talk show in 1976, the Sex Pistols were introduced by the host, Bill Grundy, who told his viewers, "They are punk rockers—the new craze, they tell me." Grundy did his best to seem underwhelmed by the spectacle of the four band members, accompanied by four of their punk friends, smirking and sneering. "You frighten me to death," he said sarcastically, goading them to "say something outrageous." Steve Jones, the guitarist, was happy to oblige, calling Grundy a "dirty fucker" and a "fuckin' rotter." A contemporary viewer might be less startled by the profanity than by the fact that one of the punks was wearing what was then a common punk accessory: a swastika armband. But the appearance fixed the reputation of the Sex Pistols as the ultimate punks, in both the new and the old senses of the word. (It also helped fix the reputation of Grundy, who was suspended for two weeks, for "sloppy journalism," and whose career subsequently declined; he died, of a heart attack, in 1993, and was eulogized in *The Guardian* as "a delightful companion except when overtaken by his low tolerance level for Scotch.") When my mother noticed that the Sex Pistols were one of the bands I was suddenly obsessed with, she dimly remembered them as the unpleasant young men who had caused such a fuss back in the seventies.

Punk rockers scorned the music business, and the big-time rock bands that ruled the concert circuit and the album charts. Members of the Sex Pistols were photographed in a Pink Floyd T-shirt, modified with the words "I HATE." But the Sex Pistols broke up in 1978—twelve years before I discovered them on that mixtape, wedged alongside their many musical descendants. By the time I heard it, punk was old and the Sex Pistols were relics, the absent godparents of a movement that had evolved and thrived long beyond anything the antagonists on Bill Grundy's show could have imagined. In 1981, an absurd Scottish band called the Exploited released a debut album titled *Punks Not Dead*, and the rather self-defeating title marked a change in attitude. Punk would never again be considered a "new craze," but rather a stubborn old crusade that had somehow outlived its moment. The Exploited were represented on Matt's mixtape by "Sex & Violence," a song that contained no words besides the three in the title, repeated endlessly as a gnomic protest against sixties idealism. If the hippies wanted peace and love, then the punks would demand the opposite.

It didn't seem at all peculiar to me, in 1990, that the Sex Pistols, this long-ago British band, should capture my imagination. Even on a second-generation cassette, the group's music was shockingly vivid; the gregarious roar of Steve Jones's guitar and the venomous screech of the lead singer and antagonist, Johnny Rotten, were equally infectious, in opposite ways. "Anarchy in the U.K." was the band's defining single, building to an unyielding declaration of purposelessness: "I wanna be anarchist / Get pissed / Destroy." I tried to learn more by picking up *Lipstick Traces: A Secret History of the Twentieth Century*, which was the first book of music criticism I ever encountered. It was published in 1989, and I read it, or tried to read it, two years later, while riding a train from Connecticut to Boston. The author was Greil Marcus, a visionary rock critic whose career predated punk but who found himself startled by the incandescence of the Sex Pistols. In Marcus's view, Rotten was the unlikely (and perhaps unwitting) heir to various radical European intellectual traditions. Marcus noted, meaningfully but mysteriously, that Rotten's birth name, John Lydon, linked him to John of Leiden, the sixteenth-century Dutch prophet and insurrectionist. I quit reading somewhere in the book's more esoteric second half, but I was excited by Marcus's determination to connect punk to the wider world, and by his description of the Sex Pistols' music as "a breach in the pop milieu"—an impossibly obnoxious phenomenon that made all sorts of other phenomena suddenly seem possible.

How did punk survive so long? One answer is that it didn't, really. The incarnation of punk that I heard on that mixtape, and that converted me, had strayed from the trail blazed by the Sex Pistols. By 1990, "punk" had become a grab-bag term, referring to a wide range of bands that played music that was angry, or rowdy, or funny, or strange, or just loud. My gateway mixtape included a song by Hüsker Dü, a hardcore punk band from Saint Paul, Minnesota, that left hardcore behind, perfecting love songs that were histrionic but tuneful. Hüsker Dü was often classified as "post-punk," because the members were part of a world that grew out of the punk explosion; or "college rock," because they played a style of music beloved by college radio DJs; or "alternative," a word that was increasingly applied, in the decade to come, to any moody band with distorted guitars. There was room in my idea of punk for the Red Hot Chili Peppers, at least until 1992, when "Under the Bridge," an earnest ballad, transformed them into the kind of mainstream rock act I had come to disdain. If memory serves, their newfound earnestness annoyed me at least as much as their newfound success. My musical diet in those years was full of jokey and sometimes offensive acts like the Dead Milkmen, from Philadelphia, whose body of work included an upbeat song called "Takin' Retards to the Zoo." The promise of punk was that it offered room for practically everything—in its broadest sense, loving punk meant being nonmainstream, a slippery and seductive identity that was often more appealing than the music itself.

Music, in fact, sometimes seemed somewhat extraneous to the development of punk. In 1977, a handmade British punk fanzine called *Sideburns* published a marvelously crude illustration showing how to play three simple chords (A, E, and G) on the guitar. The text was stern but inspirational:

THIS IS A CHORD

THIS IS ANOTHER

THIS IS A THIRD

NOW FORM A BAND

The implication was that there was nothing special about making music— anyone could do it, and everyone should, the simpler the better. Many punks were eager to demystify and democratize popular music, although this democratic spirit did not prevent them from sneering at normal folks and their normal interests. Punk rhetoric tended to be simultaneously populist and elitist: you took up for "the people" while simultaneously decrying the mediocre mainstream crap they listened to. In *Lipstick Traces*, Marcus quotes Paul Westerberg, from the unpretentious American post-punk band the Replacements, who loved punk because he related to it. "The Sex Pistols made you feel like you knew them, that they weren't above you," Westerberg said. But the Sex Pistols and all the other punks didn't seem like anyone *I* knew. They were weird and scary, and their music sounded as if it had crossed an unimaginable cultural gulf, not to mention an ocean and a decade, to find me in my bedroom in Connecticut.

I was born in England, in 1976, a few months before the Sex Pistols terrorized Bill Grundy, and my family lived in Ghana and Scotland before arriving in America, shortly after my fifth birthday. I understand why listeners sometimes hunger to hear their identities reflected in music, but I also suspect that the hunger for difference can be just as powerful. My parents were born and raised in Africa: my father, Black, in the Gambia; my mother, white, in South Africa. They both taught at Harvard and then Yale, and they both loved classical music, as well as *Graceland*, the landmark 1986 Afropop album by Paul Simon. As a teenager, I was drawn to punk for the same reason that I was not drawn to, say, the majestic Senegalese singer Youssou N'Dour, or the great composers whose work I practiced at—and, less consistently, between—my weekly violin lessons. I loved punk because I *didn't* really see my family represented in it, or myself, at least not in some of the major identity categories that my biography might have suggested: Black, brown-skinned, biracial, African. It was thrilling to claim these alien bands and this alien movement as my own. Punk was the exclusive province of me and Matt and hardly anyone else we knew.

The do-it-yourself spirit of punk did inspire me to find ways to participate. In the years after my conversion, Matt and I broadcast our favorite records to an audience of no one over the airwaves of our ten-watt high school radio station. We formed bands that scarcely existed, releasing tapes and even a record that were never really distributed. We published a few issues of a homemade punk-rock magazine—a fanzine, or zine—called *Tttttttttt*, a name we chose solely because it was unpronounceable. I also started dressing the part, a little bit. I modified my hairstyle, turning a half-hearted hip-hop flattop into something a bit more freakish: I kept the sides of my head shaved, while twisting the top into a scraggly collection of braids, or maybe dreads, decorated over the years with a few plastic barrettes, a piece of yarn or two, a bit of bleach.

Even so, when I said I was a punk, I realized that I was not a punk in the same way that the members of the Sex Pistols or the Exploited were punks. They emerged from rebellious and decadent social circles, where I was polite and conscientious. My dedication to the punk lifestyle went not much further than a slightly strange hairstyle, along with a small number of T-shirts and a larger number of albums and cassettes. (Matt and I resolved to stretch our musical budgets by never making duplicate purchases; if one of us bought an album, the other one was entitled to a free copy, dubbed onto a tape.) In the New Haven area, where we lived, punk concerts were rare, and most of the clubs barred anyone younger than twenty-one. I finally found a loophole on one of the last days of 1990, when I discovered that our local concert hall, Toad's Place, allowed underage patrons to attend if they were accompanied by legal guardians. Matt was evidently unable to persuade his parents that this discovery was significant, but I had more luck with mine, which is how I was able to see my first punk concert: I took my mother to see the Ramones, the pioneering New York City punk band. And while she watched (or, more likely, didn't) from the safety of the bar area, I spent a blissful hour amid a sweaty group of aging punks and youthful poseurs, all shoving one another and shouting along.

When I picture myself as a fourteen-year-old in that crowd, saluting the Ramones with a triumphant pair of middle fingers merely because it seemed like the "punk" thing to do, I think about the smallness of the punk revolution. In casting aside the Rolling Stones and adopting the Ramones, I had simply traded one elderly rock band for a different, slightly less elderly rock band. The appeal of punk was not really the music, which I still love but which doesn't sound any better or more adventurous to me now than Bell Biv DeVoe's clattering R&B classic "Poison," or Madonna's stylized club track "Vogue," which were two of the dominant MTV hits at the moment of my punk conversion. And the appeal wasn't really the community, either, or the do-it-yourself spirit. For me, the thrill of punk lay in its negative identity. Punk demanded total devotion, to be expressed as total rejection of the mainstream. This was a quasi-religious doctrine, turning aesthetic disagreements into matters of grave moral significance. Punk was good and other music was bad, meaning not just inferior but wrong. While rock 'n' roll sometimes conceived of itself as an eternal spirit, present in every group of believers, the ideology of punk had more in common with the stern message Jesus Christ delivers in the Gospel of Luke: "If any man come to me, and hate not his father, and mother, and wife, and children, and brethren, and sisters, yea, and his own life also, he cannot be my disciple."

Punk taught me that having strong opinions about music was possible and maybe inevitable; it taught me to love music by teaching me to hate music, too. Over the years, the objects of my musical scorn shifted and dwindled—having learned, at fourteen, to savor the perverse charms of punk, I eventually came to hear just about the entire universe of popular music as perversely charming, or potentially so. In that sense, it was the spirit of punk that also drew me, eventually, to hip-hop, and pop music, and country music, and just about everything else. The philosophy of punk is both incoherent and inescapable. At least, it has been for me.

There is nothing so unusual about any of this. Lots of teenagers are lucky enough to have a private passion, something that mysteriously captures first your attention and then your personality, and never quite lets go. But my punk obsession turned out to be quite widely shared. Even as I was nurturing my punk-rock disdain for mass culture, the genre was, maddeningly enough, going mainstream. In 1991, fourteen years after *Never Mind the Bollocks*, a band called Nirvana, led by a Sex Pistols fan named Kurt Cobain, released *Nevermind*, a snarling blockbuster that turned punk-inspired music into a national craze. I was a high school junior when the album arrived, and I wanted nothing to do with it—to my ears, Nirvana was merely a rock band, not a punk band, as attested to by the sudden ubiquity of "Smells Like Teen Spirit," the breakthrough Nirvana single, on MTV and at my high school. Still, there was no way to ignore the fact that the black Doc Martens boots I liked to wear, as a marker of punk identity, were increasingly commonplace. (In 1992, one influential downtown New York retailer told *The New York Times*, sniffily, "Every mall store sells Doc Martens now.") Nirvana toured Europe with Sonic Youth, a noisy but sophisticated post-punk band that was suddenly playing to huge crowds. The members of Sonic Youth were the subjects of a documentary about the tour called *1991: The Year Punk Broke*. The film took its title from a scene showing Thurston Moore, the band's cofounder, sitting in a restaurant, delivering a wry report on the state of music. "Ninety-one is the year that punk finally breaks. Through. To the mass consciousness of global society," he says, deadpan. "Modern punk, as featured in *Elle* magazine."

The strangest thing was the way punk *kept* breaking. Cobain died, by suicide, in 1994, just as a Bay Area punk band called Green Day was finding a place—a permanent place, it turned out—in the rock-star firmament. After Green Day came blink-182, a punk band with a pop sensibility, and then Avril Lavigne, a pop star with a punk sensibility; by the early 2000s, MTV was promoting punk music as the natural successor to teen pop. (In 2003, an MTV executive enthused about the current crop of punk bands, like Good Charlotte and the Used. "People are gravitating towards it," he told me, "because these are great pop songs.") Even as punk went pop, punk-inspired underground scenes remained remarkably fertile, spawning punky throwback bands, like the Strokes, but also a wide range of musical disruptors: Ezra Koenig, from the crafty indie band Vampire Weekend, grew up listening to punk rock, and so did the polymathic Canadian singer-producer known as Grimes. And while successive generations of teenagers had more musical choices than I did, many of them still gravitated, year after year, to various forms of punk music. They gathered at basement concerts or, motherless, at all-ages club shows, shouting and sometimes shoving as bands played music inspired, however indirectly, by the Sex Pistols. Punk and post-punk heroes like Iggy Pop, Patti Smith, and David Byrne were revered as sages, often by young listeners eager for a connection to an older, punker world that they were too young to have experienced.

Punk helped enshrine the idea that popular culture was split between a vacuous mainstream and a worthy underground, or "alternative." The spirit and logic of punk helped spark alt-country, alt-rap, alt-versions of whatever genre had come to seem a bit too mainstream, although none of these other "alts," which tended to be rather high-minded and old-fashioned, seemed as startling to me, or as inspiring. Initially punk had been derided as a brainless fad—a "largely one-dimensional" genre that had mainly "petered out," as one *Newsweek* critic declared in 1978. And yet punk has endured, in the twenty-first century, not as a bad joke but as an artistic ideal, evoking defiance and integrity. Starting in 2005, the annual Afropunk Festival celebrated "alternative black culture," a formulation that was strategically ambiguous and therefore inclusive: just about any Black artist, it seemed, might be deemed "Afropunk" if they were cool enough, or original enough. At various times in my life, the vagueness and versatility of "punk" has struck me as strange, or hilarious, or embarrassing, but it's not hard to see why the concept has proven so useful. Punk represents the universal human desire to be a little less universal—to separate whatever it is you care about from whatever it is that other people care about. Greil Marcus put it well. "Punk drew lines," he wrote. "It divided the young from the old, the rich from the poor, then the young from the young, the old from the old, the rich from the rich, the poor from the poor, rock 'n' roll from rock 'n' roll." This determination to tell and show the world that you are different is, perhaps, rather immature. The same, though, might be said about popular music itself, and about the passions that lead so many of us to care so much about it in the first place.

Rock 'n' Roll at Its Finest

When I discovered punk, I had three years left in high school, and I devoted them to an ongoing treasure hunt: if "punk," broadly defined, meant "weird," then I resolved to hunt down the weirdest records I could find. I was monomaniacal and, doubtless, insufferable. I remember selecting for my senior yearbook quote a snippet of chimp-like gibberish from an album called *Soul Discharge*, by a delirious Japanese noise-rock band called Boredoms, which I played until I understood its scrambled logic, or thought I did. (Even now, *Soul Discharge* inspires in me that combination of awe and warm nostalgia that many of us derive from whatever music we worshipped in high school.) When I arrived in the fall of 1993 at Harvard University, I was looking for punk-rock compatriots, and I found them within a week at the college radio station, in the dusty basement of Memorial Hall, one of the grandest buildings on campus. Like most college radio stations, WHRB was full of obsessives who loved to argue about music. Unlike most college radio stations, WHRB aspired to academic rigor. Students hoping to join the punk-rock department, which controlled late-night programming, first had to take a semester-long class in punk-rock history. Enrollment was limited to applicants who passed a written examination, which included both open-ended essay questions and a quick-response section, in which they—we—were played unlabeled snippets of songs, and instructed to write down reactions. I remember hearing a few twangy notes of unaccompanied electric guitar and immediately knowing two things for certain: that the song was "Cunt Tease," a sneering provocation by a self-consciously crude New York–based group called Pussy Galore; and that I would never again be as well prepared for a test as I was on that day.

Many years after that entrance exam, I was interviewed for the art and culture magazine *Bidoun* alongside my friend Jace Clayton, a fellow writer and music obsessive, who also happens to be, very much unlike me, an acclaimed musician. Jace and I went to college together—we first met at the radio station, taking that punk-rock exam, which repelled him just as totally as it seduced me. "By the end of the test, I was just writing satirical, increasingly bitter answers to these ridiculous questions, knowing that I would never, ever get in," he remembered. He said that WHRB was "the worst radio station ever," and indeed he got his revenge by taking his talents two subway stops away, to the MIT radio station, where he began to hone his own marvelously free-form approach, playing whatever records he liked.

For me, though, WHRB's devotion to punk-rock orthodoxy was a revelation. I had assumed that the spirit of punk was, in Johnny Rotten's words, "anarchist," anti-rules. But of course every culture, every movement, has rules, even or especially those that claim to be transgressive. As aspiring DJs, we were taught that punk wasn't some all-embracing mystical essence, to be freely discovered by every seeker, or even a universal ideal of negation, but a specific genre with a specific history. Every week that fall, we were presented with a lecture from a veteran DJ about some aspect of punk history, and a crate of ten or so canonical albums; before the next lecture, we had to listen to them and write down our reactions. We were free to say we hated this music—no one there liked all of those records, and some people disliked most of them. Once we became DJs, we would be expected to express ourselves by writing miniature reviews on white stickers affixed to the album covers, or the plastic sleeves that held them. But first, we had to study.

As a high school punk, eager to differentiate myself from the mainstream, I had little interest in any punk record that sounded too much like rock 'n' roll. But the relationship between punk and rock 'n' roll has always been intimate; many of the earliest punks wanted not to destroy rock 'n' roll but to purify and perfect it. When critics began to use the term "punk rock," in the early seventies, they applied it to a wide range of rock stars; *The New York Times* described the music of Alice Cooper, the theatrical hard-rock star, as "punk rock" in 1972, and described Bruce Springsteen the same way, the next year. But "punk rock" was also a backward-looking term, used to identify a savage, scruffy spirit that some listeners found lacking in much seventies rock. In 1972, a farsighted New York guitarist named Lenny Kaye put together a double-LP compilation called *Nuggets*, which gathered twenty-seven weird or rude rock songs from the late 1960s and which occupied an important place on the WHRB syllabus. The track list included "Dirty Water," the riotous Standells song that became an unofficial

Boston anthem, and a version of "Baby Please Don't Go" by the Amboy Dukes, the band led by the guitar hero Ted Nugent. In the liner notes, Kaye lionized this barely bygone age as a "changeling era," when rock 'n' roll was still wild and primitive. He described the groups on the compilation as "decidedly unprofessional," which he meant as high praise. "The name that has been unofficially coined for them—'punk-rock'—seems particularly fitting in this case," he wrote, "for if nothing else they exemplified the berserk pleasure that comes with being on-stage outrageous, the relentless middle-finger drive and determination offered only by rock and roll at its finest."

Kaye wrote in the wistful past tense, although some of these oldies were only a few years old. (The "nuggets" came from four years, 1965 through 1968.) Even as he was assembling his compilation, though, a handful of American bands were seeking to sustain, or revive, this spirit. In New York, during the *Nuggets* era, a band called the Velvet Underground emerged, under the patronage of the artist Andy Warhol, as perhaps the first "underground" band in rock 'n' roll history, with squally guitars and sometimes sordid lyrics that conjured up a world of druggy decadence. And in Michigan, a pair of similarly "berserk" bands emerged: MC5, known for shaggy and furious live shows; and the Stooges, who were even more furious, and even better, led by a snarling and slithering instigator who called himself Iggy Pop. In 1970, the critic Lester Bangs described the Stooges as the antidote to the "pompous edifice" of the "supremely ridiculous rock 'n' roll industry." Not that the Stooges weren't ridiculous in their own way: their sublime signature song was "I Wanna Be Your Dog," based on a crude declaration of lust and an even cruder progression of three descending chords. Bangs loved it, and he loved the way Iggy Pop flailed around, onstage and off it, like a menacing clown. "None of them have been playing their instruments for more than two or three years," he wrote of the Stooges. "But that's good—now they won't have to unlearn any of the stuff which ruins so many other promising young musicians: flash blues, folk-pickin', Wes Montgomery–style jazz, etc." Thanks to bands like the Stooges, rock 'n' roll could break its bad habits and be born again.

In Bangs's view, naivete was one thing that separated bands like the Stooges from similarly raucous peers like Led Zeppelin, which was then helping to invent the genre of heavy metal. Bangs loathed Led Zeppelin: the music sounded to him bombastic and pretentious, and he referred to the band members, at various times, as "talentless nonentities," "lumbering sloths," "jaded fops," and "big babies." From a distance, the budding punk movement and the budding heavy metal movement had plenty in common, starting with a commitment to noisy rock 'n' roll. But where heavy-metal pioneers like Ozzy Osbourne, from Black Sabbath, sometimes presented themselves as high priests, presiding over powerful musical rituals, the early punks took a more casual approach, treating nightclub stages as extensions of the streets outside. In the early seventies, the New York Dolls built a small following and a big reputation, armed with little more than some rudimentary rock 'n' roll, some garish women's clothing, and lots of attitude—certain audiences, it turned out, loved to be sneered at. Kaye himself played with Patti Smith, a singer and poet who began her career by declaring, in the first lines of her first album, in 1975, "Jesus died for somebody's sins / But not mine." By 1976, when the first Ramones album appeared, it was becoming clear that the spirit of the Stooges had helped inspire a growing subculture, with CBGB, a grotty downtown nightclub, as the unofficial headquarters. The Ramones dressed like street hustlers, in tight jeans and black leather jackets, and they streamlined rock 'n' roll into songs that were fast and loud and mindless, or seemingly mindless. They expanded the titular formula of "I Wanna Be Your Dog" into a whole suite of "wanna bes": "I Wanna Be Your Boyfriend," "Now I Wanna Sniff Some Glue," "I Don't Wanna Walk Around with You," "Now I Wanna Be a Good Boy," "I Wanna Be Well," and, most of all, "I Wanna Be Sedated," a maniacally upbeat song about boredom that has endured as a punk-rock anthem, perfectly evoking the genre's twin preoccupations with fun and hopelessness.

When I first heard "I Wanna Be Sedated," during my initial punk-rock catechism, I loved it because it seemed like the beginning of a tradition, pointing away from all the conventional things a rock 'n' roll band might do, and pointing toward anything and everything else. But the weekly lectures at WHRB taught me to hear it a little more the way Bangs heard it: as the culmination of years of furtive rock 'n' roll ferment, and as a reassertion of the values that rock 'n' roll ought to have been championing all along. In fact, Bangs wasn't entirely enthusiastic about the late-seventies punk explosion—he worried that the hopelessness was drowning out the fun, as well as the meaning. Punk rock at its best, he argued in 1977, "embodied the who-gives-a-damn-let's-just-slam-it-at-'em spirit of great rock 'n' roll"; punk at its worst was merely nihilistic. He wrote, "So much of what's doled out as punk merely amounts to saying I suck, you suck, the world sucks, and who gives a damn—which is, er, ah, somehow *insufficient.*" Bangs's view of punk was literally conservative, because he saw punk as a reactionary and remedial force, come to roll back the misguided innovations that were ruining rock. The WHRB approach was conservative, too, providing an old-fashioned indoctrination into a genre that was, in many important ways, stubbornly retro. Anyone who wanted to claim punk as an inherently progressive movement, broad-minded and liberatory, had to wrestle, first, with its history.

Punk Explosion

There is a different view of how punk came to be, linked to a different place. Punk in New York was an accidental phenomenon, the product of a cluster of bands and a handful of observers. *Punk*, a music magazine based in New York, published its first issue in 1976, helping to popularize a term that was already widely—if loosely—applied. Punk in London was not at all an accident. It was more like a plan, maybe even a conspiracy. Malcolm McLaren was a canny and mischievous English gadabout who had spent some time in New York, where he served for a while as the de facto manager of the

New York Dolls, whose lives were often as dissolute as their lyrics. (At one point, he had the band dress up in red leather and perform in front of a hammer-and-sickle flag, relishing the unlikely combination of real sleaze with fake communism.) As the New York Dolls were dissolving, in 1975, McLaren returned to London, where he was the proprietor, with the designer Vivienne Westwood, of an outré fashion boutique called SEX. McLaren figured that London could use some Dolls of its own, and he found some new clients: young men who hung around the shop and played music together, too. The Sex Pistols were really the SEX Pistols, named after the boutique the same way sports teams are named after their cities.

There was only one dull song on *Never Mind the Bollocks*: "New York," which gave the Sex Pistols a chance to acknowledge their obvious debt to New York bands by excoriating them. (When Rotten sang, "You're just a pile of shit, you're coming to this / You poor little faggot, you're sealed with a kiss," he seemed to be aiming at the New York Dolls, making derisive reference both to their wardrobe of women's clothes and to one of their best-known songs, "Looking for a Kiss.") The rest of the album was just about as rude, and much more exciting. Unlike most of the New York bands, reveling in their own squalid world, the Sex Pistols seemed eager to bait the public, the media, and the music industry—the album's seething finale was "EMI," about the British record company that had signed the Sex Pistols and then dropped them. The Sex Pistols were as much a publicity stunt as a band, and a successful one, rebranding punk as a quasi-revolutionary British movement, known for its deviant fashion and its defiant politics. The signature accessory of British punk was the safety pin, worn as an earring or else a cheek piercing. Legs McNeil, one of the founders of *Punk* magazine, was shocked by the sudden ubiquity of British punk. In *Please Kill Me*, his oral history of the movement, McNeil remembered thinking, "Hey, wait a minute! This isn't punk—a spiked haircut and a safety pin? What is this shit?" A 1978 report on punk, on the *Today* show, told American audiences, as if it were an established fact, "Punk began in Britain."

In a way, though, punk did begin *again* in Britain. "God Save the

Queen," the Sex Pistols' sarcastic tribute, was a deft act of provocation—it rose to No. 2 on the British pop chart, despite being effectively banned from British radio. (It began, "God save the Queen / The fascist regime.") But it was scarcely the most venomous song on the album. "Bodies" was a song about abortion, with no coherent message beyond frustration and contempt and disgust: "Fuck this and fuck that / Fuck it all, and fuck the fucking brat." And in "Problems," Rotten refuses to shut up as the song winds down, snarling "problem" over and over again, ignoring the rest of the band. This, it turns out, was a fairly faithful depiction of the state of intragroup relations: Steve Jones, the guitarist, was trying to make a great rock 'n' roll album, while Rotten was more interested in making trouble. Rotten's seething disdain combined with McLaren's sense of theater to create the widespread and enduring impression that the Sex Pistols were something more than just a rock band. After the Bill Grundy affair, the *Daily Mirror* put the Sex Pistols on the front page, accompanied by a headline that was an even better advertisement than anything McLaren could have written: THE FILTH AND THE FURY! Sometime during my high school years, I acquired a black Sex Pistols T-shirt featuring a collage of photographs and tabloid headlines, including that one.

It is easy to chuckle at the cynicism of the British newspaper editors, feigning shock in order to titillate their readers. But there really was something shocking about the Sex Pistols, and that shock is part of what sparked young acolytes to start filthy and furious punk bands all over Britain, and all over the world. Unlike its American counterpart, British punk was, at its inception, less a remediation than a rejection. The nihilism that Bangs detected and disliked was in large part an import from Britain, sent over by the Sex Pistols. Bangs thought that "Fuck this and fuck that" was not a philosophy likely to inspire continual musical flourishing, but this sentiment turned out to be the Sex Pistols' most important contribution to popular music, precisely because it was so vague: an all-purpose negation, linked to no particular positive program. The demise of the Sex Pistols came after a chaotic American tour that ended in San Francisco in 1978, with a sullen cover version of "No Fun," by the Stooges. As the music finally stopped, Johnny Rotten provided a mirthless epilogue: "Ah, ha ha! Ever get the feeling you've been cheated? Good night." Less than a year later, Sid Vicious, the band's bass player, was charged with murder, after his girlfriend was found stabbed to death in their New York hotel room; he died, from an overdose of heroin, in 1979, before he could stand trial.

Some of the Sex Pistols' acolytes paid tribute by following their example, or a cartoonish version of it. In the years after the Sex Pistols' demise, a punk uniform emerged: you could advertise your punkness by wearing a black leather jacket adorned with studs and slogans, and by shaving the sides of your head and spiking the remaining hair into a Mohawk, a look that was all but unknown among earlier punks. The Exploited and scores of other bands strove to be punker than the Sex Pistols—faster, or drunker, or angrier, or more anti-establishment. These punk dead-enders have always been easy to mock, and perhaps that's part of why I always found them so charming. Not long after arriving at WHRB, I first heard an excellent English group called Discharge, known for black-and-white album covers, and for warp-speed songs with gruff lyrics about atomic bombs and other horrors of the modern world. Discharge helped inspire the style known as crust punk, which was associated with radical politics and a boozy, nomadic lifestyle. You could measure Discharge's influence by counting the like-minded bands that emerged, some of which adopted similar names: Disfear, from Sweden; Disclose, from Japan; Distraught, from New York. Old-fashioned music buffs loved to wax poetic about creativity and individual expression. What, then, could have been punker or more radical than an army of musical clones, bashing out blurry black-and-white songs about nuclear annihilation while pursuing its alcoholic equivalent?

And yet it turned out there were lots of other ways to be punk. When the Sex Pistols appeared on Bill Grundy's show, one of the punks standing behind the band was Siouxsie Sioux, then known as one of the most stylish habitués of the London clubs, who soon proved herself to be an inventive and influential musician in her own right. As the leader of Siouxsie and the Banshees, she released a series of danceable, dissonant records that helped launch the next musical uprising. By the early 1980s, England was full of former punks experimenting with synthesizers and brightly colored clothes; these bands, variously labeled "post-punk" or "new wave" or "new pop," had no allergy to commercial success, and some of them made a show of embracing it. Siouxsie's band far outlasted the Sex Pistols: in 1991, Siouxsie and the Banshees went to No. 23 on the *Billboard* pop chart with "Kiss Them for Me," a beguiling ode to Jayne Mansfield, the fifties movie star, that I remember seeing in rotation on MTV. (At the time, I didn't know that it was about Mansfield. I didn't know, either, that Siouxsie Sioux was a godmother of British punk, or that the song was based on a clever sample of a track by the pioneering rapper Schoolly D.) Johnny Rotten was on MTV then, too, a regular presence on *120 Minutes*, the network's showcase for alternative music, which had been launched in 1986. Having reclaimed his birth name, John Lydon, he spent the eighties and early nineties leading Public Image Ltd, a band that paired his unabashedly acerbic singing with beat-driven music that ranged from gloomy to vivacious. *120 Minutes* was hosted by a London transplant named Dave Kendall, and I'm not sure I ever stopped to wonder why, in those pre-Nirvana years, alternative rock in America so often had an English accent.

One of the most cherished records on the WHRB syllabus was *Wanna Buy a Bridge?*, which was new to me and, as far as I remember, to all the other aspiring DJs, too—hearing it was like hearing a secret history. It was a battered artifact from 1980, released on an English independent label called Rough Trade. And it gathered fourteen tracks from fourteen bands that were making scrappy but sweet music in the immediate aftermath of punk. There was a spidery, violin-powered ode to lovesickness by a band called the Raincoats; a punchy, playful song called "Mind Your Own Business," by the Delta 5; and "Man Next Door," by the Slits, who were inspired by the ghostly, disorienting sound of Jamaican dub reggae. The album was exciting because it captured the moment when the energy of the punk explosion was beginning to disperse, shooting out as screaming chaos and bashful love songs and a dozen other things besides. Most of this music didn't sound like punk rock, but it was still closely linked to punk, and the relationship was reflected in a gentle, rather amateurish song by a group called Television Personalities. Dan Treacy, the main member, led what sounded like a bedroom sing-along, poking fun at young people practicing their "punk" moves at home—"But only when their mum's gone out." The verses were rather judgmental, but by the time he got to the chorus, Treacy sounded more like a small boy watching a delightful parade:

> *Here they come*
> *La-la la-la la, la*
> *La-la la-la la, la*
> *The part-time punks*

There were good reasons, no doubt, why a song like this would resonate among a bunch of Harvard undergraduates for whom punk indoctrination was merely one of many extracurricular activities. There was something ridiculous about the WHRB ethos—but then, there has always been something ridiculous about punk, which cultivated an image of chaos and insubordination that no human being could possibly live up to, at least not for long. (What would it mean, really, to be a *full-time* punk?) After passing my punk exam, I completed my semester-long audition and became an official member of the WHRB staff, a giver of punk-history lectures, and, eventually and inevitably, the director of the department, responsible for ensuring that the station's late-night broadcasts continued to be recognizably punk.

I was probably a better lecturer than I was a DJ, and I was definitely a better DJ than I was a director. But I liked the challenge, for a while, of being the keeper of the orthodoxy, tasked with setting and enforcing the rules that other DJs would inevitably and appropriately rebel against. Would the Federal Communications Commission leave us alone if the DJs referred to a delightful old punk band as "the Snivelling 'S'-Hits," rather than "the Snivelling Shits"? How big could a record label get before it was considered a "major" label and its releases banned from our airwaves? How extensively could DJs explore other nonmainstream genres, like techno or heavy metal or hip-hop? (WHRB also broadcast an influential hip-hop radio show, but only once a week, on Saturday nights, an arrangement that some people quite rightly found strange, or worse than strange.) If punky cult bands from the sixties like the Monks—who shaved tonsures into their heads and recorded a frenzied banjo-driven album while serving as GIs in Germany—were welcome on our air, then what was our policy on punky *mainstream* bands from the sixties, like the Rolling Stones? (I had by then disavowed my disavowal of the Stones—lured back, perhaps, by their savage 1965 cover version of "She Said Yeah," by the rock 'n' roll pioneer Larry Williams.) I can't remember exactly what answers I devised to these questions. But I remember thinking hard about the complex and codependent relationship between musical rules and musical rule breakers. Listeners and for that matter DJs who delight in mixing and matching genres necessarily rely upon the existence of recognizable genres, recognizable musical identities. And musical identities are always exclusive, even if they don't claim to be. Any musical movement that claims to be all-embracing is probably lying, both to the outside world and to itself.

Punk Politics

Every movement needs a symbol, although not every movement chooses its symbol wisely. In the early days, the unofficial punk logo was the swastika, which showed up on the arm of one of the Bill Grundy punks and many places besides. In *Please Kill Me*, the oral history, Ron Asheton, whose deceptively simple guitar riffs propelled the Stooges, talked about how he had been obsessed with Nazi Germany since boyhood. "I'd wear SS pins to school, draw swastikas all over my books, draw Hitler mustaches on everyone's pictures, and draw little SS bolts on my arm," he said. Asheton evidently had not outgrown this obsession by the time he cofounded the Stooges, and he sometimes performed in full Nazi uniform, including a swastika armband. During the British punk explosion, Sid Vicious was often photographed in a swastika T-shirt, and Siouxsie Sioux sometimes wore a swastika armband; Vivienne Westwood, the designer who helped create the look of British punk, sold an ambiguous T-shirt that read "DESTROY" above the image of a swastika, an upside-down Jesus, and the Queen on a postage stamp. The Ramones evoked the Nazi Wehrmacht with "Blitzkrieg Bop," using ominous language to describe the innocent frenzy of "kids" at a rock 'n' roll concert. And one of the songs the Sex Pistols played at their final concert was "Belsen Was a Gas," a taunting song about a Nazi concentration camp: "Belsen was a gas, I heard the other day / In the open graves, where the Jews all lay."

Many punks insisted that they had no hidden agenda: their embrace of Nazi imagery, they said, was mere provocation, an attempt to shock mainstream society by flaunting symbols of evil, symbols of the enemy whom their parents' generation had not long ago defeated. (In the seventies, at the dawn of punk, the Nazi era was only thirty years in the past—about as far away then as the grunge era is today.) In *Please Kill Me*, Legs McNeil described Nazi chic as a reaction to the 1970s obsession with smiley faces and niceness; punks just wanted to be nasty instead. Bangs wasn't so sure. In 1979, in *The Village Voice*, he published "The White Noise Supremacists," an essay about racism in the punk scene. He had noticed the proliferation of swastikas at punk concerts in New York, and he understood that the symbol was a "way for kids to get a rise out of their parents and maybe the press." He worried, though, that "after a while this casual, even ironic embrace of the totems of bigotry crosses over into the real poison." He wrote that when he played a record by the soul singer Otis Redding at a party full of punk musicians and *Punk* journalists, he was asked, "What're you playing all that nigger disco shit for, Lester?" The essay was Bangs's apology for having once been, as he saw it, part of the problem—he, too, had used the word "nigger," ostensibly ironically. "Took me a long time to find it out," he wrote, "but those words are lethal, man, and you shouldn't just go slinging them around for effect."

The Otis Redding story is telling because it hints at the link between punk's rhetorical identity and its musical identity. The mainstream rock 'n' roll of the late seventies was often bluesy or funky, and the mainstream pop often had a disco beat. To choose the brisk and unfunky songs of the Ramones, instead, was to choose a white band that was ostentatiously uninterested in contemporary Black music—a white band that made rock 'n' roll seem like white music, much the way heavy metal had done, only with a more confrontational spirit. In America, this was the complicated way that punk rock paid tribute to the success and ubiquity of Black music: by classifying it as mainstream, by turning away from it, by insisting that a grimy newish form of rock 'n' roll was somehow more authentic than the multiracial sound of the radio. In *Please Kill Me*, one of the other founders of *Punk*, John Holmstrom, objects to Bangs's diagnosis of racism within the New York punk scene. "I mean, we weren't racists," Holmstrom says. "But we were unashamedly saying, 'We're white, and we're proud.' Like, they're black and they're proud."

With the rise of the Sex Pistols, punk acquired a new slogan, "Anarchy in the UK," and a new, markedly less polarizing symbol: the circled "A." The Sex Pistols were not espousing any particular political program: "anarchy" meant "chaos," and the circled "A" was a tribal identifier, or an open-source logo, scribbled and scratched and spray-painted on walls around the world. But some punks tried to take this slogan more seriously than the Sex Pistols did, celebrating not mere anarchy but *anarchism*, the political philosophy; they agitated for a society that would be radically egalitarian and radically free. Starting in 1977, a band called Crass helped popularize a style that some people called anarcho-punk. The band headquarters was an intentional community in the English countryside, from which Crass issued a series of prolix but invigorating punk records, with tinny guitar sounds and unexpectedly jaunty basslines. The band called for "anarchy and peace," denouncing consumerism and the Falklands War with equal vigor and specificity. One of the earliest Crass songs, "Punk Is Dead," argued that the genre had failed to live up to its own rhetoric. Steve Ignorant, the singer, disparaged Patti Smith and the Sex Pistols as mere corporate entertainers, not insurgents: "I watch and understand that it don't mean a thing / The scorpions might attack, but the system stole the sting." When the Exploited released "Punks Not Dead," three years later, it was partly a response to Crass, whom the singer and leader of the Exploited, known as Wattie, called "a big bunch of wankers." Wattie was an anarchist, too, but not one with an interest in political philosophy. He sang, "I'm not ashamed about getting drunk / And I don't care what you say / 'Cause I believe in anarchy."

At a Sex Pistols concert in July 1976, the opening act had been a brand-new band called the Clash. The members were fans of the Sex Pistols and soon became rivals: the self-titled debut album by the Clash arrived early the next year, six months before *Never Mind the Bollocks*. The members of the Clash were not quite anarcho-punks, and they recorded for a major label, CBS Records, as Steve Ignorant, from Crass, was happy to point out. (He sneered, "CBS promote the Clash / Ain't for revolution, it's just for cash.") But the Clash offered an idealistic alternative to the seething fury of the Sex Pistols. Perhaps the members knew that Malcolm McLaren viewed punk as a mischievous publicity stunt, but that didn't mean that they couldn't take it more seriously. The first single by the Clash was "White Riot," inspired by the Black rioters who fought with the police at the 1976 Notting Hill Carnival. The song was a boisterous sing-along anthem, with lyrics that expressed a complicated mixture of solidarity, envy, and guilt: "White riot, I wanna riot / White riot, a riot of my own."

From the beginning, the Clash's music bore the influence of reggae, which had been adopted as the rebellious young sound of Black Britain. At a concert in New York, in 1981, the band selected Grandmaster Flash and the Furious Five, the pioneering hip-hop group, as its opening act. (This cross-pollination of punk and hip-hop evidently didn't much impress the Clash's American fans, who booed Grandmaster Flash offstage.) The band members were ambitious and sometimes unpredictable: the Clash discography includes a patchy triple album named *Sandinista!*, in honor of the Nicaraguan socialist party; it also includes "Rock the Casbah," a convivial, disco-influenced track that became a Top 10 pop hit in America, and an eighties MTV staple. These musical hybrids and agitprop ballads could be awkward, but they also showed how far punky idealism could stretch, and how popular it could be. When Lester Bangs went to England to visit the Clash, in the late seventies, he wasn't sure what to expect, but he came away convinced that the music was good, and that the band members were, too. "There is a mood around the Clash, call it whatever you want, that is positive in a way I've never sensed around almost any other band," he wrote. "Something unpretentiously moral, and something both self-affirming and life-affirming." This seemed to him like proof that punk rock could be a force for decency.

The Clash did more than any group to combat the perception that punk was inherently nihilist, or maybe even fascist. The rise of punk in Britain was roughly coterminous with the formation, in 1976, of an avowedly antifascist activist group called Rock Against Racism, which had been founded in reaction to a couple of rock stars. One of them was David Bowie, the shape-shifting rock 'n' roll auteur, who had recently reinvented himself as a decadent and sinister character called the Thin White Duke, and who said, in a 1976 *Playboy* interview, "I believe very strongly in fascism." The other rock star was Eric Clapton, who the same year reportedly interrupted a concert in Birmingham to inveigh, drunkenly, against immigration: "Send them all back," he reportedly said. "The Black dogs and coons." Alarmed by what seemed like a trend, the RAR organizers recruited punk and reggae bands to push back. This movement partly reversed the logic of the initial punk explosion: now the punks were being cast as advocates of liberal tolerance, denouncing the shocking views of mainstream rockers. (Bowie recanted in 1977, saying, "I am *not* a fascist"; Clapton, more circumspect, wrote, in his 2007 autobiography, "Since then I have learned to keep my opinions to myself.") The Clash was one of the headliners at a 1978 RAR concert that drew something like a hundred thousand attendees to Victoria Park in London. Onstage, the Clash's singer and guitarist Joe Strummer wore a T-shirt emblazoned with a different shocking symbol: not a circled A, and certainly not a swastika, but a red star and a submachine gun, which were the logo of the Red Army Faction, also known as the Baader-Meinhof Group, the leftist German guerrilla movement.

I didn't listen to the Clash in high school. Perhaps I was frightened away by MTV's embrace of "Rock the Casbah." Or perhaps the band's impassioned but midtempo rock 'n' roll just didn't sound "punk" enough for me. And yet I absorbed, second- or thirdhand, the Clash's conviction that punk should be linked to progressive politics. I ordered a bunch of buttons from some hippie mail-order catalog—anti-racism, anti-war, pro-choice—and affixed them to the front of my nylon flight jacket, which was black with orange lining, in keeping with punk-rock tradition. I was a founding member of the gay-rights group at my high school, and I started reading *High Times* magazine not because I had any experience with marijuana, or interest in it, but strictly because I believed in drug legalization. I sought out more peripheral causes. On record-buying trips to New York, I picked up copies of *Revolutionary Worker*, a Maoist newspaper, and *The Shadow*, an anarchist newspaper. Affixed to the wall of my bedroom, printed on sprocket-holed computer paper, were the lyrics to "Stars and Stripes of Corruption," a thoroughgoing Dead Kennedys polemic in which Jello Biafra brayed about the evils of the American empire, and the passivity of a citizenry that didn't realize or care that it was being "farmed like worms." For me, punk meant rejecting mainstream music and rejecting mainstream politics, too.

There is a tension between these two kinds of rejection, although it didn't trouble me then. Part of the appeal of punk was that most people didn't like it; punks loved to antagonize the non-punk world. (Dead Kennedys also had a song called "MTV—Get Off the Air," which lambasted the network for appealing to "the lowest common denominator.") But if the whole point of punk was to be different, then what was the point of punk politics? Did we really hope to attain and wield political power? To remake society? I never expected that America would belatedly come around to the Dead Kennedys. So why would I have expected that America would ever come to share my various political convictions? There is nothing wrong with supporting unpopular causes, of course: sometimes those causes spread and triumph, and sometimes causes that never catch on are nevertheless righteous. But there is something especially perverse about adopting unpopular causes in part because they are unpopular, and then pretending to be outraged by that unpopularity. This paradox is probably built into punk, which can never quite decide if it wants to win over the mainstream or just enjoy an autonomous existence in the margins. And it might also be built into the idea of "radical" politics, which tend to attract a certain number of people who love being out of step with most of the population, and want to remain that way.

There is no reason, of course, why punk politics need be left-wing, or liberal. One of the many British punk albums that arrived in 1977 was *All Skrewed Up*, by Skrewdriver, a band that was less well-known for its rowdy songs than for its rowdy fans, who made it hard for the group to book concerts. Skrewdriver was closely associated with the skinhead movement, which was famously tough and often working-class but not necessarily political. Most of the early Skrewdriver songs were about not much in particular: "Backstreet kids, just drink and fight / Backstreet kids, well that's all right." But after a couple of years, Skrewdriver disappeared; the lead singer, Ian Stuart, returned in the early eighties with a new lineup, and a new sense of purpose. One of the band's comeback singles was called "White Power," which became an anthem for the band and for a worldwide movement of neo-Nazi punk. The new mission required a new sound, so the band's gruff, slipshod punk gave way to earnest hard rock, with Stuart's rather wobbly vocals very loud in the mix, to make sure everyone could hear the words. I have sometimes wondered how different—how much scarier—the eighties punk scene might have been, if Skrewdriver had been more musically formidable.

Stuart's movement never conquered the punk world, where neo-Nazis remained a despised minority. But neither did it go away. A small but alarming cohort of like-minded bands emerged around the world, turning Stuart into a neo-Nazi ringleader. (He died in a car crash in 1993 and was eulogized as a martyr to the cause of white power.) In 1987, the Anti-Defamation League released an influential report warning that there were several hundred "skinhead activists" in America, "preaching"—and some-times practicing—"violence against Blacks, Jews, and other minorities." This report helped push coverage of skinheads into the mainstream: the next year, Oprah Winfrey interviewed a pair of white-power skinheads on her new talk show. The ongoing threat posed by neo-Nazis inspired some punks and some skinheads to fight back, sometimes through groups like Anti-Racist Action, which turned out, like so many punk phenomena, to be more enduring and more influential than anyone might have predicted. Organizations like ARA inspired the modern antifa movement, which seized news headlines during the Donald Trump era by being willing and indeed eager to fight a new generation of enemies on the right, including the Proud Boys, a "Western chauvinist" group that favored the same kind of Fred Perry shirts that British skinheads had worn. Both the rise of antifa and the rise of the Proud Boys represented, among other things, yet another manifestation of punk politics, even if relatively few people realized it.

Tougher Than Punk

At the dawn of the 1980s, a punk-rock hooligan called John Joseph left his native New York. He had enlisted in the navy and moved to Norfolk, Virginia, where one night he drove off-base to see a punk band, or what he thought was a punk band. What he found, though, was something else: an all-Black group from Washington, DC, with a background in jazz and a growing interest in Rastafarianism, playing so fast and with such eerie intensity that they seemed to be vibrating. In his autobiography, Joseph remembered thinking that he had just witnessed "the greatest band in the world." The debut Bad Brains single, "Pay to Cum," was released in 1980, around the time of Joseph's encounter, and it made punk rock sound, by comparison, like whatever punk rock had been supposed to replace. (It buzzed along for ninety seconds at about three hundred beats per minute, which was nearly twice the tempo of an average song by the Ramones.) The music of Bad Brains, and of a generation of similarly aggressive American bands, came to be known as hardcore punk, commonly shortened to "hard-core." And in the early eighties, hardcore took root in cities around America, often adopted by young men—"kids," they called themselves—like John Joseph, who were looking for something tougher than punk.

Hardcore was both an intensification of punk and a rejection of it: a double-negative genre, rebelling against the punk rebellion from within. Instead of cultivating bright, spiky hairdos, some of the kids shaved bald, sometimes out of kinship with British skinheads. Where traditional punks just bobbed up and down ("pogoing," they called it), hardcore kids jumped off stages and collided with one another on the dance floor, forming violent "pits" that resembled fistfights, and often inspired them. In *American Hardcore*, Steven Blush's lively oral history of the movement, Joseph recalled that when he returned to his hometown, the city's punk scene suddenly seemed rather quaint and weak. "We'd get in the fucking cars, go to New York, and wreak havoc," he said. "People didn't even know how to stage-dive."

New York, which helped lead the American punk explosion, was late to adopt hardcore, which arrived in force elsewhere first. After Joseph left the navy—secretly, and illicitly—he stopped first in Washington, DC, which nurtured a fistful of other hardcore bands besides Bad Brains. Joseph knew some of the kids there, including Ian MacKaye, the leader of Minor Threat, which was for a few years the platonic ideal of a hardcore band, assembling perfect little bundles of musical adrenaline, frantic but tuneful. (In high school, I listened obsessively to the band's *Complete Discography* CD, which contained twenty-six songs and which just about fit on one side of a ninety-minute cassette.) MacKaye's lyrics were feisty but not avowedly political, and in an interview years later, he recalled that he had avoided singing about President Ronald Reagan, whom he loathed, because he wanted his music to outlive Reagan's presidency. Perhaps. But perhaps he just wasn't all that interested. Hardcore was an insular genre, less concerned with grand political debates than with small intra-tribal disputes. Minor Threat's first record included a forty-six-second-long song called "Straight Edge," in which MacKaye found a combative way to deliver a mild message:

I'm a person, just like you
But I've got better things to do
Than sit around and fuck my head
Hang out with the living dead

All he really meant was that he didn't use drugs or alcohol, unlike some of the punks he knew. And yet this declaration became the basis of an unlikely subculture: ever since the early eighties, there have been "straight-edge" acolytes and bands around the world, using militant language in defense of sobriety. For many years I was straight-edge, too, though somewhat ironically, and mainly by default, since none of my friends really cared about getting high or getting drunk. (By the nineties, the militance and self-righteousness of the straight-edge movement had become a running joke, even among those of us who were, in fact, straight-edge.) If punk rock was antisocial, hardcore was often anti-antisocial, combining a general truculence with a pious commitment to community-mindedness. "Don't go out alone, go with a friend / You might need him in the end," MacKaye sang. He was expounding on the joy of fellowship, and the necessity of self-defense. Or maybe it was the other way around.

MacKaye's best friend was Henry Rollins, who was working in a

Washington, DC, ice cream shop and leading a bare-bones hardcore band called S.O.A., for State of Alert, when he agreed to move across the country to join Black Flag, one of the first and biggest and best bands in the hardcore universe. Ever since the late 1970s, there had been a fashionable and creative punk-rock scene in Hollywood, but Black Flag was different: a feral fraternity in street clothes, from the unhip Southern California town of Hermosa Beach. Police officers often raided Black Flag's concerts, and this conflict inspired a furious, scene-centric protest song called "Police Story": "This fucking city is run by pigs / They take the rights away from all the kids!" The band's leader was Greg Ginn, a guitarist whose scabrous and squally playing made Black Flag sound at once angry and slightly psychedelic. Rollins was a theatrical front man, shouting about depression and insanity while growing increasingly muscular and increasingly shaggy—in the course of a few years, he went from looking like a skinhead to looking like a caveman. After Black Flag broke up, in 1986, Rollins became an all-purpose countercultural icon, touring the world with his own band and as a poet and speaker, and working as an actor, a model, and a radio DJ. In 1994, he published the tour diaries he kept during his time in Black Flag, which provided an edifying record of the atmosphere at Black Flag concerts. One entry, written after a 1983 London gig, documented the emerging cultural divide between English punk and American hardcore. "A man with a mohawk started to fuck with Greg and I beat him up," Rollins wrote. "His mohawk made a good handle to hold onto when I beat his face into the floor. The bouncers were afraid to break it up. They stood nearby and asked me to please let the guy go. Punk rock shit head."

Hardcore scenes emerged all over the country, reflecting their host cities. There were hockey-obsessed hardcore bands in Boston, and quirky, political hardcore bands in Austin, Texas. The Bay Area had not just Dead Kennedys but also Flipper, which mocked the generic reputation of hardcore by releasing a deadpan debut album known as *ALBUM—GENERIC FLIPPER*, or *GENERIC FLIPPER ALBUM*, and which was not really hardcore, and not at all generic. Inevitably, hardcore took hold in New York, too, as a strange and streetwise mishmash. Bad Brains resettled there and increasingly reinforced their frenetic songs with off-speed passages known as "mosh" parts. (The word may have derived from the Jamaican term "mash up," meaning "destroy"—a rough analogue of "kill," in the show-business sense.) A band called Agnostic Front used skinhead imagery to build a fearsome reputation, denouncing "Nazi hypocrism" while also disparaging "minorities" with "gold chains" who were abusing the welfare system. (The lead singer, Roger Miret, was a Cuban immigrant, and so, by many definitions, he was a minority, too.) John Joseph returned to town and became the lead singer of a band called Cro-Mags, which in 1986 released a tough and swaggering album called *The Age of Quarrel*. (The title was derived from a Sanskrit term, and it reflected Joseph's affiliation with the Hare Krishna movement.) A bratty hardcore band called the Beastie Boys found huge success, but only by becoming a bratty hip-hop group. And the scene was transformed, in the second half of the decade, by the arrival of Ray Cappo, a Connecticut transplant whose band, Youth of Today, led a straight-edge revival by playing youth-friendly matinee concerts at CBGB, the same club that had nurtured New York's decadent punk scene a decade before. Cappo was clean-cut and athletic-looking—suspiciously so, I thought, when I was discovering punk and hardcore a few years later. I had embraced punk in search of strangeness, and much early-nineties hardcore struck me as distastefully normal and not a little macho. Cappo barked, "Physically strong / Morally straight / Positive youth / We're the Youth of Today!" That sounded to me like the opposite of punk. In time, though, I grew to love the odd hybrids and innovations of New York hardcore. (It was transformed yet again in the nineties, as bands embraced the rhythms and rhymes of hip-hop, creating an early version of rap-rock.) I loved, too, the way hardcore bands kept finding new ways to redefine punk, or indeed rebuke it.

The first hardcore show I saw was in Boston, in 1991—the same trip during which I first encountered Greil Marcus's writings. The headliner was Fugazi, a band from Washington, DC, that included Ian MacKaye, who was then working to expand the possibilities of hardcore. Fugazi was one of my favorite bands: restless and imaginative, with reggae-inspired basslines and impressionistic lyrics, many of them murmured or moaned, rather than shouted. And I think I was expecting an audience full of fans as reverent as I was. But Fugazi drew lots of unreformed hardcore kids, and so the atmosphere inside the club was tense. (It was St. Patrick's Day in Boston, which tends to be a rowdy occasion, even when there isn't a hardcore show going on.) I saw skinheads there for the first time in my life, and I tried to figure out how scared I should be. MacKaye regarded the crowd with patient disapproval, searching for some way to get everyone to stop shoving and hitting and stage-diving. At one point, when the music calmed down but the slam-dancers did not, he said, "I want to see, sort of, the correlation between the movement—*here*—and the sound—*there*." And then he sang a song called "Suggestion," about sexual assault, pausing near the end to dedicate it to a woman who had been "molested," he said, at a recent Fugazi concert.

There must have been a couple thousand people there that afternoon, and one of them was Mark Greif, a scholar and cultural critic, who mentioned the concert in a perceptive essay about his own formative but complicated experience with punk and hardcore. He adored Fugazi, and he remembered being "mesmerized," on that afternoon, by the "pointless energy" of the kids in the pit but also dispirited by it. "I sorrowed that all this seemed unworthy of the band, the music, the unnameable it pointed to," he wrote. I was struck by those words, because I remember having a nearly opposite reaction. The tension and hints of violence were thrilling, because they made me feel I was not simply watching a concert but witnessing a drama, and not one guaranteed to end well. And I thought that Fugazi's artful music was enriched, not diminished, by the fact that it attracted so many fans who seemed not to completely understand the people onstage, nor be understood by them. I heard the music differently after that—now it was inseparable from the noise and menace of that show. The unruly crowd seemed like proof that Fugazi was not merely a band but a *hardcore* band, still, and the people in that club seemed to agree that the distinction meant something, even if they would not have agreed about what that was.

An Incantation

A year after that concert, in the summer of 1992, Fugazi played outside the United States Capitol, as part of what was billed as a protest against "the radical rightward swing of the Supreme Court." Clarence Thomas had been appointed to the court the previous year, despite having been accused of sexual harassment, and the court had recently ruled to make it easier for states to regulate abortion. The members of Fugazi played in front of a banner that read, TURN OFF YOUR TV!, and one of the first songs in the set was "Reclamation," which begins with what resembles a pro-choice statement of principles: "These are our demands / We want control of our bodies / Decisions will now be ours." Fugazi was less insular than Minor Threat had been, and more willing to engage the wider world. Halfway through the set, the band's other main singer, Guy Picciotto, briefly addressed the Supreme Court. "If their laws don't reflect our reality, we don't have to fuckin' obey 'em," he said, as if he were leading an insurgency—and in a sense he was.

Within the hardcore-punk subculture, though, Fugazi was not an insurgency but the establishment: one of the most popular and influential underground bands in the country, able to sell hundreds of thousands of copies of its albums through its own label, Dischord Records, which Mac-Kaye had cofounded in 1980. By the time of the 1992 protest concert, Mac-Kaye had been hardcore royalty for over a decade, and like many of the most powerful figures in the worlds of punk and hardcore, he and his band-mates were all white men. You might say that the true insurgents on the 1992 bill were the members of Bikini Kill, which played first: three women and a man, bashing out urgent and unapologetically primitive punk rock, and sometimes switching instruments between songs. Often, the center of attention was Kathleen Hanna, finding new ways to be confrontational—to be *punk*. On a grainy video of the concert, you can watch her jump, shake, bang her head, and suddenly stand still on her tiptoes, declaring, "I can sell my body if I wanna / God knows you already sold your mind."

Bikini Kill had been a band for less than two years and didn't have anything like Fugazi's fan base. But already Bikini Kill had become one of the most contentious—and, it was becoming clear, important—bands in the country: the soundtrack of an emerging movement called riot grrrl, which was devoted to the proposition that punk rock and feminism sorely needed each other. In 2010, the cultural scholar Sara Marcus published *Girls to the Front*, an indispensable history that documented the way riot grrrl took root, simultaneously, in Olympia, Washington, where some key members, including Hanna, attended the Evergreen State College, and Washington, DC, where the hardcore scene was a source of both inspiration and frustration. MacKaye was one early supporter, and he produced the group's first record, a six-song mini-album called *Bikini Kill*, which appeared later in 1992. But Marcus discovered that MacKaye didn't want to share the stage with Bikini Kill at that Capitol protest. "He felt that having two bands would tip the event from being a rally to being a concert," she wrote. "Plus, he said, two bands meant twice as much time for the cops to come and shut off the power." The backdrop was a source of tension, too: Marcus reported that MacKaye wanted a banner that read 30 YEARS, in reference to the idea that the forthcoming presidential election would shape the court for a generation, while a representative from the riot grrrl movement wanted something more specific, like ABORT THE COURT. (Apparently neither side loved or hated TURN OFF YOUR TV!, which is why it was selected.) The members of Fugazi were kicking against the political hierarchy, but the members of Bikini Kill were kicking against the hardcore hierarchy, too.

Riot grrrl was as much a literary movement as a musical one, perhaps more so: its breakthrough hit was not a record but a zine, *riot grrrl*, which appeared in 1991, the work of a group of like-minded women, including Hanna. It wasn't clear who was in charge—indeed, that was part of the idea, as a future issue explained: "There is no editor and there is no concrete vision or expectation, or there shouldn't be." The 1990s were a golden era of zines, enabled by a technological interregnum: cheap copy shops were everywhere, and they hadn't yet been made obsolete by the Internet. (A few years later, I had a friend who worked at Kinko's, the corporate copy shop, and stole hundred-dollar copy cards, which he sold at hardcore shows for ten dollars apiece to kids who had fanzines or flyers to print.) That first issue of *riot grrrl* described an uprising that was already underway:

> There has been a proliferation of angry grrrl zines in recent months, mainly due to the queezy feeling we girls get in our stomachs when we contemplate the general lack of girl power in society as a whole, and in the punk rock underground specifically. In this long hot summer we are presently experiencing, some of us girls thought it was time we put our collective angry heads together and do a mini-zine, and put it out as often as possible.

One of the movement's goals was to rewrite punk history, to show that women had played an important role. The riot grrrls championed precursors like the Go-Go's, who emerged from the Los Angeles punk scene to become eighties pop idols; Poly Styrene, the gale-force lead singer of X-Ray Spex, from the initial British punk explosion; and Joan Jett, the rock star who brought punk attitude to mainstream radio in the eighties. (A group called Bratmobile paid tribute by recording a puckish version of "Cherry Bomb," the 1976 single by the Runaways, Jett's first band.) Another of its goals was to expand the idea of what punk could be and do. The members of Bikini Kill published a zine to be distributed at concerts, which was full of instigation and advice: how to start a band; how to understand "white privilege"; how to respond to anti-gay slurs; how to cope with harassment; how to fight back. Most important, the members of Bikini Kill made the whole enterprise seem like mischievous fun, like joining a secret society. "The revolution is about going to the playground with your best girlfriends," one manifesto declared. "You are hanging upside down on the bars and all the blood is rushing to your head. It's a euphoric feeling. the boys can see our underwear and we don't really care." Bikini Kill's best-loved song was "Rebel Girl," which starts with a brilliant bit of misdirection, as Hanna cries out, "That girl thinks she's the queen of the neighborhood!" It sounds like an indictment, but the song is a celebration and a vindication: the girl who thinks she's the coolest turns out to be absolutely correct.

It is not hard to understand why the riot grrrls felt alienated by the "punk rock underground," where all-male bands were very much the norm, and where all-male bands that made it a point to talk about sexual assault during concerts, as Fugazi did, were very much the exception. The world of punk was a violent place, figuratively and often literally; many punks viewed mainstream pop music as disagreeably soft and feminine, while celebrating their own bands as gratifyingly hard and masculine. (This attitude was an inheritance from rock 'n' roll, where "soft rock" was often an insult. Few punk bands, likewise, ever bragged about playing *soft*core punk.) What is more puzzling about the riot grrrl movement is why these women, many of them conversant in feminist theory and sympathetic to any number of left-wing causes, were dedicated to something as regressive— as conservative, much of the time—as punk rock. In Marcus's *Girls to the Front*, Michelle Noel, a DJ from Tacoma, Washington, explained that her punk identity preexisted her riot grrrl identity. "There was a possibility that I could change punk, 'cause I belonged there," she said. "It didn't feel possible to change the rest of the world—because I didn't feel *part* of the rest of the world." And Marcus describes a riot grrrl party from 1993, when the movement's energy was beginning to wane, where someone kept playing

"Closer to Fine," by the Indigo Girls, the folk duo. It is an astonishing song, a fervent ode to uncertainty that found a place on MTV, and the Indigo Girls sometimes put their celebrity in service of activism. (A few months before that riot grrrl party, the Indigo Girls had been surprise guest performers at the March on Washington for Lesbian, Gay, and Bi Equal Rights and Liberation.) But one of the riot grrrls was not impressed. "If I hear that goddamn 'I went to the fountain' song one more time," she said, "I'm gonna kill people." After all, the Indigo Girls may have been feminist, but they weren't really punk.

Should that have mattered? It was easy enough to accept the argument that punk rock needed feminism. But what about the corollary, that feminism needed punk rock? In the early nineties, there was no shortage of music made by women. Why shouldn't a liberal, feminist-minded listener have gravitated toward folk music, instead, or gospel, or R&B, or Afropop, or any number of genres *not* primarily associated with bellowing white guys? Many riot grrrls wondered this, too. *The Riot Grrrl Collection*, a 2013 compendium of zines and other artifacts, reproduces a series of questions that Hanna wrote in a notebook in 1991. The first one strikes at the heart of the new movement she was helping to lead: "How can we make our scenes less White in both numbers + ideology? How can we best support/ educate + draw from non-punk feminists? Should we?" A couple of years later, a zine author named Ramdasha Bikceem described her mixed feelings about a recent riot grrrl convention. "I think I was one of the only 3 black kids there," she wrote. "I mean Riot Grrrl calls for a change, but I question who it's including." In theory, riot grrrl was open to every woman and girl who wanted to fight sexism. In practice, part of what gave the movement its identity and its energy was its devotion to a particular variant of rock 'n' roll. A 1994 flyer for a band called Heavens to Betsy offered an earnest apology: "We often centered on white middle class sexism and white middle class girls and therefore excluded women of color and white working class women's issues from our discussions." A more inclusive movement might have drawn in a more representative cross-section of American women—but then, it probably wouldn't have had anything to do with punk, or perhaps with music.

Riot grrrl was very theoretical. It was influenced by feminist theory, helping to push academic ideas about gender oppression into the world of popular culture. But it was also theoretical in a different sense. "Riot Grrrl always existed first and foremost as an incantation," Sara Marcus wrote. There were relatively few riot grrrls and only a handful of prominent riot grrrl bands, and even Bikini Kill, by far the most popular of them, spent most of the movement's heyday touring as an opening act or else headlining small clubs, before disbanding in 1997. In mainstream accounts, riot grrrl often came across as a jumble of punkish fashions ("round-collared, cinched-waist dresses" and "heavy black high-top boots," according to *The New York Times*), confrontational slogans ("They write SLUT on their tummies with Magic Markers," *Rolling Stone* explained), and noise. The term got applied to just about any woman who happened to be in the vicinity of an electric guitar, especially if she could be described as somehow angry. In 1995, an interviewer from *Rolling Stone* asked Alanis Morissette, then a rising star, if she had ever been called "a poseur, a prefab riot-grrrl substitute"; she laughingly said she had not. To many people who weren't paying close attention, the ultimate riot grrrl seemed to be Courtney Love, who led the band Hole. She was a riotous figure in her own right, but one who was actively hostile to the movement. Love reportedly once hit Hanna, backstage at a music festival. And *Live Through This*, Hole's volcanic 1994 album, ends with Love sneering at unnamed revolutionaries from Olympia: "Everyone's the same / And so are you!"

While riot grrrls endured plenty of abuse, much of it from within the punk scene, the movement had broad appeal and lasting influence. It seems likely that the riot grrrl moment made both listeners and record executives pay more attention to women rock acts of all sorts, from the indie singer-songwriter Liz Phair, who emerged in 1993, to Meredith Brooks, who had a huge hit in 1997 with a song called "Bitch." ("I'm a bitch, I'm a lover / I'm a child, I'm a mother," she snarled, although the main message was much more conciliatory: in the song, a woman offers gratitude and even sympathy to the man who loves her.) It seems possible that without riot grrrl, there might never have been a pop group from England, the Spice Girls, that was devoted to the concept of "girl power." One of the movement's most enduring figures turned out to be Carrie Brownstein, who played in a riot grrrl band called Excuse 17 before cofounding the acclaimed and long-running indie band Sleater-Kinney and satirizing Pacific Northwest culture on the television show *Portlandia*. And there is no better example of riot grrrl as incantation than Pussy Riot, the Russian punk rock band and protest act, which many people have heard of and precious few have actually heard. The most amazing thing about the old riot grrrl zines and records is how contemporary the language is. "White privilege" and "safe space" and anger at "slut"-shaming: in many ways, the arguments of riot grrrl are the arguments of modern feminism, modern politics, modern culture. The music has remained a bit of a secret, but the incantation is everywhere.

Feasting on Crumbs

It is possible to construct an entire history of popular music around the changing role of scarcity. In the seventies and eighties, relatively few records were distributed nationwide, and only a fraction of them were readily accessible. Listeners were restricted by the tastes of their local radio DJs and record-store clerks. Some magazines made adventurous recommendations, but many of those magazines were obscure, too. Most important, you could only listen to as much music as you could afford to buy, and this financial constraint encouraged a certain amount of aesthetic conservatism: taking a chance on a new band, or a new genre, could be expensive. By the 2000s, of course, the Internet was making it easy and virtually free to discover and sample music, and in the 2010s, many listeners were migrating to streaming services, which offered unlimited music for free, or for a nominal fee. In retrospect, the eighties and nineties were a period of transition and limited abundance, as a cottage industry sprouted up alongside the mainstream music business. Obscure records increasingly appeared in local record shops, some of them imports from Britain and elsewhere, and some of them homegrown, maybe handmade. After I discovered punk, there was no activity I liked better than record shopping. Matt and I would head to downtown New Haven, to scour the local outlets: Strawberries, a four-story shop that was part of a regional chain; Cutler's, a beloved local mom-and-pop store; and, best of all, Rhymes, a dimly lit punk shop above a movie theater. My mother would give me five dollars so I could buy myself lunch from Subway. But we had as much food as I wanted at home and not nearly as many records as I wanted, so I would skip lunch and invest the money in my musical education.

In England, the punk explosion was followed by an eruption of colorful new wave and pop music, and it spun off some mainstream-rock acts, including the Police, who conquered arenas with an extraordinarily agile mixture of rock and reggae, and Billy Idol, a former London punk who became a cartoonish rock star in America, to the enduring puzzlement of many Brits, who seemed glad to be rid of him. The punk explosion also made room for the emergence of moody, semipopular bands like the Cure and the Smiths, who occupied a small but secure niche in the musical establishment. As a newly minted punk, I had no interest in buying records like that—they seemed both too sedate and too theatrical. (I remember making a sharp if rather arbitrary distinction between punks, like me, and goths, who wore black and took themselves seriously, and whose musical tastes ranged from synthesizer pop to heavy metal to dance music.) In time I was won over by these English bands that found ways to cool the hot rage of punk into something smoother and slyer, often emphasizing songwriting instead of noise-making. The punks prized audacity, but I'm not sure if there was ever a punk band as audacious as the Smiths, led by a singer known only as Morrissey, who refused to apologize for his odd, half-crooning voice, or for his half-ironic lyrics about despair and desire. He all but dared listeners to take his self-pity seriously:

> Now I know how Joan of Arc felt
> As the flames rose
> To her Roman nose
> And her Walkman started to melt.

In the United States, Talking Heads, led by David Byrne, managed a similar trick, emerging from the seventies punk scene to create a series of wry, bittersweet post-punk records. And probably no American post-punk act was more important than R.E.M., an Athens, Georgia, band known for strummy songs that were cryptic but somehow openhearted. Nothing about R.E.M. suggested grandeur, but by the end of the eighties, the band was emerging as one of the most popular in America—so popular, in fact, that it never occurred to me to listen to an R.E.M. album until years afterward, let alone buy one.

Many of the records that Matt and I bought were, instead, products of the proudly independent labels that had emerged in the aftermath of the punk explosion. This was not an entirely new development: small record labels had helped fuel the rise of R&B and rock 'n' roll and just about every other genre, and many of the major labels had once been independent, including Atlantic Records, which was founded in 1947 and didn't become part of a corporate conglomerate until twenty years later, when it was bought by Warner Bros. But traditionally, small labels were just as hungry for sales and hits as big ones, and often hungrier. By contrast, the punk-inspired indie labels—Alternative Tentacles, Dischord, Epitaph, Homestead, Lookout! Records, SST, Touch and Go, and countless more—had a paradoxical mission. They aimed to engage in commerce without quite going commercial. A successful indie label, like any small business, built up its customer base by cultivating a reputation for quality and reliability. And the scarcity of music was what made those labels so influential: a large but limited number of indie albums wound up on the shelves of shops nationwide, and so those that did were virtually guaranteed to sell at least marginally well. (I would often spend my sandwich money on a tape by an unfamiliar band, solely because I trusted the label that released it.) But the labels also had to find ways to assure customers that they weren't merely in it for the money. Dischord, for instance, made a point of keeping prices unusually low, contributing to a general perception that the major labels, especially, were a rip-off. The indies offered a good deal, with an implicit message: life could be better and more affordable in the margins.

Like many small-business owners, the musicians and proprietors who created this world tended to be industrious and thrifty. In *Our Band Could Be Your Life,* his 2001 book about the American independent-label scene in the eighties, the critic Michael Azerrad noticed how hard everyone seemed to be working. The outrageousness of seventies punk was fading, replaced by a more pragmatic sensibility, which he cherished. "It was liberating on many levels, especially from what many perceived as the selfishness, greed, and arrogance of Reagan's America," he wrote. "The indie underground made a modest way of life not just attractive but a downright moral imperative." Azerrad emphasized not the chaotic atmosphere at Black Flag concerts but the "selfless work ethic" of the band members— Greg Ginn, the guitarist, founded and ran SST, one of the scene's most influential labels. Steve Albini, from the caustic Chicago band Big Black, insisted on doing band business through handshake deals, with no paperwork. And even as Albini became one of the rock world's most celebrated producers, with clients that included Nirvana, he refused the title of "producer," which he found pretentious, insisting on a more modest "recorded by" credit, instead. Sonic Youth was known in America for occupying a middle ground between punk band and art project, and for carefully dissonant and tangled guitar lines. But one member, Lee Ranaldo, told Azerrad that during tours of Europe, he noticed that the local bands didn't have the "work ethic" of American indie acts. He sounded proud, maybe even a bit patriotic.

I was nowhere near prescient enough to have had any idea that this world of little bands and labels and record shops might not last forever. In college, I was sometimes tasked with taking unwanted major-label records and CDs to the local record shops, to trade them in for a smaller number of obscurities that we might actually play. I loved record stores so much that I became an employee, working shifts at a handful of them, starting with Discount Records, a Harvard Square institution that had evolved into a charmless corporate CD store—"No discount, no records," as my punk friends liked to remind me. (The highlight, by far, was the day I sold a copy of Hole's *Live Through This* to PJ Harvey, the intense English singer and songwriter. She barely spoke, and I wasn't even sure it was her until she presented her credit card.) Eventually I took a leave of absence from Harvard so I could spend even more time around records. For a year, I worked weekdays in the warehouse of Newbury Comics, a local retail chain, where my main responsibility was to affix price tags to CDs. On the side, I worked as a clerk and buyer at a small shop in Harvard Square, where I got a chance to try not to be one of those obnoxious guys behind the record-store counter. Actually, I'm not sure that record-store clerks truly deserved the reputation they acquired for being "snobs" and "totally elitist," as a customer in the 2000 record-store movie *High Fidelity* put it. Even when record stores were prospering, a job behind the counter was typically a low-paying position in the service sector. And like most retail professionals, we record-store clerks sometimes struggled to meet the exacting and contradictory demands of the people we served. Many of them, I noticed, wanted or expected me to share their enthusiasm about whatever they were buying: "This record is *amazing*, right?" It was always a stressful question, because it obliged me to work out a response that was both friendly and truthful, and to do it quickly. In an exchange like that, even a brief pause might be interpreted as evidence of judgmentalism.

From behind the counter, I also got a better sense of how the record-store economy worked. In his book, Azerrad couldn't help but sound disapproving when he explained that many popular indie bands, including Sonic Youth, ended up signing contracts with conglomerates. "Once they went to a major label, an important connection to the underground community was invariably lost," he wrote, about the eighties stalwarts. And yet the profusion of record stores in the 1990s was in large part a tribute to the success and power of major labels. For a store like the one I worked at, new independent-label releases were essentially a tool to bring customers through the door; the two- or three-dollar margin just wasn't worth much, especially when you subtracted the wholesale cost of records you ordered but couldn't sell. Used records and CDs, often mainstream titles, were more profitable, especially if you could acquire them cheaply: from someone cleaning out a garage, say, or from a business going under. (I remember getting a strange feeling of déjà vu one afternoon, while flipping through used records at a different shop. I talked to the owners and learned that they had bought out the stock of Rhymes, in New Haven, which had gone out of business years earlier—I was staring at all the records I had painstakingly decided *not* to buy, back in high school.) Even better, for a little record store, were promotional copies, which were known as cutouts, in reference to the holes that were punched into the jackets, to indicate that they were not to be sold. Little shops like ours didn't care, and we loved the fat margins, so the resourceful women who owned the shop were in touch with mysterious characters who somehow acquired boxes full of promotional copies of whatever CDs were in demand. Even at a quirky Cambridge record store like ours, most people who came through the door wanted to buy *popular* music. There was a whole industry devoted to giving those people what they wanted—an industry so big and so profitable, especially in the nineties, that all sorts of funny little businesses could thrive underfoot, feasting on crumbs.

Stubborn Purists

In the fall of 1994, a year after I arrived at Harvard, Boston was the site of one of the year's biggest and most notorious punk-rock shows. Green Day had agreed to play a free concert in conjunction with the local alternative-rock station, WFNX, at the Hatch Shell, an outdoor venue alongside the Charles River. There are many theories of what went wrong. It was certainly a bad idea, in retrospect, to allow Snapple, a sponsor, to distribute free bottles of juice to the crowd—Snapple bottles turned out to be more aerodynamic than anyone had realized. But the main problem was that Green Day was simply too popular. *Dookie*, the band's breakthrough album, had arrived earlier that year, and it was on its way to becoming a blockbuster, eventually transforming Green Day into probably the most popular punk band ever. About seventy thousand people reportedly turned up at the Hatch Shell, overwhelming the barriers and eventually the band, which managed about half a dozen songs before retreating in the face of flying Snapple. There were dozens of arrests, and the local television stations had to tell their audience who, exactly, had inspired such a fuss. "They have been called 'punk rock's hyperactive problem children,'" one anchor explained, and perhaps some older viewers felt a warm pang of nostalgia. Nearly two decades after the Sex Pistols' encounter with Bill Grundy, punk rock was still causing trouble.

The nineties punk revival had begun, accidentally, in 1986, with the launch of one of those American independent labels. This one was called Sub Pop, and it was based in Seattle, where, like many of the best indie labels, it cultivated a distinctive style. Sub Pop bands were unusual, in the post-punk world, for their fascination with hard rock, and they found ways to recuperate the kind of meaty, bluesy riffs that many punk bands had been eager to abjure. In 1989, as Sub Pop was becoming an indie-rock brand name, one of the label's musicians told a reporter that the local sound was "hard music played to a slow tempo." The reporter was Everett True, an English journalist in town to report on the underground scene. And the musician was Kurt Cobain, who loved punk rock but didn't aspire, exactly, to play it. In the indie-label world that nurtured Nirvana, "punk" was used in both the broad sense, the way Matt used it when compiling my miscellaneous "punk" mixtape, and a narrower sense, the way the Exploited used it when hollering, "Punk's not dead!" In an interview with MuchMusic, the Canadian cable channel, in 1991, Cobain was asked whether his band was punk, and he supplied a fittingly contradictory answer. "I don't think we've ever been labeled as 'punk rock' in the first place, we've just played in the underground circuit," he said, rather sullenly. And then, with a shrug, he brightened slightly and switched directions. "We like punk rock more than any other style of music so, um—yeah! We're punk rock."

By the time he gave that interview, Cobain and his bandmates had left Sub Pop for a major label, and had become the standard-bearers for the Seattle sound, which was known as "grunge," a term that hardly anyone involved seemed to like, or use. It sometimes seemed, though, that the further Cobain got from the punk scene, the more punk he felt. The sudden, worldwide success of Nirvana turned him into a spokesperson for everything associated with the band, including punk. In 1992, he appeared on the cover of *Rolling Stone* wearing a T-shirt with a handwritten message: "CORPORATE MAGAZINES STILL SUCK." (This was a reference, as long-time Nirvana fans probably would have known and newer ones probably wouldn't, to the punk label SST, which sold T-shirts and stickers that read, "CORPORATE ROCK STILL SUCKS.") And Cobain went out of his way to share Nirvana's spotlight with lesser-known bands from the punk and post-punk underground. In the liner notes to a 1992 Nirvana compilation, *Incesticide,* he wrote a moving story about his successful effort to track down a member of the Raincoats, the long-defunct spidery English post-punk band that I first encountered a year later, at WHRB. I didn't learn about the Raincoats earlier because I didn't read those liner notes because I didn't listen to Nirvana because I peremptorily decided that

Nirvana was insufficiently punk. That kind of self-righteous punk purism is hard to defend. And yet I'd like to try.

The Seattle scene that supported Nirvana was relatively easygoing, and some of the people in it responded to Nirvana's success, and the subsequent frenzy of attention from media outlets and record companies, with resignation and sarcasm. (In 1992, an informant from the Seattle scene provided *The New York Times* with a "lexicon of grunge," which the newspaper duly published. It turned out to be an excellent prank: cool kids in Seattle did not, alas, refer to "hanging out" as "swingin' on the flippity-flop.") But Green Day was from the Bay Area, and the punk scene there was fiercely and scrupulously anti-mainstream. *MAXIMUM ROCKNROLL*, or *MRR*, based in San Francisco, was a smudgy black-and-white zine that functioned as punk's American publication of record—and sometimes its moral arbiter, too. Across the bay, in Berkeley, some of the same people ran 924 Gilman Street, a punk club defined by its precepts: all ages, all volunteer, drug- and alcohol-free, nonhierarchical, anti-corporate. And in the late eighties, no label documented Bay Area punk better than Lookout! Records. One of the Lookout! standouts was Operation Ivy, which mixed frantic punk with the slightly less frantic sound of ska, the upbeat Jamaican genre. Another was Green Day, which, starting in 1989, released a series of strikingly sweet-natured pop-punk records. While Operation Ivy was known for impassioned songs about violence in society and at punk shows, Green Day's favorite topics were love and lovesickness. Billie Joe Armstrong, the lead singer, sang with a trace of an English accent, as if he were paying tribute to the old seventies punks even while delivering lyrics that might have made some of them retch: "Staring across the room / Are you leaving soon? / I just need a little time."

Green Day's music was obviously and unabashedly accessible. And after Nirvana's breakthrough, in 1991, record executives were suddenly eager to find punk-inspired bands of their own. So it shouldn't have been a shock when Green Day left Lookout! and signed with Reprise Records, a major label. And yet it was. The band was banished from 924 Gilman Street, which had been its unofficial home. *MRR* had previously been modestly supportive, praising the band's "catchy choruses and irresistible hooks." But now, Green Day was banned from the zine's review section and excoriated in its pages. Tim Yohannan, the founder and editor, wrote that major-label punk bands like Green Day were part of a corporate "attack" on the "punk/indie/underground scene," and likened the invaders to the neo-Nazi skinheads who had tried to establish a presence in punk in the eighties. ("No difference, except this time the thugs are smarter and richer," he wrote.) One contributor compared Green Day to Billy Idol, which was meant as a brutal criticism. The popularity of *Dookie* was a vindication, but Armstrong said that it didn't feel that way. In *Smash!*, a book about the nineties pop-punk explosion, he recalled that success felt more to him like exile from the Bay Area scene. "I felt like I was being run out of town," Armstrong said. "It was, like, 'Oh, the fucking *rock star* is here.' It was just so alienating. I just wanted to be a normal punk like everybody else." With *Dookie*, Green Day achieved mainstream success by being a bit less cheerful: the album's hit singles were about anxiety ("Basket Case") and masturbation ("Longview") and general anomie. A few years later, the band recorded an unusually vituperative song, "Platypus (I Hate You)," that seemed to be about Yohannan, the *MRR* editor. The lyrics describe a "dickhead fuckface" who is dying of cancer—as, indeed, Yohannan did, in 1998.

You might think that the Bay Area punks should have made an exception for a band as exceptional as Green Day. But the scene's egalitarian ethos meant that the rules had to apply to everyone, "friend or stranger," as Yohannan put it. *MRR*'s ambition was both inclusive and exclusive: it aimed to provide a forum for all the punk bands in the world—and none of the non-punk ones. The Green Day affair came amid an extraordinary, yearslong debate in the zine's pages over the meaning of punk. The proscription against major labels was widely accepted, but some wondered how strict the anti-corporate edict should be. In one issue, Yohannan criticized Bikini Kill for agreeing to play a concert with the Go-Go's, because the concert was sponsored by Budweiser. Others wondered about musical boundaries: if *MRR* was a punk zine, did that mean it only covered bands that sounded, more or less, like the Ramones? In October 1992, Yohannan announced that the zine would no longer review records that were "more on the metal side of life, or the hard rock side of life, or the folk side of life," even if they came from established independent labels. One of the columnists, Kent McClard, objected to the magazine's eagerness to draw boundaries, suggesting that "politics and honesty" should be more important than musical categorization. McClard left soon after to found a new zine, *HeartattaCk*, which was devoted to the proposition that "hardcore is a state of mind, not a musical style," and which therefore promised to write about "all records and CDs that are sent in for review regardless of musical style," as long as they did not have universal product codes. ("The U.P.C. code is big business," McClard explained.) And yet McClard was not, of course, agnostic about musical style. In addition to the zine, he also ran a label, Ebullition, that was devoted to furious, screaming hardcore. Indeed it seems likely that he would never have cared enough to argue about barcodes if the argument hadn't been linked to a genre he loved—just as, perhaps, the members of Green Day might never have formed a band and devoted their lives to it, if they hadn't discovered a scene where punk meant something more than music. Music and idealism can be mutually reinforcing, each making the other more appealing.

The Green Day controversy inspired some of the best issues *MRR* ever published, and it also marked the end of the zine's golden age. To many, it seemed as if Yohannan's dogmatic leadership was to blame. But by all accounts, *MRR* was always dogmatic. The difference is that, in the 1980s, there was more consensus about what was punk and what wasn't. The zine's rules and boundaries only grew conspicuous when the consensus began to fray: when more big corporations began releasing credible punk records; when more punk labels began experimenting with *non*-punk records; when more casual fans started gravitating toward the music, lured in by the popularity of Nirvana and Green Day and many others. (Two months after

Dookie, a Southern California band called the Offspring released *Smash*, which likewise sold millions and conquered the mainstream, prompting *Rolling Stone* to ask, "Can it be that the whole world has gone punk?") The punk underground didn't disappear: *MRR*, less influential, kept going, and so did 924 Gilman Street, which even welcomed back Green Day, in 2015, for a secret benefit concert. But the nineties punk gold rush inevitably changed the meaning of punk, dissolving the tense but fruitful relationship between stubborn purists like Yohannan, who dreamed of a unified and egalitarian scene, and restless musicians like Armstrong, a so-called normal punk who couldn't help but be exceptional.

There is a simple reason why I didn't attend the chaotic Green Day show at the Hatch Shell: I had no idea it was happening. In the divide between mainstream punk and underground punk, I was strictly on the side of the underground, and I didn't see myself as having anything in common with the masses of fans who ran amok in Boston that night. That same fall, I was part of an effort in Boston to start a hardcore punk collective, bringing together idealistic hardcore kids from around the city. The inaugural event was a vegetarian potluck dinner in somebody's living room, and maybe it was similar in spirit to one of the early riot grrrl meetings. We discussed bands and record labels, art projects and political causes. (I remember being puzzled, at a gathering not long afterward, when a few of the participants were talking excitedly about going to the circus. Luckily I realized, before saying anything stupid, that they were talking about going to *protest* the circus's treatment of animals.) The collective transformed my experience of punk rock, making me feel like part of a citywide network of friends and allies. But the collective itself was a failure, and the meetings soon ceased, because after a few months it became clear that there was only one objective that people really cared about: organizing punk shows. And that is what we did, working together and individually to put on cheap, friendly, all-ages concerts in out-of-the-way places, like the basement of a health-food store, or the common room of a sympathetic church. I played at a few of those shows myself, with one or another of the bands I formed, none of which ever impressed anyone. (*MRR* once described a band I was in as playing "one screechingly harsh hardcore song over and over again," which was about as close as I ever came to receiving a musical compliment.) I saw how, far from the incentives of the mainstream music industry, like-minded punks could create their own world. But I found out something, too, about the nature of punk idealism. We had first come together as a collective because we believed that hardcore punk wasn't just about music. But for many of us, evidently, it was.

The Opposite of Punk

The rise of Green Day paved a path for many tuneful punk bands to reach non-punk fans, and none was more successful than blink-182, a fun-loving trio from San Diego County. Even more than Green Day, blink-182 embraced the idea of pop-punk—the idea, that is, of playing catchy, slaphappy rock songs designed not to affront listeners but to gratify them. Where the members of Green Day were, in their own self-effacing ways, serious and ambitious musicians, the members of blink-182 cultivated the impression that they were a bunch of idiots. (The stage banter on their live album can be summed up in two words: "dog semen.") In the video for "All the Small Things," from 1999, they dressed up as members of an inept boy band, but as the song ascended the pop chart, eventually reaching No. 6, the parody began to seem like a prophecy. The group's success marked the beginning of a new, cozier relationship between punk and pop. Unlike the members of Green Day, the members of blink-182 had no interest in punk credibility, and punk credibility had no interest in them.

It should have been a bad sign, then, when blink-182 released, in 2003, a rather glum self-titled album—fun and funny bands are not usually improved by seriousness. But the album produced one of the group's most enduring songs, "I Miss You," which arrived just as a new punk-rock wave was cresting, the product of yet another punk movement with roots in Washington, DC. The name of the movement was popularized by an article in a 1986 issue of *Thrasher*, the skateboarding magazine, which told readers about a cohort of bands making impassioned music. "Crowds are said to be left in tears from the intensity," the magazine reported, and it explained that this new subgenre was known as Emo-Core or Emotional Core. The name, often shortened to emo, stuck, much to the horror of many of the people involved. One of them was Ian MacKaye, who between Minor Threat and Fugazi was the lead singer of Embrace, which was one of the bands mentioned in *Thrasher*. At a concert not long afterward, MacKaye ridiculed the article, and the term. "'Emo-core' must be the stupidest fucking thing I've ever heard in my entire life," he said. "As if hardcore wasn't emotional to begin with."

Perhaps the name was redundant, but so are many musical genre names. (Yes, hardcore was "emotional" to begin with, but one might equally object that punk rock was "hardcore" to begin with.) By emphasizing the value of "emotional" lyrics and music, emo taught generations of bands that one way to be punk was to emphasize and even exaggerate the emotion in your music—joy, sometimes, but more often anguish and melancholy. The first emo album, and still one of the greatest, was the self-titled 1985 debut by Rites of Spring, a Washington, DC, band led by Guy Picciotto, who a few years later joined MacKaye in Fugazi. It was a volatile album, with Picciotto screaming lyrics that a different singer might have chosen to whisper, instead: "I woke up this morning with a piece of past caught in my throat / And then I choked." In the years that followed, other emo bands found other ways to be impassioned: by composing hushed, atmospheric songs; by throwing clamorous, unintelligible tantrums; by writing love songs that were even more sentimental than Green Day's. And in the 2000s, when blink-182 released "I Miss You," emo was ascendant. Angsty, theatrical bands like Fall Out Boy, My Chemical Romance, Panic! at the Disco, and Paramore thrived on MTV, making music that was unabashedly commercial, and unapologetically adolescent. (Fall Out Boy's best-known refrain was a spiteful insult to an ex: "I'm just a notch in your bedpost / But you're just a line in a song.") Chris Carrabba, a tattooed singer-songwriter who recorded under the name Dashboard Confessional, emerged as an emo heartthrob. And so did Conor Oberst, a rumpled troubadour who formed a one-man band called Bright Eyes, singing songs so emotionally vivid that they permanently recalibrated my musical perception. The rise of emo marked a new punk generation gap: graying Green Day fans could disdain this music, feeling some of the same revulsion and superiority, no doubt, that many eighties punks felt in the nineties, when Green Day took off.

None of the decade's emo bands ever became quite as big as Nirvana or Green Day. By the end of the 2000s, rock was shrinking and MTV was dying, and emo no longer seemed like the next big thing. But while "emo" may be a stupid word, it points to a tendency so broad that it can probably never go away. A number of the bands didn't. Fall Out Boy soldiered on in the 2010s as a kind of all-purpose hitmaking rock act, and Brendon Urie, from Panic! at the Disco, found a second career on Broadway, even while keeping his first career alive. You could hear the spirit of emo, if you wanted to, in the plaintive and sometimes accusatory songs of Taylor Swift, the country-pop star, who like many musicians her age (she was born in 1989) grew up on emo, and who, in 2019, recorded a hit duet with Urie. You could hear it, too, in the woozy, melancholy music of Post Malone, who told me he smuggled the spirit of Bright Eyes into his hip-hop hits. In fact, some of the most popular young musicians of the 2010s were a trio of singing hip-hop stars—Lil Peep, XXXTentacion, and Juice WRLD—who expressed in their music the moody and sometimes resentful spirit of emo. These names will likely forever be linked, not just because of their overlapping sensibilities but because all three died young. XXXTentacion was shot to death in 2018 during a robbery. And Lil Peep and Juice WRLD died from accidental overdoses of opioids in 2017 and 2019, respectively. This is one of many ironies of emo: that a tradition originally associated with the straight-edge scene in Washington, DC, came to be linked, decades later, to America's opioid epidemic.

There has long been something embarrassing about emo, both the name and the music itself, which tends to be earnest and expressive in a way that can feel profoundly uncool. That sense of excess is part of what I love about it, although I understand why it makes some people cringe, especially older people; at emo shows in the 2000s, I sometimes felt (and surely looked) more like a chaperone than one of the so-called kids. In a sharp and influential essay from 2003 called "Emo: Where the Girls Aren't," the critic Jessica Hopper wrote about how emo sometimes seemed to consist of nothing but breakup songs, with boys singing to girls, including the girls who often predominated in the audiences, but not really singing *about* them:

> Girls in emo songs today do not have names. We are not identified beyond our absence, our shape drawn by the pain we've caused. Our lives, our day-to-day-to-day does not exist, we do not get colored in. Our actions are portrayed solely through the detailing of neurotic self-entanglement of the boy singer—our region of personal power, simply, is our impact on his romantic life.

Hopper's essay exposed the solipsism that has always been part of emo, and the meanness that has sometimes been added to it. She acknowledged that the problems of emo were in many ways the problems of rock 'n' roll, equally detectable in the music of the Rolling Stones. But she saw no reason why the punk-rock community should not be working to change that. Even as Hopper wrote, though, emo was growing less connected to that community. And when Juice WRLD emerged as the emo idol for the next generation, his breakup songs were, if anything, more spiteful than the ones Hopper had written about, a decade and a half earlier. In his biggest hit, "Lucid Dreams," Juice WRLD moaned, "You were made out of plastic, fake / I was tangled up in your drastic ways / Who knew evil girls had the prettiest face?" XXXTentacion was far more disturbing. His astonishing music ranged from acoustic sing-alongs to demonic rapping. And the anguished lyrics reflected a violent life, including time spent in jail on charges of false imprisonment, witness tampering, and the assault and battery of his pregnant ex-girlfriend. The gruesome saga ended, for XXXTentacion although not for his fans or for his victims, when he was killed. His ability to create popular—and, in my view, compelling—music, regardless, was a grotesque reminder that sometimes, lyrics about emotional turmoil reflect real problems, real abuse, real harm.

Compared to stars like Juice WRLD and XXXTentacion, whose tracks were streamed billions of times through online services like Spotify, many punk-inspired bands of the 2010s lived a humbler, gentler existence. They played small clubs and basements, and they built on old ideas of punk idealism. At websites like AbsolutePunk, which had previously chronicled the emo boom of the 2000s, writers and commenters grew increasingly concerned with abusive behavior in the punk scene, and increasingly self-conscious of punk rock's history as a genre full of straight white men. You could see evidence of this new sensibility in the emergence, in the late 2010s, of initiatives like Safer Scenes, which aimed to combat sexual assault and harassment at punk shows and beyond. You could see it, too, in the efforts to hold bands accountable for misbehavior. Brand New, one of the most beloved emo bands to emerge from the 2000s, was effectively shut down after it was revealed that the lead singer had solicited explicit photographs from an underage fan, and a number of less prominent bands were also criticized or blacklisted, sometimes for less clear-cut violations. When I went to see these shows, I was always struck, sometimes moved, occasionally dismayed, and often amused by all the wholesomeness on display. I saw nth-generation emo bands like the Hotelier and Modern Baseball playing thoughtful (and memorable) songs for polite audiences—for them, there was nothing particularly "punk" about bad behavior. The idea that punk should be distinguished from mainstream music above all by its niceness would have startled many of the seventies pioneers, who were proud of their nastiness. And so, too, would the notion that a punk concert should be "safer" than the rest of the world, rather than more dangerous; in some ways, this new punk scene was the opposite of the old one. There were and are plenty of bands eager to re-create the noise and menace of the bad old days. But part of what was great about twenty-first-century punk was that it didn't seem cowed by all those decades of punk history. Some versions of it found new ways to chase fun and try to chase away hopelessness. Other versions of it echoed the idealism of the Clash, without seeming indebted to the band itself. These kids seemed convinced that "punk" could be whatever they wanted it to be.

Hipsters Everywhere

When Michael Azerrad wrote his book about American indie labels in the 1980s, he ended on a note of disappointment. It wasn't that the labels were disappearing: though a number of high-profile bands were wooed away by big conglomerates, plenty remained, and the sudden popularity of so-called alternative rock increased the audience, or potential audience, for any band trying to make a living away from the mainstream. Azerrad worried, though, that the boisterous world he chronicled had grown dull. Once, bands like the Butthole Surfers had terrorized clubs across the country, subjecting patrons to howling feedback and grunted lyrics about who knows what, along with occasional displays of fire and genitals. (When I was in high school, I devoted one of my bedroom walls to an enormous and unpleasant Butthole Surfers poster, featuring four grainy images of an emaciated figure with a horribly distended belly.) "Indie rock," Azerrad wrote, "became increasingly the preserve of the more privileged strata of American youth, who favored cerebral, ironic musicians like Liz Phair, Pavement, and Palace Brothers." In a way, the underground music market had become *too good* at giving listeners what they wanted. And so "independent," a punk-inspired way of working, hardened into "indie rock," a likable genre with a recognizable sound. One way to chart this change was to consider the slow disappearance of the term "post-punk," a once-helpful catchall that became less helpful as the bands grew less "punk" and more "post."

In the 2000s, the nonthreatening normalcy of indie rock became one of its defining qualities, and sometimes a bit of a joke. In a famous scene from the 2004 film *Garden State*, Natalie Portman's character looks soulfully at Zach Braff's character, telling him, "You gotta hear this one song, it'll change your life, I swear." Then she hands him some big headphones and beams expectantly as he listens for the first time to "New Slang," a gentle and slightly off-kilter song by the Shins, who recorded for Sub Pop, Nirvana's old label, and whose popularity helped revive it. Often, indie rock in the nineties was neither acerbic nor ironic. You bought a CD by Death Cab for Cutie, or Feist, or Wilco, not to make a statement or flaunt your taste—nobody would have been impressed—but because you loved listening to it. (This "indie" rock didn't even have to be on an independent label: Wilco recorded for Reprise Records and then, after a nasty split, left and signed a new contract with Nonesuch Records, another subsidiary of the same big company, Warner Music.) Songwriting was often the focus of this music, which is part of what made it rather conservative. Instead of competing to be more rebellious, or more adventurous, these singers and bands competed to write more affecting, more memorable songs, a bit the way country songwriters in Nashville did. The era of record shopping as treasure hunting was over, because music was moving online, making scarcity obsolete. Indie-rock records were easy to find, and often they were easy to listen to as well.

Who was this music for? Punk and its variants had been tribal. Punk felt like a tribe to me when I joined it in the summer of 1990, turning away from the rest of the musical world. And no doubt it felt like a tribe to Billie Joe Armstrong a few years later when he was exiled from it, or felt he was. But by the 2000s, indie rock was big and vague, with no purity tests required. It was perfectly designed to appeal to members of an amorphous group that suddenly seemed to be everywhere: hipsters. This was a slang word dating to the jazz era, but in the 2000s it was reborn to fill a particular need. The cities were filling up with young people who were cool and recognizably nonmainstream, but not linked to any subculture in particular. So they were called hipsters, almost always pejoratively—unlike "punk rock," the term "hipster" was a flag that no one really wanted to wave. The only avowedly "hipster" publications were parodies, like *The Hipster Handbook*, a rather wan 2008 satire, and Hipster Runoff, a scabrous and sometimes cruel website written in the voice of a horny cad obsessed with indie credibility and corporate synergy. (A representative post asked, "Will buying a banjo make my personal brand more authentic?") "Hipster" was a good insult because there was no way to refute the charge, and trying only made it worse: Who but a hipster would get bent out of shape about being called a hipster?

It's easy to make fun of what happened to the culture that Azerrad chronicled. A seething and proudly autonomous underground evolved, in a couple of decades, into a worldwide alliance of semi-cool hipsters, loyal to no genre in particular. But I understand how it happened, partly because it happened to me. As a teenager, I found the defiant spirit of punk to be irresistible, but also destabilizing. I gravitated first to punk, and then to music that seemed weirder, fiercer, more extreme. But what did that mean? In high school, I fell in love with something called "noise music," experimental compositions that resembled pure static. (Much of this music was produced in Japan and available on expensive imported CDs, and I think part of what I enjoyed about it was the sheer perversity of paying twenty-five dollars for an hour of music that sounded more or less like the garbage disposal unit in my parents' kitchen downstairs.) At WHRB, I learned to hear punk as a mutant form of rock 'n' roll, and I learned to appreciate its rowdy, unpretentious spirit; it turned out that many punk and hardcore bands made noise music, too, and not always on purpose. Inevitably, though, I got curious about other genres. I discovered a chaotic form of dance music called jungle, a British genre with rhythms so fast and unpredictable that you had to ignore them and dance to the basslines instead. I heard a bizarre hip-hop album by a character called Dr. Octagon, which lured me back to the rap music I had loved as a boy. One night, I went to a concert in Boston by the dancehall reggae star Bounty Killer that was more frenetic than any punk show I had ever seen. I had paid in advance for a ticket, which bought me the right to be plucked out of a heaving crowd and pulled into the venue by a bouncer just in time to see Bounty Killer, who strutted and hollered through twenty breakneck tracks in fifteen minutes and then sprinted off-stage and directly into the back seat of a truck, which sped out of the parking lot before anyone quite knew what was going on. At least, that's the way I remember the show, which remains one of the most exciting and disorienting concerts I have ever seen, and which taught me that some other genres might be even more "punk" than punk.

How do you stay loyal, anyway, to a genre built on defiance? And why would you? Punk rock is fundamentally incoherent, an anti-traditional tradition that promises "anarchy," or a whiff of it, while providing its devotees something tidy and recognizable enough to be considered a musical genre. By the time I returned to college, after my yearlong record-store sojourn, I was spending more and more time listening to hip-hop, R&B, and dance music, and I modified my appearance to be less genre specific: I shaved off my scraggly dreads and started wearing collared shirts instead of punk tees. (Occasionally, on the subway, I would catch myself glancing at a kid in a punk T-shirt and then stop, remembering that I no longer looked like a sympathetic fellow punk—I looked like the enemy.) Years later, I fell in love with country music, which represented a more radical break with the radical values of punk rock, and therefore, perversely, a more profound embodiment of them. I listened to all sorts of music, always alert for unlikely triumphs and unexpected developments. In other words, I became a hipster, and as I think about it now, I can't see any very good reason to reject the term. Many proud identities, after all, began as insults. It must have seemed even stranger, half a century ago, when a small number of rock musicians began voluntarily identifying as punks.

The difference, of course, is that hipsters do not form a community, and so the hipster identity conveys little sense of belonging. I think part of the reason why people react so negatively to the term is that it reflects a widespread fear that the old musical communities—the old tribes—no longer function as they used to, having been replaced by a hazy mega-tribe of connoisseurs who don't truly care about anything in particular. But of course hipsters can be earnest and obsessive about music, too. (I should know.) And it's odd that our old tribal musical boundaries seem to be dissolving, at precisely the moment when people are worried about an *increase* in tribalism, particularly political tribalism. Perhaps this is no coincidence. I sometimes wonder whether political convictions are replacing musical convictions as the preeminent marker of subcultural identity. Perhaps some of the kinds of people who used to talk about obscure bands now prefer to talk about obscure or outré causes, instead. And perhaps political advocacy and organizing supplies some of the sense of belonging that people once got from tight-knit punk scenes. That would not necessarily be an unhappy development—although now, as then, there are likely to be plenty of poseurs mixed in with the true believers. But the adolescent impulse that fueled punk has not disappeared, and neither has the primacy of popular music. And historically, the moments when everyone seems to be listening to the same songs are the moments when some people are brave and immature enough to say fuck this and fuck that and start something new, or halfway new. That will probably always sound like a good idea to me.

5

HIP-HOP

Rap Music Don't Have to Teach You Anything

HALFWAY THROUGH SIDE ONE of *A Wolf in Sheep's Clothing*, the classic 1991 debut album by the hip-hop duo Black Sheep, some protesters interrupt the music.

"Yo, man," one guy says. "Why don't you be kicking some records about, you know, the upliftment of the Blacks?"

Another asks why Black Sheep is silent about "the eating of the dolphins."

Someone else mentions "the hole in the ho-zone," turning environmental degradation into a dirty joke—perhaps unwittingly.

In response to all these demands for instruction, the guys from Black Sheep can only chuckle. Something about hip-hop makes listeners greedy for more words, better words. But Black Sheep made a brilliant album. What more could anyone want?

People have been arguing over hip-hop ever since it first emerged, in the Bronx, in the seventies. It was soon the most controversial genre in the country, a distinction that has not, somehow, been erased by time or by popularity. As the genre became first successful, and then mainstream, and then finally dominant, it never became unobjectionable. Hip-hop was born in poor Black neighborhoods in the Bronx, and over the decades it has retained a singular connection to poor Black neighborhoods nationwide— and, for that matter, poor and not-necessarily-Black neighborhoods world- wide. This connection accounts for some of the demands placed upon the music: many listeners have felt that the genre ought to be politically aware, or explicitly revolutionary, and they have been disappointed to find that rappers' priorities have tended to be inconsistent, and sometimes inscruta- ble. Often, hip-hop insiders and hip-hop outsiders have found themselves united in their conviction that something is seriously wrong with the genre, even if they haven't always agreed on what that is. And rappers have per- sistently tended to say things that get them in trouble: hip-hop is obsessed with respect, and yet it has flourished and endured by shirking the de- mands of respectability. The best of it has often been deemed both irresist- ible and indefensible, sometimes by the same listeners—sometimes even by the rappers themselves.

Like many hip-hop heroes, the members of Black Sheep were trickster virtuosos: a pair of New Yorkers who grew up partly in North Carolina, and who loved hip-hop too much to take it entirely seriously. Mista Lawnge, the group's resident producer, built effervescent beats from snippets of old R&B and rock records. And Dres, the lead rapper, balanced sly jokes with unex- pected flourishes of erudition. He could compress a muzzy nightclub scene into a neat but unpredictable little packet of syllables, delivered with mock formality:

> When you see a honey by the strobe light,
> Black, I hope you got good sight.
> For honey that you see,
> like the Shakespeare soliloquy,
> may or may not be
> all that.

Despite their playful arrogance, the members of Black Sheep were also self-conscious about their position in a shifting hip-hop hierarchy. This was not an unusual state of affairs. Rapping often makes people self-conscious. Singers can hide their words—no matter how formulaic or spurious or inscrutable—beneath a tune. (Pierre Beaumarchais, eighteenth-century French playwright, turned this observation into an aphorism: "Whatever is not worth saying can be sung.") But rappers are more exposed than singers, because their form of expression is more similar to speech. And so rappers spend lots of time explaining who they are, what they're doing, and why they deserve your attention. The earliest rappers were essentially emcees, hired to host parties, and they never got out of the habit of introducing themselves. The opening lines of the first verse of the first hip-hop hit ever released—"Rapper's Delight," by the Sugarhill Gang, from 1979—contained an introduction: "I am Wonder Mike, and I'd like to say hello / To the Black, to the white, the red and the brown, the purple and yellow." A dozen years later, Black Sheep's album offered a slicker version of the same sentiment: "Dres, D-R-E-S, yes, I guess I can start / If it's all right with you, I'll rip this here joint apart." Calling out your own name can be a way of boasting, but it can also be a courtly gesture, a way of checking in with listeners and putting them at ease, the way any good host would.

For similar reasons, rappers are famously eager to engage with their detractors—more than singers, they must worry about social standing, because that standing is what gives them the right, and the credibility, to speak and to be believed. "Rapper's Delight" provoked a furious response, on record and in interviews, from a pioneering rapper named Grandmaster Caz, whose lyrics appeared, uncredited, on the track. And two of the most beloved rappers of all time, Tupac Shakur and the Notorious B.I.G., engaged in a vicious feud in the 1990s. But there are slyer ways to acknowledge criticism. The members of Black Sheep knew that their album, which included a track called "Hoes We Knows," might be called sexist, so they included a skit in which they faced exactly that charge; to the group's credit, the feminist journalists in the skit seemed more sympathetic than the rappers themselves. In 1991, when the album appeared, the genre and the country were mesmerized by the rise of so-called gangsta rap, and so the duo opened the album with a gangsta parody, preemptively mocking the notion of street credibility before the group could be accused of lacking it. In the parody, Dres is a cold-blooded killer, eating breakfast and getting ready for school: "Hungry as fuck, said my grace / Pop kept screaming, so I shot him in the face!" The track ends when Dres wakes up and sheds his delusion. "I dreamt I was *hard*," he says.

The fake protesters who interrupt the Black Sheep album, complaining about the "ho zone," reflected a different hip-hop sensibility that was then emergent. Starting in the late eighties, Public Enemy honed a form of hip-hop that was militant, incandescently righteous—the group's records made rapping seem like serious business. Ever since, there have been listeners who hear Public Enemy as not just a great hip-hop group but the ideal to which the genre ought to aspire. Just as Bob Dylan helped popularize the idea that singers should be truth tellers, Public Enemy helped popularize the idea that rappers should be revolutionaries. Black Sheep was not entirely opposed to earnestness; *A Wolf in Sheep's Clothing* included, amid the wisecracks, rhymes about the legacy of racism and the importance of persevering in the face of low expectations. But in 1992, in an interview with *The Source*, which for years was hip-hop's most important magazine, Mista Lawnge complained that too many hip-hop acts were rushing to meet the demand for "message"-oriented music. "Nobody else has stereotyped any other particular music as being something that has to teach," he said. "Rap music don't have to teach you anything." Hip-hop is entertainment, but more than other genres—more than country, or R&B, or even rock 'n' roll—hip-hop has often been asked to provide something greater than mere entertainment.

I'm pretty sure I heard Black Sheep's greatest hit, "The Choice Is Yours," when I was in high school—I think I remember a DJ playing it at a school dance. But I didn't hear the rest of the album until a few years later, when I rediscovered hip-hop. As a boy, I had acquired and memorized cassettes by Run-DMC, Kurtis Blow, and the Beastie Boys. This music wasn't generally played on the local Top 40 radio station, but it didn't seem obscure, especially because all the other boys at school were listening to it, too. Virtually all of those boys were white, but I don't remember being surprised that they were obsessed with Black music. And although one Black boy in my grade exuded hip-hop cool, no one would remember *me* as having been particularly hip-hop, despite my attempt at a rapper's haircut: a flattop, neither as sharp nor as flat as the ones on the record covers. Hip-hop was certainly African American music. But to me then, it mainly seemed American: it belonged not to the world of my African parents but to the world of my friends. That, of course, was part of the appeal: the rappers didn't seem like me, or even "look like" me, though we were part of the same racial category. They were much cooler than that.

Hip-hop got a major mainstream outlet in 1988, when MTV launched *Yo! MTV Raps.* I remember catching glimpses of it at friends' houses and paying closer attention the next year, when my family got its own cable box. By then, hip-hop was finding its place on the charts: MC Hammer released "U Can't Touch This," a ubiquitous smash, in January 1990, and Vanilla Ice's "Ice Ice Baby" arrived in August, by which point I was a freshly minted punk rocker, newly but fully converted to the ideology of anti-mainstreamism. Hip-hop was party music, MTV music, pop music; hip-hop was what my popular high school classmates listened to when they weren't listening to classic rock. The mainstream Americanness of hip-hop, which had seduced me as a boy, now seemed like a reason to reject it. The music was interesting, perhaps, but not really for me, not anymore. I thought I had outgrown it.

The album that brought me back to hip-hop was neither a big hit nor a pop crossover, which is why I found it so seductive. I was in college—actually, out of college, taking my yearlong sabbatical at a record-store warehouse. Control of the warehouse stereo was determined by a strict but complicated rotation system, and one day in the spring of 1996, one of my coworkers put on a new album by a guy who called himself Dr. Octagon. This, I later discovered, was a new musical identity for a hip-hop veteran known as Kool Keith, who had achieved some renown with a cult-favorite eighties group, Ultramagnetic MCs. As Dr. Octagon, Kool Keith delivered his own absurd version of a hip-hop introduction: "Dr. Octagon, paramedic fetus of the East / With priests, I'm from the Church of the Operating Room." The album was dizzying, full of technical jargon and nonsense boasts, and it helped me see, rather belatedly, that hip-hop could be audacious and strange—indeed, that it always had been, and that I just hadn't realized it.

Rappers and their fans have often championed hip-hop as an authentic reflection of life in some of America's toughest neighborhoods, and as an indispensable chronicle of the African American experience. "Rap is black America's TV station," Chuck D, from Public Enemy, told *Spin* magazine, in 1988. "The only thing that gives the straight-up facts on how the black youth feels is a rap record." As a defense of hip-hop, this may be effective, but as an analysis of the music, it is not particularly insightful, not least because it doesn't make hip-hop sound like much fun. In fact, hip-hop has *not* always told the truth; often, the practice of rapping has seemed less like reporting and more like bullshitting. The key to the genre's continual rise has been its insistence on being, decade after decade, outrageously entertaining. It's not hard to understand why many concerned listeners and musicians—including Chuck D—wanted to reshape hip-hop, hoping to transform it into a genre that would be a more unambiguous force for good in the world. Hip-hop remained proudly unreformed, but it kept seducing listeners. It may be the quintessential modern American art form, the country's greatest cultural contribution to the world. And yet, for most of its history, hip-hop has been regarded as the kind of music that one loves despite its alleged flaws—a guilty pleasure. In a sense, this is the highest possible praise: testament to just how much pleasure hip-hop has managed to provide.

The (New) Sound of Young America

The inventors of hip-hop didn't think of themselves as creating a genre, because they were too busy throwing parties. One of the most important inventors was DJ Kool Herc, a Jamaican immigrant living in the Bronx who became known, in the early seventies, for playing music you couldn't hear anywhere else. This was the dawn of the disco era; about ten miles south, in downtown Manhattan, the pioneering disco DJs were concocting their own form of dance music. But the burgeoning disco scene was artsy and cosmopolitan: gay and straight, white and Black and Latino, were all welcome in the DJ booths and on the dance floors. (Although not equally welcome, all the time.) The scene at Kool Herc's parties, some of which were held in the community room of his apartment building, was Blacker, straighter, rougher. In *Yes Yes Y'all*, an important oral history of the genre's early days, another early hip-hop DJ, Disco Wiz, remembers being a "thuggish" teenager, looking for a hospitable place to party. "We weren't socially accepted at disco joints; we were pretty much segregated," recalled Disco Wiz, who is Latino. (Perhaps his stage name was a sign of how influential the disco movement nevertheless remained.) "When Kool Herc finally hit the scene, we started getting the buzz that something was different."

While disco DJs learned to remix and extend their favorite R&B records, making them last forever, Herc's style was less smooth. His favorite records included "It's Just Begun," a saxophone-driven funk track by the Jimmy Castor Bunch, and "Apache," a rubbery instrumental by an obscure group called Michael Viner's Incredible Bongo Band. What Herc really loved was the "break": the part of the record where most of the band dropped out, leaving behind little more than a hard, syncopated beat. Using two turntables, he devised a way to play the break over and over, to the delight of the dancers in the crowd—break-dancers, they would eventually be called. One of many Herc fans was a skillful young tinkerer who took the name Grandmaster Flash, and who realized he could draw a crowd by putting on a show. Grandmaster Flash taught himself how to switch between turntables even faster, spinning one record backward while the other was playing, so that he could thrill the dancers by repeating their favorite musical phrases back-to-back, uninterrupted.

When I first moved to New York, in 1999, I was an editor and writer in need of office space, so I rented a desk in Chelsea from a guy named Bill Adler, a lifelong music fan and scholar whose many careers included a stretch in the eighties as the head of public relations for Def Jam Records, the preeminent hip-hop record label. Bill's circle of friends was almost as impressive as his arsenal of war stories, and for a few years we shared the office with a third person, a hip-hop veteran named Kool DJ AJ, who had been part of the seventies Bronx scene and who had found that hip-hop notoriety was not necessarily remunerative. (At the time, one of AJ's main business ventures was concert ticket arbitrage—"scalping," to use a pejorative term.) AJ, who died of stomach cancer in 2015, was justifiably proud of his status as a hip-hop pioneer; the front cover of *Yes Yes Y'all* is a photograph of him, concentrating on his turntables. But he was always forthright about his abilities: unlike Grandmaster Flash, he was not a virtuoso, or even a record obsessive. He was well-known and well-connected, the kind of guy who could help ensure that a night would end reasonably predictably, with payments made and equipment unstolen. For him, hip-hop was as much a social phenomenon as a musical one. "I didn't go to a party really to concentrate on Herc that much," AJ remembered in the oral history. "I went to a party to party."

The early DJs learned that one way to keep the partygoers partying was to talk to them, and soon they were bringing along emcees—or "MCs"—who worked the microphones like amped-up radio personalities, calling out catchphrases: "Yes, yes, y'all"; "To the beat, y'all"; "Keep on to the break o' dawn"; "Hip, hop, it don't stop." (Before it was a genre name, "hip, hop" was a command.) By 1978, the most popular DJs were working with teams of MCs who performed routines, tossing rhymes back and forth. Grandmaster Flash had a highly regarded troupe that eventually became known as the Furious Five, and the members bragged about themselves and about their boss: "Flash is the man that can't be beat / Because he never ever heard the word 'defeat.'" And Grandmaster Caz, known for his story rhymes, performed with a few different groups before joining the Cold Crush Brothers.

These performers were paid well to pack clubs in the Bronx and Harlem, and they weren't necessarily eager to become recording artists, especially since it wasn't clear that their art was recordable. Their job was to play other people's records, and to spend a few hours talking to the people on the dance floor. How do you make a song out of that?

It seems fitting, for a genre obsessed with authenticity: a number of the earliest hip-hop records were in some sense bogus. In 1979, a funky R&B group called Fatback Band decided to pay tribute to the new dance craze that was simmering in the Bronx, so the group released "King Tim III (Personality Jock)," which had workmanlike rapping by a guy one of the band's crew members knew. This was, by some accounts, the first hip-hop record, even though it didn't emerge from the Bronx hip-hop scene. Neither did "Rapper's Delight," by Sugarhill Gang, which appeared a few months later, and became a novelty hit. The three members, pulled together by the record producer Sylvia Robinson, were not known as rappers: one of them, Big Bank Hank, had spent some time managing the career of Grandmaster Caz; when an acquaintance asked if he wanted to make a record, he brought some of Caz's lyrics into the studio with him. (When Big Bank Hank raps, "I'm the C-A-S-N, the O-V-A and the rest is F-L-Y," he is spelling out Caz's old stage name, Cas[a]nova Fly.) "Rapper's Delight" wasn't quite the real thing, but it was perfect: a catchy, cheerful song that introduced the world to a new genre, which was helpfully named in the chorus. "I said a hip, hop, the hippie, the hippie / To the hip, hip hop, you don't stop."

In those early years, hip-hop undoubtedly struck many listeners as quirky rather than radical: stilted poetry, declaimed over disco records. And the early hits tended to confirm this impression. Kurtis Blow was the first rapper to sign a major-label contract; his debut single, released a few months after "Rapper's Delight," was a holiday jingle, "Christmas Rappin'." Blondie, the punkish pop band, went to No. 1 in 1981 with "Rapture," which was built around a goofy, free-associative rap by Debbie Harry, the lead singer. Rapping seemed easy and fun: comedians did it, including Mel

Brooks, who rapped in character as both Louis XVI and Hitler; Stevie Wonder even did some rapping on his 1982 single "Do I Do." Few groups did more to popularize the genre, in its earliest incarnation, than the Fat Boys, three performers who functioned as hip-hop ambassadors, using fatness as an expedient punch line. (This joke seemed less funny when, in 1995, Darren Robinson, the so-called Human Beat Box who gave the group its musical identity, died from a heart attack, at age twenty-eight.) The Fat Boys placed a handful of songs on the R&B chart, including "Jailhouse Rap," a jokey track about being arrested for stealing food; they collaborated with the Beach Boys on "Wipeout," which was a crossover hit; and they launched an unlikely movie career, which culminated with the three starring in *Disorderlies*, a slapstick comedy.

The success of "Rapture" helped teach the country what rapping was, but it didn't push the genre into the musical mainstream. In fact, in 1984, *Billboard* reported that some previously rap-friendly stations in New York, the genre's birthplace, had begun playing rap only "sporadically," perhaps because they thought the fad was fading. But somehow, the genre found a receptive home at my elementary school in Cambridge, Massachusetts—and, as far as I can tell, at elementary schools nationwide. I bought a cassette of *Ego Trip*, an album by Kurtis Blow, because it contained "Basketball," a very kid-friendly ode to the game's most famous players. (The album also included "AJ Scratch," in which Blow paid tribute to his DJ, the same AJ who would eventually be my officemate. Hip-hop has a way of making connections across time and space.) My favorite group was Run-DMC, which had a brash style, using simple beats that they sometimes combined with squealing electric guitars. This was a novel hybrid, and also a canny way of attracting rock fans, although I had no idea, then, that electric guitars were unusual in hip-hop. Mainly I think I liked the way the rappers shouted their emphatic lyrics, which were easy and fun to memorize. In one stanza from "King of Rock," the title track from their 1985 album, Run started each line so that DMC could finish it decisively:

Now, we crash through walls / Cut through floors
Bust through ceilings / And knock down doors
And when we're on the tape / We're fresh out the box
You can hear our sound / For blocks and blocks

If you were, as I was, a not particularly mature eleven-year-old boy in 1987, hip-hop seemed like a genre that had been invented to amuse you. My friends and I all had copies of *Licensed to Ill*, the 1986 debut album by the Beastie Boys, three white rappers who had previously performed as a hardcore punk band and whose whiteness intrigued me less than the fact that they seemed like Run-DMC's delinquent little brothers. (I was slightly scandalized by the album's most notorious lines, which described either an assignation or an assault: "The sheriff's after me for what I did to his daughter / I did it like this, I did it like that / I did it with a Wiffle ball bat.") And I remember filling the cover of a three-ring binder with lyrics from the first album by DJ Jazzy Jeff & the Fresh Prince, who were known for long, cartoonish story rhymes. It wouldn't have surprised me to learn that the Fresh Prince, as Will Smith, would transform a few years afterward into a sitcom star, although his later incarnation as an action hero would have been harder for me to imagine.

One of the most startling facts about these early hip-hop successes is that many of them were connected to a single person: Russell Simmons, the most influential figure in 1980s hip-hop. He managed Kurtis Blow, who became the genre's first star even though he was never considered a particularly skilled rapper. His brother was Joseph Simmons, also known as Run, from Run-DMC, whom Russell likewise managed; he also managed DJ Jazzy Jeff & the Fresh Prince. The Beastie Boys recorded for Def Jam, the hip-hop record label that Simmons built with his partner, Rick Rubin. So did Public Enemy, and so did LL Cool J, a rapper and actor who launched one of the most successful careers in the history of hip-hop. Simmons did not manage the Fat Boys, but Madonna's manager evidently thought he did and called Simmons looking for them; Simmons told him about the Beastie

Boys instead and got his group a gig as the opening act on Madonna's first tour. Both the Beastie Boys and Madonna later said they enjoyed this pairing, although Madonna's fans, who reportedly jeered and threw things, apparently did not.

One of the many perks of sharing an office with Bill Adler, the former Def Jam publicist, was having access to his filing cabinets, which were full of photographs and articles from hip-hop's early years—things no one else was wise enough to save. This collection is now housed at Cornell, as the Adler Hip Hop Archive, and one of its delights is a draft of a 1989 letter from Adler to Bryant Gumbel, who was then a host of the *Today* show on NBC, and who had recently interviewed DJ Jazzy Jeff & the Fresh Prince. "We represent all the top rappers in the business," Adler wrote, on behalf of Simmons, exaggerating only slightly. He suggested that those rappers were the modern equivalent of the Rolling Stones, Elvis Presley, James Brown, and Bob Dylan, and made a strategic comparison. "We feel that we can make the same claim for our artists in the eighties that Berry Gordy made for the Motown artists in the sixties: they are 'the sound of young America,'" he wrote. A few years earlier, this claim might have seemed far-fetched. A few years later, it would be conventional wisdom.

Music in Every Phrase

People sometimes talk about "rap and hip-hop," as if the terms denote two distinct genres, but they have usually been used interchangeably. The difference, if there is one: "rapping" can also mean talking, more or less. And so the history of rapping predates hip-hop—by years, or decades, or maybe even centuries, depending on your definition. (Any recitation of vernacular poetry, from any culture or era, might plausibly be described as rapping.) Before there was hip-hop, there were smooth-talking R&B

radio DJs like Frankie Crocker, who was already asking, in the sixties, "Aren't you glad you live in a town / You can hear the Frankie Crocker sound / When the sun goes down?" A few years later, in Kool Herc's native Jamaica, performers like U-Roy began unspooling loose, half-improvised rhymes over instrumental tracks: "I'm tougher than tough, and that ain't no bluff / Maybe because I've got the musical stuff." (The practice was known as deejaying, probably in tribute to the American radio DJs who helped inspire it.) If you like, you can trace the tradition back to the wordy "talking blues" records of the 1920s, or the slangy jazz singing of Cab Calloway in the thirties and forties: "Do you get in the groove? Does the beat make you move? / Do you send yourself, Jack, and then trilly on back 'cause you know that it's smooth?" Countless preachers and comedians could be considered proto-rappers, and so could Muhammad Ali, who understood that taunts and provocations were more memorable if they rhymed. One of the most directly influential precursors was the comedian Pigmeat Markham, who had an R&B hit in 1968 with "Here Come the Judge," a rhyming comic monologue delivered in a muscular voice and set to an equivalently muscular beat, which practically every early rapper would have known.

Rappers were preceded, too, by a crop of Black oral poets, street-oriented and revolution-minded, whose records arrived starting in 1969: the Watts Prophets, the Last Poets, Gil Scott-Heron. (Even people who have never heard Scott-Heron's records, or his rich speaking-singing voice, may nevertheless be familiar with his rallying cry: "The revolution will not be televised!") These poets specialized in caustic verses—often unrhymed, as if to underscore the seriousness of the words. The Last Poets hollered, "Niggers are scared of revolution," and "The white man's got a God complex," as if they were hoping that some passerby would dare to disagree. The unapologetic brashness of this music anticipated the unapologetic brashness of the rappers who came afterward; ever since hip-hop, most other forms of music have seemed rather self-effacing, by comparison.

What is most surprising about all the proto-rappers, though, is just how "proto" they all were: what happened in the Bronx really was different from what came before. There is a marvelous live recording, from 1978, of Grandmaster Flash and the Furious Five, where you can hear this shift happen. Melle Mel, a key member of the Furious Five, was one of the most inventive of the early rappers, and he welcomes the dancers, sounding a bit like a radio DJ:

> *Welcoming you and yours, truly, to the place where the elite meet*
> *Where those who have pride stride*
> *Where everybody around town comes to get down*

The meter is loose and uneven, as if Melle Mel is giving a toast. (Indeed, in Jamaica, talky deejays like U-Roy were also known as toasters.) Then he starts paying closer attention to the beat, and suddenly he locks in. Where before he sounded like an announcer accompanied by a rhythm section, now Melle Mel sounds like part of the rhythm section, exaggerating the stress patterns to accentuate the backbeat, turning certain words into snare drums. Over the course of a few lines, he has transformed himself from a guy with a microphone into a *rapper*:

> *I'm Melle* Mel, *and I rock so* well
> *From the World* Trade *to the depths of* hell

This was a crucial change, because it helped listeners perceive rappers as musicians, not merely people talking over music. You didn't need to care about the lyrics, or even understand them, in order to nod along with the rhythm of the rhymes. (Few people listen to speeches or books on tape over and over, but hip-hop seems to have just as much replay value as any other kind of music.) This basic template became the hip-hop standard: say your name, make a claim, emphasize the backbeat.

At first, rappers provided service with a smile. They were party hosts, after all, and they sometimes wore glamorous leather outfits or suits; they said things like, "Clap your hands, everybody!" (This was the first line of Kurtis Blow's second single, "The Breaks.") Their voices were ingratiating, and they sometimes filled pauses by saying, "Huh-huh-huh-*huh*," as if they were eager to avoid silence—"dead air," as radio DJs call it. But Run-DMC arrived with a different attitude. "That was the end of our era, when Run-DMC and them came into the game," Grandmaster Caz remembered, in the oral history. The guys in Run-DMC came from Hollis, Queens, far from the clubs that nurtured hip-hop, and they were defiantly unglamorous: they wore jeans, Adidas sneakers, and black fedora hats; they didn't smile, and they weren't slick. Where the old disco grooves were warm and enticing, Run-DMC's approach was radically stark, with empty space between the beats, and between the lines. In 1984, the same year that the debut Run-DMC album appeared, the music historian David Toop published *The Rap Attack*, one of the first major books about hip-hop. Toop described the "piston beat" that drove the early Run-DMC singles, and he declared that the group represented "the austere and increasingly freakish end of the genre." Run-DMC records are not generally considered "freakish" today, not because Toop was wrong, but because the records themselves changed the way hip-hop was made, pushing the genre away from disco. Rappers have been scowling ever since.

Within a few years, Run-DMC, too, would seem old-fashioned, because by the mideighties, the genre had entered its so-called golden era. A new generation of hip-hop acts was emerging, and one of the first was Eric B. & Rakim, a duo that released its debut single, "Eric B. Is President," in 1986. Rakim's style was stern but astonishingly smooth, and full of poetic flourishes. He loved unexpected shifts in rhythm and rhyme scheme, and he helped popularize the practice of pushing a thought or a phrase past the end of a line, which poets call "enjambment":

> *He's kickin' it, 'cause it ain't no half-steppin'*
> *The party is live, the rhyme can't be kept in-*

side of me's erupting, just like a volcano
It ain't the everyday style, or the same ol'
rhyme...

Hip-hop's golden era was made possible not by radio play but by the emergence of a hip-hop audience so big, and so dedicated, that rappers could sell records without radio play. (The first Eric B. & Rakim album, *Paid in Full*, appeared in 1987, and although it sold something like a million copies, and is widely regarded as a classic, it earned little national radio play, and never rose higher than No. 58 on the *Billboard* chart.) Salt-N-Pepa, an exuberant duo, was an exception: the group was responsible for one of the era's most memorable singles, a suggestive dance track called "Push It," which turned out to be the start of a decade-long run of hits. Other rappers made careers—though not necessarily fortunes—away from the mainstream, honing distinctive and sometimes eccentric styles. Slick Rick was a cunning storyteller with a foppish image and a half-English accent that was honestly acquired: he and his parents, who were Jamaican, had immigrated to the Bronx from England when he was eleven. MC Lyte, from East Flatbush, Brooklyn, suggested a different direction for the genre with "Paper Thin," her 1988 single. It was notably candid and unpretentious, an implicit rebuke to the genre's many shouters and braggarts, and it began not with a proclamation but with an admission. "When you say you love me, it doesn't matter / It goes to my head as just chit-chatter," she rapped, matter-of-factly, as if she were working out how she really felt, in real time. And KRS-One, from a Bronx crew called Boogie Down Productions, was regal and grandiloquent, referring to himself as a hip-hop "teacher"; he explained, "See, kings lose crowns, but teachers stay intelligent / Talking big words on the mic, but still *irrelevant.*"

Here, too, Russell Simmons played a central role. Simmons's client Kurtis Blow had ended his debut album with a hilariously misguided cover version of "Takin' Care of Business," the seventies rock song. But with Def Jam, Simmons and Rubin aimed to release what Rubin later called "down-and-dirty hip-hop records," youthful and rebellious. What I didn't realize as a boy was that Simmons and his partner, Rubin, a white guy raised on punk, succeeded not by teaching rappers to imitate pop stars but by teaching rappers *not* to imitate pop stars. LL Cool J, the label's first star—and hip-hop's first true heartthrob—rose to fame while keeping pop music at arm's length. His brash breakthrough single was a kind of anti-radio radio record: "I Can't Live Without My Radio," an ode to the boom box. (Despite his popularity and evident charisma, LL Cool J didn't have a Top 10 pop hit until 1991, with "Around the Way Girl," a bubbly track from his fourth album.) And although the Beastie Boys were originally mistaken for a novelty act, they turned out to be loving and obsessive students of hip-hop—indeed, they stayed loyal to the ideals and sounds of 1980s hip-hop long after their peers had mostly faded away and the genre had mainly moved on.

One of Def Jam's most important achievements was to help turn Public Enemy into an unlikely success story—successful enough to change the public perception of what hip-hop was supposed to do and sound like. The group emerged from Long Island, led by Chuck D, who had a commanding voice and a militant sensibility. He was relatively old, twenty-six, when the group made its debut, and in the boisterous world of hip-hop, Chuck D's seriousness made him unusual. One of the Beastie Boys' signature refrains was "You gotta fight for your right to party!" Public Enemy responded with "Party for Your Right to Fight," an exhilarating rallying cry that put the group in the lineage of the Black Panther Party:

> *Power and equality and I'm out to get it*
> *I know some of you ain't with it*
> *This Party started right in '66*
> *With a pro-Black radical mix*

The lines were rapped by two voices simultaneously: Chuck D's, sober and authoritative, and Flavor Flav's, excitable and roguish. Flavor Flav, known for his oversize clock necklace and febrile dance moves, was an entertaining foil, and his presence allowed Chuck D to seem all the more serious by comparison. "Fight the Power," the group's defining track, appeared in the Spike Lee film *Do the Right Thing*, and Lee shot the music video, which showed the group leading a political march through Brooklyn in April 1989, repeating an all-purpose slogan of resistance: "We've got to fight the powers that be." To generations of listeners, Public Enemy was the ideal vision of a hip-hop group: fiery and politically engaged, marching through the streets to demand change. In fact, Public Enemy was an anomaly. Explicit political commentary has played a consistent but relatively minor role in the genre's evolution. If generations of fans and outsiders have nevertheless yearned, ever since the late eighties, for hip-hop to rediscover its political essence, that is the result of Public Enemy's lasting legacy, and also the result of a certain amount of wishful thinking. There is an aural illusion at work: rapping can sound a bit like speechifying, especially if you have a voice as resonant as Chuck D's. But hip-hop has generally been party music, not Party music. And the continued success of the genre has relied on the ability of rappers to get listeners to stop thinking about words and to hear the music in every phrase, no matter how militant.

Making Records Out of Records

In the original incarnation of hip-hop, DJs were in charge, because they provided the music that fueled the parties. But when hip-hop moved from clubs to records, the rappers took over, and DJs assumed a more marginal role. By convention, they were often given top billing, as if they were still the stars and the rappers were sidekicks: first Grandmaster Flash, then the Furious Five; first Eric B., then Rakim. On the records themselves, though, DJs could be minor or elusive presences. Listeners curious about what made Flash so great could hear for themselves on a 1981 single called "The

Adventures of Grandmaster Flash on the Wheels of Steel," which was a recording of Flash at work, recombining and transforming some of his favorite records. The next year, Grandmaster Flash and the Furious Five released *The Message*, which was an international hit and a defining moment for early hip-hop: it paired hard hand claps and gleaming synthesizers with rhymes about life in the ghetto. ("God is smiling on you, but he's frowning, too / Because only God knows what you'll go through.) But it was an odd sort of triumph for Grandmaster Flash himself, because by all accounts he played no role in writing, producing, or performing it. According to the emerging conventions of recorded hip-hop, rappers were out front, delivering the lyrics, and producers were behind the scenes, composing the tracks. DJs sometimes seemed rather extraneous.

For a time, the sound of eighties hip-hop was squiggly and staccato, overlapping with an emerging dance genre known as electro. Afrika Bambaataa, one of the Bronx pioneers, had an international club hit in 1982 with "Planet Rock," which combined old-fashioned party raps with a bleeding-edge beat based on a track by Kraftwerk, the avant-garde German electronic group. But as the golden era began, producers were finding new ways to make records out of records. Marley Marl, from Queens, combined old vinyl with new technology to evoke the trebly noise of a raucous party, and years later he posted a series of videos explaining how he did it. For "The Bridge," in 1986, by a rapper called MC Shan, Marley Marl used a digital "sampler" to record a crisp drumbeat from an obscure seventies funk record by a group called the Honey Drippers, and then used an early drum machine to trigger—or "play"—those drum sounds in the pattern and tempo he wanted. For noise, he found a horn part he liked on an old disco record and then ran it backward, creating a disorienting blast that grew louder and then suddenly cut out. The sampling era turned hip-hop into a genre ruled by record collectors: you used your vinyl library to create your musical identity. Public Enemy was known for chaotic collages created by a group of in-house producers, the Bomb Squad. "Fight the Power," the group's signature song, begins with Chuck D declaring, "1989, the number, another summer / Sound of the funky drummer." He was naming the year, but he was also naming the source of the beat: "Funky Drummer," a 1970 James Brown single that includes, near the end, a sublime eight-bar showcase for his drummer, Clyde Stubblefield. "Funky Drummer" had been a minor hit (No. 20 R&B, No. 51 pop), but thanks to Stubblefield, it became one of the most frequently sampled records of all time.

By embracing sampling, hip-hop scrambled musical history, creating a canon that gave new life to big names like James Brown, elevated obscurities like the Honey Drippers, and challenged old ideas about what was cool. In *Making Beats*, a book about hip-hop sampling, Joseph G. Schloss, an ethnomusicologist, considered "Say No Go," a lighthearted but exasperated track about drug addiction from De La Soul's 1989 debut album, *3 Feet High and Rising*. The song is built around a fistful of samples, most prominently a snippet from "I Can't Go for That (No Can Do)," the feathery 1981 pop hit by Hall and Oates. Schloss cited an academic analysis of De La Soul's track, which called it a prime example of "the art of ironic sampling," because it transformed "the cheesiest pop song imaginable" into something "hip." But when Schloss relayed this analysis to Prince Paul, who helped produce the track, Prince Paul demurred, saying there was nothing "ironic" about his enthusiasm for Hall and Oates. "That's pretty deep," Prince Paul told Schloss. "But I think the bottom line is just: That was a good song!"

De La Soul's approach to sampling may not have been ironic, but it was certainly mischievous. The release of *3 Feet High and Rising* marked the dawn of a new, self-critical era in hip-hop. The album was playful and odd, full of non sequiturs and in-jokes. (One member was known as Trugoy the Dove, which was an alteration of his name, "Dave," and a backward acknowledgment that he loved yogurt.) Before then, many rappers had aimed to show and tell the world that they were better than their peers, but De La Soul seemed more interested in being different. One track consisted mainly of snippets of rappers promising to "rock" the audience—the group was inviting listeners to test their knowledge of hip-hop history, while also, perhaps, showing how formulaic the genre could be. Another track lampooned hip-hop fashion, from Adidas sneakers to bomber jackets. Instead of promising to delight crowds, the members of De La Soul promised to do nothing more or less than express themselves with integrity: "Right is wrong when hype is written on the Soul—De La, that is / Style is surely our own thing, not the false disguise of show biz." The group sometimes promised to usher in a "D.A.I.S.Y. Age"; the letters stood for "da inner sound, y'all," a formulation that suggested that hip-hop didn't need to be party music at all.

De La Soul had allies in its effort to rethink hip-hop: the group was part of Native Tongues, a collective that was often perceived as an alternative to the genre's mainstream. The Jungle Brothers, another Native Tongues act, wore Afrocentric clothes and found unexpected ways to connect hip-hop to the African diaspora. *Done by the Forces of Nature*, the group's second album, included a sample of voices saying, "Ooga-chaka, Ooga-ooga-ooga-chaka." Some listeners might have imagined it was an African field recording, but actually it was a nonsense chant from a Swedish version of an English version of an American pop song, "Hooked on a Feeling." (World music, after all—just not the kind listeners were expecting.) The first album by Queen Latifah, *All Hail the Queen*, also arrived in 1989, dignified but danceable. "Ladies first, there's no time to rehearse / I'm divine and my mind expands throughout the universe," she rapped, and in later decades she was so successful as an actress and singer that some fans probably have no idea, now, that she used to rap. Black Sheep was a Native Tongues act, too, although Dres and Mista Lawnge liked to think of themselves as misfits within this misfit crew—their group name reflected their status as the impish "lowlifes" of the family. And then there was A Tribe Called Quest, which in 1989 released *People's Instinctive Travels and the Paths of Rhythm*, an album with a long-winded title and a streamlined approach—it used beats and riffs from seventies jazz and R&B records to create a sophisticated, grown-up sound. Over a sample of the keyboardist Les McCann, Q-Tip transformed an aimless night in New York into a bucolic literary scene:

> *A Jeep is blasting from the urban streets*
> *Loops of funk over hardcore beats*
> *The moon dabbles in the morning sky*
> *As the minutes just creep on by*

Sometimes, sampling was a way to stitch together obscure snippets to create a new composition that sounded vaguely familiar, though maybe unplaceable. And sometimes sampling was closer in spirit to a venerable rock 'n' roll tradition: the cover version. In the years after Kurtis Blow sang "Takin' Care of Business," rappers tended to avoid straightforward cover versions, perhaps because listeners generally expected hip-hop lyrics to be original, each verse the singular expression of the person delivering it. (For decades, the structure of a hip-hop track remained remarkably strict: an eight-bar refrain, two verses of sixteen bars, and an optional third verse of either eight or sixteen bars; this formula was so well-known that "sixteen" became a slang term for a hip-hop verse.) In 1986, the members of Run-DMC were considering writing a track based on "Walk This Way," an old hard-rock hit by Aerosmith that had an appealingly brisk, rap-friendly beat. But instead of using a snippet of the old record, they were persuaded by Rick Rubin, who was helping to produce them, to remake the entire song, with help from Steven Tyler and Joe Perry, from Aerosmith. The sample became instead a cover version, a collaboration, and a blockbuster hit, reinvigorating Aerosmith's career and putting Run-DMC into heavy rotation on MTV.

It is surely no coincidence that a number of the first blockbuster hip-hop hits were, like "Walk This Way," based on older songs. In 1989, a rapper named Tone Lōc used the riff from another hard-rock song—"Jamie's Cryin'," a 1978 Van Halen favorite—as the basis for his hit single "Wild

Thing." To underscore the connection to rock, he filmed a music video that parodied "Addicted to Love," the chart-topping 1986 song by the British rock star Robert Palmer. Amid a copse of models pretending to play electric guitars, Tone Lōc mugged for the camera, delivering casual rhymes about casual sex in a raspy voice: "Took her to the hotel. She said, 'You're the king' / I said, 'Be my queen, if you know what I mean, and let's do the wild thing." The next year, an entrepreneurial Oakland rapper named MC Hammer perfected this kind of musical recycling with "U Can't Touch This," pairing perfunctory rhymes with a four-word refrain, some frenetic dance moves, and a classic groove. I was thirteen when "U Can't Touch This" suddenly took over MTV and radio, and at first I had no idea that it was built on the Rick James funk hit "Super Freak," from 1981. But for older or savvier listeners, the appeal of "U Can't Touch This" was partly nostalgic—it revived a song that was halfway between recent and ancient, in pop terms. (MC Hammer's label delayed releasing a cassette single in order to force fans to buy the album; as a consequence, the song only went to No. 8, but the album became the first hip-hop album ever to be certified diamond, for US sales of over ten million copies.) A few months after MC Hammer, Vanilla Ice did almost exactly the same thing: his breakthrough single, "Ice Ice Baby," used the bassline from a different 1981 hit, "Under Pressure," a collaboration between Queen and David Bowie.

Those two hits, "U Can't Touch This" and "Ice Ice Baby," were widely mocked and loathed, respectively—MC Hammer was a charming hustler in billowy pants, while Vanilla Ice was a preening idol with a defensive streak. For years, rappers had been battling the perception that sampling was a lazy and unimaginative way to make records. (In 1988, after the jazz and R&B musician James Mtume criticized sampling, a group called Stetsasonic released a track called "Talkin' All That Jazz," rapping, "A sample's just a tactic, / A portion of my method, a tool—in fact, it's / Only of importance when I make it a priority.") The ubiquity of "U Can't Touch This" and "Ice Ice Baby" only heightened this perception. One representative newspaper review of MC Hammer's subsequent arena tour suggested that he relied on samples because he didn't have any good ideas of his own. "Once he borrows something worthwhile," the critic complained, "he rarely knows what to do with it, folding the snippets into drearily repetitious tunes."

For hip-hop fans, the debate over sampling was shaped by the fact that rappers, not producers, were generally considered to be the authors of hip-hop tracks, which meant that the questions of originality typically centered around lyrics and cadence. It was considered shameful to swipe someone else's rhymes, as Big Bank Hank did, or to imitate someone else's rhyme style. And serious hip-hop listeners tended to dismiss the big pop hits. (Reviewing MC Hammer's album, *The Source* declared, "We don't know one rap fan who has bought it or even listened to it.") But within hip-hop, everyone agreed that there was nothing inherently shameful about rhyming over someone else's beat—done properly, it could even be seen as an act of self-assertion. In 1990, the rapper Ice Cube, a former member of the group N.W.A, released a track called "Jackin' for Beats," in which he rapped over other rappers' music. The track ended, provocatively, with a snippet from the first record N.W.A had made without him. He snarled, "Ice Cube will take a funky beat and reshape it / Locate a dope break and then I *break it*."

It turned out that the aesthetic debate over sampling was less consequential than the legal one. In the early days of hip-hop, copyright questions were settled on a case-by-case basis. The music on "Rapper's Delight," the breakthrough Sugarhill Gang hit, came from a studio band re-creating the break from "Good Times," the disco hit by Chic; to fend off a lawsuit, Sugarhill Gang's record label agreed to grant sole songwriting credit to Nile Rodgers and Bernard Edwards, from Chic. But no one knew exactly how to settle the claims raised by sampling, especially since some tracks sampled more than one song. (What if you sampled three musicians, and all three of them demanded sole songwriting credit?) Jimmy Castor, the funk musician who helped inspire hip-hop, won a settlement after suing the Beastie Boys for sampling a drumbeat and a vocal snippet—"Yo, Leroy!"—from an old record of his. The Turtles, a sixties rock band, reportedly won a seven-figure settlement after De La Soul used one of their songs as the basis for an interlude on *3 Feet High and Rising*. It seemed clear that De La Soul's usage could only have increased the popularity of the Turtles; there was no plausible scenario in which a shopper in the market for a Turtles greatest-hits compilation would have decided to buy the new De La Soul album, instead. An attorney for De La Soul's record label told the *Los Angeles Times*, "I'm not saying there is no sample of the Turtles, but other things are also involved [on the track] that are not the Turtles." It was becoming clear, though, that rappers had little leverage in negotiations with the artists they sampled, especially after the fact. This was proven in 1991, when the singer-songwriter Gilbert O'Sullivan prevailed in court against the prankish rapper Biz Markie, who had sampled one of his songs. The judge ordered Biz Markie's album pulled from the record stores, and referred him for criminal prosecution for theft; at the last minute, the case was settled out of court, but it taught the hip-hop industry that sampling was essentially indefensible, legally speaking. In order to safely sell copies of any hip-hop album, a record company needed to sign agreements with every artist sampled on it.

This precedent turned sampling from an act of appropriation into an act of collaboration, the product of a negotiation between lawyers on both sides. In the eighties, many rappers figured they could safely sample, especially if they were using only small snippets from obscure records. But after the Biz Markie case, producers realized that this approach could make things difficult or impossible for the lawyers, who might be sent on a series of scavenger hunts. If a sample was likely to be expensive in any case, why not pay to use a big, popular refrain, instead of a random snippet? Sean "Puffy" Combs, the producer and rapper also known as Puff Daddy, perfected this approach in the late nineties. He became a constant presence on the radio by retrofitting old hits with new hip-hop verses. He helped turn "I'm Coming Out," by Diana Ross, into "Mo Money, Mo Problems," by the Notorious B.I.G.; after B.I.G. was murdered, he helped turn "Every

Breath You Take," by the Police, into "I'll Be Missing You," a tribute. In "Feel So Good," a 1997 hip-hop hit that combined a recognizable Kool and the Gang riff ("Hollywood Swinging," 1974) with a recognizable Gloria Estefan chorus ("Bad Boy," 1985), Combs's protégé Ma$e bragged about this efficient strategy: "Take hits from the eighties / But do it sound so crazy." Combs was a flamboyant figure, known for his shiny suits, and plenty of hip-hop connoisseurs scoffed at him, especially because it wasn't exactly clear what he did. He was a producer, and yet his productions tended to be group efforts; he was a rapper, and yet he relied on ghostwriters. But in some ways he was a throwback to the earliest days of the genre, when rapping wasn't quite so important. Back then, DJs ruled, and their most important skill was the ability to choose some old records and use them to create a memorable party.

Street-Corner Rhymes

The album cover told you nothing about the music, and everything about the sensibility. It was an image of a Black hand with gleaming rings holding a sheaf of hundred-dollar bills. There was no face, just a torso: a slick suit with a wonderfully redundant button on the lapel, depicting a Black fist holding a stack of bills. "HUSTLERS CONVENTION," the pin read, and if you looked closely you could see a shiny bracelet that spelled out a name, Lightnin' Rod. The album appeared in 1973, and many buyers probably did not know that Lightnin' Rod was the alter ego of an oral poet named Jalal Mansur Nuriddin, who was a member of the Last Poets, the fearsomely righteous spoken-word group. Backed by a band of accomplished R&B musicians, Nuriddin tells one long story in verse—a series of sextains, with a loose sense of meter and a strict A-A-B-C-C-B rhyme scheme. Nuriddin chronicles a world of pimps, gamblers, gangsters, and dope dealers; the story culminates, naturally, with police and prison, but the mood throughout is jocular. This is a tall tale, one that can't help but glorify the demimonde it documents: a place where "There'll be money for the making / Bitches for the taking / And all you can shoot, snort, smoke, or drink."

The *Hustlers Convention* album drew from a long tradition of African American street-corner rhymes—ribald stories told and retold over the decades. The most famous of these is the tale of "the signifying monkey," which is said to have roots in Yoruba mythology, brought to America by enslaved Africans. In 1964, Roger D. Abrahams, a folklorist, collected many of these street-corner tales in an indispensable book called *Deep Down in the Jungle: Negro Narrative Folklore from the Streets of Philadelphia*, based on research he conducted while studying at the University of Pennsylvania. The stories Abrahams collected were vivid and often profane: "My blood began to boil, my ass began to itch / I jumped up and shot that rotten bitch." This language was not meant to offend unsuspecting listeners, because it was not meant to reach unsuspecting listeners. These were private stories, made only marginally less private by virtue of their inclusion in a scholarly book about urban folklore.

With the rise of hip-hop, though, this private tradition became public, and eventually profitable. While most of the early hip-hop hits were purposefully inoffensive, another hip-hop lineage was quietly emerging. A Philadelphia rapper named Schoolly D released a single in 1985 called "P.S.K. (What Does It Mean?)." What "P.S.K." meant was "Parkside Killers," a local gang, and Schoolly D's lyrics sounded like variants of the stories that Abrahams had collected in the same city, two decades before: "Put my pistol up against his head / And said, 'You sucker-ass nigga, I should shoot you dead.'" (A few years later, Schoolly D even recorded his own version of the old folktale about the monkey, calling it "Signifying Rapper.") Shortly after the song's release, Schoolly D told a Dutch documentary crew that unlike more popular rappers, he offered an unexpurgated chronicle of street life. "Our style is raw—very raw," he said. "If Run-DMC's buddies do crack, they not gon' say it, because the record companies won't let 'em say it, first of all. 'You can't be affiliated with drugs.' But, you know, if it's happening, *we* gon' say it." In *Spin*, the insightful cultural critic John Leland praised Schoolly D, using a term that few people knew: he wrote that "P.S.K." was "the ultimate gangster rap record"—musically "cool," but morally "bad." In New York in 1986, a similarly uncompromising rapper, Just-Ice, proclaimed himself "the Gangster of Hip-Hop." In Oakland, a rapper named Too $hort took inspiration from the local drug dealers and sex workers; starting in 1985, he released a series of albums full of street-life stories. Most influential of all was Ice-T, who moved from New Jersey to Los Angeles as a boy, and who had already lived a full life (soldier, thief, failed drug dealer, part-time pimp) when, in 1986, he released "6 in the Mornin'," which contained ten verses of rhymes about crime and, in much smaller quantity, punishment. This was a commercial product, not a street-corner tale, and yet Ice-T's rhymes sounded like private stories, which gave them a voyeuristic appeal. "The batter rams rolling, rocks are the thing / Life has no meaning and money is king," he rapped, and listeners could congratulate themselves for knowing that "batter rams" were what the Los Angeles Police Department used to bash down doors, and "rocks" were crack cocaine. Where a rapper like Rakim claimed hip-hop credibility because of his dazzling technique, Ice-T claimed a different kind of credibility: like Schoolly D, he offered himself as an authentic voice of life on the streets.

The appearance, in 1987, of an independently released single called "The Boyz-n-the Hood" seemed at first like merely one more example of this street-corner tradition, updated for the hip-hop age. The voice was reedy and the lyrics were cheerful but brutal: in the second verse, the narrator shoots a former friend; in the third verse, he slaps a "stupid bitch" for impertinence. But buyers who looked closely may have noticed something unusual: the rapper on the track was Eazy-E, and yet the songwriting credit was assigned to a different rapper, Ice Cube. This might have undermined Eazy-E's credibility, if he were the type of rapper to brag about his way with words, but he wasn't—he presented himself not as a virtuoso but as a neighborhood tough guy, backed by a crew. That crew called itself N.W.A, or Niggaz with Attitudes, and the group's 1988 debut album, *Straight Outta Compton*, is among the most consequential hip-hop albums ever released.

Part of what made the album so important was that it was so well made. The group included a handful of producers, including Dr. Dre, who was then unknown; they used warm samples and cold drum-machine beats to build tracks so sturdy they seemed to be encased in armor. Eazy-E, the group's leader, and Ice Cube, the group's best rapper, pulled the album in different directions. Eazy-E rapped about partying and gunplay, in the street-corner tradition. Ice Cube was both fiercer and more high-minded. "Fuck tha police," he snarled in the incendiary track of the same name, but his verse was a lucid complaint about police harassment: "Searchin' my car, lookin' for the product / Thinkin' every nigga is sellin' narcotics." The track generated a furious backlash. The Federal Bureau of Investigation sent a letter of complaint to N.W.A's record label, and at a concert in Detroit, in 1989, police officers physically prevented the group from performing. N.W.A's success helped convince the broader public that hip-hop was not some goofy fad but a serious cultural development, and a potentially pernicious one. *Newsweek* put hip-hop on the cover in 1990, with a headline that rhymed, though not well: RAP RAGE: YO! STREET RHYME HAS GONE BIG TIME, BUT ARE THOSE SOUNDS OUT OF BOUNDS? The same year, the Black lifestyle magazine *Ebony* worried about rap's "image problem," noting that many rappers had "street-tough attitudes" and that they delivered lyrics "that would be completely unintelligible were it not for the heavy doses of four-letter words mixed in for effect."

Thanks almost solely to *Straight Outta Compton*, which was both a bestseller and a national obsession, "gangster rap," a formulation that seemed rather exotic when John Leland used it in the pages of *Spin*, became a term everyone knew, even if people didn't quite agree on what it meant. The word "gangster"—or, more and more, "gangsta"—suggested a link between hip-hop and the distinctive gang culture of Southern California, although the members of N.W.A did not rap explicitly about Bloods or Crips. Sometimes "gangsta rap" referred to a subgenre: a tough-talking, bass-heavy form of hip-hop that thrived in Southern California, carried forward by rappers (DJ Quik, MC Eiht) who never really crossed over to the pop charts. More often, the term was used as shorthand for any rapper whose rhymes featured "heavy doses of four-letter words," as *Ebony* put it. Gangsta rap was what happened when Black street-corner tales found their way into the mainstream, and the mainstream recoiled in horror. In 1990, Rick Rubin was running a new label, Def American, when he encountered a problem: his major-label partner, Geffen Records, refused to distribute an album by a Houston group called the Geto Boys, because it contained gruesome rhymes about murder and rape. (A subsidiary of Warner Bros. eventually agreed to distribute the album, and the Geto Boys are now regarded as hip-hop pioneers; in 2019 the group's greatest rapper, Scarface, ran for a seat on the Houston City Council and won more than a third of the votes.) Often, people talked about gangsta rap as if it were an alien invasion, conquering a once-exalted genre and bringing it low. In 1997, an article in *Ebony* asked, "Will Gangsta Rap Sink Hip-Hop?"

Hip-hop didn't sink, but neither did it return to the way it was before *Straight Outta Compton*. Older acts scrambled to adapt. As gangsta rap was exploding, Run-DMC appeared on *The Arsenio Hall Show,* and one member, Run, tried to reassure viewers that his group's new album wasn't inoffensive. "We've got a little bit of cursing on there," he said rather piteously. "Run-DMC has *always* been rough." Even hip-hop acts, like Black Sheep, that lampooned the excesses of gangsta rap nevertheless tended to use language that would have sounded out of place on, say, the first Run-DMC album. And the founding fathers of gangsta rap enjoyed extraordinary sustained success. I remember seeing an Ice-T music video on MTV when I was thirteen, sometime in late 1989: he was onstage at what looked like a rock concert, lip-synching the words alongside some musicians who seemed to be playing entirely different songs, and the scene was so chaotic and confusing that it convinced me to head downtown and buy his new album. (The album was called *The Iceberg: Freedom of Speech… Just Watch What You Say!*—this was the album with the introduction by Jello Biafra, from the punk band Dead Kennedys, that helped inspire my conversion to the doctrine of punk rock.) Years later, Ice-T would become a familiar presence on television, on *Law & Order: Special Victims Unit.* It was an unlikely evolution. In 1992, with his metal-influenced side project, Body Count, Ice-T created a national uproar with a song called "Cop Killer." On *Law & Order: Special Victims Unit*, he has spent two decades playing a gruff but heroic detective in the New York Police Department.

Perhaps because the gangsta rap movement was based in Southern California, it flourished on-screen: films like *Boyz n the Hood*, in 1991, and *Menace II Society*, in 1993, helped dramatize the world that N.W.A had rapped about. And Ice Cube, the most venerable of the original "gangsta" rappers, left N.W.A to become not just a successful solo artist but a bona fide movie star, too. His departure sparked a yearslong feud and destabilized N.W.A. The follow-up to *Straight Outta Compton* arrived in 1991, bearing a backward title, *Efil4zaggin.* It was less idealistic and in some ways more provocative—more in the street-corner tradition—than its predecessor. The first half was mainly about violence, and the second half was mainly about sex, although sometimes these themes combined, as in a brief but unsettling interlude called "To Kill a Hooker." It became the top-selling album in the country, despite not spawning any hit singles, and the group disbanded not long after the album's release. (Eazy-E persisted as a solo act until his death, from AIDS complications, in 1995.) In retrospect, *Efil4zaggin* is remembered less for the rhymes than for the sublime clarity and sheen of the beats, which were largely the work of Dr. Dre, who turned out to be a new kind of virtuoso. Dr. Dre had a knack for mixing together samples with electronic sounds and live instruments to create a streamlined and futuristic style that evoked seventies funk, and his 1992 solo album, *The Chronic*, proved that so-called gangsta rap could sell like pop music without *sounding* like pop music. Although he had a rich and resonant voice,

Dr. Dre was primarily a producer, not a rapper—he generally outsourced the writing of his rhymes to rapper protégés. Gangsta rap was widely reviled for its lyrics, and yet the movement's biggest star turned out to be a guy who was more interested in music than words. Dr. Dre launched the career of Snoop Dogg; he produced Tupac Shakur's biggest hit, "California Love"; he helped Eminem and then 50 Cent become two of the most popular rappers of the contemporary era; and eventually he cofounded Beats Electronics, an audio equipment company that was acquired by Apple in 2014. The deal confirmed Dr. Dre's status as a hip-hop immortal, reportedly earning him hundreds of millions of dollars and allowing him to do something that many rappers had promised to do but few had managed: leave hip-hop behind.

I'm Not a Rapper

Once upon a time, rappers were proud to be rappers. Rappers rapped mainly about rapping: first they introduced themselves, and then they told you what they were doing. "What you hear is not a test, I'm rapping to the beat," Wonder Mike explained in "Rapper's Delight," as if he couldn't quite believe it. Run-DMC had a different attitude, but a similarly self-referential approach; as DMC once explained, "I rock the party with the words I speak / And Run says the rhymes that are unique." Rakim, from Eric B. & Rakim, was known for his innovative flow and mystical imagery, but he, too, often found himself rapping about how great he was at rapping: "The heat is on, you see / smoke, then I'm finished when the beat is gone. I'm no / joke." Other golden-era rappers rapped about what they were doing in slightly different terms. By portraying himself as a teacher, KRS-One was giving himself an altered identity while still acknowledging his vocation; every lyric could be a lesson, every listener a pupil. Chuck D liked to remind listeners that he was both a rapper and a rabble-rouser, exclaiming, "Power of the people, say, 'Make a miracle, D, pump the lyrical!'"—in essence, a rhyme calling for protests calling for more rhymes. And in tracks like "Can I Kick It?" and "Check the Rhime," A Tribe Called Quest framed rapping as a form of social recreation, a semi-competitive game played with friends.

One reason why gangsta rap took over is that it helped give rappers something else to rap about. Instead of rhyming endlessly (if inventively) about lyrical skill, rappers could disappear into their rhymes: each album could be a series of stories, with the star as the daring protagonist. You can hear the transition on *Straight Outta Compton*, which artfully blurred the line between literal and figurative boasts. When Ice Cube rhymed, "Here's a murder rap to keep y'all dancin' / With a crime record like Charles Manson," he was punning on the dual meanings of "rap" and "record," allowing listeners to decide for themselves whether he was an actual criminal or just a rapper obsessed with the language of crime. In the years that followed, many gangsta rappers dispensed with this ambiguity altogether, portraying themselves as gangsters by nature, and rappers only by necessity or by happenstance. (In 1993, hundreds of thousands of people bought *Bangin on Wax*, the debut album by a group called Bloods & Crips; the selling point was that these were real-life gang members, not professional rappers.) On *The Chronic*, Dr. Dre and his streetwise and sleepy-voiced young protégé, Snoop Dogg, made it even easier for listeners to forget that they were rappers. As they extolled their allies and menaced their enemies, including Dr. Dre's former musical partner Eazy-E, they insisted that they were real gangsters—"real Gs," as Dr. Dre put it. In this formulation, and in hip-hop more broadly, the word "real" was all-important.

For decades, the phrase "keep it real" had been used as a vague, slangy imperative. ("You gotta keep it steady, baby / Got to keep it real," Daryl Hall sang in a Hall and Oates song from 1974.) But sometime around 1995, the phrase exploded, emerging as the new guiding imperative of the hip-hop world. It appeared in a number of hip-hop tracks that year, including one by the group Cypress Hill, and another by California's newest hip-hop star, Tupac Shakur, who advertised his integrity: "Tryin' to maintain in this dirty game / Keep it real, and I will, even if it kills me." The phrase had come to be associated with a strain of gangsta verisimilitude—in a way, it was an updated version of the "outlaw" ethos of seventies country. But not everyone appreciated it. In 1995, an artist manager complained in *Billboard* that the ethos was undermining rap's popularity. "The music is poisoning itself because it doesn't have enough diversity in its messages—just this 'keep it real, keep it hard' attitude," he said. But "keep it real" proved to be a versatile directive, because depending on the context it could mean "keep it gangsta" or, perhaps contrarily, "be yourself." In an interview from around the same time, the Notorious B.I.G., the Brooklyn rapper who became Shakur's rival, was asked for advice for aspiring hip-hop stars. "Basically, just to keep it real, you know what I'm saying? Stay real to yourself," he said.

Shakur first emerged in the early 1990s as a rather bohemian figure: a good-looking rapper who was also a poet and actor, the son of Black Panther Party activists, named after an eighteenth-century Peruvian insurgent. As a rapper, he spelled his name 2pac, and developed a reputation for brash but earnest rhymes about the injustice of Black life in America: "To my homies on the block, gettin' dropped by cops / I'm still around for ya, keepin' my sound underground for ya." But by 1995, when he released an influential album called *Me Against the World*, he was a scandalous figure. He had survived an altercation with off-duty police officers, he had been convicted of sexual abuse, and he had been shot and robbed in a recording studio. Shakur was in prison when the album was released, and when he regained his freedom he was hungry for revenge against the Notorious B.I.G., whom he believed had set him up to be shot. Part of the appeal of *Me Against the World* was that it encouraged listeners to draw parallels between what they heard in the lyrics—which were, by turns, defiant, resentful, and fatalistic—and what they knew about Shakur's life.

Shakur's rival, B.I.G., was born in Brooklyn to Jamaican immigrants, and although he didn't resemble a movie star (he called himself "chubby" and "ugly" in lyrics), he was perhaps the best writer in the genre's history. B.I.G.

used heavy stress patterns to make his lines swing, and sly humor to make them stick, bragging, "We're smokin', drinkin', got the hooker thinkin', / If money smell bad, then this nigga Biggie stinkin'!" Even more important, he knew how to turn himself into a memorable character. On *Ready to Die*, his 1994 debut, he chronicled his life from birth to death, by suicide, suggesting that crime had saved him from poverty, and that hip-hop had saved him from crime—some crime, anyway. ("I'm the triple-beam dream," he crowed, mentioning a professional-grade scale as a way of asserting that he was literally a former dope dealer, or that his music was figuratively dope.) B.I.G. was an unusually compelling protagonist, which may explain why, when he released a track called "Who Shot Ya?" shortly after Shakur was shot, Shakur interpreted the lyrics as a provocation, even though they had been written earlier. Shakur responded with some contemptuous tracks of his own, and soon the feud had drawn in others; because B.I.G. was from Brooklyn and Shakur was based in California, many people interpreted it as a kind of hip-hop civil war, East Coast versus West Coast. It was transfixing, and slightly sickening: two of the genre's biggest stars, ringleaders in a transcontinental dispute, in an atmosphere of real violence. Shakur was murdered in September 1996, and B.I.G. was murdered six months later; neither case was solved, which means no one can say whether the killings were the result of the feud. But the episode illustrated both how dangerous a hip-hop feud could be, and how compelling. A hip-hop feud evokes the early days of the genre, while also helping turn rappers more fully into characters. Part of the power of hearing B.I.G. sneer, "Who shot ya?" is that even now we can hear it the way Shakur evidently did, as something more specific—more *real*, perhaps—than an idle threat.

The deaths of Shakur and B.I.G. drew extra attention to hip-hop, helping make the genre more popular than ever. Shakur lived on, on murals and T-shirts around the world, as a hip-hop saint, and dozens or hundreds of rappers copied his image, down to the way he sometimes wore a bandanna knotted across his forehead, and his habit of drawing out syllables for emphasis. B.I.G. lived on, too: the outpouring of grief helped turn his executive producer, Sean "Puffy" Combs, into a mainstream pop star, and elevated a number of his protégés and contemporaries. One of them was Lil' Kim, who remade hip-hop in her own image, fierce and glamorous. She was sometimes treated as a novelty: promoted as the first—that is, only—lady of B.I.G.'s crew, Junior M.A.F.I.A., celebrated and sometimes criticized for rhymes that made her seem as bloodthirsty and sex-obsessed as her male counterparts. She rapped, "Nobody do it better / Bet I wet ya, like hurricanes and typhoons / Got buffoons eating my pussy while I watch cartoons." Like her mentor, Lil' Kim also had a rival, a similarly self-possessed rapper named Foxy Brown; together (which is to say, very much apart), they helped invent an enduring new gangster archetype.

Another rapper who thrived in the wake of B.I.G. was Jay-Z, who honed a cleverly low-key approach: he rapped like one of those mob bosses who were so tough they didn't need to raise their voices. (Instead of threatening to shoot someone, Jay-Z might simply declare, airily, "Believe you me, son / I hate to do it just as bad as you hate to see it done.") Jay-Z helped popularize another revolution in hip-hop narrative: he didn't just emphasize his credentials as a former street hustler, he sometimes minimized his considerable lyrical skill, encouraging listeners to pretend he wasn't a rapper at all. He once rhymed, "I'm not looking at you dudes, I'm looking past ya / I thought I told you characters: I'm not a rapper." This was a subtle threat—a way of warning adversaries not to assume that he didn't mean what he was saying. But it was also a way of acknowledging that the hierarchy had shifted.

Back in the eighties, a rapper was a glamorous thing to be. But by the late nineties, the top rappers seemed to want to be thought of as mafiosi, instead, or perhaps tycoons. Rappers were expected to start fashion lines and record labels and other ventures; while rock stars once feared being described as sellouts, hip-hop stars were eager to tell fans about their business dealings. "I'm not a businessman / I'm a business, man," as Jay-Z once put it. As more rappers achieved huge success without forsaking the "gangsta" ethos, success and its trappings became the genre's main subjects. You could become rich by bragging about being rich, and so assets like cars and diamonds, or "ice," provided proof that you were as good as your word. The late nineties and early 2000s were sometimes known, in hip-hop, as the "bling-bling" era; the term was popularized in a 1999 hit by the New Orleans rapper B.G., which asked, "What kinda nigga got diamonds that'll—bling!—blind ya?" And as fascination with the drug-dealing life increased, a pair of upstart hip-hop magazines, *F.E.D.S.* (Finally Every Dimension of the Streets) and *Don Diva*, built avid readerships by publishing profiles of infamous kingpins, who shared war stories and old snapshots, often from behind bars. Why dally with gangsta rappers when you could have the real thing?

This was the climate in which rappers became self-hating rappers, reluctant to talk much about craft in interviews, let alone on record. In 2001, when I asked Jay-Z to talk about the old days, when he was first emerging as a great rapper, he politely corrected me. "It wasn't about *rap*, it was more about life, for me," he said, as if his meticulous rhymes about joy and pain were merely a by-product of everything else that was going on. "All those things that was happening in *Reasonable Doubt*? They was *happening*." That album, *Reasonable Doubt*, was Jay-Z's first, from 1996, and it includes a track called "D'Evils," a kind of meta-allegory about the art of rapping. In the second verse, a hustler kidnaps a young mother because he's looking for her lover, who has betrayed him. The hustler pays her to squeal, and there's an implication of violence—"My hand around her collar"—as he stuffs her full of bills: "About his whereabouts I wasn't convinced / I kept feeding her money till her shit started to make sense." This was how the hip-hop industry often worked, feeding its stars money and power in exchange for a convincing story. A *real* gangster, of course, would never "rap"—this was the paradox at the heart of "gangsta rap."

In the 2000s, this paradox helped change the way hip-hop sounded, forcing rappers to find new ways to explain—and justify—what they were doing. Eminem, a white rapper who emerged in the late nineties as Dr. Dre's newest protégé, scrambled the gangsta rap approach. His rhymes, sometimes delivered by an alter ego named Slim Shady, exploded with *too much* sex and violence, making gangsta bravado seem ridiculous. Instead of hoping that everyone would forget that he was a rapper, Eminem used his cascading syllables to remind listeners that it was his job to exaggerate and provoke:

> *How many retards'll listen to me*
> *and run up in the school, shootin', when they're pissed at a tea-*
>   *cher? Her? Him? Is it you? Is it them?*
> *"Wasn't me! Slim Shady said to do it again!"*

Eminem's dense, carefully enunciated lyrics made him a star, but also an outlier. In the early 2000s, hip-hop was heading in a different direction, under the influence of rappers like 50 Cent, a mischievous hitmaker allied with both Eminem and Dr. Dre. In keeping with gangsta tradition, 50 Cent used his biography to enliven his rhymes: all of his fans knew that he loved to pick fights with fellow rappers and that he had survived an ambush in which he was shot nine times. (He scoffed at his would-be killers: "These pussy niggas puttin' money on my head / Go on and get your refund, mo'fucker—I ain't dead.") The shooting left him with a slight speech impediment, but his slurry voice turned out to be an important asset. It was the aural equivalent of Jay-Z's nonchalant attitude, conveying the sense that 50 Cent was a bit too cool for his day job. He broke through with "In da Club," one of the biggest hits in hip-hop history; I remember listening to the radio the night it was released, as the DJ played it over and over for what seemed like half an hour. There was a gleaming, infectious beat, co-produced by Dr. Dre, but the main attraction was 50 Cent's tuneful and nonchalant flow: rappers sometimes talk about "spitting" lyrics, but 50 Cent came closer to murmuring them. Singing them, even. 50 Cent was one of a handful of hip-hop stars who realized that listeners would be happy to listen to rappers carry a tune, or try to. If it was no longer cool to brag about being a rapper, then perhaps it wasn't so cool to sound like one, either. This development produced a string of imaginative and charming hit records, but it also raised an awkward question. If rapping—rhymed, rhythmic talking—was now optional, then what, exactly, was hip-hop?

The Real Face of Rap

What is hip-hop? There have always been two overlapping answers to this question. Hip-hop is rapping. And hip-hop is Black music—more specifically, music created and nurtured by young Black innovators, often living and working in Black neighborhoods in major cities. Like country music, it is both an artistic tradition and a cultural identity. Anyone can rap, and throughout the history of hip-hop, plenty of anyones *have* rapped. But because of the particular history of rapping, outsiders often emphasize their own cultural connections to the hip-hop world, or affinity with it. When Blondie recorded "Rapture," Debbie Harry began her rap by mentioning Fab 5 Freddy, a noted hip-hop scenester, and the video featured a graffiti wall and a brief appearance by Jean-Michel Basquiat, the graffiti-inspired visual artist. You can often see a version of this impulse whenever non-Black people from outside the hip-hop world are rapping, whether accompanying a favorite record or trying out some jokey rhymes of their own. Often, sometimes subconsciously, they find themselves making unfamiliar hand gestures, moving their bodies in ways they associate with Black people.

It seemed reasonable to wonder, early on, whether hip-hop would be overrun by pop acts like Blondie and whether it might swiftly follow the path of rock 'n' roll, which by the seventies was widely perceived as a white genre, albeit one with Black roots. It didn't happen. True, white rappers received outsize attention and outsize success. Four of the bestselling rap albums of all time are by white rappers: two by Eminem, as well as *Licensed to Ill*, by the Beastie Boys, and *Devil Without a Cause*, by Kid Rock, a rapper who is generally considered a rock star, instead—which is part of the point. (White rappers have had more success crossing over into other genres than their Black counterparts have.) But the genre's major performers have been Black, with relatively few exceptions.

What about the listeners? In 1991, *The New Republic* put on its cover a photograph of a preppie-looking white guy, alongside the headline THE REAL FACE OF RAP. The implication was that the genre's Black identity was somehow fraudulent, belied by its popularity among white listeners. The author, David Samuels, wrote that "although rap is still proportionally more popular among blacks, its primary audience is white and lives in the suburbs," and he suggested that rappers were increasingly "packaged as violent black criminals" for the delectation of these white listeners. But good demographic information about pop listening habits was hard to find, and the article's only specific datum came from an MTV executive, who said that the audience for *Yo! MTV Raps* was "primarily white, male, suburban, and between the ages of 16 and 24." It seems clear enough that hip-hop has long been popular among white audiences—more popular, in many times and places, than the other major Black genre, R&B. No doubt there are plenty of possible explanations for this, but we should not neglect the simplest one: that white people love hip-hop because hip-hop is awesome. Why wouldn't *anyone* love it?

Hip-hop has been shaped, too, by the fact that so many of its leading voices have been male—and, in many cases, eager to remind listeners of it. Often, rappers who aren't Black men have had to figure out exactly how they fit, how they're supposed to sound, even which words they're supposed to use. The n-word, commonplace among Black rappers, is off-limits to white rappers, although it has often been used by rappers of Puerto Rican descent, especially in New York. The word has a gender connotation, too: Black women rappers have had to figure out whether it refers to them or only to their male counterparts. Rock stars often aspired to universality, as if they were singing on behalf of the whole world; whether big names or obscure punks, they typically assumed they could speak to—and, perhaps, for—everyone in the room, all at the same time. Hip-hop stars, by contrast, tended to be unapologetically particular. When I started going to hip-hop concerts, I was struck by the way the rappers made a point of acknowledging both the men and the women in the crowd, as if these were two separate audiences that needed to be entertained in parallel; one familiar but effective way to warm up a crowd was to find a way to pit the ladies against the fellas. In one of her best-loved tracks, Lil' Kim put it less delicately: "Bitches, squeeze your tits / Niggas, grab your genitals."

As sexually explicit hip-hop came closer to the mainstream, its maleness became more conspicuous. At the dawn of the nineties, the one hip-hop group even more controversial than N.W.A was 2 Live Crew, a Miami act known for tracks that were danceable and absurdly raunchy—obscenely so, in the view of Jose Gonzalez, a federal district judge, who found that the group's 1989 album, *As Nasty As They Wanna Be*, was meant to inspire "'dirty' thoughts and the loins," and that it was "utterly without any redeeming social value." A record-store proprietor who insisted on selling the album anyway was arrested in June 1990, and soon after, three members of the group were arrested, too, for performing tracks from it. All of them were eventually acquitted, but the case made 2 Live Crew one of the best-known hip-hop acts in America, and it inspired an argument over race and sex that never really ended.

One of the expert witnesses who testified in 2 Live Crew's defense was Henry Louis Gates, Jr., a scholar of African American literature. In an op-ed column in *The New York Times*, Gates placed 2 Live Crew in the tradition of African American street-corner rhymers, explaining that the rappers were partaking in a competitive oral tradition where the winner is "the one who invents the most extravagant images, the biggest 'lies.'" He acknowledged what he called the "flagrant" sexism in the tracks, but he also said he detected in the bawdy rhymes a subversive social message—"a parodic exaggeration of the age-old stereotypes of the oversexed black female and male." And he argued that the state's attempt at censoring the group was a kind of artistic lynching. (At college, I got to know Gates while working at *Transition*, an academic journal that he coedited.) Some critics were more bothered by the way 2 Live Crew rapped about women, and more ambivalent about the idea that they were free-speech martyrs. In an essay published in *Boston Review*, the legal scholar Kimberlé Crenshaw responded by doing what Gates could not, at least not in the pages of the *Times*: quoting some unexpurgated lyrics, including, "I'll break you down and dick you long / Bust your pussy then break your backbone." Crenshaw wrote about what it was like to follow this debate, as "a black woman living at the intersection of racial and sexual subordination"—she had coined the term "intersectionality" to describe precisely this sort of multifarious oppression. Crenshaw argued that neither the legal system prosecuting 2 Live Crew nor the advocates defending the group took any special interest in the Black women who were, in her view, demeaned and abused in the group's lyrics.

In the end, 2 Live Crew won not only the legal argument but the cultural argument, too. Today, *As Nasty As They Wanna Be* sounds unusually single-minded, perhaps, but not unusually graphic—rough and sometimes brutal sex talk long ago became commonplace in mainstream hip-hop. And while Crenshaw's theory of intersectionality is more influential than ever, hers isn't the only possible interpretation of 2 Live Crew's lyrics. I suspect many listeners, both male and female, heard exuberance, rather than menace, in those lyrics. (Unlike heavy metal, which has often drawn a largely male audience, popular hip-hop, no matter how foul-mouthed, has tended to draw plenty of women listeners, even when there has been a relative paucity of popular women performers.) Crenshaw assumed, for instance, that "I'll break you down and dick you long" was a threat, or a taunt, rather than a crude offer. And indeed, nowadays, you can hear an echo of 2 Live Crew in ferocious and funny tracks like "WAP," or "Wet Ass Pussy," a similarly bawdy hip-hop hit by two women, Cardi B and Megan Thee Stallion, which became one of the most popular tracks of 2020: "Never lost a fight, but I'm looking for a beating," Megan declared. In focusing on 2 Live Crew's lyrics, both Crenshaw and Gates were in agreement with Judge Gonzalez, who pronounced that "a central characteristic of 'rap' music is its emphasis on the *verbal* message." It is possible, though, that 2 Live Crew's most important member was not the hard-hustling front man, Luther Campbell, but the producer, Mr. Mixx, who used unexpected samples to create raucous and imaginative party music, and who has inspired generations of producers and DJs in hip-hop, dance music, and beyond.

Raging Sexism

Perhaps because of my formative experience with punk, I tend to sympathize with performers like 2 Live Crew, whose music is deemed beyond the pale, whether by government entities or corporate executives or community activists. I am drawn to music that starts fights, music that offends people. Listening to music is a social experience, and yet often the most consequential music is deemed to be antisocial, at least at first. But I sympathize, as well, with 2 Live Crew's critics. It really *was* strange, in 1990, that radio stations were effectively barred by the government from airing profanity, and that theaters were prevented by industry agreement from selling certain movie tickets to patrons under the age of seventeen, while 2 Live Crew's anatomically precise refrains were essentially unregulated, despite the prevalence of Parental Advisory stickers. And if many thoughtful observers, including Crenshaw, found the album to be profoundly offensive—well, they weren't wrong. Street-corner rhymes traditionally thrived outside polite society; they were self-consciously dirty, and in that sense indefensible. I don't really think the members of 2 Live Crew set out to satirize society, using foul language to indict the foulness of the world around them. (The street-corner tradition is not by nature a self-righteous tradition, although groups like N.W.A blended the provocative language of "signifying" with the sterner language of protest.) They were trying to be funny and have fun. And it is understandable not to find 2 Live Crew funny, or to be angered or horrified by the group's lyrics. As Rick Rubin once said about the Geto Boys, "I don't think it's unreasonable for anyone not to like it."

But it's not that simple. Because hip-hop is Black music, many Black listeners, in particular, have felt an obligation *not* to simply not like it. They have felt compelled to grapple with it and not to reject it, lest they seem to be rejecting African American culture itself. In 1994, Tricia Rose published *Black Noise*, one of the first scholarly studies of hip-hop, and it was not a celebration, or not solely one. Rose identified herself, near the beginning, as "a pro-black, biracial, ex-working-class, New York–based feminist, left cultural critic," and she accurately perceived that for someone with her political and cultural commitments, hip-hop was an unreliable ally. She celebrated tracks that expressed Black political resistance, like "Who Protects Us from You?," a full-throated indictment of abusive policing by Boogie Down Productions. But she was more ambivalent about what she called the music's "'non progressive' elements," including its celebration of conspicuous consumption, which sometimes sounded to her like an endorsement of capitalism itself. Rose also heard and decried "raging sexism" in the music, and suggested that women rappers played a complicated role: when they belittled men by "hinting at their possible homosexuality," for instance, they, too, affirmed "oppressive standards of heterosexual masculinity."

Rose was ahead of her time: her book was based on the dissertation she wrote for her PhD, which she received from Brown University in 1993; it was reportedly the first dissertation ever written about hip-hop, which in the decades that followed became a popular topic of academic inquiry. Some of the controversies that once roiled the genre have quieted, such as the fight over rappers' use of the n-word, a practice that has grown more common and less polarizing as norms have shifted. (A CBS news report about N.W.A, from 1991, began with a correspondent saying, "The group's name itself is controversial: Niggers with Attitude." Nowadays, the name would be considered far less controversial than the sound of a white person saying it in full, especially with what is called a "hard 'r.'") Lyrics about violence and gang membership, too, grew less taboo, despite sporadic complaints from politicians and pundits. Snoop Dogg used to be coy about his affiliation with the Crips, but in 2006 he released an album called *Tha Blue Carpet Treatment*, named for the Crips' signature color, which included a sleek and menacing song called "10 Lil' Crips." He has since become a beloved mainstream celebrity, and his many successful ventures have included *Martha & Snoop's Potluck Party Challenge*, a cheerful variety show he cohosted with Martha Stewart, the lifestyle guru and entrepreneur.

Even as some of these other battles faded, though, the role of gender in hip-hop grew only more incendiary, as words and attitudes once associated with gangsta rap, or 2 Live Crew, became a permanent feature of the entire genre. Joan Morgan was a longtime hip-hop listener and critic who grieved over this development. In 1999, she published *When Chickenheads Come Home to Roost*, detailing her own vexed relationship with the genre. She made it clear that this relationship had helped shape her life, while also noting that it had been abusive. "All the love in the world does not erase the stinging impact of the new invectives and brutal imagery—ugly imprints left on cheeks that have turned the other way too many times," she wrote. It was a memorable and discomfiting analogy, especially since the sexual violence of hip-hop lyrics had sometimes been echoed by real-life violence against women. (In 1991, Dr. Dre assaulted a woman journalist, Dee Barnes, who he thought had disrespected N.W.A; he pleaded no contest to misdemeanor battery and was sentenced to community service, probation, and a small fine. He has also been accused of assault by many other women, including Nicole Young, who married him in 1996 and filed for divorce in 2020.) In her book, Morgan decided to treat hip-hop less like an abusive partner, whom one might be advised to leave, and more like a troubled brother, whom she resolved to try to help. "My decision to expose myself to the sexism of Dr. Dre, Ice Cube, Snoop Dogg, or the Notorious B.I.G. is really my plea to my brothers to tell me who they are," she wrote.

"I need to know why they are so angry at me. Why is disrespecting me one of the few things that make them feel like men?"

It should be said that in many ways N.W.A was unusual: top-selling rappers of the 1990s and 2000s generally did not tell elaborate tales about murdering the women they had sex with, as N.W.A did in "One Less Bitch." (As it happens, that track evoked a rock 'n' roll predecessor, "Used to Love Her," by Guns N' Roses, from 1988, which included the same phrase: "I had to kill her.") By the dawn of the 2000s, hip-hop lived both on radio and on cable networks like MTV and BET, which broadcast glitzy music videos that showed rappers surrounded by women in nightclub attire, or less than that. Derogatory language about women was ubiquitous, embedded alongside the n-word in cheerful hits by likable rappers like Ludacris, a former radio personality from Atlanta who had a string of multimillion-selling albums. In "Area Codes," Ludacris bragged about all the different places he had "hoes," declaring himself "the Abominable Ho-Man"; "Move B***h," an exuberant club track, wasn't mainly about a "bitch" at all—it was an all-purpose expression of enthusiasm and impatience. Did that make it okay?

In the post–2 Live Crew era, the argument wasn't about the legal definition of obscenity; it was about what kind of music should be admitted into the lucrative world of mainstream culture. As a hip-hop fan, I suspected that claims about the ill social effects of hip-hop were unfounded, and that the genre's cynical and sometimes contemptuous view of male-female relations echoed broader social trends, rather than generating them. But I had no way to dismiss the possibility that widespread musical usage of words like "bitch" and "ho" and "pimp" contributed to the oppression of women, especially within African American communities. Perhaps this language was even *more* pernicious when it was used in otherwise agreeable radio hits. One flashpoint emerged at Spelman College, the historically Black women's school in Atlanta, in 2004, when a group of students objected to a planned appearance by the top-selling St. Louis rapper Nelly, partly because he had filmed a video in which he leeringly slid a credit card through a woman's thonged backside—a kind of visual pun, making reference to the common sight of patrons throwing cash at exotic dancers. (Years later, in the first verse of "WAP," Cardi B used similar imagery, rapping, "Put this pussy right in your face / Swipe your nose like a credit card.") Nelly's invitation was withdrawn, and the protest helped inspire *Essence*, the Black women's lifestyle magazine, to launch a yearlong campaign, Take Back the Music, aimed at combating "degrading" portrayals of Black women in hip-hop. Diane Weathers, the editor in chief, suggested that contemporary popular music was "a cultural swamp," and published an essay by a young woman who described her "music-video habit" as an addiction that she had learned to fight by turning off the television. The problem, really, wasn't that hip-hop existed, but that it had become ubiquitous without ever becoming respectable or well-behaved—it was as if death metal had somehow conquered the pop charts. Did this music, insanely popular but sometimes foul-mouthed and offensive, really deserve to be welcomed onto a college campus, or celebrated in the pages of a refined magazine for Black women? Maybe not. There were listeners who badly wanted hip-hop to be more upstanding and less insulting, for the sake of the broader community. My own desires were more selfish: I wanted the genre to keep pumping out great records, even at the expense of full mainstream acceptance.

Many observers assumed that eventually America would come to its senses and firmly reject the language and attitudes of gangsta rap. When the #MeToo movement finally arrived, though, focusing public attention on abusive men, no musician fell as far as R. Kelly, the R&B singer, whose career appears to have been effectively ended by brave testimony from women who revealed decades of sexual abuse. In hip-hop, the biggest story concerned not a gangsta rapper but Russell Simmons, the industry godfather. In 2017, four women told *The New York Times* that he had raped or assaulted them, and three years later, the documentary *On the Record* featured allegations of assault and harassment by four additional women. The response was muted, perhaps because Simmons had mainly moved on from music—if he had still been hip-hop's leading power broker, perhaps the accusations would have prompted more reappraisal.

When it came to rap lyrics, some red lines had emerged: anything that seemed to endorse or condone rape, for instance, was generally taboo. The rapper Rick Ross was asked to apologize in 2013 for condoning rape, after he rhymed about drugging a woman in order to assault her: "Put molly all in her champagne, she ain't even know it / I took her home and I enjoyed that, she ain't even know it." ("I would never use the term 'rape' in my records," he said afterward. "Hip-hop don't condone that, the streets don't condone that, nobody condones that." He said it was all "a misunderstanding with a lyric, a misinterpretation.") Often, though, rappers remained defiantly unreformed, especially compared to male performers in other genres. Eminem, once denounced for his semi-sarcastic use of anti-gay epithets, desisted without ever really apologizing. Kendrick Lamar, justifiably the most acclaimed rapper of the 2010s, had a big hit in 2017 with "HUMBLE.," in which he snarled, "Bitch, sit down, be humble"; it wasn't clear whether he was reprimanding a romantic partner, insulting a rival rapper, or giving himself advice. And hardly anybody even seemed to notice when, in a 2019 hit, the rapper DaBaby declared, "I tell a bitch to shut up / You 'bout to fuck my nut up." This didn't sound like a particularly provocative couplet—it just sounded like hip-hop.

Self-Conscious

In 2008, Tricia Rose published *The Hip Hop Wars*, a follow-up to *Black Noise* that was decidedly more pessimistic. Hip-hop, she wrote, was "gravely ill," because it had spent too much time and energy "pandering to America's racist and sexist lowest common denominator." But throughout the book, she was careful to specify that she was only talking about "commercial" hip-hop—the dominant form, but not the only one. She wanted readers to be aware of a second tradition, less popular but more substantive, which she called "socially conscious" or "progressive" hip-hop. In the underground, Rose wrote, out of reach of the "powerful corporate interests" that controlled the media and the music industry, a cohort of rappers had emerged as the genre's best and maybe last hope; they were making thoughtful and politically minded music, leaving behind what she called "the gangsta-pimp-ho trinity." Even as she praised "socially conscious" hip-hop, Rose expressed some reluctance about the term, because it was reductive, and because it divided the hip-hop world in a way that many rappers found unhelpful. "Being called 'socially conscious' is almost a commercial death sentence" for a rapper, she wrote, because the label led listeners to expect lyrics that were explicitly political, and possibly rather humorless. "From this sober perspective on consciousness, gangstas appear to be the only ones having fun." Even so, she was so alarmed by the state of "mainstream" hip-hop that she felt it important to help support an alternative: she ended one chapter of her book with a list of resources, including an alphabetical roster of "progressive" hip-hop acts she endorsed, from Afu-Ra to Zion I.

"Socially conscious" was an old term, used for decades to describe people who wanted to change the world around them, or at least think about changing it. In 1937, in *The New Yorker*, James Thurber published a brief satire about a gaggle of "leftist, or socially conscious, literary critics" trying and failing to explain themselves to "an average worker." In eighties hip-hop, "socially conscious" denoted so-called message records, like *The Message*, by Grandmaster Flash and the Furious Five. The term fit Public Enemy, the group that seemed to be inaugurating a new, more political militant era in hip-hop. But in May 1989, a month after Spike Lee filmed Public Enemy's "Fight the Power" march in Brooklyn, Professor Griff, a non-rapping member, gave an interview to *The Washington Times* in which he said that Jews were to blame for "the majority of wickedness that goes on across the globe," and declared that he was not afraid of their "faggot little hit men." The quotes inspired a furious response from Jewish advocacy groups and others, and by the time the "Fight the Power" video arrived that summer, the group was in turmoil. Public Enemy seemed to break up and then re-form; Griff was fired and then rehired; Chuck D apologized, but Griff did not. It was surreal, the idea of parsing the statements of an auxiliary member of a hip-hop group, as if he were a major political figure—but then, the members of Public Enemy *were* major political figures, and so Griff's espousal of anti-Semitic conspiracy theories was a legitimate political scandal. The controversy, and Chuck D's equivocal response to it, undermined the sense that the group members were fearless and clear-eyed revolutionaries. Perhaps more important, hip-hop fans were lured away by newer acts, with newer stories. Public Enemy released many more albums and even made some more hip-hop hits, but the members never looked more impressive, or more consequential, than they had on that spring day in Brooklyn, leading an all-purpose revolution.

This was one problem with political hip-hop: rappers did not always make great politicians. Ice Cube, the leading voice of gangsta rap, was transformed by the 1992 protests and riots in Los Angeles into a kind of spokesperson—suddenly, his furious rhymes seemed entirely in step with the nightly news. But his 1991 album, *Death Certificate*, included an admonition to the "Oriental one-penny-countin' motherfuckers" behind the counters of convenience stores; imprecations aimed at N.W.A's former manager, a "white Jew," whom he blamed for breaking up the group; and a warning to any "devil," especially a "fuckin' homo," who might take advantage of him. Lines such as these were all but impossible to defend as political rallying cries. The most persuasive defense of Ice Cube was essentially the aesthetic, not the political: that he was a spellbinding rapper whose music made it easier for listeners to understand why he felt the way he did, and perhaps why others did, too. One of the era's most prominent examples of hip-hop activism was much less confrontational: "Self-Destruction," a 1989 collaborative single credited to the Stop the Violence Movement, a coalition led by KRS-One that included Public Enemy, MC Lyte, and a number of other top rappers. (The purpose was to raise money for the National Urban League, and to draw attention to the causes and costs of "black-on-black crime"; this was simultaneously a charity drive, a protest movement, and a pep talk.) In a long-form video, KRS-One expressed his hope that the project would not only help combat violence, but that it would also transform hip-hop itself. "I believe that it's because of movements like Boogie Down Productions, 'Stop the Violence' movement, Public Enemy, that has saved rap music literally," he said. "If rap had gone on with its egotistical, sexist attitude it would be dead right now."

The idea of hip-hop activism aimed at saving hip-hop sounds rather circular, but it turned out that the salvation of hip-hop was a growing preoccupation. The success of so-called gangsta rap had given the genre a new idea about what success might look like. (A previously obscure California rapper named Coolio rose to fame in 1994, using the sound and style of gangsta rap to create two of the era's biggest hip-hop hits, "Fantastic Voyage" and "Gangsta's Paradise.") And the melding of gangsta and pop presented a problem for many rappers who were neither, and who found themselves out of place and unwelcome on newly dominant hip-hop radio stations. In 1996, De La Soul, the group once known for whimsical rhymes about the "D.A.I.S.Y. Age," released *Stakes Is High*, a rather stern album with a black-and-white cover. On the title track, the rapper known as Dave (he no longer went by Trugoy the Dove) made a case that much contemporary hip-hop was both boring and pernicious:

> *Sick of R&B bitches over bullshit tracks*
> *Cocaine and crack, which bring sickness to Blacks*
> *Sick of swoll'-head rappers with their sickening raps*
> *Clappers of gats, makin' the whole sick world collapse*

More and more, the hip-hop that was considered socially conscious—"conscious," for short—was defined by its opposition to the mainstream. Like the outlaw country movement in the seventies, the conscious hip-hop movement of the nineties was simultaneously conservative and progressive, blending a groovy, countercultural spirit with a stubborn conviction that they just didn't make hip-hop the way they used to. "I Used to Love H.E.R.," a 1994 track by the Chicago rapper Common, helped galvanize this new sensibility. Common described hip-hop as a woman who had lost her way and gone Hollywood—"Stressin' how hardcore and real she is / She was really the realest before she got into show biz"—and vowed to "take her back." (In seeking to criticize violent and sexual imagery, these reformists could sound both anti-macho and anti-feminist.) An avowedly revolutionary duo, dead prez, had a hip-hop hit in 1999 with "Hip-Hop," an incandescent bit of music criticism. Like De La Soul, dead prez suggested that R&B music, popular and nonthreatening and maybe somewhat feminized, represented hip-hop at its most impure: "I'm sick of that fake thug, R&B-rap scenario, all day on the radio." Like the gangstas, these reformers often promised to keep it real, even as their rhymes showed how ambiguous that directive could be. Black Thought, from the Philadelphia group the Roots, issued an unsparing verdict: "The principles of true hip-hop have been forsaken / It's all contractual and about money makin'."

These rappers wanted hip-hop to be taken seriously, and they wanted hip-hop to take itself seriously, too. Some prided themselves on the syllabic density and intellectual sensibility of their rhymes. Black Thought was one of many who preferred to be called an MC, rather than a rapper, because it made him seem more like an earnest student and practitioner of his craft and less like a shameless hustler. "To me, a rapper is someone who's involved in the business side yet has no knowledge of the past of the culture," he told *Vibe* in 1996. The Roots were unusual because they were a live band, co-led by a virtuoso drummer known as Questlove, and they liked to remind listeners that hip-hop was part of a broader tradition of Black music. (Two albums included willowy collaborations with Cassandra Wilson, the jazz singer.) There was a tension between this devotion to "true hip-hop" and this urge to leave hip-hop behind—in fact, ambivalence about hip-hop was something that "conscious" rappers shared with their gangsta counterparts. In New York, Lauryn Hill, from a group called Fugees, sought to defend hip-hop from pretenders who rapped "for all the wrong reasons," while simultaneously making it clear that she could do more than just rap. Hill's breakthrough was a faithful version of "Killing Me Softly with His Song," the 1973 Roberta Flack hit; there was a heavy hip-hop beat and some mumbled encouragement from her fellow Fugees, but no rapping whatsoever. Hill made her solo debut in 1998 with *The Miseducation of Lauryn Hill*, the high-water mark of the conscious-hip-hop movement. With her half-raspy rapping and singing voice, Hill eased between tough rhymes and balladry, creating a hip-hop album with the spirit and sweetness of seventies soul.

Perhaps I should confess that despite liking and even loving many of these records, I did not think of myself as being on the side of "conscious" or "progressive" hip-hop. The movement to reform hip-hop, like similar movements to reform country and R&B, proceeded from the assumption that something had gone wrong with the genre. But it has never been obvious to me that anything was particularly wrong with hip-hop—certainly not anything likely to be fixed by an infusion of high-mindedness. I didn't think that literary references or polysyllabic words were necessarily anything to celebrate, or that rhymes about politics and racism were guaranteed to be more memorable, or less hackneyed, than rhymes about killing and fucking. Some hip-hop musicians and fans seemed envious of the exalted status of jazz, a once disreputable form that was often celebrated, in the second half of the twentieth century, as America's classical music, and nurtured by many of the same nonprofit institutions that serve as guardians of America's high-art heritage. But I didn't think the status of jazz was any reason for jealousy. If anything, I was grateful that hip-hop had been protected from institutionalization by its stubborn vulgarity, and its abiding failure to become respectable. So I couldn't help but get nervous whenever I thought I saw a sign of creeping respectability: when Lin-Manuel Miranda dazzled Broadway and the nation with his hip-hop history lesson, *Hamilton*; or when Common was invited to perform at the White House;

or when Kendrick Lamar was recognized with not only a shelfful of Grammy Awards but a Pulitzer Prize in music, the first ever given to someone from outside the worlds of composed music and jazz.

What was conscious hip-hop? In the 2000s, groups like the Roots, respected and semipopular, were often held up as exemplars of artistic integrity. (Jay-Z paid the group a backhanded compliment by suggesting that he cared too much about selling records to follow their example: "My bills through the roof / Can't do numbers like the Roots.") But the group's most important contribution may have been its offshoot, the Soulquarians, a loose-knit collective led by Questlove; working with an innovative producer named J Dilla, he helped create an extraordinary series of albums by the rappers Mos Def, Talib Kweli, and Common and the neo-soul singers D'Angelo and Erykah Badu, among others. Questlove also established himself as a DJ and music historian, and in 2009 got the Roots hired as the house band for Jimmy Fallon, the late-night host; by the end of the 2010s, Questlove was one of the most recognizable people in hip-hop, more mainstream than most of the genre's hitmakers. Just as the gangsta rap pioneers of the late eighties forged bigger and longer careers than most people would have guessed, so did the conscious hip-hop cohort of the late nineties, even though its most spectacular success story followed no one's dictates but his own.

Kanye West was already one of hip-hop's most celebrated producers when he began to reveal himself as an odd but mesmerizing rapper. As a producer for Jay-Z and others, he was known for taking snippets of old soul tracks and speeding them up, creating tracks that sounded familiar but slightly off-kilter. As a rapper, he was sympathetic to conscious hip-hop but also keenly aware of his own contradictions and hypocrisies. On his first album, in 2004, West used a piece of a Lauryn Hill song to rhyme about being "self-conscious," rather than socially conscious. He rapped—or maybe bragged—about blowing one of his first big checks on jewelry, criticizing conspicuous consumption while also fessing up to it: "I got a problem with spending before I get it / We *all* self-conscious, I'm just the first to admit it." The ironies that informed West's music only got richer as he did. By creating futuristic electronic tracks and arranging unexpected collaborations, he evolved from a "self-conscious" oddball to arguably the most influential figure in hip-hop. By embarking on a successful second career in fashion, he turned his shopping obsession into a lucrative and influential brand. By marrying Kim Kardashian, he became not merely a revered musician but one of the most closely watched people on the planet. By criticizing President Bush and being criticized by President Obama and praising President Trump and running, sort of, for president in 2020, all while groping toward a political philosophy of his own, he built and shattered and remade his own reputation. And by releasing a patchy but powerful gospel album, *Jesus Is King*, in 2019, he declared his allegiance to one of the most august traditions in the history of American music.

Part of what's dispiriting about the idea of conscious hip-hop is that so often "conscious" refers to a rather cramped range of cultural and ideological influences: great seventies soul records, unimpeachable observations about Black pain and Black power. For that reason, I sometimes think of many of my own favorite rappers as making "unconscious" hip-hop instead: reckless, rather than responsible; dreamlike, rather than logical; suggestive, rather than conclusive. But if it makes sense to talk about "conscious" hip-hop, then surely West's restless and unpredictable and hypersensitive body of work fits the definition. He sometimes seems intent on reconciling within himself all of hip-hop's incompatible tendencies, shadowboxing with his many critics as he cycles through roles, from party host to rabble-rouser to antihero. He believes stubbornly in his own genius, yet he can be intensely vulnerable to criticism. Battling mental illness, he demands attention even when he seems to need privacy. Again and again, he has linked his identity as a Black man in America to his conviction that the country needs radical and perhaps revolutionary change, even if he can't quite express what that would mean. As he recently put it, "I got the mind state to take us past the stratosphere / I use the same attitude that done got us here." What could be more socially conscious than that?

Ambition and Hunger

In hip-hop, maybe even more than in other genres, every faction believes itself to be the true defender of the faith. In the months after the bizarre Dr. Octagon album reordered my priorities in 1996, I dove back into hip-hop, trying to figure out what I had missed and which versions of the hip-hop catechism were most convincing to me, or most entertaining. As a punk-rock obsessive, I was used to seeking out the niche and the marginal, on the theory that great music was generally allergic to major labels and big marketing budgets. And there was, in the late nineties, a growing scene of nonmainstream hip-hop: not just the bohemians in the "conscious" movement but a cohort of even more firmly anti-commercial acts like Company Flow, a mixed-race crew from New York known for tracks that were gritty and grouchy and incessantly wordy, with endless verses and absent choruses. I think I once saw the members of Company Flow perform at Fat Beats, a second-story Greenwich Village record store that served as a hub for underground hip-hop; there was a problem with the microphone, so the rappers had to shout their lyrics through a pair of headphones instead. El-P, from Company Flow, spent years building his reputation as a rapper and producer, and found belated success in the 2010s, as half of a fiery and loquacious duo called Run the Jewels.

In general, though, I was surprised and after a while pleased to find that the rules of punk did not apply: the most thrilling hip-hop records were often relatively mainstream—successful commercial releases, if not necessarily blockbusters. I bought and, almost by accident, memorized the debut album by the Notorious B.I.G., whom I had previously known only for the silky radio hit "Big Poppa." I listened for the first time to *Illmatic*, the astonishingly fat-free 1994 album by Nas, from Queens, who represented a kind of platonic ideal of hip-hop virtuosity, streetwise but not quite gangsta, thoughtful but not exactly "conscious." (Nas had a breakthrough hit two years later with "If I Ruled the World," a reimagined version of an old Kurtis Blow song; the original had been cowritten by my onetime officemate DJ AJ, who, when I met him, was still cashing royalty checks from Nas's hit.) Above all, though, I was astonished by Wu-Tang Clan, a collective from Staten Island, New York, that released a dizzying debut album in 1993, followed by a series of charismatic and mysterious solo records.

I am old enough to remember the first time I used the Internet: I was standing at a kiosk in the college library, paging greedily through the Original Hip-Hop Lyrics Archive, an unlicensed website that contained lyrics to all the major hip-hop albums, including everything by Wu-Tang Clan. (Hip-hop albums have almost never been packaged with lyric sheets; you could only read them by listening to them.) The group members had inscrutable names like Raekwon the Chef, and their rhymes drew from local slang, kung fu movies, and the theology of the Five Percenters, a New York–based offshoot of the Nation of Islam. The Clan's in-house producer, known as RZA, liked to splice together snippets from movie soundtracks and dusty old soul records, making listeners feel as if they had stumbled into a secret lair. Some codes were decipherable: when Raekwon rhymed, "Yo, bombin' / We usually take all niggas' garments / Save your breath before I vomit," he was slyly turning the first part of his group's name into an acronym. But sometimes, there was nothing to do but savor the sounds and the syllables. During the gangsta-rap boom, it was easy to believe that hip-hop was intelligible, possibly to a fault: those scowling guys on MTV seemed to mean nothing more or less than what they said. A group like Wu-Tang Clan, intimidating but also enigmatic, made it clear that hip-hop did not need to be so literal-minded—and that probably it never really had been.

Obsessed with hip-hop, I arrived in New York in the summer of 1997, having secured an internship at *The Source*, a onetime hip-hop newsletter that had grown fat and glossy along with the genre it covered. It had been cofounded by a white hip-hop fan named David Mays, who had been, like me, an undergraduate at Harvard, and a DJ at the college radio station. I don't think I ever really met Mays, beyond perhaps a perfunctory hello. What I remember was a loud and bustling office, full of editors, mainly young and Black, all of them steeped in the music and culture of hip-hop. *The Source* was less glamorous than *Vibe*, its self-consciously upscale rival, which had been founded by Quincy Jones, and which covered hip-hop alongside R&B. But *The Source* was justifiably proud of its reach, and of its knowledgeable and diverse readership. (It circulated widely within the prison system, and its subscribers seemed to include a number of people who subscribed to no other magazines—*The Source* alone could claim them.) The magazine's chief asset was credibility: the hip-hop world paid attention when an album was awarded "five mics," the magazine's highest rating, and rappers were eager to be featured in the "Hip-Hop Quotable" column, where each month the editors transcribed a verse that impressed them.

I tried my best to be helpful at *The Source*, though I'm sure I learned much more than I contributed. The magazine's offices were not quite as celebrity-studded as you might expect; if any big-name rappers ever dropped by to say hello, I missed it. Even so, I did sometimes feel as if I was at the center of the cultural universe, because in 1997, New York hip-hop was suddenly a national obsession. The Notorious B.I.G. had been killed a few months earlier, and Sean Combs was ascendant; their hits provided the soundtrack to the country's summer, and Combs, with his mogul-chic image, was helping to invent the idea of hip-hop as a luxury brand. (The next summer, he installed himself in the Hamptons, the exclusive Long Island beach region, throwing parties so spectacular that they created a permanent place for the hip-hop elite in New York high society.) In June, Wu-Tang Clan released *Wu-Tang Forever*, which made its debut atop the album chart, selling more than half a million copies in a week despite having nothing even vaguely resembling a hit single. And Jay-Z, who would release his second album later that year, was already positioning himself to inherit the title—King of New York—that B.I.G. left behind; another claimant was Nas, who had recently emerged as a hitmaker and was trying to form a supergroup with Dr. Dre. One of Combs's signature hits that year was "It's All About the Benjamins," named for the man on the front of the hundred-dollar bill; it had a radically minimalist one-note beat, and five verses by five different rappers, including Lil' Kim. "Ain't nobody's hero but I wanna be heard / On your Hot 9-7 every day, that's my word," Combs proclaimed, as if a New York hip-hop radio station was the most glamorous destination in the world. That summer, it seemed to be. And by the end of 1997, *The Source* was selling more newsstand copies than any music magazine in the country, including *Rolling Stone*.

The unabashed ambition of my favorite rappers helped me to think differently about truly popular music. For a group like Wu-Tang Clan, the commercial mainstream was not a corrupting cesspool to be avoided but territory to be conquered. If you were a fan, you couldn't help but cheer as the group's unlikely empire expanded to include a fashion line, a video game, and a fistful of major-label record deals, with members negotiating separately. Because hip-hop was originally party music, it was originally social music, and rappers, much like comedians, measured success by judging the audience reaction. Rakim once rapped, "To me, 'MC' means 'move the crowd,'" and the story of hip-hop can be told as a story of rappers finding more ways to move bigger crowds. Ambition and hunger were at the core of the genre's identity, and so it seemed perverse to me—and probably unjust—to begrudge these rappers their obsession with "Benjamins." On the contrary, hip-hop's money-hungry lyrics often reflected the disorienting and bittersweet feeling of growing up poor in a wealthy nation and then suddenly becoming rich, or kind of rich. (Wu-Tang Clan was known for "C.R.E.A.M.," which stood for "cash rules everything around me"; that phrase sounded different after you heard the song's verses, which were bleak narratives of drugs and jail.) Once I learned to enjoy this spirit of unapologetic American ambition within hip-hop, it was easier for me to enjoy it in all other forms of music, too. Through hip-hop, I came to love the smooth seductions of contemporary R&B, the garish confections of mainstream pop, even the resolutely unhip ballads of modern country music—all of it simultaneously earnest and shameless in its desperation to "move the crowd." Hip-hop helped me hear that every genre was in some sense a hustle, an attempt to sell listeners some things they wanted, and some things they didn't know they wanted.

Over the decades, the idea of hip-hop as a hustle complicated many efforts to establish or maintain the genre's purity. This idea also complicated the mission of *The Source*, which aimed to celebrate and promote hip-hop and, from time to time, critique it. Like *Rolling Stone* in its early days, *The Source* traded on the idea that, unlike mainstream publications, it could chronicle its chosen culture from within. (One issue, from 1993, promised readers that the album reviewers were active participants in hip-hop: "70% of them either rhyme or produce beats themselves.") The magazine was relatively skeptical of gangsta rap. In 1996, a review of the hard-boiled Queens duo Mobb Deep fretted that "hip-hop's preoccupation with the gangsta aesthetic is problematic." And after Eazy-E's death, the magazine ran a strikingly ambivalent editor's note, regretting his promotion of "Black-on-Black crime, moral-less capitalism, and the further objectification of women" while nevertheless praising the "rebellious and aggressive revolutionary energy" of his music. And yet the magazine's criticisms tended to be muted; where rock magazines sometimes delighted in declaring popular bands terrible and their fans clueless, *The Source* generally took a more conciliatory approach. There have been plenty of influential hip-hop writers, but there has never been a hip-hop equivalent of Robert Christgau, who was only half kidding when he declared himself Dean of American Rock Critics, and who believed that the best way to show respect to the music he loved was to be brutally, gleefully honest in assessing it. (Christgau and I once served as onstage judges at a competition between cover bands composed of staffers from two music magazines, *Spin* and *Blender*; if I recall correctly, it ended in tears.) *The Source* sometimes poked fun at rappers through a monthly caricature feature, drawn by the illustrator André LeRoy Davis. But it is impossible to imagine the magazine beginning a review of a new album from a revered artist with anything like the phrase that *Rolling Stone* once used to begin a Bob Dylan review: "What is this shit?"

The Source's coverage of hip-hop came to be complicated, too, by its relationship with one rapper in particular. While David Mays was an undergraduate at Harvard, he got to know a streetwise local group called the Almighty RSO, led by a rapper named Benzino; for a time, he was the group's manager. It is hardly unprecedented for the publisher of a music magazine to have close and potentially compromising relationships with musicians; Jann Wenner, the cofounder of *Rolling Stone*, was friendly with a number of rock stars, including Mick Jagger. Unfortunately, Benzino cannot fairly be described as the Mick Jagger of hip-hop. In 1994, after the editors of *The Source* declined to profile the group, Mays circumvented them, surreptitiously inserting a laudatory profile into the November issue, on pages set aside for advertising. A number of editors quit in protest, and Mays was eventually able to recruit replacements—by the time I arrived, I was only dimly aware of the controversy. For reasons no one has ever satisfactorily explained, Benzino's role at the magazine only grew; years later, he started to appear on the magazine's masthead, listed as "Co-Founder and Chief Brand Executive," or "Co-Founder and Visionary." Benzino, who never built a fan base, became embroiled in a mystifying feud with Eminem and 50 Cent, two of the genre's biggest stars, and the magazine eagerly took his side. The February 2003 issue was particularly bizarre: it included an admiring cover story about the rapper Ja Rule, who was feuding with 50 Cent; a rather censorious essay about Eminem; a respectful five-page profile of Benzino, in which readers were told about his "plans to save hip-hop"; and a fold-out poster of Benzino holding Eminem's severed head and spine.

The anti-Eminem crusade damaged the magazine's reputation and also its finances, because a number of record labels pulled their advertising in response. More damage came in 2005, when Kim Osorio, the editor in chief during the Benzino-poster era, sued the magazine, Mays, and Benzino for sexual harassment and other mistreatment; she was awarded $15.5 million, which was reduced to $8 million on appeal. In 2007, *The Source* declared bankruptcy—by then, both the magazine industry and the music industry were struggling to adapt to the rise of online media. Mays tried other media ventures, and Benzino eventually found a congenial home on television, as a member of the cast of *Love & Hip-Hop Atlanta*, a soap-operatic reality show. In retrospect, it is possible to see the late-nineties hip-hop boom as a mixed blessing for a magazine like *The Source*, which thrived for a time as a specialist title but grew less authoritative as hip-hop's audience grew increasingly broad and the hip-hop magazine marketplace grew increasingly cluttered. (Alongside *Vibe*, there was also *XXL*, founded by exiles from *The Source*, and *Blaze*, *Vibe*'s hip-hop-oriented spin-off. And beyond New York there was *Rap Pages*, in Los Angeles; *Ozone*, first in Orlando and then in Atlanta; and *Murder Dog*, a quirky Bay Area title that was about as unfiltered as the rappers it covered.) To read old issues of *The Source* today is to be confronted with articles and advertisements that combine to create the sense of a self-contained world, with its own slang and fashion, its own pantheon of geniuses and celebrities. Thanks in part to *The Source* itself, that world came to seem a little less self-contained with every issue.

Escape from New York

It is probable that no issue ever published by *The Source* had as much lasting influence as the night of August 3, 1995, when the magazine hosted its second annual Source Awards. The ceremony took place in the theater below Madison Square Garden, in New York, and it celebrated a hometown hero, the Notorious B.I.G., who won four awards. But much of the night belonged to the West Coast. There was an all-star performance featuring Dr. Dre and Snoop Dogg, both of whom were then associated with the pugnacious Los Angeles record label Death Row Records. The label's proprietor, Suge Knight, taking the stage in a Blood-red shirt, sent a greeting to Tupac Shakur, who was then in prison, and who had recently allied himself with Death Row. Knight disparaged an unnamed "executive producer" who he claimed was hungry for fame, and everyone knew he was talking about a local guy, Sean Combs; the insult helped to establish the perception that East Coast and West Coast rappers were at war. When Dr. Dre was named Producer of the Year, some in the audience booed him, and Snoop Dogg took offense. "The East Coast don't love Dr. Dre and Snoop Dogg?" he asked angrily and incredulously. It was not a particularly celebratory night; Questlove, from the Roots, was in the audience, and in an interview with the music site Pitchfork, he said that he remembered "fights in the audience" and feeling as if "a bomb was going to detonate." John Singleton, the director of *Boyz n the Hood*, tried to ease the hostility. "We've got to kill all this East Coast, West Coast, South, Midwest dissension in rap," he told the crowd.

Outsiders sometimes saw this "dissension" as mere arrogance run amok, but really it was a sign that hip-hop had begun to fragment. The real heroes of the night turned out to be the two members of OutKast, from Atlanta, who were also booed, after being named New Artist of the Year. One of them, André 3000, responded with a defiant and resonant declaration of regional pride. "The South got something to say," he said. OutKast had released its debut album in 1994, perfecting a soulful Southern variant of gangsta rap and then spiraling outward, using live instruments and alien electronics to create a kind of hip-hop psychedelia. Big Boi was the group's motormouthed virtuoso, finding ways to upgrade traditional hip-hop boasts: "I'm cooler than a polar bear's toenails / Oh, hell / There he go again, talkin' that shit." And André 3000 was a peerless storyteller, using scrambled rhyme schemes and unequal line lengths to keep his verses vivid and unpredictable. In one track, he described the scene in his native Atlanta, from the cars (vintage Chevrolets upgraded with pearlescent paint) to the criminals:

> *Live, from home of the Brave,*
> *with dirty dollars and beauty parlors and baby ballers and*
> *   bowling-ball Impalas and street scholars*
> *majoring in culinary arts—you know,*
> *how to work bread, cheese, and dough*
> *from scratch.*

But see, the catch
is, you can get caught—
know what you're selling, what you bought.

The members of OutKast should have been easy for a New York hip-hop fan to love: they were students of the genre's history, creating a strikingly Southern variant of the city's lyrics-driven style; André 3000, in particular, was in some sense a Southern inheritor of the Native Tongues sensibility. His defiant Source Awards speech became a battle cry, and it served as the bittersweet conclusion to OutKast's astonishing album *Aquemini*, which fully justified André's bravado, while also serving as an early sign that hip-hop's future was in neither New York nor California.

Other Southern rappers were less eccentric but in a sense more radical, because they challenged the genre's unwritten rules. In 1998, the same year OutKast released *Aquemini*, a rapper from New Orleans named Juvenile released an album called *400 Degreez*, which showed how hip-hop was evolving, far from the tastemakers in New York. The album's breakthrough single, "Ha," barely even sounded like a hip-hop track. A drum machine emphasized each beat about evenly, instead of clobbering the backbeat, the way traditional hip-hop tracks did. And Juvenile's verses were hardly verses at all—he was just listing things, almost talking, adding a kind of grunt at the end of each line:

> *That's you with that bad-ass Benz, ha*
> *That's you that can't keep a old lady, 'cause you keep fuckin' her*
>   *friends, ha*
> *You gotta go to court, ha*
> *You got served a subpoena for child support, ha*

It sounded like a novelty song, or rather a novelty that hadn't yet been formed into a proper song—in other words, it sounded, to many hip-hop listeners, the way hip-hop had once sounded to everyone else. While the rest of the country hadn't been paying attention, New Orleans had developed its own dance-oriented variant of hip-hop, known as bounce music, which in turn influenced the keyboard-driven sound of many New Orleans hip-hop records, including *400 Degreez*. The album was full of unfamiliar words like "whoadie," a friendly male term of address that turned out to be derived from "ward," the civic units that divide New Orleans. Juvenile's voice was gluey and greasy, and he didn't seem particularly worried about making himself understood; like many of the best rappers, he seemed to be rapping exclusively for the benefit of people in his neighborhood. He was signed to a label called Cash Money, and also performed with a group, the Hot Boys, that included B.G., the rapper whose hit popularized the word "bling." Juvenile's own defining hit turned out to be "Back That Azz Up," a genial club track, which became a perennial, popular everywhere from strip clubs to weddings, where the censored version, "Back That Thang Up," often prevailed. As a consequence, *400 Degreez* was a surprise blockbuster, selling about four million copies within two years in America. This was perhaps the most radical thing about *400 Degreez*: that so many people loved it.

In the nineties, many cities had built their own local scenes, enabled by regional CD distributors that helped rappers build networks of supportive shops. Often, these rappers achieved substantial success without much support from gatekeepers, including music critics; many of the writers covering hip-hop considered these regional kingpins rather unsophisticated. And so, after that summer of 1997 at *The Source*, I started writing occasionally about this music. I interviewed Juvenile and the rest of the Cash Money crew for a short piece in *The Boston Phoenix*, an alternative weekly. (I asked them to spell "whoadie," and everyone had a different suggestion.) After I moved to New York, in 1999, I wrote for *The Village Voice* about Trick Daddy and Trina, who were creating the new sound of Miami, and Three 6 Mafia, a strange and woozy group whose tracks had become Memphis's most prominent export. By the time I was hired as a pop critic at *The New York Times*, in 2002, the notion of an East Coast–West Coast battle had long faded, but geography was more important than ever. The country was full of rappers hoping to build a local reputation and then go national and global, hoping to do in their cities what Juvenile had done in New Orleans, and Nelly had done in St. Louis, and Ludacris had done in Atlanta.

All of this regionalism made the 2000s a rather miscellaneous time in hip-hop. The era of blockbuster albums seemed to be ending, and a new format was emerging. Hip-hop fans had long collected mixtapes, which were cassette compilations of new tracks and remixes. But in the 2000s, rappers routinely collaborated with mixtape DJs to create CD mixtapes that were effectively unlicensed—and, in a sense, illegal—albums. (Rappers often did this to build excitement for their "official" albums, though it seems clear that some of them became distributors, too, effectively bootlegging themselves and cutting their record companies out of the action.) At the *Times*, my job was to cover a wide range of pop music, and the job taught me both humility and confidence. I learned that, no matter how much I listened and read, I would never know as much about any genre as the true experts, both the professionals and the fans. But I learned, too, that if I did the research, I could learn enough about any kind of music to enjoy it and to have an opinion about it. Even so, I took special pleasure in celebrating the chaotic world of hip-hop in the pages of the *Times*. Ever since the eighties, there had been a ready audience for writers willing to argue that hip-hop was misguided or pernicious; even among hip-hop specialists, a reflexive disdain for so-called mainstream hip-hop had hardened into conventional wisdom. (A representative article from *Rolling Stone*, in 2000, noted in passing, as if it were obvious, that the genre "desperately" needed "resuscitation.") As far as I was concerned, hip-hop was the most exciting music in the world—terms like "mainstream" or "gangsta" only concealed the riotous variety of a genre that sounded different in just about every city.

In Houston, a generation of rappers was building on the legacy created by DJ Screw, who remixed records by slowing them down; this sound was linked to Screw's favorite drug, codeine-enhanced cough syrup, which also led to his death, via overdose, in 2000. Three 6 Mafia, from Memphis, discovered that there is something more valuable than a hit: "It's Hard Out Here for a Pimp," the group's rather workaday contribution to the film *Hustle & Flow*, was named Best Original Song at the 2006 Academy Awards, instantly bringing the members a kind of mainstream renown that they surely never expected and didn't quite know what to do with. Around the same time, a rapper named Yo Gotti was emerging as the new king of Memphis. He had a marvelously squelchy voice, rapping as if he were simultaneously sucking on a Jolly Rancher. His lyrics were deft but rather terse, depicting a world where no one had time to do anything but chase cash and cheat death: "Yo Gotti got the money and the power / You a part-time snitch and you a full-time coward." (Once, on a trip to Memphis, I happened across a Yo Gotti interview in the local weekly, the *Memphis Flyer*. The reporter noted that his most recent album and mixtape had both been reviewed in *The New York Times*. Yo Gotti's response was perfect. "I heard about it," he said, "but it didn't mean nothing to me.") As New York became less dominant, the city's hip-hop empire started to seem like just one more quirky regional rap scene. Cam'ron, from Harlem, was famous for his flamboyant take on gangsta chic, like a pink fur coat with a matching pink fur headband, and for his similarly flamboyant rhymes. At the Apollo Theater, in 2004, I watched agog as Cam'ron celebrated the release of his album *Purple Haze*, doing something like gangsta dada: "Bucket by OshKosh B'Gosh / Golly, I'm gully: 'Look at his galoshes!' / Gucci, gold-, platinum-plaque collages."

Most important of all, though, was OutKast's native Atlanta, which was transformed in the 2000s from a regional hip-hop powerhouse to the genre's new home—the hip-hop Nashville. It was strange, in the 2000s, to be living and working in New York and to increasingly feel as if the spirit of hip-hop had somehow escaped the city; even our local radio stations seemed slow to adopt the latest hits from Atlanta, which were changing the genre. OutKast's exuberant records were going mainstream, and a new sound was emerging there, slower and meaner, following the lead of a star named T.I., who declared, in 2001, that he rapped "for the niggas and the j's in the trap." The "j's" were junkies, and "the trap" was one of the tumbledown houses that often served, in Atlanta, as drug dealers' headquarters. ("Trap" became a verb, too: trapping was what trappers did in the trap.) Soon people were talking about "trap music," an Atlanta style characterized by grand and eerie keyboards, and lyrics that were monomaniacally focused on drug dealing. The style created other stars, including Young Jeezy, who called himself the Snowman, with a wink, and Gucci Mane, whose discography includes about a dozen "trap"-themed mixtapes and who became a kind of hip-hop folk hero. What made Atlanta extraordinary, though, was the wide range of performers that have thrived there ever since, orbiting the local hip-hop scene, from the screaming hitmaker Lil Jon to the innovative slow-jam specialist The-Dream, from the rowdy trio Migos to the wholehearted R&B singer Summer Walker. Some of these acts carried onward the legacy of OutKast, which achieved massive popularity just as the two members began to drift apart. CeeLo Green, from an OutKast-affiliated group called Goodie Mob, forged a left-field pop career in the 2000s, alone and as part of an alternative-rock duo, Gnarls Barkley. Future, a rapper who got his start hanging around OutKast's studio, became one of the most important figures in 2010s hip-hop. Killer Mike, once an OutKast protégé, emerged as the other half, with the rapper El-P, of the duo Run the Jewels, and as one of hip-hop's leading political figures. During the 2020 protests against police violence, it was Killer Mike who stood beside the city's mayor, Keisha Lance Bottoms. "Atlanta's not perfect," he said. "But we're a lot better than we ever were. And we're a lot better than cities are."

Unlike Nashville, Atlanta had trouble figuring out how to turn its musical heritage into a tourist attraction: a visitor who arrived in the city eager to see the home of hip-hop wouldn't have known where to start, or what to see. (Indeed, I sometimes felt that way when I went to Atlanta, where so many of the important landmarks turned out to be rather nondescript buildings in plain-looking neighborhoods; once, doing research with a friend for a book of photography, I spent a strange and enjoyable night at a teen dance party held in a dark and unfurnished room in a suburban office park.) One difference, of course, is that hip-hop is Black music, typically emerging from neighborhoods without much wealth, and therefore without the resources needed to build and maintain a sturdy infrastructure. Coach K is one of the most influential figures in Atlanta hip-hop, a manager whose clients have included Young Jeezy, Gucci Mane, Migos, and many others. He told me that for Atlanta hip-hop, "the streets" were not merely a source of inspiration but a source of capital, too. "There was no labels here, no media, no banks," he said. "The money came from out the black market—it came from out the streets—to build the shit." To him, this explained both how Atlanta hip-hop had managed to thrive, and also how it had managed to avoid being swallowed up by the New York–Los Angeles record industry. In his view, the "gangsta" in "gangsta rap," far from ruining hip-hop, had helped the genre stay tied to the community that created it, and stay relatively independent. Writers unhappy with hip-hop in the 2000s often pointed to the malign influence of corporate money—the assumption, which I always found too convenient, was that if it weren't for those pesky record executives, the supposedly good music would be more popular. But what I generally observed was more like the opposite: grassroots local hip-hop scenes all over the country, and record executives desperately scrambling to keep up.

Serious Rapping

One of the only downsides of life as a pop critic is the obligation to stay at every concert until the end, no matter the weather. In 2003, Hot 97 held its annual Summer Jam concert at Giants Stadium, in New Jersey, where the headliners were 50 Cent, Eminem, and lots of rain. Like many

New York–area hip-hop concerts, this one attracted an enthusiastic and integrated crowd. And like many hip-hop concerts in general, it didn't sound all that great. Although hip-hop began as a strictly live phenomenon, the genre has long had a strained relationship with live performance. Rhymes that are marvels of timing and texture on record have a tendency to turn sloppy and shouty onstage. (It is no coincidence that hip-hop has failed to create a significant live-album tradition; apart from the early years, there are few examples of classic live hip-hop recordings.) Often, hip-hop shows are exciting less for the sound that's created than for the undeniable thrill of being in the same place as the superheroic character from the records.

Summer Jam, in particular, was known for excitement: much like the old Source Awards, it brought together rappers who sometimes regarded one another as competitors, or even enemies, and the results could be unpredictable. At the 2001 edition, Jay-Z had unveiled a new song, "Takeover," in which he insulted Prodigy, from the group Mobb Deep, and taunted Nas, sparking a feud that lasted for years. In 2003, the second-to-last act was 50 Cent, whose set of hits was energetic but sloppy. Then it was time for Eminem, the other headliner. But it had been raining for hours, and I noticed that many of the fans were doing what I wished I could have done: they were leaving. A striking number of those who left after 50 Cent were Black, and a striking number of those who stayed for Eminem were white. It was in some ways a predictable divide, suggesting that in this stadium, at least, the Black concertgoers cared more about the Black headliner, and the white ones cared more about the white headliner, even though 50 Cent and Eminem were allies and friends. Of the two, 50 Cent was more interested in making crossover radio hits. Eminem was more focused on *serious* rapping, obsessed with beats and rhymes. Which one was more hip-hop?

The diverging responses to 50 Cent and Eminem were a sign that in the twenty-first century, an old question persisted: What did it mean to be a rapper? The members of De La Soul had the biggest hit of their career with

"Feel Good Inc.," a 2005 collaboration with the British band Gorillaz. But in America, the song was a rock radio smash and a nonentity on hip-hop radio, despite De La Soul's impeccable hip-hop credentials. Similarly, late-career Beastie Boys hits like "Intergalactic," from 1998, and "Ch-Check It Out," from 2004, were embraced by alternative-rock stations, even though both records consisted of rapping and sampling, with scarcely any singing or electric guitars. In 1998, an executive from the group's label, Capitol Records, told *Billboard* that the Beastie Boys' background made them a better fit for rock stations, despite what their music sounded like. "They were punks first," the executive said, "and they aren't trying to pretend to be something they aren't, like disenfranchised street kids." This was a clumsy but revealing way of explaining something true: not every successful rapper had a place in contemporary hip-hop.

The rap-rock boom of the late nineties had been propelled by white men who were eager to establish that they belonged in hip-hop. In 1999, Fred Durst, from Limp Bizkit, told *Rolling Stone* that as a boy, he had been harassed for loving hip-hop. ("Until the Beastie Boys came out, I was called 'nigger lover,'" he said.) He craved hip-hop credibility, even though he knew he was unlikely to earn hip-hop sales. "I don't want the hip-hop world to *buy my record*," he said. "I just want 'em to go, 'Hey, man, at least we know that guy's for real.'" In the 2000s, the rap-rock boom gave way to a hip-pop boom, propelled by white women who trod more lightly on hip-hop turf. Fergie was the designated singer in the Black Eyed Peas, a hip-hop group that evolved into a pop juggernaut, thanks partly to her; as a successful solo act, she sang and sometimes rapped, never taking herself too seriously. Gwen Stefani, from the ska-inspired rock band No Doubt, became a solo success, too, working with the Neptunes on "Hollaback Girl," a playful hip-hop hit. In 2009, Jon Caramanica wrote an incisive essay in *The New York Times* about the increasing prominence of white women rappers, inspired by Ke$ha, who rapped the verses and sung the choruses in her break-through hit, "Tik Tok." In his eagerness to insist that Ke$ha wasn't trying to be hip-hop, Barry Weiss, the chairman of her record label, RCA, coined an exquisite euphemism. "I never thought of her as rapping," he told Caramanica. "I just thought of it as her particular vocal phrasing on certain songs."

Even as hip-pop thrived, so, more quietly, did its opposite: a slightly old-fashioned world where verbal virtuosity was what really mattered. A few years after I joined the staff of *The New Yorker*, I profiled an emerging hip-hop crew called Odd Future, a young collective based in California, although really the members seemed to live on the Internet: Odd Future was one of the first major hip-hop acts to build its audience exclusively online, with virtually no help from major labels. The ringleader was a boisterous polymath named Tyler, the Creator, but the crew's virtuoso rapper was a mysterious teenager known as Earl Sweatshirt—mysterious because by the time the crew began its rise, in 2010, he had disappeared. It turned out his mother had arranged for him to be sent to a boarding school in Samoa, partly because she was worried about how hip-hop celebrity might affect his mental development. Earl Sweatshirt was sixteen when he went away, known for playful and profane lyrics full of sneaky rhymes: "I'm half-privileged, think white and have nigga lips / A tad different: mad smart, act ignorant." (His mother is Cheryl I. Harris, a respected legal scholar, and his father is Keorapetse Kgositsile, a liberation-minded poet from South Africa who is two generations removed from hip-hop: one of his poems inspired the name of the Last Poets, the proto-hip-hop group.) He was still incommunicado when I wrote my profile, but he agreed to break his silence by answering some questions by letter, in hopes of convincing his fans to stop harassing his mother, whom they blamed for his absence. In his handwritten response to me, he assured fans that he wasn't being held against his will and talked about his favorite music. He mentioned Eminem as an influence, although he said he found Eminem's most recent album, *Recovery*, to be unforgivably earnest. (He complained that Eminem's new ethos seemed to be "Let's hold hands and cry a whole lot.") And he expressed his admiration for MF Doom, a New York legend who had been releasing albums since 1991, developing a diffident but compelling style, full of mumbled non sequiturs. Earl Sweatshirt reemerged the next year, but instead of claiming his accrued celebrity, he disappeared into his rhymes, releasing a series of albums that were excellent but rather moody—rather MF Doom–like. This was not hip-hop for casual listeners. On the contrary, it seemed designed to drive casual listeners away.

This distinction, though, between "serious" and "casual" listeners can be misleading, because a sense of seriousness is precisely what a lot of casual listeners are after. Nothing did more to transform Eminem from a polarizing provocateur to a beloved symbol of hip-hop integrity than the release, in 2002, of *8 Mile*, a movie in which he played a more lovable version of himself—a working-class white kid in Black Detroit, obsessed with showing off his skills in the local rap battles. The film inspired two different *New York Times* op-ed columnists, both baby boomers, to make the case for Eminem: Frank Rich, a former Broadway critic, wrote that Eminem was at last "entering the American mainstream," while suggesting that the film made "a credible case" for "hip-hop as a positive social good"; Maureen Dowd, known for writing about politics, did some casual ethnographic research, reporting that "a gaggle of my girlfriends are surreptitiously smitten with Eminem." In the film, Eminem's character is obsessed with the art of battle rap, in which competitors compete by trading rhyming insults; Eminem's character wins the climactic battle by declaring, "Fuck everybody, fuck *y'all*, if you doubt me / I'm a piece of fuckin' white trash, I say it proudly." The film helped popularize battle rapping, and in the years afterward, battle-rap leagues went mainstream, with their own championships, broadcast via pay-per-view, and their own stars, who tended to remain unknown outside the battle-rap subculture. This was hip-hop reduced to pure punch lines—reduced so much, in fact, that the contestants customarily rapped a cappella, with no music at all.

The *8 Mile* soundtrack gave Eminem his first No. 1 hit, "Lose Yourself," an intense and generally inoffensive motivational anthem. More crossover hits followed, including "Love the Way You Lie," a duet with the pop singer Rihanna. But Eminem didn't embrace a film career and mainly went back to what he was doing before: rapping fast and furious, often in a pinched, aggrieved voice that was increasingly at odds with the casual, slangy sound of mainstream hip-hop. He acknowledged that his whiteness helped account for his massive popularity, and he talked about his Black peers and forebears with humility. (A few months before *8 Mile* was released, Eminem declared himself, in rhyme, the *ninth*-best rapper of all time, and he named the eight rappers, all of them Black, whom he ranked ahead of himself; the list included Jay-Z, Tupac Shakur, the Notorious B.I.G., André 3000, and Nas, as well as some lesser-known figures.) All of this helped earn Eminem respect from the hip-hop world, even though, as I discovered on that rainy night in a football stadium, he wasn't especially popular among the Black listeners who have traditionally been central to hip-hop. In 2019, DJ Vlad, who runs a popular YouTube channel, interviewed Conway the Machine, a Black rapper from Buffalo, New York, whom Eminem had signed to his record company. Conway was, as you might expect, effusive about Eminem, praising both his skill and his devotion to hip-hop. But Conway also conceded that, to some potential listeners, those credentials didn't much matter. "I'm from the hood, and I'm in the hood," Conway said. "And there's *nobody* in the hood that's riding around to an Eminem album."

Your Voice Too Light

Ever since I became obsessed with hip-hop, I have been marveling at my good fortune: how lucky to be alive at a time when exuberant and ingenious spoken rhymes, emerging from working-class African American neighborhoods, constituted one of the most influential artistic traditions in the world. There was no reason to think that this particular musical form would maintain indefinitely either its deep connection to African American youth culture or its broad popularity. And by the end of the

2000s, with album sales slumping and hip-hop album sales slumping disproportionately, it seemed possible that the genre's long hot streak was at last beginning to cool. Certainly the place-based infrastructure of 2000s hip-hop, which enlivened the genre with a procession of local scenes and sounds, was melting away, thanks partly to digital distribution, which helped musicians and listeners hear what was happening outside their hometowns. Lil Wayne first emerged as a member of the same Cash Money crew, from New Orleans, that included Juvenile. (It was Lil Wayne who rapped the chorus on the 1999 hit "Bling Bling," which was released when he was only sixteen.) On a series of mixtapes and albums in the 2000s, he emerged as one of the genre's biggest stars: he had a froggy voice, marvelously enriched by his New Orleans accent, and he rapped eloquently about his hometown. But as the decade ended, he was reinventing himself again: he was spending time in Miami, where he morphed into a kind of fun-loving rock star, infatuated with skateboarding and getting high, learning to play the electric guitar. This second transformation didn't improve his music—quite the opposite. But it did magnify his influence, turning Lil Wayne into a touchstone for younger rappers who viewed his woozy music and decadent lifestyle as a kind of emancipation from hip-hop orthodoxy. This version of Lil Wayne liked to remind listeners that he was a "Martian," and his continued success was proof that hip-hop was growing less parochial, less obsessed with street corners.

Once I was no longer a music critic at a daily newspaper, I stopped going to so many concerts but kept listening to lots of music—new music, especially. Less of it, no doubt, than a full-time critic, but much more of it, I daresay, than your average middle-aged dad. By the 2010s, I had more or less abandoned both CDs and vinyl, because I valued efficiency over either collectibility or fidelity: as a listener, my goal was not to build an exquisite library but to figure out what music was being made, and how I might enjoy it. Using first iTunes and then Spotify, I developed some rules designed to maximize my exposure to new music, and to eliminate the paralyzing obligation of having to decide, again and again throughout the day, what I felt like listening to. I collected interesting tracks from the past year or so onto playlists, and then listened to the playlists in shuffle mode, with no skipping allowed—any track I didn't feel like hearing got permanently kicked off the playlist. Each week, on the day when most new music was released (traditionally Tuesday in the US, although that switched in 2015 to Friday, which is now the the worldwide music release day), I dumped new albums and singles into the playlists, and tracks that were more than a year old were deleted, if they had made it that long. I named my two main playlists "singing" and "rapping," and used them as the soundtrack to family dinners and solo commutes, respectively. I eventually began to notice, though, that this seemingly simple division—indie rock and country music and mainstream pop and R&B and electronic music on one list; hip-hop on the other—was growing more complicated. My process got more time-consuming, as more and more artists released albums that required judgment calls: I would have to scan through entire albums, deciding in a few seconds which tracks belonged in "singing" and which belonged in "rapping." This seemingly self-evident distinction was no longer so obvious.

Maybe it never had been. In the 1990s and 2000s, the story of hip-hop was really only half a story. On the radio and in nightclubs, the genre lived side by side with R&B, in a kind of gender-balanced power-sharing agreement: hip-hop tracks for the fellas, R&B jams for the ladies. A hip-hop station like Hot 97 was actually a hybrid station, playing "Blazin' Hip-Hop and R&B," as its longtime slogan promised. For anyone wondering why listeners didn't tire of hip-hop's endless machismo, or why the hip-hop audience wasn't more impatient with the fact that so many rappers were men, this was one answer: because hip-hop evolved in symbiosis with R&B. Sometimes the genres worked together, as when rappers and singers teamed up to compete for the Grammy Award for Best Rap/Sung Collaboration. Sometimes they veered apart, as when rappers foreswore R&B, or when an R&B singer like Usher promised, in contradistinction to his hip-hop counterparts, "I just wanna take it nice and slow." And often they borrowed from each other, as when R. Kelly and Mary J. Blige brought hip-hop swagger into R&B, or when hip-hop producers transformed R&B snippets into beats for rappers to use. A few performers refused to choose, like Missy Elliott, a visionary from Virginia who usually rapped, unless she felt like singing. Elliott and her frequent collaborator, the producer Timbaland, created their own form of mutant hip-hop. Elliott's biggest hits were dance tracks: "Get Ur Freak On," from 2001, based on a brilliantly minimal sample of bhangra music, and "Work It," from 2002, known for a chorus where the lyrics are played partly backward. But one of my favorite Missy Elliott moments comes from a lesser-known 1997 track, "I'm Talkin'," in which she declares, "My style of rapping / I'm su-su-such a good rapper." Only she is not rapping at all—she is singing, mischievously and rather prettily.

Rappers had long used melody to enliven their rhymes—in the 1990s, Bone Thugs-n-Harmony, from Cleveland, pioneered a sing-rapping style that was melodic but heavily rhythmic and lyrically dense. When Nelly emerged in 2000, he showed off a more easeful form of sing-rapping, making songs that transcended hip-hop, even though he never stopped being categorized as a rapper. (Nelly later teamed up with country acts, including Tim McGraw and Florida Georgia Line, becoming a mixed-genre hitmaker.) Kanye West had his first major hit with "Slow Jamz," a 2003 collaboration in which he sang the first verse, using only a few notes but using them effectively. And the same year, André 3000, from OutKast, made a spectacular transition with "Hey Ya!," a kind of funky new-wave pastiche that went No. 1, becoming one of the decade's biggest hits—it wasn't really hip-hop at all, except by pedigree. In an earlier era, André 3000's success might have inspired anxiety: he was one of the greatest rappers in hip-hop history, and he had gone pop. But by the 2000s, the old formula had been reversed—more and more, pop was going hip-hop, instead. Mainstream singers were working with hip-hop producers, singing over hip-hop beats. Timbaland, the inventive Virginia producer who worked with Missy Elliott, and who created hip-hop classics like Jay-Z's "Big Pimpin'," also produced "Cry Me a River," the song that helped establish Justin Timberlake, from the boy band *NSYNC, as a solo star. The Neptunes, also from Virginia, had a similar trajectory, boosted by the fact that the duo included Pharrell Williams, who was also a singer and sometime rapper, and who became a star in his own right, possessed of both pop and hip-hop credibility.

No musician did more to enlarge this singing-rapping tradition, or to frustrate my ridiculous "singing" and "rapping" playlists, than Drake, a hip-hop star whose massive success in the 2010s showed just how much the genre had changed. He came from Toronto, the son of a Black man from Memphis and a Jewish woman from Canada, and he began his career not onstage but on-screen, playing a wheelchair-using boy named Jimmy in *Degrassi: The Next Generation*, a Canadian teen television drama. But he had a remarkable ear for beats and melody, and an audacious sense of himself: instead of acting hard, like so many rappers before him, Drake was defiantly soft, a lovesick heartthrob known for his impressive collection of sweaters. ("I have a sweater obsession, I guess," he once said.) Drake's first big hit was "Best I Ever Had," from 2009, in which he mostly sang the chorus and mostly rapped the verses, borrowing a melody from a track by Lil Wayne, who was in some sense his boss—Drake was signed to Lil Wayne's record label, Young Money. If you think of the chorus as the heart of the track, then "Best I Ever Had" is an R&B song, setting a mellow mood that is enlivened and not ruined by the conversational rhymes in the verses. But if you concentrate, instead, on the influence of Lil Wayne, and the sly arrogance of Drake's verses, then "Best I Ever Had" belongs in a "rapping" playlist, not a "singing" playlist. For Drake, switching between genres was also a way of emphasizing different parts of his persona—the rapper and the singer, each shameless in his own way. In the second verse, he tried to suggest that he was both a ladies' man and a guys' guy: "When my album drop, bitches'll buy it for the picture / And niggas'll buy it, too, and claim they got it for they sister." Nicki Minaj, a hip-hop star who was also signed to Young Money, switched personas and genres even more sharply than Drake did. She was a venomous rapper who could also sing pop songs, going from a whisper to a roar, employing multiple voices: she could evoke New York, where she grew up; or Trinidad, where she was born; or a kind of parody girly-world, reflecting her fascination with Barbie-doll imagery. (Her fans were known as Barbz.) Even as they made pop hits, Drake and Nicki Minaj stayed loyal to hip-hop, and influential within it—together, they taught a generation of fierce women and emotive men that hip-hop had a place for them, too.

In 2009, Jay-Z predicted the future of hip-hop, getting it exactly right and exactly wrong. He released a track called "D.O.A. (Death of Autotune)," railing against the ubiquity of pitch-correction software, which could add melody to any vocal line, turning a tuneless rapper into a tuneful cyborg singer. The technology had first risen to prominence in 1998, when Cher used it to computerize her voice in "Believe," a dance-pop single that went to No. 1; by 2009, so many singers and rappers had used auto-tune that it was tempting to believe, as Jay-Z did, that the technology was a waning fad. He suggested that auto-tune was making hip-hop too pop and too playful, and he called for the return of a tougher, ostensibly more masculine sound, jeering, "You niggas' jeans too tight / Your colors too bright / Your voice too light." He was right about the trend, but wrong about it being on its way out. In the 2010s, hip-hop became more popular and dominant than ever, thanks partly to the possibilities that auto-tune allowed. It sometimes seemed as if hip-hop *was* popular music, with everything else either a sub-genre or variant of it, or a quirky alternative to it. On streaming services especially, you might look at the chart and see that just about all the most popular songs in America were hip-hop, or hip-hop-ish.

This was a triumphant moment for the genre, although it didn't always *sound* triumphant: hip-hop, the world's greatest party music, had grown even more popular by cultivating its depressive streak. The rapper Future showed his peers that auto-tune could be used not just for pop choruses but for dark, woozy atmospherics—he valued the technology not because it kept him in tune but because it made his voice sound wobbly, as if he were rapping from a different world. Future cared about texture and mood much more than lyrics, and some of his rhymes consisted of little more than offhand drug references: "Only God can judge us / Take a bar and I love it." Future's music both reflected and popularized the recreational use of prescription sedatives within hip-hop, and for that matter within the country: he rapped about swallowing tablets—or "bars"—of Xanax, and about sipping codeine-fortified cough syrup, the same drug that fueled DJ Screw, the architect of modern Houston hip-hop, and also killed him.

Ever since the eighties, drug use had been generally disdained in hip-hop, with the obvious exception of marijuana. But the popularity of prescription cough syrup, known as lean, dissolved the taboo, while also dissolving the once-solid sound of hip-hop itself. As Lil Wayne grew more closely associated with syrup, his music grew more light-headed and more uneven. ("I got a full cup of lean that I saw in the fridge / I started to swig, but ended up drinkin' all of that shit," he croaked.) You could hear the influence of Future, and maybe also the influence of lean, in a generation of young rappers, sometimes derided as "mumble rappers," who made hip-hop that was blurry and impressionistic: Young Thug, from Atlanta, was a brilliant mumbler and yelper and howler; Travis Scott, from Houston, built immersive tracks by treating his voice as one more electronic instrument; the melancholy emo rappers Lil Peep, XXXTentacion, and Juice WRLD built links between hip-hop and punk. Perhaps the canniest star to emerge from this world was Post Malone, a seeming mumbler (the first song on his first album began, "I done drank codeine from a broken whiskey glass") who revealed himself to be an uncommonly deft pop singer and songwriter. Once, during an interview in the kitchen of his mountain hideaway in Utah, I asked Post Malone about his evolution, and he told me that he started out imitating his favorite rappers, and gradually found his way to a more unclassifiable sound, reflecting a wide range of genres. "I owe *everything* to hip-hop," he told me, but then he revised the thought. "I owe everything to rock. I owe everything to fuckin' *music*." Indeed, one of his many hits is a collaboration with both Travis Scott and the heavy-metal pioneer Ozzy Osbourne, and it would be surprising if he didn't eventually find a way to scale the country chart, too. Post Malone is white, and in a sense he is merely one more white performer drawing from hip-hop, and then rising to higher heights than virtually all of his Black peers. But he is also a good example of the increasing fuzziness of hip-hop, a term that more and more describes neither a community nor a way of making music but, like rock 'n' roll, a spirit or essence—one that might even be detected in the sound of a white guy singing a song with Ozzy Osbourne. Hip-hop has two traditional definitions: hip-hop is rapping, and hip-hop is Black youth culture. What happens when neither definition reliably applies?

Mixed Up

Like rock 'n' roll, and maybe even more than rock 'n' roll, hip-hop has taken root all over the globe, inspiring local scenes that sometimes follow American examples rather too faithfully and other times take the form of marvelously distinct genres. You could hear the spirit of hip-hop in funk carioca, a frenetic genre that emerged in the late eighties, in Brazil, borrowing from and enlarging the musical legacy of 2 Live Crew; in kwaito, a loping style, partly derived from house music, that helped define postapartheid South Africa; and in countless other hybrids and offshoots. In Jamaica, which helped spawn hip-hop in the first place, a brash and verbose variant of reggae known as dancehall evolved for decades in parallel with American hip-hop, nurturing an extraordinarily rich vocal tradition that was not quite singing *or* rapping. (In the Jamaican press, dancehall reggae stars were typically referred to as "deejays," like their seventies precursors, or as "artistes," a suitably open-ended term.) Dancehall reggae stars occasionally scaled the American pop charts, as Sean Paul did, and frequently helped inspire American rappers; this was especially true in New York, where many performers had connections to the Caribbean, including the Notorious B.I.G., who was the son of Jamaican immigrants. All of these far-flung genres were recognizably hip-hop, in a broad sense: exuberant and defiant, with more-or-less spoken lyrics that rhymed, linked to poor neighborhoods and marginalized populations. And yet all of them, too, were recognizably *not* hip-hop, in a narrower sense: separated by language and genre from the tracks played on American radio. Indeed, these countries invariably had orthodox hip-hop scenes, too, surviving and sometimes flourishing alongside these mixed-up hybrids.

In England, in the 2000s, a clamorous genre called grime emerged, drawing from dancehall reggae and from the fidgety rhythms of homegrown electronic music. In the United Kingdom, it sparked a moral panic, and something like a cultural revolution, elevating and emboldening a generation of Black British voices. But the music made scarcely any impression in the American hip-hop world, in which the British accents and beats sounded unacceptably exotic. Hip-hop grew more transatlantic in the 2010s, as a Chicago-born variant of gangsta rap, known as drill music, inspired a lyrically and musically brutal counterpart in England, known as UK drill. This style *did* resonate in America, because it inspired a cohort of rappers from Brooklyn who created their own version, Brooklyn drill, often collaborating with British producers. Brooklyn drill was irreducibly global and intensely local: it was built, like its UK predecessor, on smudgy basslines and onomatopoeic gunshot-noise interjections, but the lyrics tended to focus on neighborhoods and gangs, as if to suggest that even in the social media era, it was not necessarily easy to escape whatever was outside your door. Pop Smoke, the first major star to emerge from Brooklyn drill, was murdered in February 2020, a few months before the release of his debut album, which topped the *Billboard* album chart.

The most consequential diversification of American hip-hop came from Latin music genres, some of which had helped fuel early hip-hop and had grown alongside it. Puerto Rican musicians have played a particularly important role in hip-hop since its creation, and yet in New York, as in the rest of the country, Latin music and hip-hop have remained generally separate worlds. That was still true in the 2000s, when the Puerto Rico–bred genre known as reggaeton exploded in popularity; radio stations across the country switched to an all-reggaeton format, attracting young listeners from a wide variety of Latino backgrounds. This burst of excitement created stars like Daddy Yankee, who noted in 2006 that reggaeton had "unified the Latin masses," and Don Omar, who was the headliner at a celebratory concert I attended in 2007 at Shea Stadium—a momentous event, even though most non-Latino New Yorkers probably had no idea it was happening. It wasn't until 2017 that Daddy Yankee reached the top of the pop chart, with "Despacito," a pop-reggaeton collaboration with the Puerto Rican singer Luis Fonsi and the Canadian heartthrob Justin Bieber, who added to a remix of the song a few months after the original was released. "Despacito" became a global sensation, one of the decade's biggest hits, in any country or language. It also revealed how the globalized music industry had shifted: where once Latin music stars were asked to sing and speak in English in order to achieve "crossover" success, now it was Bieber hoping to cross over, delivering a brief English-language introduction and then switching to Spanish for the chorus. There are, by most measures, more native Spanish speakers in the world than native English speakers. And on streaming services like Spotify, where all streams count the same, the term "crossover" makes less sense—beyond a certain threshold of popularity, any hit will look like a crossover hit.

By the time "Despacito" conquered the world, a new hybrid was taking off: some people called it Latin trap, and it blended the sing-rapping style of reggaeton with the woozy atmosphere and synthetic snare drums of modern hip-hop. Latin music became a kind of universal party music, versatile and seductive. Madonna released a Latin-influenced album in 2019, and the Black Eyed Peas released a wholly Latin hybrid album in 2020. After decades of talk about Latin music crossing over, it was great fun to watch anglophone American stars straining to match the appeal of someone like Bad Bunny, a Puerto Rican maverick whose echoey and sometimes melancholy Latin trap tracks made him a global celebrity—either the most influential hip-hop star of his era, or a sign that hip-hop's worldwide supremacy was beginning to fade, depending on how you defined "hip-hop." The Anglophone hip-hop industry didn't ignore these developments, of course. The first Latin trap song to top the *Billboard* pop chart, in 2019, was "I Like It," by the rapper Cardi B, a former reality-television star from the Bronx whose accent evoked Spanish-speaking New York neighborhoods and whose heritage was partly Latina. (Her mother was from Trinidad, and her father was from the Dominican Republic.) "I Like It" was based on "I Like It Like That," the sixties boogaloo hit, and it featured Bad Bunny and J Balvin, from Colombia, who was a big name in reggaeton—in other words, it was a carefully engineered pop blockbuster that worked every bit as well as its creators intended.

I'm still not sure whether the increasing fuzziness of hip-hop is a sign that the genre remains too versatile to fade away, or a sign that its identity has already begun to evaporate. Some musicians push back against this fuzziness, of course. Kendrick Lamar is a brilliant rapper, known for tangled verses that reveal an astonishingly clear-eyed view of life and death. ("The Blacker the Berry," from 2015, is a furious exploration of race hatred and self-hatred, with each verse foreshadowing the track's final question: "Why did I weep when Trayvon Martin was in the street / When gangbanging make me kill a nigga blacker than me?") But both his careful attention to rhyme and meter and his equally careful attention to Black identity and Black neighborhoods mark Lamar as a hip-hop anomaly, much like Public Enemy in the late eighties: proof of what the genre is capable of, at its extreme, but not representative of what the genre is *generally* like. That is no criticism—and besides, we typically judge an artistic tradition by the best of what it produces, not by the average. But I can't help but wince when people talk about hip-hop as the high-minded, Pulitzer Prize–winning genre they feel it should be, rather than the rowdy and messy genre it usually has been. And I wince partly because I'm not sure that a purely high-minded version of hip-hop would have lasted so long, or spread so far, or inspired so many. Kendrick Lamar's rhymes are studied in school—quite rightly, too. But surely hip-hop benefits from the continuing existence of rappers whose music doesn't sound remotely like homework.

There are signs, in the social media age, that hip-hop won't always be the world's dominant youth culture. There are more ways than there used to be for charismatic characters to draw a crowd, even if they don't have money or connections. Distinctively African American terms and memes, the kinds of things that might once have only spread through hip-hop music, can now metastasize on TikTok or Instagram, with no song attached. Sometimes rappers go viral, but sometimes they can seem conspicuously and perilously behind the times, rushing to keep up with an online culture that might evolve even faster than hip-hop does. Rapping is important; done well, it is sublime. But if hip-hop was merely rapping, with no intimate connection to Black youth culture, no ability to adapt to shifting trends, then it would cease to be recognizably hip-hop—it would merely be poetry, or one more form of American roots music. The genre's tendency to evolve in unpredictable ways explains why it has continued to draw both crowds and critics, and why people who love it tend eventually to be heartbroken by it. Tricia Rose was dispirited to see hip-hop conquered by "commercialism," as represented by rappers like Jay-Z. And Jay-Z was appalled, in turn, to see hip-hop reimagined by an army of auto-tune clones. I have no reason to be sure that I, too, won't have my heart broken by hip-hop one day. But it hasn't happened yet.

6.

DANCE MUSIC

What Else Is Music For?

NILE RODGERS TRAVELED THROUGH half a dozen American subcultures before he discovered one that felt like home. He was raised in New York, in Greenwich Village, the child of parents whom he later recalled as beatniks: his mother and her partner shared a love of jazz and a love of drugs, both of which turned out to be heritable. As a boy, Rodgers discovered rock 'n' roll, learned to sniff glue, joined the Black Panthers, and eventually earned a place as a guitarist in the house band at the Apollo Theater, in Harlem, faking an encyclopedic knowledge of R&B until he no longer had to fake it. For a time, Rodgers thought he was going to start the great American "avant-garde classical-jazz-rock-fusion" band. But then, in the mid-1970s, he found something even better—something he described, in his memoir, as "a new way of living" and a "fledgling counter-culture lifestyle," one that was "even more expressive, political, and communal" than the hippie movement of the sixties.

This "new way of living" was called disco. And if Rodgers's description of it seems somewhat overheated, that is precisely the point. He was a disco auteur: the cofounder, with his friend Bernard Edwards, of a band called Chic, and a producer of some of the most artful dance music ever made.

Like most stories about dance music, the Nile Rodgers story is a conversion narrative: the tale of a guy who found salvation in a nightclub, and saw the world differently ever after. With the aid of a prescient and intrepid girlfriend, Rodgers explored New York's flourishing club scene, where he gave himself over to a nonverbal liberation movement. "We held our meetings and demonstrations on the dance floor," he remembered, adding that dancing had become, somehow, "a powerful communication tool." (A great night out, he discovered, could be "every bit as motivational" as a speech by Angela Davis, the fiery Black Panther.) Rodgers looked back on those days with both fondness and defensiveness; like many dance-floor revolutionaries, he couldn't help but suspect that if you weren't there, you would never really understand. Some of this defensiveness was related to the peculiar history of disco, which went, in less than a decade, from the margins to the mainstream and back again. Rodgers strained to praise disco because he knew that, even decades later, many people would rather bury it. He knew that, too often, pop music history is organized around great albums, rather than great parties. Often, that means dance music gets written out.

The first Chic song was called "Everybody Dance," and it was a miracle of musical engineering, based on a groove so airy that you hardly noticed its insistent thump. When the track was first recorded, in 1977, it had no lyrics at all except for a chorus that sounded tantalizingly unfinished ("Everybody dance / Do-do-do / Clap your hands, clap your hands"), and therefore endlessly replayable. Not even Rodgers quite understood what he and Edwards had created, but the recording engineer liked it enough to bring an acetate—basically, a demo on a disc—to an after-hours club called the Night Owl, where he was a DJ. The engineer invited Rodgers to visit, and Rodgers discovered that his demo had become a smash hit, at least in one New York club; the DJ would play it over and over, for something like an hour at a time, and somehow the dancers' enthusiasm never faded. "I had never seen anything like that," Rodgers recalled. "I realized the power of a groove, and the power of the DJ to talk to the audience, just through your groove record." In time, Chic acquired a record deal, and the song acquired a couple of verses, which were perfectly lovely, and perfectly unnecessary. "Everybody Dance" barely made it into the Top 40—its peak was No. 38— but it rose to the top of the *Billboard* dance chart, and the first Chic album, *Chic*, eventually sold more than five hundred thousand copies. By the end of 1977, Rodgers was emerging as a new kind of celebrity, one that hadn't existed a decade earlier: he was a disco star.

If this was a new musical role, Rodgers was nevertheless an old-fashioned candidate for it. Unlike many of the most important figures in the disco revolution, Rodgers was a virtuoso, in a traditional sense: a great guitarist, master of the funky, quick-strummed style he called "chucking"; his partner, Edwards, who died in 1996, was an extraordinarily nimble and funky bass player. Other great musicians helped create disco, too, including Earl Young, the drummer for the house band at Philadelphia International, the R&B label. Young's playing was innovative and unusually precise—he was a human drum machine, at a time when club DJs were demanding perfectly consistent tempos to enable seamless transitions between records. Young popularized the beat that became the backbone of disco: four-four time, with a bass drum thumping evenly on all four beats, and a hi-hat hissing on the off-beats. In *A House on Fire*, a history of Philadelphia Soul, John A. Jackson explained how, on a 1975 track called "Bad Luck," by Harold Melvin & the Blue Notes, Young's hi-hat was accidentally recorded too loud and couldn't be quieted in the final mix; this mistake may have helped make loud hi-hats a foundation of the disco sound.

In the popular imagination, though, disco was thought of as machine music, and in many ways it was. "Disco" is short for "discothèque," which is French for "record library." Some of the earliest discothèques seem to have sprung up in Europe, in the 1940s and '50s: in England, Jimmy Savile played records in dance halls and hotels; in Paris, disc jockeys ruled an influential club called the Whisky à Go Go, which inspired similarly influential "Whisky à Go Go" clubs in America. At the time, the idea of a discothèque might have seemed like one giant leap backward. It was sort of like listening to the radio, only without the miraculous technology of radio broadcasting, which allows sound to travel at the speed of light. Compared to that, a discothèque was positively crude: patrons were crowded into the same room as the disc jockey, watching a live person play recorded music. Even so, the innovation quickly spread. In 1965, *Billboard* published a special report on the discothèque industry, telling its readers that "discotheque is the most heavily promoted French import since the bikini." In these sixties discothèques, the star was often a jukebox, not a DJ—part of the appeal, for bar owners, was that discothèques provided unusually cheap entertainment. (In the United Kingdom, the rise of the discothèque inspired a legal challenge from the musicians' union, which worried that its members were being underbid.) Above all, discothèques thrived because they emphasized the social nature of listening to music: with no live band to gawk at, revelers were encouraged to gawk at each other instead. In *Billboard*, an executive from Seeburg, a jukebox company, explained the importance of social engineering. "You need a happy mixture of both guys and dolls to make a discotheque click," he said, and he was right, in general, about the importance of a "happy mixture"—even though, in the decades to come, a number of discos would prove him very wrong about the precise ratio required.

In 1965, the same year that *Billboard* declared that "discotheque" was the new "bikini," a starry-eyed record collector named David Mancuso rented a loft in downtown Manhattan, at the corner of Bleecker Street and Broadway. Tim Lawrence, a historian of American dance music, has written about how Mancuso used his loft to host LSD parties, compiling what he called "journey tapes" to help his guests enjoy their experiences. "They drew on everything from classical music to the Moody Blues," Mancuso wrote. "Somebody might get up and start dancing around the room at some point, although they weren't dance sessions." Starting in 1970, though, Mancuso grew more purposeful: his loft came to be known as the Loft, and he began to host a regular party there, playing records for people he knew, although he knew a lot of people. (He created membership cards, which were required for entry.) The party was called Love Saves the Day, and it was largely gay, but by no means exclusively so; Mancuso prided himself on attracting a racially and sexually mixed crowd, which was charged two dollars at the door. No alcohol was served, and Mancuso firmly decreed that no drugs should be sold on the dance floor—although the specificity of that decree also suggests just how permissive the atmosphere actually was. Mancuso was always on the lookout for police, who had no shortage of reasons (or excuses) to raid his loft, and who sometimes targeted gay clubs. Only a year before, police had raided the Stonewall Inn, prompting a riot, but Mancuso found that, to many of the young men who populated the city's cutting-edge dance floors, the Stonewall riot didn't necessarily seem like a watershed—gay nightlife continued, and so did pressure from the police. The Loft was raided for the first time in 1972, but the city found no evidence that Mancuso was selling alcohol, and so the party carried on; a few years later it moved a short way downtown, to a loft in SoHo, where Mancuso and his friends kept dancing well into the eighties. Lawrence told these stories and many others in an invaluable book named after Mancuso's institution. In *Love Saves the Day*, he re-created the world of New York nightclubs in the seventies, showing how music and dancing came together to create the sound known as disco, and helped invent modern dance music. Throughout much of human history, the term "dance music" would have sounded redundant. What else is music for? But disco rearranged the priorities of pop, teaching a generation that a great groove could be more important—more useful—than a beautifully written song.

The rise of disco was astonishingly fast. In 1973, three years after Mancuso started his loft parties, *Rolling Stone* published a report on the emerging "disco sound" by Vince Aletti, who became the genre's leading chronicler, and who explained that the world of disco revolved around DJs, who were "underground stars"—sadly for the Seeburg corporation, discos had outgrown jukeboxes. Three years later, in 1976, *Billboard* suggested that disco was "rapidly becoming the universal pop music." That's how popular disco was, and how omnivorous. It seemed to emerge from nowhere and take over everything. Beethoven went disco (Walter Murphy and the Big

Apple Band, "A Fifth of Beethoven"), Star Wars went disco (Meco, "Star Wars Theme/Cantina Band"), rockers like the Rolling Stones ("Miss You") and Rod Stewart ("Da Ya Think I'm Sexy") and Queen ("Another One Bites the Dust") went disco, and all of them went to No. 1 on the pop chart. But a backlash was building, one that became harder to ignore in 1979, when a couple of rock radio DJs hosted a promotion called Disco Demolition Night, during a Chicago White Sox doubleheader. Fans could buy a discounted ticket if they brought a disco record with them, and between games the records were to be blown up on the field as a musical protest. The promotion sparked too much excitement, and fans stormed the field, after which the second game had to be canceled. At the time, six of the ten most popular songs in America were disco songs; "Bad Girls," by Donna Summer, the biggest disco star of all, was beginning a five-week run at No. 1. But the rock fans' furious rebuke was a sign that disco had become uncool, and before long it became unpopular, too. Twelve months later, on the one-year anniversary of the anti-disco riot, only one disco hit remained in the Top 10, and America's favorite song was "It's Still Rock and Roll to Me," by Billy Joel.

Nile Rodgers remembered that the "Disco Sucks" movement traumatized him so badly that he decided to eliminate the word "dance" from his lyrical vocabulary, because he didn't want to be marginalized as merely a disco producer. But the death of disco didn't mean the death of dancing—it meant the rebirth of dance music, as DJs and music producers around the world found new ways to create indelible grooves, sometimes making big hits and sometimes burrowing deeper underground. "Dance music" has generally been a catchall term, or more accurately a catch-some term, referring not to *every* danceable form of popular music but only to those that are descended, however indirectly, from disco. People usually use the term "dance music" to refer to tracks that are heavily rhythmic and unapologetically repetitive. Dance music is often created not by an old-fashioned band playing live in a studio, but by a producer manipulating bits of sound—it is often, in other words, what we call "electronic" music, although this term has grown outdated. (Nowadays, there is very little music of any genre that is not in some sense electronic music.) Dance music means house and techno and rave; it means most of what was briefly called, in the nineties, "electronica"; it means EDM, which stands for "electronic dance music," a broadly descriptive term that became, in the twenty-first century, a genre unto itself, and one that was nearly as popular, and as reviled, as disco at its peak. People who love this music tend, like Rodgers, to speak the fulsome language of converts—and they tend, too, to share his suspicion that the wider world doesn't really get it, doesn't understand the revolution that these grooves inspired. Like hip-hop, dance music began as party music. But more than hip-hop, it has remained party music. And parties are ephemeral. Throughout the history of dance music, it hasn't always been clear whether the music would out-live the party, or whether it even should.

One Big Mix

Disco music was born in many places, and one of them was Douala, a West African city in what is now Cameroon. Douala was the birthplace of Manu Dibango, a saxophone player and bandleader who relocated to Paris, got himself a record contract, and, in 1972, recorded an infectious but unclas-sifiable song called "Soul Makossa," which was named after a local genre. ("Makossa" is a Douala word that means, of course, "dance.") It might have remained an obscurity in America if David Mancuso hadn't found a copy of Dibango's record in a Caribbean record store in Brooklyn and added it to his playlist at the Loft. "Soul Makossa" doesn't quite sound like what we think of as disco; it doesn't have the thump-and-hiss beat that Earl Young helped establish as disco's rhythmic backbone. But it is beguiling and unpredictable, a rather quirky assemblage of parts, with a blaring horn riff and vocals that resemble background chatter. "Mama-ko, mama-ssa, mako-mako-ssa," Dibango mutters, as if he's testing the microphone. What the song has, most of all, is a steady, heavy pulse, suggestive of the kind of perpetual motion that Mancuso and his fellow DJs hoped to encourage. The song spread to other dance floors, and then to Frankie Crocker, the star DJ at WBLS, the city's most disco-friendly radio station. In his influential 1973 disco article for *Rolling Stone*, Vince Aletti wrote that "Soul Makossa" was "a perfect example of the genre," and Dibango's import was rereleased in America, where it made an unlikely appearance on the pop charts. Until then, DJs like Mancuso had filled their sets with a mix of pop hits (Mancuso was fond of "Love Train," the R&B smash by the O'Jays) and obscurities (he also loved a funky Spanish rock band called Barrabás). "Soul Makossa" was the first obscurity that became a pop hit primarily thanks to the enthusiasm of disco DJs.

Enthusiasm, in fact, was Mancuso's greatest asset. In a town, and a demimonde, that could be unsparing, he was renowned for his niceness, for the way he filled his loft with balloons to encourage a festive mood, and for the earnest way he revered his favorite records. As proof of this last quality, he insisted on playing every song all the way through, with a small pause before and after to ensure that there was no overlap. His many peers and disciples tended to be much less reverent. Lawrence's book explained the alliances and rivalries that defined the scene. There was Francis Grasso, who was an anomaly: a straight DJ at a gay club, the Sanctuary, who liked to play the orgasmic interlude from "Whole Lotta Love," by Led Zeppelin, on top of the drumming section of "I'm a Man," by Chicago. (Grasso said that he loved playing for gay crowds because they allowed him to do "things that the straights couldn't have handled.") At a Loft-like club called the Gallery, Nicky Siano was proudly unpredictable, sometimes using variable-speed turntables to blend records together, and sometimes twisting the equalizers or even turning off the speakers, to create moments of high drama. And then there was Larry Levan, Siano's protégé (and, briefly, his lover), who learned to DJ at the Continental Baths, a bathhouse on the Upper West Side, and eventually became the resident at yet another

Loft-inspired downtown club, the Paradise Garage. Levan is sometimes praised as the greatest DJ ever, for reasons having more to do with his sensibility than his technique. He realized that danceable music need not be peppy—it could be deep and dreamlike and druggy, like Mancuso's "journey tapes" from the sixties. One of the records that Levan loved was "Heartbeat," by Taana Gardner, which the dance floor at first resisted because it was shockingly slow: fewer than 100 beats per minute, where the average disco track was closer to 120. But Levan kept playing it, and eventually the dancers were converted; like every great DJ, Levan had an ability to change the way people heard the records he played, often permanently.

At first, the disco DJs were scavengers, hunting for hidden treasures in the chaotic heap of records produced by the music industry, which tended not to recognize great grooves until DJs pointed them out, and sometimes not even then. But as executives realized that discos could drive record sales, the relationship between DJs and record companies became more symbiotic. Mancuso helped organize the New York Record Pool, an organization that helped record companies give free records to disco DJs in exchange for feedback and, if the records made it onto disco playlists, promotion. A former model named Tom Moulton thought he could be even more helpful than that: he had been compiling nonstop music mixes, on reel-to-reel tape, for the Sandpiper, a club on Fire Island, outside New York. Moulton was hired by record companies to make their tracks more disco-friendly, and he did the job with wit and precision, extending songs by splicing and looping the rhythm sections that dancers loved. Moulton helped codify a musical form that changed the face of pop: the remix. Record companies began to issue these singles on twelve-inch records, instead of the traditional seven-inch records, because they were so long, and because the extra space between the grooves allowed the records to be louder, which DJs valued. Musicians, on the other hand, did not always appreciate these innovations. Moulton's first assignment was "Do It ('Til You're Satisfied)," by a new group, B.T. Express; the members didn't like the way Moulton pared back the vocals, but dancers did, and so did many members of the broader listening public, who pushed the song to No. 2 on the pop chart in 1974. Moulton took an even more radical approach when he was handed the tracks for *Never Can Say Goodbye*, the 1975 debut album by Gloria Gaynor. He extended the three tracks on side one and put them back-to-back, with scarcely any pauses, to create a continuous dance mix. In *Love Saves the Day*, Moulton recalled that Gaynor wasn't happy to be upstaged by the beat on her own album. "I don't sing much," she said when she heard his version. "What am I supposed to do when we perform the song?" Moulton told her to learn how to dance.

The album made Gaynor one of the biggest names in disco, and the success of disco records helped spread New York club culture across the country, turning tens of thousands of local bars and nightclubs into instant discos. All that was required was a DJ and some lights—and the lights were optional. This musical tendency became, in 1977, a pop-culture phenomenon, with the opening of Studio 54, a celebrity-centric New York club that was purpose-built to generate tabloid headlines, fostering the perception that disco was for people who were glamorous, or wished they were. (Tellingly, Studio 54 was never known for great music, because many of the patrons were not there to dance but to socialize and gawk.) Even now, few faces are more associated with the genre than those of John Travolta, the star of the 1977 disco blockbuster *Saturday Night Fever*, and the three members of the Bee Gees, who provided most of the soundtrack, which was one of the bestselling albums of the decade. The Bee Gees had once been an Australian rock band, but they reinvented themselves in the seventies with a series of worldwide disco hits: "Jive Talkin'," "You Should Be Dancing," "Night Fever," and, most of all, "Stayin' Alive," a song so popular it came to define the genre.

So what was this genre, exactly? For the most part, disco was R&B, only smoother and faster and stranger. Diana Ross, working with Nile Rodgers, released the best album of her career, *diana*, at the end of the disco age. The genre was a perfect fit, too, for Donna Summer, who had sung in a rock band and appeared in a touring version of *Hair*, the rock musical, before she found disco. Where pure R&B singers sometimes sobbed or wailed, to evoke the genre's history, Summer's voice was light and creamy, summoning up the fantasy of a dance floor where all the old genre categories might melt away. Like rock 'n' roll before it, disco promised to dissolve boundaries of genre and race—the music was driven by a dream of integration. Disco was reflexively open-minded: one of the most successful disco-oriented record companies was Salsoul Records, which helped bring Latin rhythms into the US pop mainstream. The genre embraced some Black singers who were just too unusual to have succeeded in R&B, none more so than Grace Jones, a Jamaica-born model who invented her own theatrical form of dance music. And to a surprising extent, the genre retained some of its gay identity even as it went mainstream. The Village People reached No. 2 on the pop chart with "Y.M.C.A.," which was essentially an in-joke, full of suggestive lyrics about a wonderful place where "you can hang out with all the boys." (There was an in-joke hidden within the in-joke: Victor Willis, the lead singer, was actually straight.) A singer named Carl Bean had a disco club hit with "I Was Born This Way," an explicitly pro-gay anthem that was released on Motown, a label not known for political provocation. And then there was Sylvester, the glamorous so-called Queen of Disco, who had a string of dance hits, and who was among the first pop stars to publicly embrace gay identity. He made a memorable appearance on *American Bandstand*, the cheerfully square television show, in 1978, during which Dick Clark referred to him, admiringly, as "an outrageous gentleman."

Of course, this open-mindedness had its limits. Because disco was party music, it relied, like Mancuso's Loft, upon a complicated dynamic of inclusion and exclusion. Every genre has gatekeepers, but disco had literal gatekeepers: people stationed at the door, determining who was allowed in and who wasn't. Mancuso wanted to maintain a warm, welcoming environment—which meant, paradoxically, that he had to keep an eye on the membership rolls, to make sure his loft wasn't overrun by people who weren't so welcoming. Studio 54 was known for its strict door policy; one of Chic's biggest hits, "Le Freak," was originally written as a protest song, after Rodgers and Edwards were turned away. But on the occasion of Studio 54's first anniversary, Truman Capote told *The New York Times* that the club was "very democratic," citing the carefully curated diversity of its clientele: "Boys with boys, girls with girls, girls with boys, blacks and whites, capitalists and Marxists, Chinese and everything else—all one big mix!" Beyond the world of clubs, though, it was harder to control admission. Because the spirit of disco was essentially inclusive, there was relatively little talk about "real" versus "fake" disco, and therefore relatively little organized resistance when outsiders claimed the movement as their own. In 1976, a Tennessee radio DJ named Rick Dees released "Disco Duck (Part 1)," a novelty song full of cartoonish quacks that went to No. 1, and that became a useful example for anyone looking to establish that disco was objectively bad.

One of those people was Steve Dahl, a prankish radio personality who was one of the organizers of Disco Demolition Night in Chicago. Dahl told Tim Lawrence that he saw himself as a defender of rock 'n' roll, which seemed to him to be "threatened as a species." (The radio station where he used to work had recently switched formats, from rock to disco.) What he most objected to about disco, he said, was its "superficiality." This was a common complaint: a couple of days before Dahl's event, *The New York Times* had published an op-ed arguing that the world of disco was defined by "glitter and gloss, without substance, subtlety, or more than surface sexuality." Even so, Dahl and the White Sox were evidently unprepared for the enthusiasm of the attendees, who turned a publicity stunt into a kind of cultural uprising. A number of critics saw something disturbing in the spectacle of all these rock fans, mainly white, seeking to destroy the genre of disco, which was largely Black and gay. Lawrence compared the event to the repression of jazz—"Negermusik"—in Nazi Germany, and argued that the backlash against disco was inherently "homophobic." Detractors who called the music "superficial" or "artificial," he says, were using "derogatory euphemisms for 'gay.'"

No doubt the inclusive nature of disco had something to do with the backlash it generated, but it's worth remembering how mainstream the genre had become. By 1979, disco was associated with Black and gay nightlife, but it was also associated with mainstream celebrities like Rod Stewart and John Travolta. (Dahl recorded a parody of Stewart's "Da Ya Think I'm Sexy," called, "Do You Think I'm Disco," about a hapless poseur whose social life is saved by Led Zeppelin; the lyrics took aim at *Saturday Night Fever* and "Disco Duck.") The appeal of disco was always partly tribal—*Saturday Night Fever* was based on a semifictional article in *New York* magazine about Italian American disco dancers in Brooklyn, called "Tribal Rites of the New Saturday Night." It makes sense, then, that the backlash to disco was tribal, too, fueled by people who viewed themselves as non-members of this virtual club, eager to reject Studio 54 before it rejected them. Three years before the riot, *Billboard* had expressed the hope (or perhaps the fear) that disco was becoming truly "universal" music, when in fact it was becoming—like most fast-growing genres—intensely polarizing. Just as the genre itself was, in various times and ways, inclusive and exclusive, so, too, could the backlash to it seem, from different angles, like hateful retaliation or a well-deserved rebuke. Many of the connoisseurs in New York, for example, disdained the disco hits every bit as much as rock fans did, if not more. Frankie Knuckles was a former New York disco DJ, a protégé of Larry Levan who had moved to Chicago, where he played records for serious dancers at a club called the Warehouse. He watched the riot on television, and wasn't much bothered by it. "It didn't affect the Warehouse, because the Warehouse wasn't a mainstream discotheque," he told Tim Lawrence. Robert Williams, the owner of the Warehouse, said, "We thought Steve Dahl was *hilarious*."

One of the people at that White Sox doubleheader was an aspiring music producer named Vince Lawrence, no relation to the historian, who was working as an usher. He viewed the riot differently. "All of the records that were piling up at the gate weren't necessarily disco records—most of them were just Black records," he recalled, in a recent documentary. "The message was, well, if you're Black or you're gay, then you're not one of us." A number of Black musicians found that the backlash against disco made it harder for Black records to cross over to pop radio. The next month, "Good Times," by Chic, was replaced at the top of the charts by "My Sharona," a terse and punkish rock song by a new band called the Knack. "The media and the industry pitted us against the Knack," Rodgers later recalled. "The disco kings in their buppie uniforms versus the scrappy white boys. But we never saw it that way." Like most disco stars, Rodgers didn't necessarily think of himself as a disco star, and yet he learned that his disco identity was hard to shake. Rodgers continued to make music, and to make hits: he produced "Let's Dance," for David Bowie, in 1983, and "The Reflex," for the British new-wave band Duran Duran, in 1984, both of which went to No. 1. But in all the years following the bonfire in Chicago, Chic never reached the Top 40 again.

Very Much Alive

When disco first emerged, its sound was plush and orchestral, in the easeful tradition of seventies soul. But not every drummer could supply a beat as steady as Earl Young's, and some producers found that this new genre demanded some new instruments. Throughout the seventies, a handful of singers had been experimenting with drum machines. "Family Affair," a woozy composition by Sly and the Family Stone, slouched to the top of the pop chart in 1971; three years later, in 1974, George McCrae used a simple electronic beat for "Rock Your Baby," a huge hit that was disarming precisely because it sounded like a ghostly demo instead of a finished recording. Even so, when Donna Summer released "I Feel Love," in 1977, it seemed to have been beamed in from a different, more advanced galaxy. The song was produced by Giorgio Moroder, an Italian producer and experimenter based in Munich, who used a Moog synthesizer to create a flickering electronic track that evoked the sensation of being inside a rocket, endlessly accelerating upward. At the time, many people probably assumed it was a novelty record. Instead, it was a watershed. Before "I Feel Love," electronic music had often been armchair music, the purview of adventurous composers like Wendy Carlos, who created the soundtrack to *A Clockwork Orange*, and avant-garde bands like Tangerine Dream, from Germany, who existed on the ambient fringe of the progressive-rock movement. "I Feel Love" popularized the idea that electronic music could be danceable—and, in time, the far more radical idea that dance music should be electronic. Indeed, by the nineties, the terms "dance music" and "electronic music" had come to be used more or less interchangeably, thanks to the movement that was galvanized by "I Feel Love."

People sometimes used the term "Eurodisco" to describe the influx of dance records, often synthesizer-driven, that arrived in America in the late seventies. Nelson George, the R&B historian, disparaged the "metronome-like beat" that powered these records, writing that they were "perfect for folks with no sense of rhythm." (The subtext was that African American musicians were being displaced by white producers from overseas.) But the Eurodisco invasion, which helped push disco away from its R&B roots, also helped the genre establish an independent musical identity. A few months after "I Feel Love," a French producer known as Cerrone released a track called "Supernature," a ten-minute electronic voyage that made three-minute pop songs sound obsolete. In San Francisco, Patrick Cowley, a keyboardist and producer who worked with Sylvester, helped pioneer an up-tempo, heavily electronic variant of disco that was known as Hi-NRG, which became closely associated with gay clubs in the eighties. Cowley's most popular solo track was a bawdy and futuristic song called "Menergy," which topped the dance chart in late 1981. By then, of course, disco was widely considered to be dead; in truth, it was underground but very much alive.

One place it lived on was in Chicago, the adopted home of Frankie

Knuckles, who was known for his marathon Saturday-night sets at the Warehouse: he would start spinning records before midnight, and keep going until sometime around noon. The death of mainstream disco did not dampen his enthusiasm for the music, but it did mean that he had to search harder for great records because the major labels had lost interest. By the early eighties, Knuckles's playlists included latter-day disco favorites along with quirky electronic pop songs from emerging European acts like Yello and Modern Romance. His selection was so distinctive that a local record store created a section full of the kinds of things he liked, labeling it "Warehouse music," after the club. Some of the tracks Knuckles played were literally impossible to find, though, because he sometimes used a reel-to-reel machine to create his own bespoke remixes.

In 1982, Knuckles left the Warehouse to open his own club, the Power Plant, and gained a rival, Ron Hardy, who played a more frenzied variant of disco at a new version of the Warehouse, now known as the Music Box. Knuckles and Hardy shared the same problem: they needed more—and brawnier—dance tracks than the local record stores could provide. And soon a handful of local producers began turning out their own dance tracks, often using electronic keyboards, which were growing cheaper and easier to program. In 1984, a DJ named Jesse Saunders pressed up a twelve-inch single called "On and On," which was essentially a bootleg version of a disco remix he liked. (The track was cowritten by another local producer, Vince Lawrence, the Chicago White Sox doubleheader usher.) The next year, a producer known as Chip E. released a robotic rhythm track called "Time to Jack," which had almost no lyrics besides the title, repeatedly intoned as an exhortation to dancers. And in 1986, Marshall Jefferson released "Move Your Body," a comparatively lush production, with a thumping beat and an impressive piano introduction, which Jefferson recorded at one-third the tempo and then sped up, to make himself sound sort of like a virtuoso. By then, these records had adopted the name of the record-store section where they were filed: Warehouse music, customarily shortened to "house music."

Jefferson's track, with its triumphant refrain, functioned as a love song to this new genre, or perhaps a birth announcement:

> *Gotta have house!*
> *Music!*
> *All night long!*

None of these tracks went anywhere near the *Billboard* pop charts, but in Chicago this was pop music, or at any rate popular music: a top house track might sell tens of thousands of copies in area record stores, and local radios broadcast mix shows by house DJs. Meanwhile, in Detroit, a handful of tinkerers had heard about the scene in Chicago, and they were working on their own electronic tracks. These producers, like the pioneers in Chicago, were all Black, and they were equally influenced by the homegrown grooves of Parliament-Funkadelic and by the alien electronic sounds of groups like Kraftwerk, from Germany, for whom advanced technology was both a musical tool and a lyrical theme. One of these Detroit tinkerers was Juan Atkins, who adopted the name Model 500 (because it was "non-ethnic," he later said) and released, in 1985, a tough and twitchy track called "No UFO's," which became a club favorite four hours west, in Chicago. Another Detroit record that did well in Chicago was "Strings of Life," a 1987 track by Derrick May that caused excitement and astonishment on Frankie Knuckles's dance floor. There were no words, and there was no bassline, just a disorienting collage of electronic strings and piano chords, locked onto a forceful beat that would mutate, disappear for a while, and then come crashing back.

It turned out that Chicago DJs weren't the only disco stalwarts who were looking for some new dance music. An adventurous post-punk club in Manchester, England, called the Haçienda began to play some of these house records, and in July 1986, the hip British fashion magazine *i-D* sent a reporter to investigate the Chicago scene, which had been, the magazine explained, "the hot tip amongst DJs and A&R people for the last three or four months." When the article was published in September, "Love Can't Turn Around," by a Chicago house producer named Farley "Jackmaster" Funk, was heading to No. 10 on the British pop chart; the next year, another Chicago producer, Steve "Silk" Hurley, reached No. 1 with "Jack Your Body." Inspired by these successes, Virgin Records decided to introduce British listeners to a different group of Midwestern producers, and in 1988, the label released a compilation called *Techno! The New Dance Sound of Detroit*. This effort was surprisingly successful—the compilation generated a Top 10 British hit, "Big Fun," by Inner City, a group led by Kevin Saunderson, who was one of those original Detroit tinkerers. The compilation also helped name the genre: its title came from Atkins, who contributed a track called "Techno Music," and "techno" became the standard term for this Detroit-born style, which tended to be chillier and more mysterious than the house music of Chicago.

The success of house and techno in Britain was unlikely enough, especially considering the general lack of interest in America. But what happened next was even more bizarre. Some white British DJs had returned to London from a holiday in Ibiza, off the Spanish coast, where they had spent long nights and mornings listening to dance music of all kinds, including house music, and where they had grown quite fond of a previously obscure pill called MDMA, known colloquially as ecstasy, which induced a friendly sort of euphoria: it made music sound better and people seem nicer. They organized club nights in London, devoted to a similarly intemperate mixture of dancing and revelry. Where many London nightclubs were stylish and expensive, these parties were intentionally unpretentious, full of people wearing baggy clothes and smiley-face T-shirts, as if they were all on vacation. In this scene, the most influential track was not one of the British hits but an obscurity, and a curiosity: a composition called "Acid Trax," from 1987, by a Chicago group called Phuture. Chicago house was often raw, but "Acid Trax" was unusually bare-bones: there was just a rolling beat and an outrageously squiggly keyboard line, which was created by twisting the knobs on a Roland TB-303, a small synthesizer that was meant to generate electronic basslines. Ron Hardy, the rowdier rival of Frankie Knuckles, was fond of "Acid Trax," and so were the revelers in London, where it became the foundation of a subgenre known as acid house, which was also the name given to the budding party scene. It was a confusing name, since the prevalent drug in this scene was not lysergic acid diethylamide, or LSD, but ecstasy, which was often known as "e." Still, the term stuck. In February 1988, the *Record Mirror*, a British weekly music newspaper, told its readers that "acid house" was "the maddest, baddest dance sound of the moment," noting approvingly that in this music, melodies were "non-existent." (In a recent documentary produced for Channel 4, the British network, DJ Pierre, from Phuture, remembered how surprised he was when he heard about the acid-house scene in Britain. He said, "*White* people like house music?") The article mentioned the "drug-induced atmosphere" on British dance floors, and asked, "I wonder how long it will be before our 'moral guardians' start claiming that promoting the music is helping to promote drug-taking among the young?"

The answer to that question was: six months, more or less. By the summer of 1988, acid house was becoming a national obsession, with thousands of kids converging in clubs and at outdoor parties. British newspapers sounded the alarm, printing articles that practically begged young people to go and see what all the fuss was about. One headline from *The Observer* in August: DRUGS FEAR AS THE "ACID HOUSE" CULT REVIVES A SIXTIES SPECTRE. The reporter described "vacant-eyed young people" in a nightclub, and suggested that "acid house" might be "the biggest youth trend since punk." Two months later, in October, the paper ran an even more shocking headline, ACID EATS THE BRAIN LOOSE, about the dangers of ecstasy; the article called the drug "uniquely poisonous," citing research into brain damage by a Johns Hopkins neurologist. A slew of acid-centric tracks were released that year, and were sometimes pulled off the radio for promoting drug use, including "We Call It Acieeed," by D-Mob, and "It's a Trip," by Children of the Night. (A few years later, a group called the Shamen snuck onto the charts with a silly dance track called "Ebeneezer Goode"; it took the censors a little while to notice that the titular phrase was sometimes shortened to "eezer Goode.") An obscure American subgenre had inspired a national debate in Britain, and police officers were increasingly called to prevent young people from commandeering warehouses or fields for their dance parties. In November, *New Musical Express*, which had covered acid house enthusiastically, published a cover showing a police officer ripping a smiley face in half. ACID CRACKDOWN, the headline read.

For British dancers, the summer of 1988—the summer of love, people called it—was year zero, the birth of a new culture, and the era to which all other eras would forever be compared, usually unfavorably. During the acid-house craze, partiers sometimes described what they were up to as "raving," and in the years that followed, they began to use "rave" as a noun, a name for an outdoor party; these, often illegal, became the most influential sites for British dance music. By 1990, the British "acid" craze had given way to so-called rave culture, which was less Mediterranean in spirit and less American in sound—altogether more homegrown. The rave scene was rebellious: skeptical of the media, which had turned acid house into such a circus, and resentful of the police, who always seemed to be trying to ruin a good party. Organizers often tried to outwit the authorities by refusing to reveal a party's location in advance; prospective partygoers might be given a number to call, or a meeting place to find, for precise directions. For many of the attendees, the late-night scavenger hunt was part of the thrill.

The house and techno pioneers, like their disco predecessors, had been trying to make hits, because they wanted as many people dancing as possible. But British rave culture counted punk rock among its cultural antecedents, and so it harbored a certain degree of antipathy toward normal people and their normal music. Sarah Thornton, a sociologist, assessed British dance music in a shrewd book called *Club Cultures*, which was published in 1995. She observed that many of the people she met at clubs and raves shared a disdain for the uninitiated. Women who loved mainstream pop music were caricatured as "Sharon and Tracy"; ignorant lads who only knew about dance music from reading the tabloids were called "Acid Teds." Thornton noticed that these hierarchies had something to do with gender: in this scene, as in punk and metal scenes, anything deemed mainstream or superficial was apt to be described as feminine. She noticed, too, that these rituals of disparagement helped "contribute to the feeling and sense of shared identity that many people report to be the primary appeal of clubs and raves." Because rave culture considered itself to be an outlaw culture, inherently at odds with whatever was on the radio, it fought more fiercely than disco to keep control of its own identity. The Prodigy was a rather feral group that emerged from the rave scene in 1991 with a single called "Charly," driven by a syncopated beat and a collage of samples, including one from an old educational cartoon. The song was an unexpected hit, rising to No. 3 on the British pop chart, and the next year *Mixmag*, a dance-music magazine, put Liam Howlett, the group's producer, on its cover, holding a gun to his own head. The headline read THE PRODIGY: DID "CHARLY" KILL RAVE? The article inside, by Dom Phillips, argued that "Charly" was a "nightmare," a "novelty" record—the latest iteration, essentially, of "Disco Duck." Phillips wrote that the Prodigy was "the ultimate cheesy teen rave act," and that the rave scene, in general, had grown "too big, too popular, too crap." Howlett seemed mortified. "It's so hard to keep an underground respect when you've got a record in the charts," he said.

The editors of *Mixmag* were not, of course, suggesting that their readers give up on electronic music altogether. For an outsider, the most startling thing about the cover story was probably the admission, somewhere in the middle, that electronic dance music was actually quite healthy. "This has been a good year for hard house music," wrote Phillips, who later became the magazine's editor. He praised "Digeridoo," a new track by Aphex Twin, which he considered "tough but intelligent techno." He noted the increasing popularity of "melodic house." And he considered the increasing commingling of "hardcore" and "ragga." In other words, *Mixmag* was using "rave" to refer to one form of electronic dance music out of many; Phillips's point was that the scene was splintering, and that some shards were sharper than others. He was also illuminating the way dance music was creating its own taxonomy. "Intelligent techno" was a pseudo-genre linked to Aphex Twin's record label, Warp, which was known for putting out "electronic music for the mind"—which is to say, for the bedroom, not the dance floor. By comparison, many rave tracks were considered, like some of the disco hits, purely functional, and therefore rather mindless, no matter how efficiently the tracks fulfilled their function. In *Energy Flash*, an indispensable history of dance music, which was first published in 1998, Simon Reynolds, a critic and a convert, defended what he called the "radical anonymity" of utilitarian dance music. The book was driven by what Reynolds called a "counter-prejudice": a suspicion of pretension and a love of single-minded intensity. Reynolds's favorite rave records "coarsened and intensified" the sounds of house and techno, creating loud, crowd-pleasing tracks that were unashamedly "one-dimensional"; they were rock 'n' roll in spirit, though not in sound.

The splintering of dance music, and the arguments over it, were in some ways a tribute to its inescapable precursor, disco, a style so contradictory and controversial that virtually no one seems able to love it in its entirety. Many listeners who came later tried to defend disco by dividing the genre into real disco and fake disco, but they tended not to be able to agree on the divisions. Nelson George, the R&B critic, loved the soulful sound of Earl Young's band, but he wasn't impressed by the European producers and their synthesizers. Frankie Knuckles loved a wide range of disco sounds and styles, but he was strictly "underground"—not much interested in the hits. Fans of "intelligent techno" might have cherished the electronic experimentation that disco producers pioneered, but rejected its love of camp and silliness. And Simon Reynolds, celebrating the hardcore tracks that helped build the rave scene, couldn't help but regret the pretension of some dance music producers, and their yearning to be considered "real" musicians. It is an abiding truth of dance music that even the greatest tracks tend to be underappreciated, and many of the greatest musicians never shake the sense that they should, and could, be making music that is more substantial. Donna Summer, at the height of her fame and popularity, told *Newsweek* that she would "like to have as much validity" as Barbra Streisand and Aretha Franklin. Seven years later, a roaring divo from the Chicago club scene named Darryl Pandy said that he, too, was hoping to follow in Streisand's footsteps. The bittersweet truth is that, many decades later, Pandy is a cult hero of dance music, known for nothing more and nothing less than a pair of excellent Chicago house tracks.

Party Monsters

Near the end of that 1986 *i-D* article about the Chicago house scene, the reporter, Simon Witter, makes a confession: he bought thirty-five singles on his trip and later determined that many of them were "unlistenably awful." He thought that this kind of disappointment might be inherent to the genre of dance music. "In the grey light of your front room a lot of the point is lost," Witter concludes. This is a common criticism, although not everybody agrees that it really is a criticism. Many of these records were designed to be played over a great sound system, by a great DJ. Should it have mattered if they sounded underwhelming—or even "awful"—when you took them home? In the nineties, when I first got obsessed with electronic music, I used to spend time in dance-music stores, listening to twelve-inch singles on the store turntables. After an hour or so, I would always buy two or three—it seemed only fair. And then I would bring the records home, having no particular idea what to do with them. They were made for DJs, and I was not a DJ. But I don't think I ever had the experience of hearing a record that sounded great in a DJ set but terrible on my stereo. A crafty DJ can help you listen more carefully, helping you notice things you might not have bothered to notice before. And in my experience, that new perception tends to last, partly because the record is now connected to a good night out, and partly because DJ-guided insight, like any insight, tends to stick around. Once I hear something I like in a record, I usually keep hearing it.

But there is another, perhaps more profound way that a night of dancing can alter the way records sound. The British acid house scene was so closely connected to ecstasy that pills sometimes seemed more important than records. One of the most influential club nights was called Shoom, a word that was said to describe the rush of an ecstasy high—or, as *i-D* winkingly described it, "the state of ecstasy dancers aspire to." Jenny Rampling, one of the organizers, told the magazine that clubgoers could "totally relax and freak out as much as they want to without anybody standing and watching them," which was an implicit invitation to indulge. Sarah Thornton, the sociologist, decided that there was only one way to understand this world. "I'm not a personal fan of drugs—I worry about my brain cells," she wrote, recounting an experience in the women's room of an unnamed club. "But they're a fact of this youth culture, so I submit myself to the experiment in the name of thorough research." Reynolds was less reticent. "Ecstasy," he wrote, "has a particular physical sensation that's hard to describe: an oozy yearn, a bliss-ache, a trembley effervescence that makes you feel like you've got champagne for blood." He forthrightly considered the question that attaches to any druggy musical subculture: Do people only like this stuff because they're high? By way of an answer, he noted that he often listened to dance music sober, and loved it. But he added a caveat. "Whether I'd *feel it*, viscerally understand it, if my nervous system hadn't been reprogrammed by MDMA, is another matter." This seems like a judicious conclusion, although I couldn't help but wonder whether Reynolds was underestimating his own imaginative capabilities. Perhaps I have my own bias, owing to inexperience: in all my time dancing to DJs, I have never been fortified by anything stronger than alcohol and caffeine, occasionally in ghastly combination. (The mixture of Red Bull and vodka, if ever I have reason to ingest it again, will surely remind me of sitting on a lawn in Miami, half listening to the sound of a few DJs and a few tens of thousands of ravers.) But the world of clubgoers never felt any more alien to me than the world of country fans, or the world of metalheads. Just as one needn't be on a date to be moved by a romantic ballad, perhaps you needn't be on ecstasy to aspire to it—though Reynolds makes a convincing case that it may well help.

In the disco era, drugs played an important role in the nightlife economy. David Mancuso's enthusiasm for LSD was linked to the communal atmosphere he tried to encourage. There was a practical benefit, too: Mancuso didn't have a license to sell alcohol, so perhaps it was helpful to have guests who weren't particularly interested in buying it. At gay clubs like the Continental Baths, which facilitated sexual encounters, it was generally easy to find amyl nitrate, which was commonly used to enhance sexual pleasure. Many of the DJs were drug connoisseurs and a number were also addicts, including Larry Levan, a longtime heroin user who died of heart failure at the age of thirty-eight. Mostly, though, there was cocaine—which, like disco, was considered very glamorous in the seventies. Studio 54 was known for not just tolerating cocaine use but advertising it through its most famous design element: an enormous crescent moon face on the back wall, with a glowing spoon hanging next to the nose. For Nile Rodgers, cocaine was part of the nightlife culture that he loved, and he says he didn't give it up until 1994, after a psychotic episode.

In his book, Reynolds did more than just explain who was how high: he offered something like a materialist history of dance music, using drugs to explain how the British scene shifted over the decades. It didn't seem to be the case, after all, that ecstasy "eats the brain loose": the research that inspired that alarming *Observer* headline was eventually published and then retracted, when it was found that the subjects had accidentally been given methamphetamine—that is, speed—"instead of the intended drug, MDMA." Ecstasy was evidently unlikely to create either junkies or brain-eaten zombies. One of the biggest risks it posed was dehydration: it made people want to dance, and it made them thirsty; during long nights in crowded raves, that combination occasionally caused problems. Reynolds judged that it also had a desexualizing effect, creating in Britain something rarely observed in human history: a youth culture in which sexual desire played a minimal role. One of the biggest problems with ecstasy seemed to be that its efficacy waned over time, and so Reynolds argued that most rave scenes had "a honeymoon period of two years, tops," after which revelers turned to new drugs, which changed the culture and changed the music. In the midnineties, some revelers in Britain and beyond turned to speed, and to sped-up forms of techno like gabber, in which the beat is so fast and menacing that there's scarcely room for anything else. Others turned to marijuana, and to a murky offshoot known as jungle, which combined fast drums with slow basslines. "As marijuana displaced the E," Reynolds wrote, "dancing lost its mania, became less ravey and out-of-control."

Reynolds's theory works reasonably well in America, too, where localized rave scenes developed and morphed in the years after Britain's summer of love. In the Bay Area, in the early nineties, some British expatriates helped rave culture merge with the remnants of the hippie movement and an early iteration of the tech industry. In 1991, *Mondo 2000*, a magazine devoted to "cyberculture," told its readers that house music was "the best techno-shamanic cultural virus so far." For a few years, before the city cracked down and the pioneers moved on, San Francisco was known for its "psychedelic" raves, and for its neo-hippie beach parties. New York was the home of a wild roving party called Storm Rave, which burned out after a few years and was replaced by NASA, an after-hours party held in a Tribeca club called Shelter. (The dance-music historian Michaelangelo Matos credits—or blames—the NASA party for helping popularize the extra-baggy pants that came to be associated with rave culture in America.) Also, in New York, there was the Limelight, the home of the promoter Michael Alig and his high-profile Club Kids, for whom outrageous behavior and imaginative outfits were more important than either dancing or music. Alig helped make the Limelight the city's most infamous nightclub since Studio 54, and he became something of an underground celebrity, although he was increasingly dependent on heroin, and increasingly unhinged. In 1996, Alig murdered his drug dealer and dumped his remains in the Hudson River. He served seventeen years in prison, during which time he was played by Macaulay Culkin in the film *Party Monster*; he was paroled in 2014 and died, from a heroin overdose, six years later.

Despite these and other eruptions of rave culture in America, electronic dance music never established itself the way it had in Britain and throughout Europe. What Reynolds called the "radical anonymity" of the British scene seemed, from an ocean away, merely perverse, an onslaught of faceless studio tinkerers. How many American listeners could be bothered to learn the difference between the Orb, a group known for playful chill-out music, and William Orbit, a guy known for artsy atmospherics, and Orbital, a duo known for trippy dance tracks? Every few years, there would be another false alarm. In 1992, *Time* promised that the American audience for techno was "steadily growing." The next year, the magazine told readers that a "cyberpunk" culture was emerging, bringing with it a soundtrack of acid house. The biggest name to emerge from the New York scene was Moby, who in 1991 had reached No. 10 on the British chart with a rave-inspired dance track called "Go." (This was a kind of triple crossover: a British hit by an American producer inspired by a British scene built on an American genre.) In 1994, *Rolling Stone* reported that, thanks to Moby, "house and techno are now poised for a domestic breakthrough." And in 2000, *The Face* ran an article that was both triumphant and somewhat sheepish: DANCE MUSIC CONQUERS AMERICA! YES, REALLY THIS TIME.

There is a long tradition of American musicians—particularly African American musicians—who find more acclaim overseas than at home. The pioneers of house and techno sometimes viewed themselves that way, as the modern-day equivalents of legendary blues or jazz musicians, playing gigs for fans across Europe, where they were often regarded as living legends, and then returning home to relative obscurity. The situation was even stranger, because many American listeners had no idea that house and techno even had American roots; the rise of rave culture made dance music seem like a European phenomenon. America kept turning out DJs and producers who were celebrated abroad, but only there. In the nineties, New York club culture nurtured a number of important musical figures, including the Nuyorican duo known as Masters at Work, whose productions and remixes revived the polyglot spirit of disco at its fiercest. In Chicago, latter-day house DJs like Derrick Carter became European headliners, celebrated for evoking the spirit of the place where modern dance music was born. And in Germany especially, "Detroit techno" became a kind of brand name, promising integrity and authenticity. Part of what Detroit techno offered its European fans was racial authenticity: a sense that this electronic music was not a white studio creation, but the soundtrack of a Black city—even if many in the city itself knew almost nothing about it.

Different Worlds

One reason why Americans resisted the charms of house and techno and the rave revolution has to do with rhythm. The thing that gave disco its smoothness, its sense of endless motion, was the evenness of its beat: Earl Young, or an imitation of him, hitting a kick drum, or an imitation of one—*thump, thump, thump, thump*—four times per bar, roughly twice per second, indefinitely. Some early hip-hop tracks used a version of this rhythm: "Rapper's Delight," with its Chic-inspired groove, was the earliest and most prominent example. But by 1982, when Grandmaster Flash and the Furious Five released *The Message*, the beat of hip-hop had grown slower and heavier. That track lopes along at only about one hundred beats per minute, with a strong emphasis—an electronic "clap"—on the second and fourth beats. In the post-disco years, American dance floors were increasingly dominated by these sharp backbeats, which were often accented with electronic claps or snare drums, and which suggested different ways of dancing. In the early eighties, an up-tempo, herky-jerky genre called electro was popular in New York clubs, and it became a favored soundtrack for break dancing, which was athletic and precise. Electro was the style that Herbie Hancock borrowed for "Rockit," his 1983 single, which was a surprise hit. The same year, a singer named Shannon had a hit with "Let the Music Play," which introduced many listeners to a genre known as freestyle: pop lyrics married to electro-inspired beats.

In the aftermath of the disco backlash, hard-edged backbeats were a way for pop and R&B singers to show that they had gotten the message, and that they were moving on from the seventies. On the radio, there was plenty of danceable electronic music, but little of it used the disco beat. Donna Summer's biggest post-disco hit was "She Works Hard for the Money," from 1983, a snappy and up-tempo synth-pop song that sounded very eighties. Starting in the mideighties, the Cuban-born pioneer Gloria Estefan sent a series of spirited hits up the American chart, giving Anglophone listeners a small taste of all the Latin dance music they were mainly ignoring. Most of all, the eighties were the Michael Jackson years, when a hybrid form of pop-inspired R&B was ascendant. By the time the rave scene took flight in Britain, rappers were also beginning their long takeover in America. Hip-hop was propulsive, it was rebellious, and it did an excellent job of alarming newspaper columnists. Why did the country's young people need acid house, when they already had N.W.A?

For many American listeners in the 1980s, there was one gateway drug into the world of dance music: Madonna. She emerged from the world that disco had built: her musical identity was formed in New York nightclubs like Danceteria, which brought together refugees from the punk and disco scenes, and the Fun House, a scrappy late-night club where the patrons were fond of electro and amphetamines. The main resident DJ at the Fun House was Jellybean Benitez, who became Madonna's most important early musical collaborator and, for a time, her lover. He helped produce Madonna's 1983 self-titled debut album, which used the tough electronic beats of the New York scene as the basis for a set of eight playful pop songs. From the beginning, Madonna had a canny sense of the way her voice, and her career, could be enlivened by the sounds and the culture of dance music. Her second album, *Like a Virgin*, was produced by Nile Rodgers, and in 1987, she released a type of record that many of her fans had probably never previously encountered: a remix album, *You Can Dance*, full of devastatingly effective extended versions of her singles. In 1990, as house music was ascendant in Britain, Madonna released "Vogue," a tribute to the drag ball culture that helped define gay nightlife in New York, and also a surprisingly uncompromising example of electronic dance music. It is not easy to measure these things, but you could make a case for "Vogue" as the most influential house track of all time—the one most likely to reach and convert listeners who had never gone near a club or a rave.

The other way that American listeners were likely to encounter dance music was through a series of big hits that arrived on the pop charts, shorn of cultural context, and then often disappeared just as quickly. Often, these were perceived as novelty songs, or exotic imports. And often, they had secret backstories. In 1989, a previously unknown Belgian act called Technotronic materialized with "Pump Up the Jam," an energetic hip-hop-driven house track, which raced up the chart to No. 2. Most American listeners probably thought of it as European club music—most would have had no way of knowing that one of the synthesizer riffs bore a suspicious resemblance to "Move Your Body," the trailblazing Marshall Jefferson track. "The Power" (1990, No. 2), by a German group called Snap!, took its beat from a track by Mantronix, an influential electro act. "Gonna Make You Sweat" (1990, No. 1) was credited to C + C Music Factory, the duo of David Cole and Robert Clivillés, pioneers in New York's house-music scene. And "3 a.m. Eternal" (1991, No. 5), was the work of the KLF, a puckish British group known—in Britain, though not at all in America—for both embracing rave culture and mocking it. These hits and others contributed to a general American sense that dance music was popular, but only in certain contexts: in queer culture, in avant-garde nightclubs, in Europe. During the rave years in Britain, dance music gained a reputation for populism; Simon Reynolds referred to all those young people taking ecstasy and dancing in the fields as a "psychedelic proletariat." In America, dance music was considered less proletarian. It wasn't widely perceived as music for normal people, despite the hits that occasionally broke through.

By the nineties, Americans interested in dance music had a new barrier to overcome: the intimidating profusion of genres and subgenres. House music was relatively easy to identify, because it retained the central element of disco: Earl Young's thump-and-hiss beat. If a track went "Oontz, oontz, oontz, oontz" it was likely to be a house track, especially if it included disco-inspired elements like tuneful basslines and bits of singing. Techno, by contrast, tended to sound conspicuously synthetic, like machine music: maybe, "Doong-tsika, doong-tsika, doong-tiska, doong-tsika." Techno often used repetition to reveal the rhythms hidden within little blocks of sound, on the principle that nearly any cluster of noises repeated over and over will begin to sound like a beat. There was a third approach: many producers in the rave scene built their tracks around so-called breakbeats, often borrowed from old funk records or new hip-hop records. (The "break" is the section in a funk or an R&B record when everybody stops playing except the drummer.) Compared to house and techno, rave music was gleefully impure. Many rave tracks sounded like up-tempo hip-hop records, with the rapping stripped out and some squiggly acid-house basslines dubbed in, alongside sound effects and snippets of dialogue. As rave music grew harder and faster, some producers began using vocals from dancehall reggae, a streetwise genre that seemed to match the menacing energy of the beats. (This was the combination of "hardcore" and "ragga" that *Mixmag* described in 1992.) The hybrid came to be called jungle, and it marked a big shift. Unlike rave, jungle was self-consciously Black music, and it was sometimes described as Britain's belated answer to hip-hop, even though it was never driven by lyrics. What it was driven by, instead, was monstrously deep basslines, moving in slow motion against clattering rhythms. Jungle producers liked to speed up and mutate breakbeats, creating intricate rhythm tracks that sounded like a series of impossible drum solos. Jungle was perhaps the most exciting music in the world for about two years, after which it was renamed drum 'n' bass and gave birth to a whole new constellation of dance genres, each one serving to confuse the casual listener a little more.

To outsiders, this array of dance genres probably seemed needlessly complex, the work of nefarious record-store clerks and spiteful music writers who had nothing better to do with their useless knowledge. Producers and DJs sometimes felt this way, too. Near the beginning of an electrifying two-hour set, broadcast on a London radio station in 1994, a DJ named Fabio told listeners what to expect. "Later on, we've got some house music," he said, and then he caught himself. "We've got all kinds of music—it's not just jungle business runnin' tonight," he said, and then he reconsidered again. "Anyway, we don't even really classify this music as specifically jungle, really. It's just music, really, y'know?" But the categorization of dance music serves a purpose, and it has to do with the unusually social nature of the dance-music scene. In a community built around parties, it is useful to have a way to describe the soundtrack. DJs need to know which records are likely to go well together: if you want people to dance all night, it helps not to have too many jarring transitions between tracks, so that revelers can feel as if they're listening to one long song, albeit one with enough surprises to keep them entertained. Great dance tracks can't be boring, but they also can't be too proud, or too disagreeable, to fit into a DJ set. They have a job to do.

Inevitably in dance music, seemingly minor stylistic differences become linked to major cultural differences—the placement of a kick drum can help determine who comes to your parties. The techno historian Dan Sicko has written about a gig in Rotterdam, in 1992, where a crew of Canadian DJs was startled to see that their brutally aggressive techno tracks inspired the revelers to strike up a disconcerting chant: *"Joden! Joden!"*—"Jews! Jews!" This turned out to be a soccer chant with a complicated history (a way of disparaging the city's rival, Amsterdam, where the soccer team was linked to the local Jewish business community), but it nevertheless made the Canadians consider the possibility that hard, fast techno could be dangerous.

At the other end of the spectrum were styles such as "down tempo," which was essentially a languorous version of hip-hop, with no rapping, and which was often used by businesses looking to create an atmosphere that was polished but hip. In the nineties, some fans and musicians began to use the term "progressive house" to describe house music that kept the genre's rhythmic pattern but eliminated pop songcraft and emphasized texture and mood: long, wispy introductions; grand, oceanic keyboards; wistful melodies. This style was originally promoted as an alternative to sweeter, more garish forms of dance music—progressive house was for people who were serious about dancing. But by the early 2000s, so-called progressive house had morphed into perhaps the world's most popular dance genre, and it had acquired a correspondingly lousy reputation among many serious students of dance music, some of whom preferred styles so stripped down that drumbeats and basslines were reduced to clicks and hums. These may have seemed like fine distinctions, but in practice, the difference between progressive house and minimal techno was the difference between a huge nightclub full of business-casual revelers clutching expensive drinks, and a small bar stocked with music geeks in T-shirts, concentrating intently with their eyes closed. Either could be great fun, but the experiences were radically different. And even in the comfort of your own bedroom, these distinctions tended to persist: with dance music, as with most genres, different sounds help you imagine different worlds.

The Upward Spiral

Electronic dance music did finally triumph in America, but not the way people were expecting. There was no sudden arrival—no equivalent of Britain's summer of love, or of its national ecstasy panic. Instead, progress was slow and, in retrospect, fairly steady. Moby, a former punk rocker who often appeared in the media as a kind of rave spokesman, did not really help house and techno break through in 1994, the way *Rolling Stone* had promised. But that year, America embraced a different album full of electronic music: *The Downward Spiral*, by Nine Inch Nails. The group's only permanent member was Trent Reznor, who grew up in western Pennsylvania and started his music career, in the eighties, in Cleveland, under the influence of a genre known as industrial music, which combined the jagged programmed rhythms of electro with the noise and spleen of punk. Reznor used many of the same machines and sounds as dance-music producers, but he used them to create songs, not tracks. To American listeners, Reznor appeared not as a mysterious studio wizard but as the mesmerizing front man of a furious band that just happened to use lots of electronic instruments.

This became the new conventional wisdom: in America, dance music was rebranded as "electronica," and groups were often marketed not as emissaries from the world of rave, but as pioneers on the frontier of alternative rock. In 1997, the Prodigy—having survived "Charly," and even made up with *Mixmag*—released an album called *The Fat of the Land*, which sent a pair of videos into heavy rotation on MTV. Viewers were mesmerized not by the breakbeats or by Liam Howlett, the group's producer and keyboardist, but by a grimacing guy with a double Mohawk who snarled a few lyrics. This was Keith Flint, whose chief job had once been to excite the crowd during live shows. Now he was being presented, in essence, as the furious front man of a new band called the Prodigy—new, anyway, to America, where few people had any idea what "Charly" was, and where *The Fat of the Land* sold more than two million copies. The Chemical Brothers were two British producers eager not to be pigeonholed as merely making dance music. Their tracks were loud and fuzzy, similar in spirit to the Beastie Boys, and "Setting Sun," one of their best-loved singles, had vocals by Noel Gallagher, from the band Oasis. *Rolling Stone* described them as a duo that appealed to "those who favor bongs, Buds, and Bob Seger T-shirts," and Grammy voters seemed to agree, because in 1998 they won an award in a surprising category: Best Rock Instrumental Performance.

Moby eventually got his American breakthrough, not with techno but with a melancholy 1999 album called *Play*, which used samples of gospel and other old records to build tracks that were perfectly catchy, but perfectly unobtrusive. The album sold millions, and became inescapable—every track was eventually licensed to be used in a movie, a television show, or an advertisement. This was the logical conclusion of a yearslong American trend: the popularity of electronic music in commercials, and on the playlists of stores and hotels, where it was invariably used to evoke a mood of youthful energy and technological sophistication. This phenomenon may have led some American listeners to think of electronic music as inherently corporate, and Reynolds argued that it suggested a kind of mixed-up progress. "In America," he wrote, "electronica skipped the radio hegemony stage and went straight to ubiquity." As a result, by the 2000s, lots of people who had never spent much time listening to electronic music nevertheless felt they knew it—and, often, that they didn't like it. I have a friend, highly knowledgeable about music, who has the same reaction whenever he overhears me listening to house or techno, no matter the subgenre. He cocks his head, smiles slightly, and says, "I feel like I'm shopping for jeans."

But American listeners kept discovering electronic music in the 2000s—perhaps because, having never really been mainstream, the music still seemed mysterious, and maybe even cool. Madonna released a couple of well-turned albums inspired by recent developments in European dance music: *Ray of Light*, in 1998, and *Music*, in 2000. Björk, the adventurous and electronics-obsessed Icelandic singer and producer, helped a generation of listeners discover that they liked electronic music just as much as alternative rock, and possibly more, becoming one of the most acclaimed singers of the modern era—and, for that matter, one of the most acclaimed electronic composers, too. Radiohead, the prog-influenced British alternative band, released a largely electronic album in 2000 called *Kid A*, which was a gateway drug for a generation of rock fans who suddenly found themselves curious about machine music.

Daft Punk, a French duo, had been celebrated since the nineties for sparkling and sometimes waggish house tracks. But in the 2000s, mainstream American listeners finally grew interested. In 2006, Daft Punk played a set at Coachella, the California festival, which had always been hospitable to dance music, and the duo won over the crowd with an updated version of a prop that some of the original disco DJs had used: a light show, which in this case took the form of a huge, neon-lined pyramid, with the two members of Daft Punk perched near the top, wearing robot helmets that gleamed and glowed. That year, the rapper Busta Rhymes released a hit song, "Touch It," based on a Daft Punk sample; the next year, Kanye West released an even bigger hit song, "Stronger," based on a different Daft Punk sample. By the time the members of Daft Punk released their next proper album, *Random Access Memories*, in 2013, they had come to seem like American stars, even though they had never previously had a Top 40 hit. *Random Access Memories* was a pleasingly strange tribute to American music in the disco and post-disco era, and it spawned a worldwide pop hit, "Get Lucky." At the 2014 Grammy Awards, Daft Punk won in four categories including Album of the Year; the group performed with Nile Rodgers, who contributed to the album, and who followed the members to the podium to help with their speeches. (They were wearing their robot helmets, and robots don't talk.) "This is the most insane thing ever," said Rodgers, chuckling—he sounded sincere, although, considering his life and career, it is hard to imagine that he really meant it.

Part of the reason Daft Punk won, no doubt, was that the recording industry wanted to acknowledge the fact that electronic dance music had finally conquered America, and no one knew quite what to do about it. It turned out that the decisive drug was not ecstasy but globalization: as CDs were replaced first by MP3 downloads and then by digital streams, and as MTV was replaced by YouTube, the world's music markets started to merge. In 2007, Rihanna, a pop star known for shifting nimbly between genres, released a stomping dance track called "Don't Stop the Music," based on a steady house-music thump. (Rihanna also quoted the stuttering interlude from "Wanna Be Startin' Somethin'," by Michael Jackson, which was itself a quote from "Soul Makossa," one of the original disco tracks.) Rihanna's song was a hit around the world, including in America, and it helped ease the way for more thumping hits. The Black Eyed Peas, previously a hip-hop group, collaborated with David Guetta, a veteran French DJ and producer, for "I Gotta Feeling," which became one of the biggest hits of 2009. Soon pop stars were scrambling for club tracks. Guetta created follow-up hits with Akon, Flo Rida, Usher, Sia, and Nicki Minaj; Calvin Harris, a Scottish producer, made a hit with Rihanna and another using himself as lead singer; the rapper Pitbull collaborated with the Dutch producer Afrojack. America even got, eventually, a druggy Ibiza record to call its own: "I Took a Pill in Ibiza," a surprise hit by the American pop singer Mike Posner, which was released in 2015, twenty-seven years after the British summer of love.

The mainstream hits were climbing the charts in parallel with the explosive growth, at long last, of the rave scene in America. Only it wasn't being called rave anymore. Some of the young revelers were partial to dubstep, a British genre, distantly related to jungle, that was built around climactic bass drops: the tempo would suddenly shift to half speed, and a shuddering, syncopated bassline would tear through the music. A young producer called Skrillex became the American face of dubstep, inspiring furious mosh pits at his performances. (Some pop stars were paying attention: there was a twitchy dubstep break in "Hold It Against Me," a 2011 Britney Spears single, and another, more subtle, in Taylor Swift's "I Knew You Were Trouble," which was released the next year.) Meanwhile, electronic tracks that hewed closer to the house-music template were commonly referred to as "electronic dance music," or EDM, an initialism that soon came to refer to the entire scene. In America, the world of EDM revolved around a network of outdoor festivals—Electric Daisy Carnival, Ultra Music Festival, Electric Zoo—as well as a handful of big clubs, particularly in Las Vegas, that could afford to book the top acts. The numbers were astonishing: the biggest festivals were drawing hundreds of thousands of attendees, and the most popular DJs could command six figures for a single gig. In 2013, SFX, a music promoter known for EDM events, went public and reached a valuation of more than a billion dollars.

These updated raves didn't have the same countercultural spirit as the British predecessors. The venues tended to be legal and, to the extent possible, well-organized; the crowds were cheerful and energetic. As the title of Posner's hit suggests, there seemed to be a pharmacological component to the upsurge of interest in dance music. American youth culture had gone bliss-achey at last: MDMA was everywhere, often sold in powder instead of pills, and commonly known as Molly, which was said to be short for "molecule" or "molecular." In 2012, at Ultra Miami, Madonna made a brief appearance, asking, suggestively, "How many people in this crowd have seen Molly?"

The response was enthusiastic, but later, on Twitter, Deadmau5, a popular and famously outspoken EDM producer, took offense. "You have a powerful voice," he told Madonna. "EDM could use your positive influence, not 'molly' talk."

Madonna defended herself by saying she had actually been referring to "Molly," a track by the French producer Cedric Gervais, in which a robotic voice says, "Please help me find Molly." (Like many dance tracks, this one makes drug use seem both glamorous and slightly sinister, a mutually reinforcing combination.)

Later that year, Deadmau5 appeared on the cover of *Rolling Stone* and used the occasion to expand his critique. "It's like talking about slavery at a fucking blues concert," he said. "It's inappropriate." His analogy was ill-judged, but the point was familiar: like lots of dance-music stars before him, Deadmau5 knew that his chosen genre was widely perceived as silly or pernicious, and he couldn't help but worry. "Disco had a longer run than EDM has," he told the magazine, two years later. "And that died in a fucking hurry."

Get Lost

Back in the 2000s, when I was working at *The New York Times*, I had a smart and sympathetic editor who used to sigh whenever I told him I wanted to review dance music. He didn't have any moral objection to it, or even a musical aversion, really. He just thought it was kind of boring. And in some ways it was. Some obscure DJ or producer would stand behind an array of turntables or computers for a few hours in the middle of the night, going, "Oontz, oontz, oontz, oontz" (or "Doong-tsika, doong-tsika, doong-tiska, doong-tsika"), and then I would do my best to explain why what was happening was actually very interesting. I wrote about this music because I loved it: I loved the way it sounded through headphones or in my apartment, with long tracks slowly mutating and evolving; and I loved the way a great DJ could use a powerful sound system to push past monotony, helping partygoers to identify so completely with the beat that small changes in timbre and rhythm became moments of high drama. I wrote about it because even then, in those years before the American EDM boom, dance music of various sorts was drawing huge audiences around the globe—a kind of international nightlife circuit had emerged, propelled by music that was often instrumental, and therefore unobstructed by language barriers. And I wrote about it, too, because I liked the challenge of describing a kind of music that sometimes seemed resistant to words.

For obvious reasons, music writers are drawn toward whatever makes for good copy: big personalities, pithy lyrics, grand concepts, petty feuds. (Think, for instance, of Kanye West, who has provided all this and much more.) Sometimes this means that less logogenic genres get ignored, or dismissed, because the pleasures they provide don't easily lend themselves to analysis or argument. In this sense, dance-music producers have something in common with jam bands. The Grateful Dead, the godfather of the jam bands, was known for making people "boogie till dawn," as David Crosby, a contemporaneous rock star, once put it. Like dance music, the

Dead's music was rather hard to put into words: listeners describing a particularly good live set tended to wax abstract about energy and vibes. Like dance music, the Dead's music sounded rather monotonous to people who didn't like it, and who couldn't register the subtle variations andinnovations that so exhilarated fans. Like dance music, the Grateful Dead's music did not translate particularly well to albums; true believers insisted that studio recordings were no substitute for hours-long live sets. And like dance music, the Dead's music was said to be enhanced by chemical intoxication—and, by outsiders, to be intolerable without it. Disciples of disreputable genres typically respond in one of two ways. Some of them internalize the criticism, searching for ways to elevate the putatively lowly music that they love. (Over the years there have been plenty of great dance-music albums: *Richard D. James Album*, a playful and extraordinarily intricate collection by Aphex Twin; *Sessions*, an intoxicating mix of tracks and remixes by the Detroit techno auteur Carl Craig; *Midtown 120 Blues*, an acerbic but wistful critique of house music by DJ Sprinkles.) Others reject the criticism entirely: who needs great albums, or even brilliant producers, when you can get lost on a dance floor, sober or not? During my years of professional concertgoing, I sometimes felt as if I were doing something rather perverse: I was usually alone, concentrating intensely on the music, often taking notes, while people all around me were hanging out, connecting with their partners and friends. For many of them, the concert was merely an excuse for a party. In practice, virtually all popular music is party music.

The EDM explosion of the early 2010s was driven by the realization that nothing beats a great party. Promoters paid for grand light shows, costumed dancers, amusement-park rides. Sometimes the music seemed like an afterthought: online, the more wised-up fans traded guesses about which big-name DJs were secretly playing prerecorded sets, twiddling useless knobs to make themselves look busy. And yet the notion of musical genius proved hard to dislodge, because all the pageantry of big EDM events only served to elevate the genre's biggest names. Headliners like Tiësto and Avicii functioned less like DJs and more like pop stars, playing short sets full of big hits. (This was essentially the opposite of the "radical anonymity" that Reynolds had once prized.) The rise of EDM, like the rise of disco, seemed to polarize the listening public, bringing together a big and enthusiastic coalition of supporters that was nonetheless outnumbered by detractors of all sorts. EDM was disdained for many of the same reasons disco once was: it seemed too formulaic, too contemptuous of older musical values, too transparent in its desire to provide pleasure to drugged-up masses wearing silly clothes. But now, some of the sternest critics were other dance-music producers—they, too, came from the world that disco had helped create. Dave Clarke is a British DJ and producer who has been releasing no-nonsense techno records since 1990, not long after the genre's birth. One of his regular gigs was to provide musical counterprogramming at Tomorrowland, in Belgium, one of the biggest EDM festivals in the world. In a 2015 interview with *Mixmag*, Clarke made a familiar-sounding distinction. "EDM is pantomime," he said. "But techno? That's the real dark art." At one point, he connected the popularity of EDM to the ubiquity of cell phones and selfies. "EDM disrupts the attention," he said, sounding rather like a musical psychologist. "It's not hypnotic."

By the time Clarke gave that interview, signs of an EDM recession were emerging. There was no equivalent of the 1979 disco sucks riot. But even before the 2020 pandemic, which suddenly emptied just about every dance floor in the world, excitement about festivals had begun to wane, and exuberant club tracks had stopped appearing so regularly on the pop charts. In 2016, SFX announced that it was filing for bankruptcy. The same month SFX made its announcement, one of the most popular EDM acts in the world was a Norwegian producer named Kygo, who was known for a leisurely, song-oriented style that many people called "tropical house." Connoisseurs hated it, of course. A house and techno DJ known as the Blessed Madonna gave a deliciously dismissive quote to *The New York Times*: "House music is a lot of things, but a relaxation tape with an EDM beat over it? That's not house. That's the soundtrack for a yoga retreat." But Kygo's fans didn't seem to care much about the noble lineage of house and techno—in fact, Kygo's music wasn't designed for dancing as much as swaying, or maybe just hanging out. (He owed his popularity in part to his ubiquity on playlists designed for people who wanted to "chill.") It is easy enough to scoff at the real-versus-fake dichotomies that are so often used, in the world of dance music, to try and control who makes it into the party. Connoisseurs who criticize pop music for its insufficient seriousness generally sound silly in the long run, and often much sooner than that. But Clarke got something right about EDM: it wasn't hypnotic, and in that sense it did function more like traditional pop music.

The thing that has always kept dance music separate from the mainstream is not its sound, which tends to be seductive and agreeable, but its philosophy. By insisting that tracks are more important than songs, disco and its descendants continually weed out the dilettantes who only want to sing along, leaving behind the people inclined to dance for hours, getting lost in the music. This is an ongoing process, because it turns out that most of us love songs and singers and lyrics—we listen to music, especially popular music, in order to feel connected to the people who make it. But that is precisely why dance-music scenes tend to venerate mysterious producers and rather faceless (and sometimes interchangeable) rhythm tracks, while scorning hit singles: because hit singles are distracting. Hit singles tug our attention away from the endless groove and toward a series of three-minute compositions. The point of dance music, historically, has been to tug the other way; to get people to think less about who made the music and more about who's dancing to it. There is nothing radical about a kick drum going *thump, thump, thump, thump*. But there is something radical—something strange and disorienting, even if you are sober, or relatively so—about dancing all night and imagining that you might keep dancing forever.

7.

POP

Pop Revolution

I N 1984, America discovered that its radio stations had been conquered by an invasive species. The interlopers were everywhere, but the most prominent was Boy George, the glamorous lead singer of a group called Culture Club. He wore colorful dreadlocks and generous helpings of makeup, and all of a sudden he was ubiquitous. *People* put him on the cover, accompanied by a headline that both mocked him and celebrated him: IT'S A GUY, IT'S A GIRL—IT'S BOY GEORGE! In the story, the magazine informed its readers that Boy George was, in fact, a man, leading "the latest invasion of British rockers," and the singer responsible for the most successful debut since the Beatles. The same year, *Newsweek* described Boy George as a "new-wave Liberace," and argued that he was a product of Britain's "wide-open musical marketplace." This, too, was a cover story, announced by an image of Boy George alongside another new British import: Annie Lennox, lead singer of the duo Eurythmics, who was perfecting her own version of androgynous glamour. The headline read BRITAIN ROCKS AMERICA—AGAIN: FROM THE BEATLES TO BOY GEORGE AND BEYOND.

In Britain, by contrast, the rise of Boy George and his counterparts was not a rock 'n' roll invasion but a homegrown pop phenomenon. And indeed, the fact that this music was self-consciously "pop," as opposed to rock 'n' roll, was part of what made it seem so phenomenal. In 1985, an English music journalist named Dave Rimmer published a book called *Like Punk Never Happened: Culture Club and the New Pop*, which was written in a spirit of mischievous provocation. Rimmer must have known that some unsuspecting teenage Boy George fans would buy it, hoping for gossipy insight only to find that, though some gossip was included, the book was mainly a sharp treatise on musical aesthetics. Rimmer evidently loved Boy George's songs, but he also wanted to explain why the triumph of Culture Club represented "a complete dissolution of the traditional British relationship between music, style, and subculture." Rimmer viewed this as a good thing, or at any rate an interesting thing—proof that Boy George was no mere novelty, but rather the exponent of something that was genuinely new. He wanted to unsettle the kind of "serious" music fans who might have doubted that Boy George was worth taking seriously in the first place—the ones who rolled their eyes, no doubt, when American magazines compared Culture Club to the Beatles. Even Rimmer's title was a provocation, suggesting a changing of the guard: the punk insurgency, less than a decade old, was dead and buried. It had been replaced by something called "pop": the word was once a catchall term for popular music, but now, in the eighties, it was a genre unto itself.

Rimmer's central argument was that, primarily in Britain, a complicated sort of musical revolution had taken place, and as a result, "Pop music was suddenly hip." Depending on your taste and perspective, this pronouncement might seem too obvious to be interesting, or else too far-fetched to be believable. In one sense, contemporary pop music is hip by definition: pop is what's in style; that's what makes it pop. In another sense, though, popularity and hipness are forever in tension, because you can't possibly keep ahead of the teeming masses by listening to the same music as them. The hitmakers who emerged from early-eighties Britain—Culture Club, Eurythmics, and also Duran Duran, the Human League, Depeche

Mode, ABC, and dozens more—specialized, fittingly, in music that was both obvious and far-fetched. Many of them took visual inspiration from David Bowie, whose outrageous seventies stage costumes helped show a generation of rock 'n' roll fans how much fun dressing up could be. But these new mannequins didn't want to be cutting-edge rock stars, adored by misfits in every town. They wanted to be mainstream pop stars, adored by everyone.

The British pop uprising was a double revolution, an insurgency that defined itself against the insurgency that came before. Most of these new pop stars had been in and around the punk scene that seized the country in the late seventies. "By the end of 1976," Boy George recalled in his first memoir, "anyone who was anyone was punk." But punk, in his view, quickly became a "joke"; in its zeal to "reject conformity," it enforced a conformity of its own, which he found unspeakably drab, all loud guitars and leather jackets. Boy George had grown up loving Shirley Bassey, the grand English diva known for her James Bond themes, and he had no interest in marginality for its own sake. So he rebelled against punk by rediscovering his love for diva-like excess, embracing an approach that was more colorful and more fun—more "pop," in a sense. "Punk was safe," he wrote. "We were spinning forward in a whirl of eyeliner and ruffles."

This is what was really new about Boy George and his "new pop" contemporaries: their self-consciousness. Pop stars from earlier decades tended to be "pop" in a broad and sometimes vague sense. The term suggested accessibility and fun, populism as well as popularity. The Boston Pops, an orchestra formed in the late nineteenth century, was named for its devotion to what was typically called "light" music. In the twentieth century, "pop music" became a convenient way to separate the music that was played on the radio from the music that was played in the symphony halls. (Which is why recordings by the Boston Pops are now tagged as "classical"—not "pop.") The opposite of pop was serious music, or art music; jazz was once pop, until it grew sufficiently unpopular to be considered serious instead. In the sixties, "pop" was often used inclusively, to gesture at whatever was popular with the young people. "Pop" suggested youth and exuberance, and the term invited a comparison to pop art, the playful visual-arts movement.

In the seventies, though, the pop consensus began to fray. Increasingly, the word "pop" became negative, in two different senses. Often, "pop" was used to describe the *absence* of a particular musical marker: saying that a country or R&B singer had "gone pop" was a way of saying that the singer had stopped being recognizably country or recognizably R&B. To go pop was to give up your old identity and, often, some of your old fans, in hopes of replacing them with a greater number of new fans. In this way, a suggestion of betrayal was built into the idea of going pop: often, the identity was also negative in the sense of being disfavored or disreputable. Being "pop" generally wasn't something to brag about. The word was used to describe performers who were outside any particular musical community, and who were therefore viewed with suspicion by many people who considered themselves serious listeners.

Boy George and his glamorous contemporaries were among the first performers to treat "pop" as an identity to claim, a flag to wave. They would defy the anti-orthodox orthodoxy of punk rock by embracing the trappings of show business: fancy clothes, catchy choruses, unapologetic ambition. "The New Pop isn't rebellious," Rimmer wrote. "It embraces the star system. It conflates art, business, and entertainment. It cares more about sales and royalties and the strength of the dollar than anything else and to make matters worse, it isn't the least bit guilty about it." Which is to say, the "new pop" really *was* rebellious—it rebelled against the idea that hip music should be rebellious. This species of pop was negative in a third sense: it aimed to negate worn-out ideas of musical authenticity.

Some of these groups flaunted their commercial aspirations, with varying amounts of irony. ABC, for instance, was a tongue-in-cheek group led by Martin Fry, a lead singer who adopted the persona of a slick corporate executive. The first ABC single, "Tears Are Not Enough," arrived in 1981, with the group's business plan printed on the back cover, written in a pseudo-pompous third-person voice:

> Fry's own obsessions with Pop had taken him out of his bedsit but nowhere important. With ambitions to carve out a very considerable niche in the International pop world, a portfolio of arrangements and an attaché case full of surprises, he had a world view and a name, ABC. . . . What he needed, more than anything else, was a group to back it up. . . . Six months later the ABC sound had developed into a catalogue of songs that were to excite the hearts of many a record company mogul.

This was preposterously overblown, of course. "We weren't pop stars," Fry recalled, in an interview a few years later. "At the time we were five people who were on the dole in Sheffield." But the ambition was real: Fry once said that his group was opposed to "the whole hippie fear of popularity." And his group's music did go pop. "Tears Are Not Enough" rose to No. 19 on the British pop chart; "The Look of Love," released the next year, went to No. 4 in Britain, and No. 18 in America, where the "new pop" was often known, instead, as "new wave." In the video, Fry and the other band members were dressed as old-fashioned music-hall entertainers, in matching striped suits and straw hats. Heaven 17, another pop group of the time, adopted a similarly corporate image; in *Smash Hits*, one of the magazines that chronicled Britain's new-pop insurgency, one of the members described Heaven 17 as "a 100% serious attempt to be incredibly popular."

Perhaps it was inevitable that this revolution would be short-lived. After all, one of the defining attributes of pop music is its seeming disposability. Heaven 17 and ABC, for instance, each managed a handful of British hits, but they remained essentially cult acts, not the world-conquering hitmakers they wanted to be. And while Boy George was briefly triumphant, his reign lasted only a few years; in America, especially, he is generally remembered less as the leader of a musical revolution than as an eighties curiosity. By the time Rimmer published his book, Culture Club's hitmaking run was essentially over. And so the provocative title—*Like Punk Never Happened*—turned out to be misleading. It was punk that endured; even people who don't care for the music, as most people do not, are often fascinated by the righteous indignation of punk, its defiant incantations, its celebration of the underground and the radical. For many listeners today, it's more like new pop never happened.

But in another sense, Rimmer was absolutely right. By claiming the term "pop" for themselves, Boy George and his contemporaries were amplifying a running argument that has helped shape the past half century of popular music. Their eighties iteration of pop was defined not just against punk rock, but more broadly against rock 'n' roll, which many of the groups viewed as hopelessly unhip. In 1981, another English music critic, Paul Morley, detected a musical shift "away from rock, grey independence, submission, austerity"; some of the most important new groups, he wrote, were more interested in "pop, disco, colour, lights, action." In a way, this was a very punk attitude. Johnny Rotten, the snarling lead singer of the Sex Pistols, reclaimed his birth name, John Lydon, after the band broke up, and started an ambitious new group, Public Image Ltd, which helped launch the war on rock 'n' roll. "The Pistols finished rock 'n' roll," Lydon declared, in a 1980 interview with *Record Mirror*. "Rock and roll is shit and it has to be cancelled. It's vile, it's gone on for 25 years, it's dismal. A grandad dance, and I'm not interested in it." Many otherwise cheerful young English pop stars took similarly truculent stances, sneering at the supposed unhipness of rock music. Adam Ant, the leader of Adam and the Ants, was one of the most image-conscious of these performers; he styled himself as a kind of renegade anti-rock warrior. "I felt rock 'n' roll had lost all its color, all its flair," he said in 1981. Gary Kemp, from Spandau Ballet: "I've never been a lover of rock." Adrian Wright, from the Human League: "I hate rock." At the first Culture Club show in New York, in 1982, Boy George was disappointed to see that the audience was full of what he called "rock-and-roll types"—in other words, squares.

These were powerful insults, and they endured even when the music didn't. By challenging the primacy of rock 'n' roll, this movement suggested a different way to think about genres. Ever since the sixties, rock 'n' roll had been the most prestigious form of popular music, beloved both by "rock critics" (the term itself suggested this bias) and by everyday fans, many of whom were inclined to accept the idea that mainstream pop music, no matter how much they loved it, was relatively inconsequential. The new pop revolution encouraged listeners of all sorts to question this hierarchy: to consider the possibility that rock 'n' roll was boring, and that so-called pop music was the future. This sometimes meant celebrating Boy George, which is what Dave Rimmer did, probably to excess. But it also meant rethinking old assumptions about musical taste. You could elevate pop music by insisting that seemingly silly songs deserved to be taken seriously. Or you could elevate pop music by arguing, instead, that the desire to take popular music "seriously" was part of the problem. (If a hit record were merely and gloriously silly, couldn't that be enough?) The new pop revolution helped transform "pop music" from a catchall into a proper genre—and, eventually, into a way of looking at the world.

The Monster with Seven Letters

The ideology of pop music had no name, at least not at first. But anyone paying close attention to the British music press in the early eighties might have noticed a strange word appearing every now and again—a code word, almost. It was popularized by a musician named Pete Wylie, the strategically provocative leader of a rather obscure band called Wah!, or the Mighty Wah!, or Wah! Heat. (This was one of Wylie's provocations: an ever-evolving band name.) Wylie's band was the cover story in the January 17, 1981, issue of *New Musical Express*, an acerbic weekly. And the headline promised readers that Wylie was leading a RACE AGAINST ROCKISM.

This was not wholly true, but it was not wholly untrue, either. The slogan inverted the name of Rock Against Racism, the lefty punk movement. Wah! was, by most definitions, a rock band, but Wylie was eager to keep up with changing tastes, and he positioned himself as a leader in the war against a pernicious ideology that he called "rockism." The "ism," not to mention the *NME* headline, suggested that this ideology was somehow related to racism, although the cover story itself offered no precise definitions. To be rockist, it seemed, was to do things the way rock bands traditionally did them—at one point, Wylie suggested that even the idea of making albums was unduly "rockist." Given the fact that he had not, in fact, forsaken rock music, Wylie also attempted to hedge his bets, voicing the hope that rock 'n' roll might still have "the potential to be an exciting, inspirational thing." Later in 1981, in a different publication, *Melody Maker*, Wylie laughingly referred to rockism as "the monster with seven letters," saying that the term was a joke that had accidentally become a philosophy, thanks to a credulous music press. "Everyone went, 'Phew! Great new word,'" he said. "The BANE of my life—in capital letters."

It is true that rockism quickly slipped from Wylie's control. In March 1981, two months after the *NME* cover story about Wah!, the rock critic Beverley Glick quoted Marc Almond, from the pop group Soft Cell, issuing the standard disclaimer. "We're more like a cabaret than a rock band really, nothing to do with rock," he said. Glick compressed this attitude into a six-word slogan: "Death to rockists, Long live funnists!" As it happened, "funnists" never caught on, but "rockists" were getting easier to spot, as the word began to generate backlash. Later that spring, Jake Burns, from the anthemic punk band Stiff Little Fingers, took exception to the idea that rockism was anything to be ashamed of. "What does that word mean anyway?" he asked. "Just because Spandau Ballet and the like dress up in weird costumes and play synthesizers and use disco rhythms doesn't mean that Elvis Presley is irrelevant." Actually, Burns had inadvertently offered a pretty good illustration of rockism, by drawing a distinction between silly pop acts, with their electronic instruments and theatrical self-presentation, and serious rock stars, standing above and beyond the latest trends.

Musicians often disdain debates over musical terminology, which makes sense: they hate to be categorized, and besides, categorizing music is not their job. But while the word "rockism" soon faded from interviews, it continued to influence music critics, who found it a helpful term to describe a whole bundle of unexamined assumptions. The term spread to academic journals, and in one of them, the musicologist Richard Middleton offered an academic definition: rockism, he wrote, was "the tendency to install rock norms as a new discursive centre." And occasionally, it found its way into American media—arriving, much like Boy George, as a startling British import. In 1990, in *The Village Voice*, Robert Christgau weighed in on what he called "the 'rockism' debate that raged through the U.K. music press in the early '80s." He argued that this debate reflected "the growing nationalism/anti-Americanism of U.K. taste." He thought it was no coincidence that the anti-rockists often praised stylish British pop acts, or that the rock they sought to dethrone was often American. In Christgau's estimation, the struggle against rockism was also a backlash against America:

> Irony, distance, and the pose have been the secret of British rock since the Beatles and the Stones, partly because that's the European way and partly because rock wasn't originally British music—having absorbed its usages secondhand, Brits who made too much of their authenticity generally looked like fools. . . . Make no mistake: even today, American rock really is more sincere. Or to add a little precision, American rockers *act* more sincere—they're so uncomfortable with the performer's role that they strive to minimize it.

The accusation of parochialism had some truth, especially at *NME* and other British publications, where writers were expected to inflate whatever was happening in the local music scene to world-historical proportions. But that did not make the rockism debate irrelevant in America, especially as the primacy of what Christgau called "American rock" increasingly came under threat.

By the turn of the century, boy bands were triumphant, rappers were ascendant, and country and R&B were persistent. And yet, often, the language of pop criticism was the language of *rock* criticism, and rock 'n' roll still occupied a place at the top of the hierarchy. Non-rock acts were sometimes honored at the Rock & Roll Hall of Fame, and they regularly appeared on the cover of *Rolling Stone*, which was for decades the leading American music magazine. But in mainstream magazines and newspapers, rock music received a disproportionate share of critical attention, relative to its waning popularity. And often, rock 'n' roll was portrayed as being inherently more credible than other forms of music, especially pop. In 2001, when the boy band *NSYNC wanted to be taken more seriously, the members posed for the cover of *Rolling Stone* in denim and leather, accompanied by a headline proclaiming them THE BIGGEST BAND IN THE WORLD. ("Band," unmodified, invariably means "rock band," not "boy band"; the headline invited readers to compare *NSYNC to revered rock acts like Red Hot Chili Peppers, Metallica, and Green Day.) Inside, the article explained that Justin Timberlake, the group's main heartthrob, was having a salutary effect on the pop star Britney Spears, whom he was dating. The magazine noted with approval that Timberlake was "helping her move from bubblegum to more rockish stuff." A few months later, Spears released an album that included a cover of "I Love Rock 'n' Roll," the extremely "rockish" song made popular by Joan Jett, two decades earlier. But why was a Joan Jett retread supposed to be better than the state-of-the-art "bubblegum" that had made Spears—and, for that matter, *NSYNC—famous in the first place?

By the time Spears released her version of "I Love Rock 'n' Roll" as a single, in 2002—not a hit, it turned out—I was working as a pop music critic for *The New York Times*, and I was starting to feel as if the ongoing debate over rockism was a shared secret: something obsessed over by a few music critics and unknown to just about everybody else. And so, in 2004, I published an essay about rockism in the *Times*. It was called "The Rap Against Rockism," and it began with a discussion of a recent pop fiasco: the case of Ashlee Simpson, who had recently been caught lip-synching during a performance on *Saturday Night Live*. What I wrote was intended as a mild defense of Simpson, and a strong defense of pop singers, lip-synchers, and other performers who failed rock 'n' roll purity tests. I wanted to challenge the idea that music videos were necessarily more superficial than live concerts, or that the spirit of disco was somehow faker than the spirit of punk.

It was easier, of course, to denounce the clichés of rockist music criticism than to explain what, exactly, was supposed to replace them. In the essay, I named a number of acts that tended to be ignored or disdained by critics in love with the rock 'n' roll ideal. I wrote about the way mainstream hip-hop, with its flash and commercial ambition, offended some rock-oriented critics, who yearned for something scruffier and more earnest. I extolled the R&B singer Tweet, who sadly never again matched the success of her spooky and sinuous debut single, "Oops (Oh My)." I mentioned Alan Jackson, the chart-topping country singer, who seemed to escape critical notice precisely because his songs were so listenable and easygoing, rather than defiant. And I noted a paradox unchanged since the age of Boy George: that a truly anti-rockist rebellion would not seem rebellious. "You literally can't fight rockism," I wrote, "because the language of righteous struggle is the language of rockism itself." If you praise the pop star Christina Aguilera for her tough spirit and righteously feminist lyrics, then you are still praising the old rockist virtues (toughness righteousness), even while ascribing them to somebody new. In that sense, rockism had something in common with the punk enthusiasm that overwhelmed me as a teenager: it was a worldview that could be acknowledged but never really defeated.

I was pleased and mildly surprised when some dissenting letters arrived at the *Times*. Jim DeRogatis, from the *Chicago Sun-Times*, was one of the critics I had criticized; he wrote in to deny, vehemently but cheerfully, that he was "a member of this dreaded club of rockists." (On the contrary, he wrote, "I have railed against nostalgia and baby boomer myopia.") One reader argued that no attentive listener should ignore the difference between an "entertainer," like Ashlee Simpson, and a true "artist," especially one who wrote and produced her music herself—as Simpson, he noted, generally did not. Another described my essay as "devious" and "insidious," insisting that one need not be a "straight white male chauvinist" in order to love "integrity, passion, and loud guitars." The essay, and the fact that it had appeared in the *Times*, seemed to help rekindle the decades-old argument over rockism, which raged anew for months and then for years.

Some of the partisans in this argument even found a catchy name for the positive tendency that they supported in opposition to rockism. They called it poptimism, a portmanteau that gestured back to the "new pop" scene where the "race against rockism" began. Poptimism suggested a fondness for pop music, but the term also suggested a rather more complicated attitude toward the practice of music criticism. If "poptimism" was a close cousin of "optimism," then surely its adherents would want to celebrate pop music. Maybe, in this inverted hierarchy, *any* criticism of pop music could be a sign of latent rockism. In time, the rockism/poptimism debate evolved into a broader argument about excellence and popularity, about the judgment of the critic versus the judgment of the crowd. In 2006, in *Slate*, the critic Jody Rosen declared that the rockism war was over, and the anti-rockists had won. "Most pop critics today would just as soon be accused of pedophilia as rockism," he wrote.

The Triumph of Poptimism

The triumph—or the partial triumph—of poptimism seems inevitable in retrospect. By the end of the 2000s, new technologies were enabling a new enthusiasm for mainstream pop. YouTube, for instance, aided the poptimist cause immeasurably, in two different ways. Its frictionless international distribution system made the biggest songs even bigger. And its democratic design, with every video free and equally accessible, undermined the sense of exclusivity that drives anti-commercial music communities. (On YouTube, there was no underground, only viral success or failure to achieve it, as measured by each video's view count.) If an obsession with albums was, as Pete Wylie once claimed, rather rockist, then perhaps the growing importance of other formats—informal mixtapes, shareable videos, online playlists—helped further advance the poptimist cause. By the early 2010s, the R&B genius known as Beyoncé seemed to be the most admired musician in the country, having won overwhelming popular and critical acclaim while showing not much interest in rock 'n' roll. Quite the opposite: rock bands regularly genuflected to *her*.

The success of poptimism meant that it began to attract the kind of critical condemnation that was previously aimed at rockism. In 2014, ten years after I wrote about rockism, the *Times* published an essay by Saul Austerlitz called "The Pernicious Rise of Poptimism," which argued that the fight against rockism had gone too far. He suggested that music critics had grown afraid to criticize pop hitmakers like Katy Perry, lest they be accused of rockist bigotry. (In fact, the critical response to Perry's 2013 album, *Prism*, had been lukewarm; *Rolling Stone* gave it three stars out of five, praising her "sunny effervescence" while chuckling at the idea that because of her success, she now felt obliged to portray herself as a "multifaceted artist.") Austerlitz defended "music that might require some effort to appreciate," asking, "Should gainfully employed adults whose job is to listen to music thoughtfully really agree so regularly with the taste of

13-year-olds?" In the post-rockist world, music critics were increasingly anxious not to appear snobbish, and to Austerlitz this seemed like dereliction of duty. This is a fair point, although his question—about how often professional critics should agree with teenage fans—seems rather abstract. Surely the answer must depend on what music, precisely, those thirteen-year-olds happen to be listening to.

Perhaps Austerlitz's real complaint had less to do with the rise of pop than with the decline of critics. By 2014, there seemed to be very few "gainfully employed adults" working as full-time music critics: magazines were folding, and many of the remaining ones relied upon freelancers; online, the most prominent (and viral) appraisals of new music often came from fans, not professional writers. In an increasingly fan-centric culture, a new idea about criticism quietly took hold. The idea was that consumers were experts, and that they were therefore correct by definition; critics were not expected to be too judgmental. In his essay, Austerlitz had suggested that it would be ridiculous for movie critics to ignore indie films in order to "analyze the majesty that is *Thor: The Dark World*." Five years later, though, the director Martin Scorsese was widely criticized for saying that superhero movies were closer to "theme parks" than to "cinema." (People seemed shocked, somehow, to learn that Scorsese had strong prescriptive opinions about film.) Austerlitz asked, too, "What if New York food critics insisted on banging on about the virtues of Wendy's Spicy Chipotle Jr. Cheeseburger?" His prophecy more or less came to pass in 2019, when a fried chicken sandwich from Popeyes preoccupied—and, in general, impressed—food writers nationwide. At its best, poptimism broadened the horizons of both critics and fans, reminding us that nothing is necessarily too silly, too crass, or too cheap to award careful attention.

There was another current in the anti-rockism movement, though, one that made it more than merely an expression of anything-goes populism. In my 2004 essay, I mentioned that rockist criticism often lionized "straight white men," and I suggested that critics ought to pay more attention to genres, like disco and R&B, that were more closely associated with Black people, women, and gay people. A spirit of activism had been present, although muted, in the rockism arguments of the eighties. The British new-pop scene was in part a rebellion against a certain kind of rock 'n' roll masculinity. Many of the stars were queer, and all of them were glamorous; there was general agreement that the old ideal of the rock star as sweaty workingman was definitely boring, and possibly oppressive. One of the most idealistic figures in this scene was Green Gartside, leader of Scritti Politti, who loved pop music in practice and, even more, in theory. "No visual or literary culture can match the innate political strength of the pop single," he told *Smash Hits* in 1982. "It's a revolutionary text."

In at least one sense, Gartside's observation was undeniable: the text on a record does indeed revolve when you play it. But in America, in particular, the rise of poptimism coincided with a renewed attention to the political power of identity. Austerlitz and others worried that the poptimist movement was turning critics into mere "cheerleaders for pop stars," and there was plenty of that. At the same time, though, the music criticism of the 2010s was often stern, rather than cheerful. Pop stars were subjected to the kind of skeptical scrutiny once reserved for politicians: their backgrounds and interviews were checked for transgressions, and they were encouraged to issue declarations on whatever controversies or crises were galvanizing opinion online. Musicians who transgressed were often downgraded or dismissed—not "canceled," necessarily, but expelled from the realm of the reputable. Similarly, admirable musicians were often upgraded. In a semi-positive review (6.5 out of 10) of a relentlessly inspirational album by the pop-R&B singer Lizzo, in 2019, a Pitchfork reviewer considered both the music and the message. "The sound might disappoint, but there will be people moved to transformations of their own thanks to her songs," the review concluded. "And that's important, too."

In some ways, the American poptimism of the 2010s seemed rather incompatible with the British movement that indirectly inspired it. For starters, the "new pop" stars were brazen appropriators. Adam and the Ants had a No. 3 British hit in 1981 with "Ant Rap," a strange and raucous hom-age to the burgeoning hip-hop scene in New York; in 1983, George Mi-chael's pop duo, Wham!, sent a cheerful genre exercise called "Wham Rap! (Enjoy What You Do?)" to No. 8 on the British chart. But the poptimist revolution offered no help, a few decades later, to white pop stars like Miley Cyrus and Iggy Azalea, who were frequently denounced for dabbling in hip-hop without showing proper deference. (Q-Tip, the revered rapper, told Azalea, on Twitter, "You have to take into account the HISTORY as you move underneath the banner of hiphop." Speaking in the voice of hip-hop authority, he informed her that hip-hop was "a SOCIO-Political move-ment.") The new poptimists may have hated rockism, but they didn't seem to have a problem with hip-hopism, or R&Bism. For a younger and more idealistic generation of listeners, the whole point of dethroning rock 'n' roll was to replace the old gods with a more diverse pantheon—and then worship accordingly.

This marked a change from the godless approach of the early-eighties anti-rockists. At times, Dave Rimmer had seemed eager to debunk not merely one conception of good music, but the whole idea of musical good-ness, as determined by critics. He scoffed at "the idea that some music is good for you" and "some music isn't," because he thought that young pop fans were smart enough to figure out for themselves what they liked, and because he didn't think there was any authority higher than that. For him, the whole point of new pop was that it encouraged listeners to stop worry-ing about "credibility," in order to focus intently on pleasure. But the ques-tion of credibility has a sneaky way of springing back into our musical conversations, as listeners create new defenses for the music they love, thereby rendering some *other* types of music defenseless, or perhaps inde-fensible. Often, the term we have used for that indefensible music is "pop," a non-genre that became a genre without ever quite shaking its dubious reputation.

The Most Popular Records in the Country?

Rock snobbery must be just about as old as rock 'n' roll itself. But the founding document of modern rock snobbery was published in *Rolling Stone*, in 1967. Its author was Tom Donahue, a producer and radio disc jockey, who wrote a pungent essay with an appropriately pungent title: "A Rotting Corpse, Stinking Up the Airwaves." Donahue's target was not a particular song, or band, or radio station, but a type of radio programming: the format known as Top 40. The format was invented in the fifties, by a couple of radio executives who realized that what listeners really wanted was an opportunity to hear the same hits over and over again. (There was a story, not necessarily accurate, that the executives had a moment of insight while sitting in a bar in Nebraska, watching the waitress repeatedly punch the same numbers into a jukebox.) The idea behind Top 40 radio was to identify the most popular songs in the country, regardless of genre, and then play them to death. In this sense, Top 40 radio resembled H. L. Mencken's famous definition of democracy: it was based on the assumption that "the common people know what they want, and deserve to get it good and hard."

But in Donahue's view, this radio format, devoted to following popular taste, had somehow lost its way. He issued a multipart indictment. He argued that the stations' lists of popular records were biased because they were based on incomplete surveys. (Most Top 40 stations, he wrote, "ignore the R&B stores.") He argued that Top 40 stations were struggling to adapt to the post-Beatles era, in which many listeners were consuming hit albums instead of hit singles. But mainly, he argued that Top 40 stations were boring. "They will seldom take a chance on a new record, even when performed by a local group," he wrote. He noted that the ratings of Top 40 stations were declining, and suggested that free-form stations like KMPX, in San Francisco, which mixed rock 'n' roll with jazz and folk music, were the future.

In its early years, rock 'n' roll *had been* pop music, part of the cheerful, youth-oriented mishmash coming out of jukeboxes and radio stations. But as the sixties progressed, an increasing number of people began to think of rock 'n' roll the way Donahue did: not as an integral part of the pop music landscape, but as an alternative to it. Standard histories of American music portray 1967 as a rock 'n' roll paradise, possibly the greatest single year in rock history. (That year, some of the genre's most venerable names released some of their most beloved albums: the Beach Boys, the Beatles, Big Brother & the Holding Company, the Byrds, the Doors, Jimi Hendrix, Jefferson Airplane, Pink Floyd, the Rolling Stones, the Velvet Underground, the Who, and many more.) And yet according to the *Billboard* Hot 100 chart, the year's biggest single was "To Sir with Love," a schoolgirl's ode to her favorite teacher, by the British singer and actress Lulu, who also starred in the movie of the same name. By contrast, the top-placing Beatles song on the list was "All You Need Is Love," at No. 30. Donahue was not wrong to say that Top 40 radio stations were ill-equipped to contend with the emergence of the sophisticated rock 'n' roll concept albums. But it seems likely, too, that even in 1967, Top 40 radio stations were for the most part doing what they were supposed to do: playing records that lots of people loved, even if those records weren't cool. And if we think of 1967 merely as the year of the rock 'n' roll bumper crop, we mischaracterize it by ignoring many of the songs that people were actually listening to.

There are many forms of musical popularity. (By some measures, the perennial No. 1 song in America would be "Happy Birthday," or perhaps the eighteenth-century melody that is used to sing both the alphabet and "Twinkle, Twinkle, Little Star.") And the goal of Top 40 radio was not merely to passively record listeners' tastes but to interpret them. In 1973, Bill Stewart, a pioneering Top 40 radio executive, told *Billboard* that in his view, the format was supposed to be entirely genre neutral. "Top 40 radio is radio literally *of the people*," he said. "If people want to hear Chinese gong music then that's what Top 40 radio stations should play." But he also said that in his view, the format's orientation toward singles, not albums, was a strength, because it meant that Top 40 radio better reflected the tastes of a particular demographic. "We're not aiming at the people who live in the rich section of town and go down and buy six albums from their allowance every week," he said. "That's why I feel a programmer can tell more by a single sale. Because the people who buy singles can't afford to buy anything else... And they're a hell of a lot more selective in their purchases."

In retrospect, it is fair to say that the singles buyers of the seventies are not typically celebrated for their discriminating tastes. While country, R&B, and various flavors of rock deepened and developed, the pop charts of the 1970s were a riot of styles and novelties. One of the styles that Stewart wanted to defend, in that *Billboard* interview, was "'bubblegum' music," by which he meant anything marketed to kids, including the Partridge Family and the Osmonds, both of which made hit records and also hit television shows. If the pop charts of the sixties reflected the buying power of young adults, the pop charts of the seventies sometimes reflected the buying power of young children, or their parents; in 1970, Ernie, from *Sesame Street*, made it to No. 16 on the Billboard chart with "Rubber Duckie." There were plenty of novelty hits, too, which were by definition disruptive events—part of the appeal of a novelty record is that it comes as a surprise. Some of them, like "Convoy," C. W. McCall's 1975 story-song about insurrectionary truckers, are strange and memorable enough to have endured as oddball classics. (The song was a No. 1 hit and inspired a 1978 movie of the same name, directed by Sam Peckinpah.) Others were simply odd, like "Once You Understand," a kind of radio play meant to dramatize the generation gap, which reached No. 23 in 1972. All pop charts have a few songs like this, and seventies pop charts may have had more than a few; it was a time of musical fragmentation, which often meant that miscellany triumphed. Even some of the most reliable hitmakers seemed somehow miscellaneous, none more than Captain & Tennille, a married duo that sent seven songs into the Top 10, including "Muskrat Love," a surreal single that seems to be about nothing less or more than what its title implies: a pair of muskrats feeling—and, at one point, making—love.

Kim Simpson, a historian of radio, argued that if the early seventies had a signature sound, it was soft. "Hit radio became an aural massage parlor of sorts in the early '70s," she wrote, "a peaceful haven amid an increasingly complex and chaotic world." Some stations found common ground between Top 40 and the format known as MOR, for "middle of the road," which promised its listeners nothing but gentle, hummable tunes. Easygoing "soft rock" bands and ruminative singer-songwriters helped position soft music as a more grown-up, more highly evolved alternative to more raucous forms of rock and R&B. But some of the decade's most successful hitmakers were singers whose style evoked a time before rock 'n' roll. Helen Reddy, an Australian-born singer with a background in variety theater, is known for "I Am Woman," an earnest celebration that became, in 1972, one of the decade's defining songs; she had a series of follow-up hits, which smuggled the spirit of cabaret and Broadway onto the airwaves. Neil Diamond became one of the decade's biggest stars by refusing to swear allegiance to any genre besides show business, teaching listeners to love his smooth but muscular voice, and his eccentric phrasing. Barry Manilow did something similar, building big audiences and scoring big successes on the pop charts, with songs that owed a debt to musical theater—an older version of mainstream American pop.

Pepsodent Smiles

In 1971, the editors of *Rolling Stone* did something mischievous: they sent Lester Bangs to review a concert by the Carpenters. Bangs was a famously dyspeptic rock critic, always ready to attack anything he perceived as phony or trite. And the Carpenters were the ultimate pop hitmakers of the seventies, a brother-sister duo whose catchy songs were often described as "wholesome," especially by people who hated wholesomeness. Bangs was one of those people. He acknowledged, early in the review, that he actually enjoyed "We've Only Just Begun," which was one of their first hits. (Its popularity on the radio had coincided, he wrote, with a brief love affair of his.) And at the concert, in San Diego, Bangs likened their songs to ice cream: "pleasant and mildly bracing." But he found the concert "disconcerting," partly because the band's stage presence was so awkward, and partly because the crowd, ranging from "tots" to "grandparents," was so well behaved and unexpressive. Bangs recalled trying and failing to elicit a usable quote from "a well-dressed, rather cold-looking blonde girl" in the audience—although, to be fair, one would like to know what *she* made of *him*. By the end, he admitted defeat. "Band and audience both," he wrote, "just gave me the creeps."

Not everyone who wrote about the duo used language this strong. But from the beginning, the two Carpenters—Karen, the shy lead singer, and Richard, the self-possessed bandleader and producer—found themselves battling the perception that their huge popularity was something to be ashamed of. A few years after the Bangs review, *Rolling Stone* put them on the cover, accompanied by a story in which Richard Carpenter objected to his portrayal in the media. "I'm *sick* of smiling," he said. "But they're all upset if you don't. So we oblige them, and we get it back in the press. 'The sticky-sweet Carpenters—*still smiling those Pepsodent smiles!*'" If the Carpenters had come around a decade earlier, their smiles likely would not have been remarkable; in the first half of the twentieth century, it was not unusual for musicians to smile for the cameras. But the rise of rock 'n' roll, and the rock-inspired counterculture, changed the expectations. The Carpenters thrived partly for the same reason they were mocked: because they were not countercultural. In the context of the seventies, their well-sung hits and seemingly unobjectionable photographs didn't seem neutral, they seemed radical—or, rather, reactionary. "It's like we're Pat Boone, only a little *cleaner*," Richard Carpenter said, taking it for granted that nothing could be more insulting than a comparison to Boone, who was known and, by then, often reviled for his easy-listening versions of rock 'n' roll hits. "As if all we do all day is drink milk, eat apple pie and take showers. I don't even *like* milk."

In some ways, Richard Carpenter did not seem like a man with much to complain about. Although the first Carpenters album didn't sell, the second, *Close to You*, from 1970, was an immediate blockbuster, spawning a pair of big hits—"We've Only Just Begun," the one that charmed Lester Bangs, and "(They Long to Be) Close to You"—and earning the duo both stardom and a measure of industry respect. At the 1971 Grammy Awards, they were nominated for four awards and won two, including Best New Artist. And even many of their detractors found something to like in Karen Carpenter's voice, which was exquisitely controlled and slightly sphinxlike, as if she weren't divulging everything that was on her mind. In an otherwise dismissive review of a concert from 1971, John S. Wilson, the pioneering *New York Times* jazz and pop critic, noted that Karen Carpenter had "an interesting vocal quality." And Tom Smucker, in *The Village Voice*, wrote that "Karen Carpenter has a voice in the great tradition of Judy Collins, Joan Baez, and other white middle-class women." (These days, Baez would not necessarily be classified as "white," because her father's family was from Mexico.) Plenty of popular singers had backgrounds that could be described as white and middle class, but the identity stuck to the Carpenters in a way it didn't stick to many of their contemporaries, perhaps because they did not pretend to be rebelling against it.

Often, the Carpenters were defined by—and criticized for—their negative genre identity: they were not a rock 'n' roll band. "I know we're not rock," Richard Carpenter said, in a 1973 *Billboard* insert that was not a journalistic interview but rather a long-form advertisement for the group. "We're pop. But we're not that kind of bland, unimaginative pop music that is so often associated with the term easy listening." (The group did occasionally incorporate rock 'n' roll gestures into their act: their first single was a cover of "Ticket to Ride," by the Beatles; "Goodbye to Love," a Carpenters single from 1972, was augmented, though not necessarily improved, by a pair of electric guitar solos.) At times, Richard Carpenter tried to embrace his identity as a mainstream pop music star, leading the backlash against rock. "The rock thing has made so many people's thinking so freaky," he told *Billboard*. "We come along as average people and because we're not painting our face, and because we dress up for a performance, we're not 'hip.'" More often, though, he seemed inclined not to reject the values of rock 'n' roll but to try to measure up to them. In one interview, he lamented the fact that some people felt obliged to choose between pop and rock, objecting to the idea that listeners "could not appreciate Led Zeppelin *and* the Carpenters."

In the seventies, there was no word for the kind of musical prejudice faced by the Carpenters and other groups like them—rockism was both too new and too commonplace to have been given a name. The Bee Gees faced similar skepticism, later in the decade, when they evolved from an accomplished rock 'n' roll band into a world-conquering disco-pop phenomenon. Skepticism followed, too, any number of acts from other genres—country, R&B, jazz—who had the temerity to make pop music. The difference with rock 'n' roll was that the genre was so big, and so popular, that it sometimes didn't seem like a genre at all. Country fans, for instance, tended to view their genre as a community, with its own traditions and values, located somewhere outside the mainstream of American popular culture; not everyone was part of it, and that was partly the point. But rock 'n' roll was everywhere, and so it was often the standard against which pop stars were judged. Karen Carpenter probably could have had a successful country career, if she had wanted one; in 1978, the Carpenters sent a twangy single called "Sweet, Sweet Smile" to No. 8 on the country chart. And yet Richard Carpenter didn't fret in interviews about not being country enough to be taken seriously. Already, by the seventies, many pop stars found that rock 'n' roll was the default category.

It was no coincidence that rock 'n' roll, in the seventies, became installed as the normative form of popular music at precisely the moment when it was starting to seem vulnerable. It was not the dominance of rock 'n' roll but rather the fear of its commercial decline that helped create rockism. Part of what gave Bangs "the creeps" about the Carpenters was their massive popularity, which made them seem less like quirky holdouts in a rock-driven era and more like possible harbingers of a post–rock 'n' roll world. Carpenter compared his group to Led Zeppelin, a hard-rock band that was beloved by fans but not exactly ubiquitous; Led Zeppelin sold albums and filled arenas without generally sending songs onto the top tier of the pop charts. And many of the era's most acclaimed rock bands were even further from the mainstream than that. (When Robert Christgau observed, at the end of the seventies, that much of his favorite music was "semi-popular," he was talking about David Bowie, Bruce Springsteen, and a whole constellation of rockers who hadn't yet become big stars, and in some cases never would.) In 1969, many of the songs near the top of the year-end *Billboard* Hot 100 list were rock 'n' roll or rock-influenced: "Honky Tonk Women," by the Rolling Stones; "Everyday People," by Sly and the Family Stone. By 1979, rock 'n' roll was largely absent from that list, with the telling exception of "My Sharona," by a band called the Knack, which was typically—and not quite accurately—said to represent something that would have seemed unnecessary a decade earlier: a rock 'n' roll revival.

The Perils of (New) Pop Stardom

By the end of the seventies, one particular style had emerged to dethrone rock 'n' roll, and just about everything else: disco, which in a few years went from being an underground subcategory of R&B to being the definitive sound of modern pop. To many young listeners, put off by disco ubiquity, the natural alternative was punk. One of the countless punks who felt this way was a young man from Wales who called himself Steve Strange, and who remembered falling in love with the Sex Pistols. "They just seemed like the perfect answer to the bland disco music that had taken over the charts, stuff like Chic and Donna Summer," he later recalled. "I remember 'Car

Wash'"—by the American R&B group Rose Royce—"it was a hit and the title of a movie, but I couldn't help thinking how colourless it was compared to the explosive energy of punk." Like many self-assured punks, though, Steve Strange eventually reconsidered his initial dismissal of disco. After a few years, he got bored with punk and moved to London, where he became a nightlife impresario, helping nurture the sound and look of new pop. Strange, like Boy George, was inspired by David Bowie, who noticed before most of his peers that punk and disco did not need to be enemies. Both genres celebrated the outrageous, and both pushed against the newfound respectability of rock 'n' roll. Punk rock was aggrieved, out for revenge. Disco was more liberatory, embracing the beat in order to chase dance-floor euphoria. But by the end of the seventies, these punk and disco impulses were beginning to combine.

One early example of this was "Fame," Bowie's 1975 hit, a strutting, snarling funk track that became a hit in disco clubs. "I'm not a big fan of disco at all," Bowie said, a few years later. "I loathe it. I really get so embarrassed that my records do so well in discos." But he seemed fascinated by both the culture and the musical possibilities of the genre. One of his most disco-friendly singles was "D.J.," which had lyrics meant to mock disc jockeys ("I am a DJ, I am what I play / I've got believers, believing me") and a beat meant to seduce them. By the end of the seventies, a number of younger musicians were creating their own hybrids, making records that were too futuristic to be punk, and too alien to be disco. In 1979, a former punk who called himself Gary Numan had a pair of No. 1 hits in Britain, "Are 'Friends' Electric?" and "Cars," which sounded like Bowie at his most cyborg. The same year, Public Image Ltd, the new group led by the former Sex Pistols singer now known as John Lydon, released a howling, scabrous single based on an incongruously danceable beat; it was called "Death Disco." One of the most radical punk-disco songs to emerge that year was called "We Are All Prostitutes," and it was exuberantly contradictory. The musicians kept toggling between a neat, Chic-like groove and squally digressions, while the singer howled leftist slogans: "Capitalism is the most barbaric of all religions!" "Department stores are our new cathedrals!" "Our children shall rise up against us!" Given all this fury, the band's name was perfectly sarcastic: the Pop Group.

This was the scene that gave birth to the new pop movement: a mixture of punk spirit and disco innovation, coming together to nurture electronic music that sounded more and more, as the years went by, like bona fide pop. In 1978, a group of friends from Sheffield, England, released a single called "Being Boiled," which had an oozing electronic beat and lyrics about silkworms and dead children. Not surprisingly, the record didn't secure a place on the British pop chart. But the group evolved, adding a pair of new members—young women, originally hired for their appearance and dancing ability—and growing more commercially ambitious. "We always wanted to be hugely popular but we couldn't play well enough to get what we wanted," said Phil Oakey, the group's guiding spirit. "Now we have choruses and stuff and a proper producer to make sure we get what we want." He was right: Oakey was the leader of the Human League, which in 1981 had a global hit with "Don't You Want Me"; it went No. 1 in both Britain and America, helping to launch the new-pop revolution. In the wake of that success, the Human League rereleased "Being Boiled," which finally found an audience. Now that the members of the Human League were proper pop stars, "Being Boiled" was by definition a proper pop song, and it rose to No. 6 on the British chart.

To a large extent, "new pop" meant "electronic pop," a faster and sharper successor to disco; the genre's iconic instrument was the synthesizer. But the pop ethos dictated that it was uncool to get nerdy or obsessive about instrumentation—*that* was the kind of thing boring old rock musicians did. For the new-pop upstarts, the emphasis was on glamour and success, not musical minutiae. The members of Culture Club, for instance, used reggae rhythms to create a buoyant, lightweight sound, setting themselves apart from some of the more dour electro-pop groups. (The name "Boy George" was an homage to the reggae tradition of honorific nicknames like King Tubby, Prince Jammy, and Jah Woosh; Culture Club once toured with

Musical Youth, a reggae band.) But they portrayed themselves as careless playboys, rather than earnest musical obsessives. Boy George remembers that he was more interested in adulation than innovation. "Part of me wanted to be out on the artistic fringe," he wrote in his memoir. "But I was such a polite, friendly boy and I wanted everyone to love me." In the world of new pop, stardom sometimes seemed more important than music. Steve Strange, the punk-turned-club-promoter, was known as one of London's most ostentatious personalities. Inevitably, he found himself leading a new-pop band, Visage, which created a No. 8 British hit, a stylish and moody post-disco record called "Fade to Grey." But the group's long-term prospects were harmed by Strange's drug use, and also by his apathy, which may have been related. "I cared more about the things going on around the album than the music itself," he later recalled, as he remembered the band's troubled attempts to create a follow-up to its successful debut album. "I wasn't a muso, I just wanted to do my bits and go."

"With pop music there are no rules," declared Trevor Horn, a British producer who helped create the electro-pop sound of the eighties, in an *NME* interview. Horn produced hits for ABC, Frankie Goes to Hollywood, and Grace Jones. And actually, he did acknowledge one rule: pop music ought to be popular. "I think the whole point of a pop record is that however much you or I might theorise about it, if it doesn't sell, if it doesn't appeal to people who don't know you and who don't know me then it's a waste of time," he said. By commercial standards, though, most of the new pop acts were probably less "pop" than, say, hard rock bands like AC/DC, let alone rock 'n' roll warhorses like the Rolling Stones. "The Human League may sell a lot of records, but they'll never play Madison Square Garden," said Nick Rhodes, from Duran Duran, in 1982. "I think we will." He was right about the Human League and also about his own group, which played the Garden for the first time in 1984. Duran Duran turned out to be one of the more popular and enduring bands from the new pop scene, perhaps because the members presented themselves as a *band*, splitting the difference between two worlds—Rimmer described them as "combining the simplicity and solidity of the Chic rhythm section with the raw energy of the Sex Pistols." If the goal was to win a popularity contest, one effective approach was to be a little *less* pop, and a little more rock 'n' roll.

Even Boy George, who never hid his own boundless appetite for applause, soon found out that in the world of pop music, the all-consuming focus on popularity could feel oppressive. In his memoir, he explained how excited he was when "Karma Chameleon," one of the group's biggest hits, went to No. 1. At least at first. "The joy quickly turned to embarrassment," he recalled. "I got sick of hearing it on the radio and miming to it on TV. 'Karma' was the kind of song everyone bought and no one liked." What he really wanted, perhaps, was a more selective sort of popularity—the kind of musical "credibility," perhaps, that anti-rockists loved to sneer at. It is not only music critics, it turns out, who have mixed feelings about the way a seemingly silly song can become suddenly and totally inescapable. "I love music," Boy George told *Smash Hits*, a few years later. "I'm just sick of being a celebrity. I'm sick of being a pop star." Boy George may have been the leading man of the new-pop movement, but even he wasn't entirely committed to its principles. Lots of people want to be pop stars. But few of them, it turns out, want to be *merely* pop stars.

This ambivalent attitude was part of what made the new pop movement so incoherent—and perhaps so unsustainable, too. In their naked ambition to be pop stars, these musicians sometimes behaved in very un-pop-star-like ways, slyly calling attention to the kinds of music-industry machinations that are usually kept hidden. Ever since the sixties, pop stars have been eager to present themselves as artistic geniuses baring their souls, not merely hitmakers, or calculating businessmen, or do-my-bits-and-go opportunists. And fans have been just as eager to play along. Frenzied adulation, of the sort teen idols must necessarily inspire, doesn't leave much room for aesthetic skepticism. This helps explain why, over the years, the war against rockism has mainly been fought by music critics, not pop stars. One of the few eighties musicians who unabashedly embraced the anti-rockist ethos was Neil Tennant, who was one half of the Pet Shop Boys.

"We're a pop group, not a rock and roll group," he once said. He and his musical partner, Chris Lowe, specialized in electronic pop songs that were sly and carefully constructed, and the duo sent nearly two dozen songs into the British Top 10. They took delight in exposing pop artifice, with cheeky lyrics about success ("I've got the brains, you've got the looks / Let's make lots of money"), and tours propelled by prerecorded tracks instead of a backing band. "I quite like proving we *can't* cut it live," Tennant said. But then, he had an unusual history. Before joining the new pop revolution, he had chronicled it as a music critic and editor at *Smash Hits*. "Rock is meant to be significant, therefore people write about it in terms of significance," Tennant once said. "Pop is meant to be throwaway." He said this in 2012, more than a quarter century into his pop career, and it sounded as if he still wasn't entirely sure whether he should be bemoaning the bad reputation of pop music—or celebrating it.

In that same 2012 interview, with *Vanity Fair*, Tennant talked about the Pet Shop Boys' relative obscurity in the United States. "Something happened to us in America," he said. "The theory is it was the video for 'Domino Dancing.'" That music video, from 1988, depicted two young men fighting over a woman; by the end, the men were shirtless, and the woman had come to seem distinctly superfluous. "Domino Dancing" peaked at No. 18 in America, and it marked the end of an era: the group never had another American Top 40 hit. Apparently some listeners wondered whether the video was simply too gay for the American mainstream, but Tennant declined to endorse this theory. "I never really believed it," he said. "America is quite homophobic, but it's also totally gay."

In the new-pop revolution, gay identity played an important role, though not always an explicit one. Listeners may have made assumptions, but Tennant didn't publicly identify himself as gay until 1994. George Michael found success with the new-pop duo Wham!, and even more success as a solo pop star; his coming-out interview was in 1998. A few groups took a more radical approach. In 1983, Frankie Goes to Hollywood scored a worldwide hit with "Relax," an addictive dance track that had a video full of writhing men, and startlingly straightforward lyrics that seemed to describe—or, rather, prescribe—a prolonged orgasm. ("Relax! Don't do it / When you want to come.") The group members at first denied this interpretation, and then, in the liner notes to their debut album, the bassist admitted it: "When it first came out we used to pretend it was about motivation, and really it was about shagging." Boy George sometimes sought to avoid categorization (early on, he told an interviewer that he was less interested in sex than in a cup of tea), although he wrote movingly in his memoir about his complicated romantic relationship with Jon Moss, Culture Club's drummer. His coy interviews contrasted with his ostentatious appearance, and he sometimes defended his approach as a form of activism. "I'm not hiding anything," he once said. "That's the underlying statement. What I'm doing, whether I say anything or not, is making people accept effeminate men."

It's striking that the new pop movement, so scornful of rock 'n' roll machismo, was nevertheless mainly led by men. Some—maybe most—of the era's most exquisite electronic pop was made by women, including Annie Lennox; Alison Moyet, originally from Yazoo; and Kate Bush, whose otherworldly early-eighties compositions were definitely new, and probably pop, but not particularly "new pop." But women tended not to be at the center of the music-magazine arguments that helped turn this musical tendency into a movement. Perhaps women performers were less likely to forswear rock 'n' roll seriousness because they were less likely to be taken seriously in the first place by some listeners and some critics, who assumed that a woman behind a microphone was necessarily a "pop" singer. Or perhaps it's just that the original anti-rockism movement, like all musical movements, was necessarily partial: elevating some voices and skipping over others in order to tell a story that made a particular kind of sense.

Pure Pop Music

In America, where punk was more a passing curiosity than a national obsession, there was no real equivalent to the British new-pop movement. The glamorous pop bands that arrived from Britain were known as "new wave," a term that emphasized novelty while suggesting repetition, as if this was merely the latest bunch of bands washing up on American shores. At the same time, though, a handful of American acts were finding their way from punk into pop. Belinda Carlisle was a music obsessive from California whose world was changed by punk: she adored Iggy Pop, the American godfather of punk, and read all the British music magazines; under the name Dottie Danger, she played drums in an early incarnation of the scabrous Los Angeles punk band the Germs. When she and four other women decided to form their own group, though, they chose a name that suggested fun, not sickness: the Go-Go's. With the Go-Go's and then on her own, Carlisle became an eighties pop star—although maybe not quite on purpose. In her autobiography, she remembered the day she and her bandmates first listened to *Beauty and the Beat*, the Go-Go's 1981 debut, which sold millions of copies. "In the studio, we had thought we were making a great punk album," she wrote. "On hearing the final version, it sounded more pop than we had anticipated."

Debbie Harry, lead singer of Blondie, was more strategic. She was part of the punk scene in New York, but she was clear in her intention that Blondie be a "pop group," in part because she wanted to avoid the "stigma" of punk. (She once suggested that the term "punk" was "a media creation," neatly reversing the usual terms of debate by implying that pop was more authentic.) "Heart of Glass," Blondie's first big hit, was a shimmering, cool-blooded disco record, shrewdly calculated both to gall the group's old punk friends and to gratify the general public; in 1979, it went to No. 1 in both America and Britain, transforming Harry from a theoretical pop star into the real thing. A few years later, another unlikely pop star emerged from the rock clubs of New York: Cyndi Lauper, who drew from reggae and punk and dance music. Her 1983 debut album, *She's So Unusual*, was a left-field blockbuster, sending four songs into the Top 5, with an ebullient sound that helped define eighties pop. She said that she once had to defend herself in conversation with Dick Clark, whose show, *American Bandstand*, brought the sounds of Top 40 to television. "He told me that I was making disposable music," she remembered. "That's what pop music was—disposable. I said, 'No, I did not work my whole life to make disposable music.'"

One of the most important insights of anti-rockism is that many assumptions about music are driven by prejudices that are, upon examination, hard to defend. When Lauper was recording *She's So Unusual*, she fell in love with one particular sound: a gated snare drum, a percussive blast that sounded a bit artificial, evoking the staccato beats that ruled dance clubs. (The "gate" is a filter that cuts off a sound when the volume drops below a certain level; instead of fading away, a gated snare reverberates loudly and then suddenly stops.) That sound influenced some listeners, Clark possibly among them, to hear Lauper's music as more "pop," and therefore more "disposable," than if she had used untreated drums. In eighties America, "pop" often meant danceable songs with electronic elements. Even people who had never stopped to think about the genre identity learned to associate certain sounds and instruments with "pop," and perhaps with superficiality.

When I think about eighties pop, I often think about one record in particular: "Borderline," the 1984 single by Madonna, which sounds to me like a perfect distillation of pop in the post-disco era. I think I remember hearing it on the radio as a boy, and being drawn in by the soft and sentimental keyboard introduction, and then the sudden kick of the drum machine. The song is built around a basic but effective pop trick: incongruity. Cheerful, squiggly synthesizer lines push the mood skyward; desperate, lovelorn lyrics ("Feels like I'm going to lose my mind") pull it back down. Listeners who have grown used to modern pitch-correction software may notice that Madonna is strikingly—though not unpleasantly—off-pitch, and the sense that she's straining to hit the notes gives the song an added intimacy. Best of all is the way the bassline climbs up and up, creating the happy illusion that the song could go on forever. Even now, when people talk about "pop" as a genre—"pure pop," they sometimes say—they are often talking about people whose music sounds a bit like "Borderline." Katy Perry emerged, in the late 2000s, to become for a time the biggest "pure" pop star in the world, updating the Madonna formula to create her own electronic pop songs. (During one late-career concert, Madonna descended from the stage to talk to Perry, who was in the audience; Perry literally kissed the ring.) Lady Gaga was a pop star who also treated "pop star" as just one of her many identities. She sometimes seemed like the truest heir of the old "new pop" movement, embracing pop as a genre—one of her albums is called *Artpop*—while treating her own fame as merely one element in a postmodern performance. There were cult pop stars, too. Robyn, from Sweden, had a couple of American hits in the late nineties and then reinvented herself, in the 2000s, as a pop auteur, making delectable records for connoisseurs. In the 2010s, so-called hyperpop acts made tracks that were ludicrously fast and chirpy, exaggerating pop sounds and tropes until they no longer sounded pop at all. And by the end of the decade, America was finally catching up to other countries in appreciating the joys of Korean pop, or K-pop, which tends to be vivid and upbeat, and which should remind American listeners of all the global hit records that never find big domestic audiences. The extraordinary American popularity of K-pop groups like BTS and BLACKPINK could be yet another pop fad, but it could also be a sign that national pop boundaries are growing more porous, and that American listeners are growing more receptive to global pop music, especially if it sounds simultaneously familiar and strange.

The faddishness of pop has always been part of its identity: paradoxically, its popularity waxes and wanes. The eighties were a great decade for pop in America, because musicians from different genres—R&B, various strains of rock 'n' roll, the dance-music underground—were all experimenting with electronic production, and converging upon similar styles. One of the many beneficiaries was Weird Al Yankovic, the parodist, who became a surprise celebrity in the eighties by rewriting the lyrics to pop songs, secure in the knowledge that everyone had already heard them. (Not coincidentally, the eighties were a time of crisis for certain genres: it was 1985 when *The New York Times* declared, on its front page, that country music was "in decline," three years before Nelson George published *The Death of Rhythm & Blues*.) But by the nineties, the pop consensus seemed to fray. Genres reasserted themselves: country and, increasingly, hip-hop produced blockbuster albums; the popularity of grunge put rock 'n' roll in a melancholy mood, increasing the musical and emotional distance between rock and pop. In 1998, *Spin* published a revealing article by Greg Milner about Casey Kasem, who had begun hosting *American Top 40*, a syndicated radio countdown program, in 1970. For the first two decades, the show used data from the *Billboard* Hot 100 chart, which aimed to measure the most popular singles in the country based on a combination of sales figures and airplay. But in the nineties, Kasem and his producers noticed that an increasing number of hip-hop tracks were making it to the Hot 100, even though Top 40 stations (which broadcast Kasem's show) often didn't play them; these hits disturbed the show's mellow mood, and annoyed some of its baby boomer listeners. "Kasem found himself in the strange position of highlighting songs his host stations wouldn't even *think* of playing," Milner wrote. "For thirteen weeks in 1992, the notoriously straitlaced DJ was forced to introduce 'Baby Got Back,' by booty-fetishist Sir Mix-A-Lot. That same year, a hundred stations dropped his show." In search of a more "pop" Top 40, Kasem began using different, more adult-oriented charts, creating a countdown that was more musically coherent, even though that meant ignoring a number of popular hip-hop and rock songs. "I'd like to see Top 40 come back so that it includes everything," Kasem said, but he didn't sound optimistic. American pop seemed big in the eighties, with enough gravitational force to pull in musicians from other genres. (Think, for instance, of the R&B fans who fretted that Prince and Michael Jackson had forsaken them, leaving the genre behind to join the pop mainstream.) But

American pop seemed much smaller in the nineties: it was a subset of the nation's favorite music, an old-fashioned and well-behaved genre competing for market share with rowdier competitors.

You'll Grow Out of It

Perhaps Kasem needn't have been so worried. By the midnineties the comeback of pop had already begun, led by an old-fashioned phenomenon that was somehow new again: teen idols. The first Backstreet Boys album appeared in 1996, and the first *NSYNC album arrived the next year; two months after the article about Top 40 and Kasem in *Spin*, Britney Spears released her debut single, ". . . Baby One More Time," which marked the start of a new teen-pop era. Many of these acts drew from R&B: the template for the boy bands was New Kids on the Block, which was essentially a white version of the African American R&B boy band New Edition. (The producer Maurice Starr discovered New Edition in 1981, and created New Kids on the Block in 1984.) But because groups like the Backstreet Boys and *NSYNC were white, and because they favored up-tempo arrangements that weren't particularly influenced by hip-hop, and because their fans tended to be young, these acts were all classified as pop, or teen pop, and not R&B. Their success made pop popular again, and even inspired the creation of a new pop countdown show: *Total Request Live*, on MTV, which had its premiere in 1998, and which brought screaming teenagers into the MTV studios, where they could scream for their favorite videos—and, if they were lucky, scream directly at their favorite stars. Starting in 2002, *American Idol* and a handful of like-minded contests brought a clean-scrubbed version of pop music to network television, turning pop fandom into wholesome family recreation. These shows often downplayed genre, mixing together all sorts of singers. But most of them struggled to build careers in the traditional music industry. "Singing competition music" essentially became a genre unto itself.

Rock 'n' roll has long been celebrated—eagerly though not always accurately—as the music of youth. And Motown claimed, in the sixties, that its R&B was "the Sound of Young America." But pop music has often been criticized for being youthful to a fault. Bill Stewart, the radio executive who was interviewed by *Billboard* in 1973, complained that Top 40 programmers were too quick to dismiss acts that were perceived to have a young following. "When the music director or program director is totaling up the votes or sales reports that he gets from the record stores, if he sees a thing by Donny Osmond or the Partridge Family or someone he considers to be bubblegum, I think that record gets a little lower rating than it would otherwise," Stewart said. "Consequently, what should be the major staple of our product, isn't." In 1971, another trade publication, *Cash Box*, printed an editorial in defense of the new teen pop. "To many older rock fans, acts like the Jackson 5, the Partridge Family, and the Osmonds represent a too simple, unsophisticated rock format, sugar-coated with a sentimentality they would rather not admit a fondness for," the magazine wrote, urging listeners and radio executives to avoid "snobbism" and appreciate "the engaging quality of youthful spirit and melodies you can hum." Like much praise for teen pop, this was faint praise. Critics looking to defend teen pop tended to do it by pointing out that truly exceptional talents could transcend the label; invariably, they mentioned the Beatles, who were originally considered teen idols. Writing in *Billboard* in 1972, the critic Nancy Erlich voiced the hope that the Osmonds and the Jackson 5 might "grow and mature." (She was less hopeful about another teen idol, David Cassidy, of the Partridge Family.) But she noted that having a youthful fan base can be a professional liability. "After a while the little girls grow up a little," she wrote, "and the star they adore is old hat to their younger sisters."

Those "little girls," the ones who turn smiling boys and men into teen-pop sensations, have often been treated with disdain in the music press.

But in 1984, a pair of perceptive music critics, Sue Steward and Sheryl Garratt, published *Signed, Sealed, and Delivered*, a history of "women in pop" that considered fans as well as musicians. Garratt objected to the characterization of young female pop fans as "silly, screaming girls." She argued that they should be seen as a primary force in pop music, not some embarrassing auxiliary to it:

> They bought the records in millions and made a massive contribution to the early success of Elvis, the Beatles, the Stones, Marc Bolan, Michael Jackson and many of the others who have since been accepted by the grown-ups and become monuments, reference-points in the rock hierarchy. Before you sneer again, boys, remember that it's often their money that allows you your pretensions.

Garratt wrote perceptively, too, of her own years as a young pop fan, when she was obsessed with a Scottish rock 'n' roll boy band called Bay City Rollers, who had a string of British hits in the seventies; in America, they are best remembered for "Saturday Night," which went to No. 1 in 1976. Garratt explained how vivid her fandom still seemed to her, even though she had long since left it behind:

> Looking back now, I hardly remember the gigs themselves, the songs, or even what the Rollers looked like. What I *do* remember are the bus rides . . . dancing in lines at the school disco and sitting in each others' bedrooms discussing our fantasies and compiling our scrapbooks. Our real obsession was with ourselves; in the end, the actual men behind the posters had very little to do with it at all. . . . One of the most important points about most teeny groups is that almost everyone else hates them. With the Rollers, everyone but the fans continually made fun of us, insisting that the band looked stupid and couldn't play. They were right, of course, but that wasn't the point. It was us against the world—and, for a while at least, we were winning.

This may be the best description of teenage fandom ever written, precisely because it comes from the inside. And yet it's hard to figure out what, exactly, to do with it. Garratt wants us to respect the furious passion of these girls, but she doesn't insist that we must similarly respect the band they loved. That sort of circumscribed respect is more likely to feel like condescension to the fans themselves, at least in the moment. To say that a teen-pop act is forgettable but that its fans are true believers is to say pretty much the same thing that rock snobs always say: that "screaming girls" only love this music because the intoxication of fandom has turned them delusional. In other words: you'll grow out of it.

Arguments over pop music, especially teen-oriented pop music, are often arguments over precisely this: whether the music will stand the test of time. This seems like a straightforward criterion, especially in the case of Bay City Rollers, who were beginning to implode by the end of the decade, abandoned even by many of their biggest fans. And yet "Saturday Night," the group's big American hit, seems to have aged pretty well. Judging from Spotify's streaming data, the song remains a favorite. More popular than Barry Manilow's "I Write the Songs," which topped the *Billboard* chart two weeks later. And considerably more popular than "Let's Do It Again," by the critically acclaimed gospel and R&B group the Staple Singers, which topped the chart the week before.

In the album era, it made some sense to distinguish camp classics, which people might be content to hear occasionally on the radio, from beloved old favorites, which inspired perennial album sales. The critic Chuck Klosterman once suggested that this distinction followed a gender divide. "Girls who love the Backstreet Boys (or Rick Springfield, or Bon Jovi) love them in a way that made my teenage adoration for Mötley Crüe seem pale," he wrote in 2001. "But here I am—ten years later—and I'll still be buying every Mötley Crüe album that gets released, fully knowing I will probably only listen to it once. Males have a weird sense of loyalty toward the bands they like; they sometimes view record buying as a responsibility." In fact, it's not obvious that album sales reflect a bifurcation between loyal male fans and faithless female ones—at least, not in all of these cases. It is true that Rick Springfield, a hunky singer and actor, sold millions of albums in the eighties and then disappeared from the pop charts. But both the Backstreet Boys and Bon Jovi kept going, and kept selling: Bon Jovi topped the album chart in 2016, and the Backstreet Boys did it in 2019. Mötley Crüe hasn't had a No. 1 album since 1989.

Anyway, in the streaming era, old-fashioned album sales don't matter much. (The *Billboard* album chart now takes into account not just physical and online sales but also the popularity of each album's songs on a wide range of audio- and video-streaming services.) And now that listeners can hear pretty much whatever song they want for no charge, or no extra charge, it is becoming clear that most pop hits retain a fairly stable following over the decades. Often, the exact level of popularity is the result of external and rather random factors: whether a newer artist happens to sample or cover a song; whether a song is chosen for a soundtrack or commercial; whether the performer goes on to live a colorful life or die a colorful death. Sometimes the most deathless songs in the world are teen-pop hits, like "… Baby One More Time," which stormed onto the airwaves in 1998 and essentially never left. Some pop songs really do resonate across the decades, and one useful function of poptimism is to identify them.

But there is another, more radical way that poptimism can alter the way we think about music: it can make us think anew about our assumption that posterity is what matters. Most people, when they think about the value of popular music, find themselves thinking about what will last. The idea is that the passage of time will have a clarifying effect, helping us to separate good songs from bad ones. True, our ideas about goodness and badness will fluctuate over time, but in general, high-quality songs and musicians are supposed to be discovered by future generations, and low-quality ones forgotten. In the case of older music, it is easy—and sometimes fun—to mock the blinkered listeners of earlier eras, who sometimes failed to hear what is so clearly audible today. We might marvel, for instance, at how listeners in the seventies failed to appreciate the starry-eyed R&B of Shuggie Otis, and wonder why, exactly, they were so captivated by Captain & Tennille. But we tend to be less sure of ourselves when it comes to new music. When we hope and expect that our favorite contemporary recordings will stand the test of time, we are seeking validation of our tastes from listeners in the future—we want them to prove us right. If we truly adore a new album, we might call it "classic" or "timeless," words that link excellence with endurance. With old songs or new ones, the assumption is the same: that musical judgments grow more accurate with the passage of time.

But what if they don't? An anti-posterity version of poptimism might insist that, just as we should stop belittling the tastes of "little girls," we should also stop discounting the opinions of contemporaneous listeners. There is no reason why broad but evanescent popularity must necessarily count for less than a narrower, more durable sort of enthusiasm. "Call Your Girlfriend," by Robyn, is a perennial favorite that made no great commercial impact when it was released in 2011. (It peaked at No. 55 on the British chart and never appeared on the American pop chart.) "Rude," by a Canadian reggae-pop band called Magic!, was one of the biggest worldwide hits of 2014—the seventh-biggest, according to both *Billboard* and Spotify. One way to exalt pop is to celebrate the considerable merits of "Call Your Girlfriend," a melancholy but danceable electro-pop anthem that may well endure as one of the great breakup songs of all time; a decade later, it is still spinning off cover versions and viral videos. But another, perhaps more perverse way is to celebrate the unexpected (and, indeed, brief) triumph of Magic!, which means thinking about the way a hit song can cause a kind of collective madness, suffusing popular culture and then slowly disappearing, leaving the people who thought they loved it feeling dazed and maybe rather sheepish. When we agree to defer to later generations, we tell ourselves that songs and singers will tend, over time, to get about as much glory or oblivion as they deserve. But if we prioritized contemporaneous responses instead, then we would regard abandoned hits with some of the same wistfulness we feel when we hear about an obscure language that has gone extinct because the last fluent speaker finally died. It is a melancholy process, although probably, in the grand sweep of history, an inevitable one—from a great enough distance, nearly any cultural achievement seems evanescent. Maybe by bursting and then quickly fading, Dave Rimmer's new-pop revolution was doing exactly what pop does best. Why must all music be built to last? Isn't it possible that the most precious pop songs are also the most perishable?

The End of Taste

When I was working as a pop music critic, I tried not to think too much about quality—at least not directly. My belief, then as now, was that there was no useful difference between loving a song and considering it good, or between not liking one and considering it bad. (If it is possible for a song to be good without inspiring any affection in a listener, then what use is goodness?) But I knew, as all critics know, that successful criticism usually relies on finding a balance between personal taste and conventional wisdom. Stray too far from the judgments of the relevant musical communities—audiences, experts, fellow critics—and readers will think you're a crank, out of touch with the world they live in. Hew too closely to those judgments and readers will think you're a hack, saying the same things everyone else is saying. Either one makes you seem boring, and as a professional critic, your chief obligation, superseding any musical directive, is not to bore the readers.

Like most music critics, I found myself often agreeing with the crowd, and occasionally dissenting from it. That might sound cynical or strategic, but to me the process felt intuitive and, as far as I could judge, honest. I have never been particularly good at predicting hits. (Music critics who have this talent are probably toiling in the wrong profession, not to mention the wrong income bracket.) Instead, I tried to figure out what other people liked, and what I liked, and why. The pop charts were especially instructive: again and again, songs and albums I would never have selected rose to the top; not infrequently, I found that after repeated listens, I could hear what all those other listeners were hearing, too. If this was a form of Stockholm syndrome—and perhaps it was, as perhaps much pop fandom is—then it was only intensified by the experience of spending a handful of nights each week at concerts. When you listen to a record that sounds lousy, it is easy to imagine that no one could *really* like it. But at a concert, you are invariably surrounded by enthusiastic fans; you're not simply watching music, you're watching music making people happy. (I can remember a few exceptions to this rule, none more dispiriting than a shambling 2004 performance by the Vines, at Irving Plaza, during which some concertgoers trickled out but many more just stood there, stoic, as the band bashed and the singer howled, sometimes plugging his own ears.) At concerts by acts whose music didn't grab me, I often found myself trying to figure out what experiences I would have had to have in order to be as excited as the fans around me. What if I had spent a summer working in a record store with someone who was obsessed with this band? What if this song had been used in a movie that I watched half a dozen times? What if my introduction had come through a friend who did a great imitation of the way the singer moved, or who couldn't stop talking about the way that guitar sounded? Often, I ended up seduced by what I saw and heard. I remember gaping, first in puzzlement and then in awe, as Bette Midler delivered a strange and witty performance in a hockey arena in Long Island, complete with mermaids in wheelchairs, which made me think anew about what I called "the complicated relationship between ability and disability." (A couple of weeks later, David Letterman congratulated her for the review I had written, she demurred, and they had a brief—and, for me, very surreal— conversation about whether I liked her.) It was the same arena where, in 2007, I was very pleasantly surprised by Miley Cyrus's high-spirited performance as Hannah Montana. As the girls in the audience shrieked and then, as the night wore on, napped, I took in Cyrus's show—a "two-hour sugar rush," I wrote, with "a welcome hint of chaos"—and wondered what else she might be capable of.

I left the *Times* in 2008, with no complaints whatsoever, having been lucky enough to spend six years doing almost nothing but listening to music and writing about it. The 2000s were a strange time to have that job, though: both the newspaper business and the music business were in a state of existential financial crisis, menaced by the possibility that their paying customers were turning into nonpaying browsers, and I sometimes felt as if I were working in two different dying industries at the same time. I was also surprised to notice that my interests were changing slightly; I was as obsessed with music as I had ever been, but I was growing less inclined to fight about it. If the broader world insisted on ignoring a great pop single ("Lose You") by the Swedish singer Linda Sundblad, or on overlooking a pile of witty but morose CDs by a rapper known as Starlito; if fans insisted on gathering in great numbers to watch the Black Keys, who sounded to me like a perfectly dull garage-rock band—well, maybe there was no reason to object too strenuously. Every once in a while, I managed to summon up some disapproval. The last concert I reviewed was by the grandiose British singer-songwriter James Blunt, whom I found aggressively charmless; one of the words I used was "loathsome." But especially with CD sales declining, and musical subgenres multiplying, it seemed perverse to spend a few paragraphs telling *Times* readers that some semipopular musician they'd probably never heard of was not worth hearing, after all. What was the point? Why criticize anything?

Most critics ask themselves this from time to time. And perhaps the question has particular relevance for critics of popular music, who are often perceived as being culturally distinct from the audience the songs are meant for—strange and nerdy grown-ups, peering down at the "kids" whose fandom fuels the music industry. Simon Frith, a pioneering and perceptive British critic, has written about the complicated unwritten rules that shape our musical judgments. In 1987, he wrote about the inescapable ideology of rock criticism:

> The rock aesthetic depends, crucially, on an argument about authenticity. Good music is the authentic expression of something—a person, an idea, a feeling, a shared experience, a *Zeitgeist*. Bad music is inauthentic—it expresses nothing. The most common term of abuse in rock criticism is "bland"—bland music has nothing in it and is made only to be commercially pleasing.

By then, of course, it was already becoming fashionable to sneer at the rockist hunger for authenticity. And yet this hunger is hard to ignore, in any genre. Frith's formulation invites us to chuckle at the clichés of rock criticism. But he also wants to help us realize that the "rock aesthetic," defined this way, applied about as well to the new, pop-oriented critics, who tended to be just as dismissive of "bland" music as their rock-loving counterparts. (Boy George and the other leading lights of the new pop movement were absolutely *obsessed* with not being bland.) One way that critics smuggle unexamined preconceptions into their writing is by using seemingly descriptive terms that function as covert judgments. When a song is described as "soulful," that is invariably a compliment. Is it possible for a song to be soulful but lousy, or soulless but excellent? If not, then "soulful" is not a description at all—it is just a synonym for "good." Similarly, Frith is right about "bland": it is almost always an insult, and the insult conceals an argument about what music is supposed to do. It seems evident that not all lousy songs are bland. But are all bland songs lousy? The celebrated producer Brian Eno invented, in the late seventies, a wispy and beatless musical genre that he called "ambient music." In the liner notes to *Ambient 1: Music for Airports*, from 1978, Eno set down some ambient commandments, including the edict that ambient music "must be as ignorable as it is interesting." Is *Music for Airports* brilliantly bland? *Is* it interesting? Must music be interesting in order to be good?

Many people who listen to a lot of music are rightly wary of musical rules, which tend to seem true only until an imaginative musician or a radical new genre comes along to break them. (When he wrote those liner notes, Eno was doing something sly: showing us how a new kind of music can redefine a seemingly straightforward word like "interesting.") And yet our presumptions and prescriptions—our prejudices, if you like—are what allow us to make sense of music in the first place, and maybe what allow us to enjoy it. Frith argued that it is not only critics who try to separate good music from bad. "Even if as a popular music scholar I can't point authoritatively to bad music (my authority will undoubtedly be rejected), as a popular music fan I do so all the time," he wrote. "This is a necessary part of fandom." Many everyday listeners claim to like all kinds of music, and some of them may even mean it. But we wouldn't trust someone who claimed to like *all* music. How could you have a taste for music if you had literally no taste at all?

Carl Wilson is an imaginative Canadian critic who set out to answer this question. Actually, he set out to answer a different question: Why do so many people love Celine Dion, the Canadian balladeer whose songs dominated the nineties? In 2007, he published a book named after her 1997 album, *Let's Talk About Love*. The album sold more than thirty million copies worldwide and included "My Heart Will Go On," still one of the most popular songs anyone has ever recorded. The book's subtitle was *A Journey to the End of Taste*; Wilson was fascinated by Dion precisely because he couldn't bear her music. He decried her "blankness," and described her music as "R&B with the sex and slyness surgically removed" and "French *chanson* severed from its wit and soul." (This absence of a credible genre identity, of course, was part of what made Dion a *pop* star.) Wilson guessed that he had never even met someone who liked Dion, despite her millions of fans, and he worried that learning to love her music might be professionally and personally destabilizing. "Maybe I am heading down a relativistic rabbit hole," he wrote. "If even Céline can be redeemed, is there no good or bad taste, or good and bad art?"

The project was a success, or perhaps a failure. Wilson learned about Dion's life and talked to some fans; he saw her live and studied her albums. But he remained admirably true to his own taste, or perhaps pigheadedly unable to transcend it. (The closest he came was when *Gilmore Girls*, the emotionally acute television series, used "My Heart Will Go On" in a subtle scene about grief. Wilson found himself responding to Dion's grand romantic professions, at least for a few minutes.) He conceded that critics, like all listeners, are influenced by the desire to accumulate "cultural capital"—to seem cool, in other words. And so he knew that his resistance to her old-fashioned embrace of show-biz schmaltz, and to her ostentatious singing voice, had been shaped by his own desire to seem sophisticated. Pierre Bourdieu, the French sociologist, wrote that "tastes are perhaps first and foremost distastes, disgust provoked by horror or visceral intolerance ('sick-making') of the tastes of others"; we love what we love because we hate what we hate, and because we don't want to be confused with those benighted people who love what we hate. But in the end, Wilson was inclined to defend his musical taste, not because it was true but because it was his. He suggested that we think of music less like politics, which drives us to debate our fellow citizens, and more like romantic love, which we often prefer to savor in private. "When we love a person, we don't want everyone else to feel the same way," he wrote. "It's bad enough if just one other person is in love with her." This is a memorable comparison, although also a depressing conclusion, at least for anyone who delights in the way that popular music has historically made our private passions public. Especially since the sixties, arguments over music have often been arguments over social identities. It's startling to think that we might now be choosing, instead, to take our musical tastes home and curl up on the couch. It's startling to think that fifty years of argument might be coming to an end.

How Can Anyone Listen to That Stuff?

In 2001, the British novelist and critic Nick Hornby published an essay in *The New Yorker* in which he did something very unusual—at least for him. He listened to the ten most popular albums in America, as listed in the July 28 issue of *Billboard*. These were hardly obscurities, but they seemed plenty obscure to Hornby. He was known for loving music; his body of work included *High Fidelity*, the 1995 novel about a record-shop owner, which became the basis for the 2000 movie of the same name. But Hornby was, by his own admission, out of touch with contemporary tastes. He admitted, ruefully, that he gravitated toward a "private Top Ten," full of music that was "disgustingly sensitive," characterized by "thoughtful, polite ironies"; he mentioned the Pernice Brothers, a literate indie band, and the jazz musician Olu Dara. For him, the *public* Top 10 was a horror show, and he wrote a witty essay about what he found there. There was a "chirpy" pop-punk band singing about masturbation. There were a couple of hip-hop crews gleefully desecrating "liberal values." ("We're not big on guns, consumerist bragging, or misogyny," Hornby explained, speaking for the liberals.) There was sullen hard rock and "sweet-natured and competent" R&B. The only album he seemed to tolerate was by Alicia Keys; the rest of the list left him feeling rather out of touch. He thought of his own treasured record collection: how good those songs sounded to him, and how far removed from contemporary culture. "I won't kid myself that it's pop music—not anymore," he wrote.

Twenty years later, Hornby's essay has aged well, although so has some of the music that failed to impress him. (The pop-punk band was blink-182, which since then has emerged as a generational touchstone. And one of the R&B groups he mentioned happened to be Destiny's Child, which is no longer accused of mere competence.) People who write about music today tend not to be so brusque—or, perhaps, so honest about their reactions to what they hear. Skeptics, like Saul Austerlitz, once worried that so-called poptimism was leading grown-ups to praise the sorts of songs beloved by thirteen-year-olds, turning music critics into mere shills for teenybopper pop. What happened, instead, was that music critics began praising just about everything. Metacritic is a website that has been tracking, since 2001, professional appraisals of cultural products, converting each review into a number from 0 to 100, and then averaging and color-coding the results. The results are fascinating, revealing not just what critics like but how they work. By the end of the 2010s, a pattern was clear. Reviews of movies, television shows, and video games tended to range widely: the average scores were a riot of green (61 or higher), yellow (40–60), and red (39 and lower), with most titles generating plenty of disagreement. But the music reviews were different: nearly every new album, of whatever genre, got an average score that was green, typically in the 70s or 80s. Yellow was rare, and red was just about absent. This phenomenon had nothing particularly to do with teenagers, or the genre of pop; it reflected the fact that music critics, once known for their contentiousness, had all but stopped writing negative reviews.

There were plenty of good explanations for this. In an industry where writers were increasingly freelancers, it made sense that an editor would assign a review of an album to a writer who was already interested in the music, as opposed to one who might have to spend a few weeks immersed in an unfamiliar body of work. (In the 2010s, the most influential music critic in America might have been Anthony Fantano, the self-proclaimed "Internet's busiest music nerd," who was not a writer but a talker: he delivered his opinions, which were generally thoughtful and stringent, on his YouTube page, in the form of thousands of video polemics.) On social media, armies of fans sometimes swarmed writers who criticized their favorite artists; perhaps some writers wanted to avoid this kind of attention, at least subconsciously. And as the cultural climate grew more politically polarized, musicians grew more adept at presenting themselves in political or quasi-political terms, as visionary or inspirational figures. Perhaps it is more difficult to say you don't care for an album when you know that the musician behind it is widely perceived to be leading a fight for Black liberation, or women's representation, or body positivity, or mental health awareness. Easier, surely, to concentrate on writing about what you like.

This development was compatible with the emergence of a new model for pop success. In the 2010s, as record stores became obsolete, streaming services increasingly determined the way people listened to music, and helped change the sound of mainstream pop. In theory, the popularity of companies like Spotify might have driven further fragmentation, because they made it so easy for listeners to explore far-flung genres. In practice, though, Spotify and its competitors, including Apple Music and YouTube, encouraged a new pop consolidation. Freed from the burden of having to decide which albums were the ones they wanted to pay for and add to their collections, millions of listeners gravitated toward similar sounds. In the new streaming era, the pop charts were full of moody, atmospheric songs that combined slangy, conversational lyrics with hip-hop-inspired beats. The new pop stars tended to draw influence from diverse sources, and yet their songs were highly compatible, blending seamlessly together on the online playlists that were displacing albums as the dominant form of music consumption: Justin Bieber, the teen idol who conquered clubs; Drake, the lovesick singing rapper; Billie Eilish, the doleful teen prodigy; Ed Sheeran, the hip-hop-loving singer-songwriter; Lorde, the sharp-eyed singer-songwriter; Post Malone, the downbeat party guy. That development shaped this book, in which—as you may have noticed—many of the chapters conclude on a note of convergence, with broadly popular performers who are eager to shrug off the weight of genre identity. "I can't really sing, but I'll try," Post Malone told me. "If there's a cool melody—*no one* can deny a cool melody." Some critics were skeptical at first, but as Post Malone became more established as a hitmaker, the reviews grew more generous. *Hollywood's Bleeding*, his third album, was the most listened-to album of 2019, according to Nielsen, which tracks the various forms of music consumption. At Metacritic, it glowed solid green, like nearly every album released that year: 79/100.

I don't mean to sound too disparaging about this trend, because I have been part of it. In 2008, I moved from *The New York Times*, where I mainly wrote shortish music reviews, to *The New Yorker*, where I wrote longer stories about people I found interesting. Some of these people were musicians, but none of them were musicians I thought were lousy. Like more and more critics, I was practicing what Carl Wilson preached: mainly nurturing my own critical grudges and aversions in private, while exhibiting my enthusiasm in public. It has been more than a decade since that James Blunt concert, and I haven't found any occasion since then to put the word "loathsome" into print. Sometimes I wondered whether, contrary to constant fears of musical decline, mainstream pop music had simply grown better over the past few decades—whether, more precisely, it had grown more compatible with my own tastes. In the 2000s, rock 'n' roll retreated; in the 2010s, clean-cut love songs largely disappeared; the hip-hop beats that replaced them were neatly aligned with my own longtime obsessions. (I remember the Cambridge, Massachusetts, record store where in the late nineties I was thrilled to find a bootleg CD by DJ Screw, the Houston pioneer who made psychedelic remixes of hip-hop tracks by slowing them down; I would never have guessed that his woozy experiments would help shape the sound of pop music in the 2010s.) Plenty of people complained about the homogeneity of Spotify pop—but plenty more people evidently loved it. Maybe new technology had made pop music more efficient, which is to say, better at giving people what they wanted. Maybe everyone had less to complain about.

This seems unlikely, though, for reasons that would not have come as a surprise to Pierre Bourdieu. Human beings tend to disagree about music because human beings are disagreeable. When we complain about music, what we are really complaining about is other people. And that is why, although we may sometimes pause to catch our breaths, we can never really stop complaining. As Simon Frith put it, "'Bad music' is a necessary concept for musical pleasure," in much the same way that the existence of evil enables the existence of good. Ever since the sixties, music has been a means of self-identification—a way for young people, in particular, to show that they aren't like everyone else, on the way to asserting that they aren't like *anyone* else. There is no reason to assume that popular music will continue to fulfill that role indefinitely. It is possible to imagine a future in which listening to music is merely a pastime, like watching movies, rather than a way to construct identity. (Even movie fanatics don't typically change the way they dress in order to reflect their favorite directors.) Or a future in which listening to music is an activity, like video gaming, that a person might either enjoy or not enjoy. (Plenty of people don't engage with video games at all, but very few people fully decline to listen to music.) It is possible, too, that the Spotify era will give way to an era of increased fragmentation, as musicians withdraw from the dominant streaming services in order to distribute their music through smaller and quirkier platforms; perhaps the next generation of insurgents will sacrifice a degree of exposure for a degree of control, earning more money from fewer listeners. But as long as people obsess about popular music, they will doubtless find themselves seized by the conviction that they are right, and their neighbors— no matter how nice or smart they may seem—are profoundly and puzzlingly wrong.

Ever since I started writing about music, I have encountered people who say, at first, that they are nervous to tell me about their favorite music, out of fear that I will deem them ignorant or unhip. In fact, they are usually eager to share, and after some reassurance they do, confessing a not-so-embarrassing enthusiasm for some pop star who has already been reevaluated as excellent by leading critics, or an abiding fascination with some faded old favorite who now inspires more nostalgia than mockery. (When Carl Wilson published his book, in 2007, he wondered whether Britney Spears might one day be "reclaimed" by critics who appreciated her musical genius; by 2014, when he published an expanded version of the book, this had pretty much come to pass.) When I worked at a record store, I worried that customers might think I was judging them, but in casual conversations these days, I often sense that people are fighting the urge to judge *me*.

Everyday listeners, it turns out, tend to have far more merciless opinions about good and bad music than most people who write about it. They are willing to dismiss entire traditions—death metal, say, or EDM. Or they harbor implacable disdain for particular musicians: maybe they find Joni Mitchell annoying, or Linkin Park fills them with rage, or they don't understand why Toby Keith is still so popular. No matter the object of their animus, they want to know: What's wrong with people? How can anyone listen to that stuff?

Those are good questions.

ACKNOWLEDGMENTS

A number of people, over the years, have told me I should write a book. Probably some of them actually meant it. But none of them meant it more than Binky Urban, my agent, who sold this book, and Scott Moyers, my editor, who bought it. This book wouldn't exist without their faith and enthusiasm, which endured even when mine flagged.

It wouldn't exist, either, without all the people over the years who shared music and musical knowledge, both of which used to be much harder to come by than they are today. Matt Moses gave me that punk-rock mixtape that I still have somewhere, which changed everything; he still knows way more about music than I do. I'm not sure I ever learned so much so quickly as I did at WHRB, with its punk-rock library and its punk-rock librarians. And countless record-store people have been willing to trade tips and arguments with me, from both sides of the counter. I don't miss musical scarcity, but I do sometimes miss the old communities and rituals it created, as well as the feeling of anticipation you got when you paid ten bucks for an album and then took it home to discover whether or not you had wasted your money.

Over the years I had some fun playing music, but pretty soon I realized that I could have even more fun writing about it. Michael C. Vazquez, at *Transition*, valued erudition, elegance, and mischief in about equal measure; I set about imitating his approach immediately. A handful of editors were willing, early on, to publish what I wrote, and pay me for it (which seemed like a great arrangement then, and still does today), including Matt Ashare at *The Boston Phoenix*, Tracii McGregor at *The Source*, and Chuck Eddy at *The Village Voice*. In New York, Bill Adler was kind enough to lend me part of his office and a small fraction of his voluminous music knowledge. I still remember the day Darryl McDaniels—DMC, from Run-DMC—stopped by to say hello, confirming my suspicion that I had lucked into the greatest office-share in the world. When I needed to buy a new turntable, our part-time officemate Aaron O'Bryant, also known as the hip-hop pioneer Kool DJ AJ, took me to Rock & Soul, a legendary midtown shop, where he negotiated on my behalf, bargaining so energetically with the salesman that I thought a fistfight might erupt.

My goal was to become a music critic at *The New York Times*, and it soon came to pass, though I'm still not sure exactly how. I suspect it had something to do with the *Times* critic Neil Strauss, who reached out to me, and to Fletcher Roberts, an editor who made my career his business, becoming a great friend and mentor. Jon Pareles, the chief pop music critic, was both a brilliant colleague (during one of our first meetings, we went to see Björk, at Radio City Music Hall, where I was shocked to see him writing not just words but accurate treble-clef transcriptions of what he was hearing) and an uncommonly generous boss, giving me a small amount of guidance and a large amount of freedom. A whole bunch of *Times* folks helped make that job just about as awesome as I thought it would be: Ben Ratliff, Sam Sifton, Jodi Kantor, Sia Michel, and dozens more.

The longest relationship of my professional life has been with *The New Yorker*, and I hope that remains true for as long as I have something to say, or think I do. More than twenty years ago, Meghan O'Rourke, who was then an editor there, asked if I would be interested in doing something about hip-hop for the magazine. "Interested" was an understatement, and in 2001, after endless stress and a series of drafts that got incrementally better, I published a profile of Jay-Z. I wrote a few more stories for the magazine after that, and then, in 2008, I left the *Times* to become a *New Yorker* staff writer. For a writer, there is no greater luxury than knowing that an army of brilliant copy editors and fact-checkers will scrutinize every sentence you write, searching for ways to make each one more felicitous, or less false. A few quotes, ideas, and phrases from my *New Yorker* pieces found their way into this book, and so I'm especially grateful to the editors who shaped my work there, including Henry Finder, Nick Thompson, and Nick Trautwein, all of whom have been invaluable in helping me figure out what sort of writer I'm supposed to be. Above all, I'm grateful to David Remnick, the editor of *The New Yorker*, for publishing me, and for telling me that the magazine could be my home. Thanks to him, that is precisely what it feels like.

David granted me time, too, to write this book, which turned out—alas!—not to be the kind of thing you can bang out in six months. There were moments when I thought that this project might be impossible and unwise, and I owe a debt to a number of people who helped me prove myself at least half wrong. Robert S. Boynton at the Arthur L. Carter Journalism Institute, at New York University, named me a visiting scholar, which got me access to both the school's libraries and its students, including Felicity Cain, who helped with research for this book. No end of people who contributed unwittingly to it, but I should thank the witting contributors, especially Mia Council, Henry Finder, Andrew Kuo, and Jason Nocito. Sameen Gauhar put her life on hold for this book, directing scrutiny not just at the facts but at the premises and conclusions, too, often working until she collapsed in exhaustion [SG: check!]. I rejected her suggestions only occasionally, and perhaps not always perspicaciously.

When I was a teenager obsessed with cassettes, I could imagine nothing that seemed more exciting than the life of a successful musician, or for that matter a semi-successful one. The older I got, though, the easier it was for me to see how hard that life is: even a chart-topping star must usually commit to an exhausting lifelong trek from venue to venue, and even many of *those* must still piece together a living from rather miscellaneous and unpredictable sources of income. I'm grateful to all of them, including the ones whose songs I have not (yet!) learned to love. I'm grateful, too, to my fellow music writers, who documented this music as it was created, and then reconsidered it in the years and decades afterward. Fanzines, newspapers, glossy magazines, biographies, histories: this book is in large part a tribute to all that work, and I hope also a small contribution to it.

Long before I had done anything, I already owed everything to my parents, both of them scholars and teachers and authors. They cared enough to encourage some of my obsessions, and understood enough to tolerate others. Also, they introduced me to *Graceland*. My little sister, Sia, eagerly accepted my musical suggestions over the years, although much of the time I should have been soliciting hers, instead—she recognized the excellence of Boyz II Men (and many other performers) long before I did. To my two boys: if you ever read this line, let me know and I'll give you some ice cream. And last and most: thank you to Sarah, who has listened to lots of this music, sometimes on purpose. You made this possible—and everything else, too. Thank you. I love you. The book is finished!